Literacies of Migration

Drawing on the lived experiences of high school-aged young Black immigrants, this book paints imaginaries of racialized translanguaging and transsemiotizing, leveraged transnationally by teenagers across the Caribbean and the United States. The Black Caribbean youth reflect a full range of literacy practices – six distinct holistic literacies – identified as a basis for flourishing. These literacies of migration encapsulate numerous examples of how the youth are racialized transgeographically, based on their translanguaging and transsemiotizing with Englishes, both institutionally and individually. In turn, the book advances a heuristic of semiolingual innocence containing eight elements, informed by the Black immigrant literacies of Caribbean youth. Through the eight elements presented – flourishing, purpose, comfort, expansion, paradox, originality, interdependence, and imagination – stakeholders and systems will be positioned to better understand and address the urgent needs of these youth. Ultimately, the heuristic supports a reinscribing of semiolingual innocence for Black Caribbean immigrant and transnational youth, as well as for all youth.

PATRIANN SMITH is a distinguished scholar-educator at the University of South Florida whose research emerges at the intersection of race, language, and immigration. She is the author of *Black Immigrant Literacies: Intersections of Race, Language, and Culture in the Classroom* (2023), co-author of *Affirming Black Students' Lives and Literacies: Bearing Witness* (2022), and co-founder of the USAID-funded RISE Caribbean Educational Research Center (CERC: 2022).

Literacies of Migration

Translanguaging Imaginaries of Innocence

Patriann Smith
University of South Florida

CAMBRIDGE
UNIVERSITY PRESS

CAMBRIDGE
UNIVERSITY PRESS

Shaftesbury Road, Cambridge CB2 8EA, United Kingdom

One Liberty Plaza, 20th Floor, New York, NY 10006, USA

477 Williamstown Road, Port Melbourne, VIC 3207, Australia

314–321, 3rd Floor, Plot 3, Splendor Forum, Jasola District Centre, New Delhi – 110025, India

103 Penang Road, #05–06/07, Visioncrest Commercial, Singapore 238467

Cambridge University Press is part of Cambridge University Press & Assessment, a department of the University of Cambridge.

We share the University's mission to contribute to society through the pursuit of education, learning and research at the highest international levels of excellence.

www.cambridge.org
Information on this title: www.cambridge.org/9781108839037

DOI: 10.1017/9781108979542

© Patriann Smith 2024

This publication is in copyright. Subject to statutory exception and to the provisions of relevant collective licensing agreements, no reproduction of any part may take place without the written permission of Cambridge University Press & Assessment.

When citing this work, please include a reference to the DOI 10.1017/9781108979542

First published 2024

A catalogue record for this publication is available from the British Library.

Library of Congress Cataloging-in-Publication Data
Names: Smith, Patriann, 1982– author.
Title: Literacies of migration: translanguaging imaginaries of innocence / Patriann Smith.
Description: Cambridge, United Kingdom ; New York, NY : Cambridge University Press, 2024. | Includes bibliographical references and index. | Summary: "Centering race across geographies, this book paints imaginaries about how Black Caribbean immigrant and transnational youth use translanguaging and semiotics to reflect a broad range of literacies. Scholars, teachers, librarians and parents can better understand and address the urgent needs of these youth through the compelling narratives presented"– Provided by publisher.
Identifiers: LCCN 2024008598 (print) | LCCN 2024008599 (ebook) | ISBN 9781108839037 (hardback) | ISBN 9781108969666 (paperback) | ISBN 9781108979542 (epub)
Subjects: LCSH: Translanguaging (Linguistics) | Semiotics. | Immigrant children–United States–Language. | Caribbeans–United States–Language. | Youth, Black–Caribbean Area–Language | Youth, Black–United States–Language. | English language–Caribbean Area. | Black English. | Literacy–Social aspects.
Classification: LCC P115.35 .S65 2024 (print) | LCC P115.35 (ebook) | DDC 401/.4089960729–dc23/eng/20240403
LC record available at https://lccn.loc.gov/2024008598
LC ebook record available at https://lccn.loc.gov/2024008599

ISBN 978-1-108-83903-7 Hardback

Cambridge University Press & Assessment has no responsibility for the persistence or accuracy of URLs for external or third-party internet websites referred to in this publication and does not guarantee that any content on such websites is, or will remain, accurate or appropriate.

Contents

List of Figures	*page* vii
Foreword: Reimagining Sociological and Political Brilliance in the Languaging Practices of Youth	viii
ALLISON SKERRETT	
Foreword: A Courageous Conversation on Blackness, Language, and Immigration Centering the Biographical and Autobiographical	xi
AWAD IBRAHIM	
Acknowledgments and Dedication	xiii

1 Introduction: Looking through the Lens of Black Immigrant Literacies — 1

2 Why '*New Model Minority*' Youth? Understanding Black Immigrants in the United States — 24

3 Afro-Caribbean Languaging, Englishes, and Literacies of Migration across the Black Diaspora: Unmasking the Fallacy of Invented Illiteracy — 72

4 Conceptualizing Translanguaging in Black Immigrant Literacies: Multiliteracies, Raciolinguistics, Language and Raciosemiotic Architecture — 108

5 Methodologically Examining Black Immigrant Literacies: A (Decolonizing) Interpretive Analytical Design — 133

6 Translanguaging Imaginaries of Innocence: A Holistic Portrait of the Literacies of Black Caribbean Immigrant Youth — 155

7 Reinscribing Lost Imaginaries of Semiolingual Innocence: Futurizing Translanguaging for Flourishing — 211

Afterword: Imagining Pedagogical Possibilities beyond
Normative Educational Perspectives   239
RAMÓN ANTONIO MARTÍNEZ

Notes   242
References   243
Index   278

Figures

4.1 A transraciolinguistic approach   *page* 119
5.1 Translanguaging via an integrated model of multilingualism for clarifying Black immigrant literacies   151
5.2 Raciolinguistic positioning of a Black immigrant youth   152
6.1 A model for conceptualizing Black immigrant literacies   203

Foreword: Reimagining Sociological and Political Brilliance in the Languaging Practices of Youth

This book is at once timely and well overdue. In *Literacies of Migration: Translanguaging Imaginaries of Innocence*, Dr. Patriann Smith invites her readers to revisit and reimagine the ways in which we recognize and respond to Black immigrant youth and their language repertoires.

Black immigrants now make up the largest and fastest growing group of immigrants to the US. At the same time, this population has had a marked and historic presence in the US and other globally powerful receiving nations such as the UK. The assignment of immigrants of African descent to the category of the "Black immigrant," however, has been part of the seriously flawed sociological enterprise of understanding these immigrants that Dr. Smith addresses. Black immigrants are ethnoculturally and linguistically diverse; and they arrive to the US and other new homelands from a host of nations that are politically, economically, educationally, and socially diverse. Moreover, the individuals comprising particular national groups themselves reflect great diversity along these axes of differences. All of these differences mean that individual and subgroup experiences of language and literacy in new homelands demand detailed inquiry in order to generate insights that actually stand a chance of changing how we know and engage with Black immigrant youth in educational and other social spaces. Dr. Smith conducts such principled inquiry in this book, and in doing so, leads us in exploring and debunking persistent, limiting myths about Black immigrant youth. She also facilitates our reimagining of the sociological and political brilliance in these youth's languaging practices. Moving beyond more powerful and authentic understandings of the language identities and practices of a diverse set of Black immigrant youth, Dr. Smith further invites her readers, with these youth, to imagine to what broader justice-oriented uses these new understandings of Black immigrant youth can be put in communities and societies in which anti-Black racism persists.

One of the limiting myths about Black English-speaking immigrants that Dr. Smith lays bare is that they possess and deploy one sole enactment of the English language. Dr. Smith efficiently moves her readers far beyond the idea of accent, one that may sound "funny" to an American ear, to borrow from one of her descriptors, in order to examine meatier ideas. Using rich cases of participants from just a small subset of "English-speaking" (or, more accurately, English-colonized) Caribbean nations, Dr. Smith peels away layer after layer of a stunning array of language repertoires that comprise these young people's *inonsans jan nwè* or semiolingual innocence, a powerful term Dr. Smith theorizes to index the rich language practices these Black youth possess. These semiolingual repertoires, Smith convincingly argues, can be apprehended in all of their brilliance only when viewed unsullied by the "white gaze" that seeks to compare these youth's languaging practices to a mythical standardized form of a named language, and in so doing, inevitably finds some trouble with their languaging. Yes, these youth are incredibly linguistically aware of their accents and they strategically use, hide, reveal, and adapt them in order to achieve self-directed academic and social goals. However, readers grasp the deep and broad structures of the English languages (plural) these youth hold through a skillful analysis. Dr. Smith's analysis reveals that these young people's semiolingual innocence includes languages that move beyond named E-languages such as "English" that are deemed superior, embodied multiliteracies, and translanguaging practices that reflect the linguistic dexterity they have developed in response to being language users across national borders. Ever conscious of the racialization to which they and their language practices are subjected in the US, the linguistic project in which these Black immigrant speakers of Englishes are involved as they lead rich transnational lives is aptly theorized by Dr. Smith as their building of a raciosemiotic architecture.

Another of the well-worn yet simultaneously reenergized (due to rising rates of Black immigrants) myths about the Black immigrant that Dr. Smith debunks in this book is that of the "model minority" Black immigrant. This myth has been durable across time with its suggestion that Black immigrants academically and economically outperform their African American counterparts. Yet ongoing accumulating research evidence consistently debunks this myth by displaying the heterogeneity in academic attainment of all Black ethnoracial groups in nations such as the US while also revealing the varied challenges with racism and linguicism *all* Black people experience in white-dominated societies. Dr. Smith elegantly enters this delicate and fraught space of supposed difference. She carefully presents from the larger literature as well as her own wealth of research data that illuminate the precarious position and experiences of Black immigrant students. Far from a unified story of academic success and broad social acceptance, Dr. Smith provides views into an educational system that ignores, undervalues, and sometimes denigrates the particular types of Black Englishes Black students from the Caribbean bring to school. She offers for our reflection the thoughtful analyses that Black English-speaking Caribbean students conduct of their literacy education experiences, one in which they struggle to be recognized as having mastery in an official "E-language" of the world of school, as well as possessing a formidable additional set of languages that they skillfully develop and deploy across myriad contexts and relationships beyond school. Who and what, then, asks Dr. Smith, does this persistent myth of the model minority Black immigrant serve? Dr. Smith sets a justice-oriented agenda, asking literacy scholars and educators to take up a critically oriented language pedagogy with diverse Black youth that allows them to notice and name rampant raciolinguicism and collaborate across Black linguistic diversity to demand that their Black Englishes and other Black languages be prioritized in literacy education and other social projects.

Within the pages of this book, readers discover stunning views of multilingual and multicultural, ethnoracially Black young people. Dr. Smith leaves her readers with a serious project to take up after engaging with the translanguaging lives of these youth. Through her theorizing of translanguaging imaginaries of semiolingual innocence, she calls us to partner with youth in their projects of flourishing through language and literacy toward a shared humanity where there is greater linguistic justice for all.

Allison Skerrett
The University of Texas at Austin

Foreword: A Courageous Conversation on Blackness, Language, and Immigration Centering the Biographical and Autobiographical

What happens when Blackness meets language, which in turn meets immigration? An intricate cartography of a courageous conversation is created, one where we are made to vacillate between the poetic and the empirical, the biographical and the autobiographical, Blackness and language, colonial white gaze and *innocence noire*, and ultimately Black containment and Black flourishing. This is the beauty of *Literacies of Migration: Translanguaging Imaginaries of Innocence*. Immigrating while Black seems to flip the script. Here, linguistics is turned into applied linguistics, semiotics into raciosemiotics, and the intersection of race and language is infinitely conjugated into raciolinguistics, translanguaging, transsemiotics, transraciolinguistics, and so on. This is because, when Blackness meets language and immigration, a moment of *métissage*, an ever complicated and radically new rhizomatic space, is created.

Literacies of Migration tells the story of six Black Caribbean immigrant youth who find themselves in the US. While doing so, the book centralizes race and language as it examines the literacy practices of these Black Caribbean immigrant youth; it uses translanguaging, transsemiotics, and transraciolinguistics as an intersectional epistemic framework; it investigates holistic literacies as a way to bridge academic and home languages; it extends our understanding of literacy in relation to racialized Black language speakers; and offers, in conclusion, a decolonial interpretive framework that helps us as academics, teachers, and policymakers to become mindful, not to say literate, of the ever complicated cartography where Blackness meets immigration, which in turns meets literacy.

Interestingly enough, even though the Black Caribbean immigrant youth are English speakers, they discovered in the US that their English is neither "standard" nor valorized; instead it is racialized, linguicized, and raciosemiotized. So, they use their long-standing acumen with translanguaging and transsemiotizing as a masterful move to resist this devaluing of their language, a brilliant way to fight yet "flourish." In doing so, they empower themselves by working through the tension of consciously and knowingly using their ("devalued") linguistic repertoire which they brought with them as immigrants and code-switch it with the idealized and so-called standard linguistic norms.

By highlighting this tension, *Literacies of Migration* invites us as "scholars, educators, teachers, and policymakers to create institutional mechanisms for empowering Black immigrant youth, their teachers, and their parents ... as they engage with tensions arising from translanguaging that rob them" of what Dr. Smith calls *'linguistic innocence.'* Only then, *Literacies of Migration* argues, can these youth spell their own name, write their own story, challenge the divide-and-conquer dichotomy of underachieving and model minority Black, understand their particular and peculiar ontological situation and identity-formation process, and finally locate themselves in time and space and at the same time question the adequacy of that location. Only then can they declare that their best is here and their absolute best is yet to come.

Awad Ibrahim
University of Ottawa

Acknowledgments and Dedication

The birthing of *Literacies of Migration: Translanguaging Imaginaries of Innocence* emerges at last, after four long years, a testament to the revelatory inspiration of the Spirit of God, and an ode to the unwavering will of Black ancestors inscribed by faith and persisting across centuries, indelibly engraved on the imaginaries of descendants yet unseen. I am grateful today for and humbled by the opportunity to serve as a vessel along this cherished ancestral journey of joy through which the truths presented here should become more visible. I will be forever thankful for those sacred beating hearts of humans in the Caribbean that came before mine, choosing to brave, through sacrifice, any oppression threatening to obscure the futures of hope that, through faith, they saw Black people begin to occupy today.

It is because of you, dear ancestors, that I write this book, a book that dares Black consciousness to recall, to remember, to reclaim the shared but often forgotten ancestry and (linguistic) innocence of Black American, Black African, and Black Caribbean peoples, whose intertwined humanities persist today with that of all others, as they did before the divisive tools of slavery and colonialism – a peoples whose subconscious yearning for solidarity became clearly visible in the inescapable attraction of *Black Panther* for so many across the globe, awakened by its inescapable call to interweave imagined futures. My heart overflows with gratitude for your persistence, dear ancestors, and for your choice to (re)inscribe imaginaries of innocence across decades, yes, even centuries, of fragile yet resilient dialectics, indelibly sealing the presence of our daily realities with the "transcendent literacies" (Willis, 2022) of an ever-present past. It is because of your faith in the always now, your genealogical lineage forever planted in the seed of every future, that this imaginary now bursts forth.

I acknowledge and dedicate *Literacies of Migration: Translanguaging Imaginaries of Innocence* to the precious children and youth of the now – my daughter, my nieces, my nephews, the Black immigrant youth whose stories are featured in and form the basis for this book, to those children and youth across the globe whom I have never met, and to the children and youth to come, whose imagined futures inspired me to commit daily to the declaration of invisible truths – long silenced. I want you to know that 'I see you' and that your God-given capacity to long for and cherish the desire for solidarity across the broad landscape that is finite humanity has infinitely moved my soul.

I viewed, with deep amazement, your righteous indignation, dear children and youth, when George Floyd's life was shockingly made to drain, visibly, remorselessly, before the collective eyes of an astonished world. I observed, with absolute reverence, your response, engraved with brilliance and hope, when beautiful young humans such as the youngest inaugural poet, Amanda Gorman, proclaimed valiantly, through her adept "semiolanguaging" at the inauguration of President Joe Biden: "We, the successors of a country and a time where a skinny Black girl descended from slaves and raised by a single mother can dream of becoming president, only to find herself reciting for one" (Gorman, 2021). In this brief but brave moment of symbolic and collective pause invoked by the daughter of a single-parent mother to the ever-present threat of the 'new Jim Crow,' I was stirred by a renewed optimism to see your unrestrained passion for crossing boundaries often seared by the lingering and blatant animosity of a historically infused racial, linguistic, and cultural past. It is because of your innocent vision for a world of transraciolinguistic justice and a desire for peace that this portrait toward solidarity now germinates, an imaginary instantiation of Dr. Martin Luther King's "I Have a Dream." Your reminder through artfully painted imaginaries such as, "The dawn is ours before we knew it" that "Somehow we do it," and "Somehow we weathered and witnessed a nation that isn't broken, but simply unfinished" (Gorman, 2021) articulates succinctly how you cultivated the soils of our collective worlds on my journey to this book.

This cultivation, for which I am grateful, was also reflected daily in my robust community of family, friends, others, and in the support of my editors as well as the numerous and lovely colleagues who motivated me, inspired me, advised me, guided me, (reverse) mentored me, 'sponsored' me, communed with me, 'carried me' in earnest these past three years through the numerous storms faced in my painting of this portrait, which now invites us to look unflinchingly through the lens of the Black immigrant, forged with a view to solidarity in *Literacies of Migration: Translanguaging Imaginaries of Innocence*. Among those for whom I am grateful are my phenomenal editor – Helen Barton – and her editorial assistant, Isabel (Izzie) Collins; the remarkable anonymous reviewers whose expertise proved critical to developing a substantive proposal as well as finalizing this book; Dr. Fenda Akiwumi and the USF Institute on Black Life; and my research assistant – Darlshawn (Shawn) Patterson – Doctoral Student of Literacy, Research Assistant, and Graduate Student Success Fellow at the University of South Florida. Among these also are my late father – Patrick; my mother – Mary Anna; my sisters – Dawn, Gilda, Patrianna; my brothers – Johnny, Ervin, Dave;

my daughter – Karice; my nieces and nephews – Jaden, Jaeda, Gheryl, Jainy, Kijana, Liam, Fiandra, Zain, Bella, Ella, Nathaniel, Destiny. And also among these are Drs. Lakeya Afolalu, Mercy Agyepong, Amma Akrofi, H. Samy Alim, Janice Almasi, Uju Anya, Susan Ariew, April Baker-Bell, Eurydice Bouchereau Bauer, Fenice Boyd, Hansel Burley, Eliza Braden, Cynthia (Cindy) Brock, Maneka Brooks, Kisha Bryan, Ayanna Brown, Ayanna Butler, the late Benjamin (Benji) Chang, Rong Chang, Jehanzeb Cheema, Yi-Hsin Chen, Ayanna Cooper, Patricia Edwards, Stephen Ekwaro-Osire, Talia Esnard, Nelson Flores, Tiffany Flowers, Paul Frazier, Mileidis Gort, Marcelle Haddix, Violet Harris, Rachel Hatten, Bridgette Hinds, Constance (Connie) Hines, Elizabeth Hordge-Freeman, Bryan Hotchkins, Andrew Hunte, Awad Ibrahim, Gay Ivey, James King, Michelle Knight-Manuel, Alex Kumi-Yeboah, Alice Lee, Guofang Li, Jaehoon Lee, Allan Luke, Dave Louis, Alison Mackey, Kofi Marfo, Ramón Antonio Martínez, Gwendolyn McMillon, LaSonya Moore, Kendra Nalubega-Booker, Shondel Nero, Kristen Pratt, Detra Price-Dennis, Aria Razfar, Saturnino Rodriguez, Victoria Risko, Jonathan Rosa, Kongji Qin, Lenny Sanchez, Jenifer Jasinski Schneider, Ruthmae Sears, Elizabeth Shaunessy-Dedrick, Allison Skerrett, Neisha Terry, Manka Varghese, Jian Wang, S. Joel Warrican, Vaughn Watson, Dianne Wellington, Arlette Willis, Colwick Wilson, Rahat Zaidi, plus the many more cherished scholar humans whose names may not appear here but who are equally valued.

I especially thank you all for being my inspiration, 'my rock,' my mentors, my thinking partners, my critical friends, and just my good friends too, across so many intersectionalities – African American, African/African immigrant, Afro-Caribbean/Afro-Caribbean immigrant, Afro-Indian, Afro-Latinx, Black, Canadian, Caribbean/West Indian, Chinese, Black immigrant, Indian, transnational, Latinx, Latin American, LGBTQIA, South Korean, white, white American, brothers, children, daughters, educators, fathers, husbands, immigrant, mothers, partners, single-parent mothers, single-parent fathers, sons, scholars, teachers, wives, others ... I stand on the shoulders of so many giants. Thank you for being a shoulder to lean on.

Like my Black ancestors and like the inspiring Amanda Gorman, you remind me daily that, "If we're to live up to our own time, then victory won't lie in the blade, but in all the bridges we've made" (Gorman, 2021). I am grateful always for the collective wisdom of ancestral and contemporary community, a reminder that "I am the daughter of Black writers who are descended from Freedom Fighters who broke their chains and changed the world"; "They call me" (Gorman, 2021). Thank you. Together, you all made this beautiful birth possible, and I dedicate this book to you.

1 Introduction
Looking through the Lens of Black Immigrant Literacies

> Wakanda
> [wuh-kahn-duh]
> The name Wakanda is primarily a female name of Native American-Sioux origin that means Inner Magical Powers. Wakanda is also a fictional country created by Stan Lee and Jack Kirby for Marvel Comics – specifically the *Fantastic Four* and *Black Panther* series.
> BabyNames.com, n.d.

> Wakanda is known as the worship of nature among the indigenous North American peoples and is a fictional African country home to the Marvel Comics superhero the Black Panther.
> Collins English Dictionary, n.d.

> The movie *Black Panther* popularized a salute, known as Wakanda Forever, as a gesture of Black excellence around the world.
> Dictionary.com, n.d.

In 2018, *Black Panther*, a film with an all-Black cast including the late Chadwick Boseman as the star, sailed past *Titanic* to become the then number three title of all time in the US, and globally, the number ten title of all time (McClintock, 2018). As a mother and *enmigwé nwè* – the St. Lucian French Creole rendering of *"immigré noire"* or "Black immigrant[1]" – in the US, my daughter had been awaiting the movie incessantly for years. She would simply not stop talking about it and I knew that our tickets had to be purchased early on. I had seen the trailer for the movie and was fascinated by the authentic languaging of the king of Wakanda. It was thrilling to watch the "cloaked, technologically advanced nation in Africa" functioning as "home to the exotic metal vibranium, the source of Black Panther's powers" (McClintock, 2018). Needless to say, though, what I would witness while watching the film far exceeded any of my wildest imaginations – the accents, the languaging, the various cultural representations of Blackness, the kinky hair, the geographies, the humor, the gestures, the clothing, the bald heads, the music, the women, the beads, the love, the goodness of Africa, the kings, the chiefs, the Black saviors. These beautiful semiotics of what I posit later as *inonsans jan nwè* – St. Lucian French Creole for *"innocence noire"* or "Black innocence" – shone beautifully, wrapped up in Black Wakanda power (Madowo & Attiah, 2018).

Black Panther surpassed my dreams, as it did my Black daughter's and that of so many millions with imagined futures for *libéwasyon jan nwè – libération noire* or Black liberation – across the world. It did so even as it reminded us of Black Panther as a movement, signaling a symbolic return to how the first modern Black political group in the US took up arms against white supremacy. Much like the Black Panther free school Breakfast Program in 1969 "fed tens of thousands of hungry [Black] kids," restoring innocence to children, "many of whom had never eaten breakfast before," this film, though fictional, dared recklessly, yet adeptly, to use languaging and semiotics. In doing so, it reinscribed Black innocence through Wakanda Forever – a symbol of unapologetic beauty, deep joy, thrilling warmth juxtaposed against a diasporic transgressiveness (Davies, 1995) emerging from the long-standing and abiding agency of Black love and truth. *Black Panther* spoke directly to Black immigrants too, bringing those whom we think of as Africans, African Americans, and Black immigrants together, to create, through the adept manipulation of languaging and literacies, a film grounded in beauty and infinitely defined by Black innocence. *Black Panther* touched deeply the lives of my daughter and me as it did Africans, African Americans, and millions of Black migrants as well as descendants of slaves across the globe. It inspired and asked that we should dare to reclaim – in solidarity with each other – the Black innocence that is rightfully ours and that lets our greatness shine through in the world. *Black Panther* challenged Black people, and indeed the world, to reinscribe an *innocence noire* that exists *sans* '(post)colonial' "white gaze" (Morrison, 2020) to reify the long-standing inherent inheritance of Black excellence. As Karen Attiah from the *Washington Post* rightly observed, "*Black Panther* [was] not just another superhero movie. Culturally, [it was] a revolutionary moment for the Black diaspora *and for white people too* [emphasis added]" (Madowo & Attiah, 2018).

I concur, because the follow up to *Black Panther* – *Black Panther: Wakanda Forever* – released in November 2022, proved to be "the [then] highest-grossing debut ever for the month of November" (Pallotta, 2022). *Black Panther: Wakanda Forever* extended the notion of solidarity among Black people, brought to life by the original *Black Panther* through languaging, to other cultures and races as well. In doing so, it exemplified how notions of *inonsans jan nwè* (defined and discussed later) hold opportunity for healing across Black, white, and all worlds. Invoking Wakanda, an Indigenous American Indian imaginary as the symbolic representation of what Dr. Arlette Willis, professor at the University of Illinois Urbana–Champaign, refers to as "transcendent literacy" (Willis, 2022, discussed later), *Black Panther* illustrated how languaging and semiotics at large function not only within the Black race to reflect excellence steeped in *innocence noire* but also operate as a mechanism for preserving solidarity across the multiple racial and cultural worlds of humanity.

Given the design of *inonsans jan nwè* intricately undergirding *Black Panther* and *Black Panther: Wakanda Forever*, and the symbolism invoked by a return to Black Panther as a political movement, it is fitting that these films and the movement are prefigured here as a precursor to the painting of innocence presented in this book, steeped in a reclaiming of the lost translanguaging imaginaries of youth's *Black immigrant literacies* (see Smith, 2020b, for a detailed discussion of the framework). Beginning this book by appealing to the brilliance of Blackness reinscribed through *Black Panther* and imbued with the symbolism of *Black Panther: Wakanda Forever*, I undertake here an extension of the long-standing decolonizing global project designed to reinscribe *inonsans jan nwè*. Inviting a co-peering through the "literacies of migration" (Capstick, 2016) of Black immigrant youth – *literacies informed by, though not always the result of, transnationalism and migration* – I invite readers on a journey that dares to reclaim what I posit in this book as lost *imajinè inosan* – "imaginaries of innocence." *Imajinè inosan*, much like is invoked in Afrofuturism, "an aesthetic and an activist movement in the arts ... [that interrogates] the intersections between speculative fiction, futurism, and African Diaspora culture" (Thomas, 2019), and in the 'unapologetically Indian' universe of Indofuturism (Chandran, 2023), has been vividly, unflinchingly, and historically present, via *"flourishing"* (Keyes, 2002), before the introduction of white gaze.

I choose to look through the lens of Black immigrant youth, whom I refer to as first-, second-, or third-generation immigrants to the US who identify as Black, who(se parents) migrate to the US from Africa, the Caribbean, or elsewhere. I do this because the Black immigrant perspective has functioned as a long-standing "prism" by scholars such as Dr. Roy Simon Bryce-Laporte for viewing American race relations (Bryce-Laporte, 1972, p. 32) and necessarily provides the basis for re-instantiating nuance surrounding notions of *inonsans jan nwè* in the increasingly and overtly racialized Black-white context of the US (Smith, 2021). Using the intersecting conceptions of multiliteracies, translanguaging, and raciolinguistics as a basis for this book, I explore the ways in which Black Caribbean youth used translanguaging to reflect a range of literacy practices by functioning as language and raciosemiotic architects (Flores, 2020; Smith, 2022d) as they used their Englishes (Kachru, 1992) as well as the broader range of their semiotic resources while racialized as Black immigrants in the US. In turn, I illustrate how contested ideologies embedded within institutions and societies surrounding race, semiotizing, and specifically languaging, as well as migration, influenced students' choices as architects. In undertaking this role, I show how the students reinscribe their Black innocence while leveraging their holistic literacies for *success* – a success reframed in this book by the degree to which youth experience overall well-being – *"flourishing"* (Keyes, 2002).

As implicitly signaled earlier in the discussion about *Black Panther*, even as anti-Blackness functions globally as a long-standing system, there remains an often-invisible divisiveness among African immigrants, Afro-Caribbean immigrants, and African American peoples in the US. This dynamic has created a situation where oppression from without is exacerbated by tensions from within. There is therefore every reason to write this book at a time when the long-standing rhetoric designed to maintain a multi-pronged divisiveness among Black people continues to increase, if not merely hold sway. I write this book about the largely heterogeneous population of Black Caribbean immigrant youth in the US largely in response to such divisiveness, exploring the contradictions faced by these youth when they are portrayed as a *(new) 'model minority'* (Ukpokodu, 2018) and juxtaposed against their often inferiorly positioned African American peers. I wished to examine the challenges they encounter in meeting the resulting and expectant high academic and social standards imposed on their personhoods and which correspond with being a *designer immigrant* or a *model minority*. In doing so, I took the concept *model minority* to represent the academic success and upward social mobility of Black immigrant youth, when compared to other immigrant groups (i.e., Latinx, Asian American) and to their Black American peers (Wilson-Forsberg et al., 2018).

From a linguistic perspective in this book, being part of the *model minority* implies proficiency in a perceived oral and written standardized English (e.g., "Standard American English": SAE), which is often thought to be crucial to academic success and the basis for upward social mobility in the US, as it is elsewhere. Yet, it has been argued that Black immigrant youth can sometimes lack proficiency in standardized Englishes[2] despite being perceived as model minorities (Ukpokodu, 2018). In addition, the Englishes spoken by Black immigrant youth from the Caribbean, often referred to as "dialects" or "Creoles," have long been thought to operate along a continuum of English/Creole and are often differentially distanced from what is regarded as Standard English (e.g., SAE) (see Alim, 2004, for a raciolinguistic problematization of the notion of "standard"; see Smith & Warrican, 2021, for a problematization of the term "dialect"). And from a social perspective, being part of the *model minority* implies acculturation, including the understanding and incorporation of comportment rules set by the "white" majority culture and institutions in and beyond the US. Such comportment rules often include communicating orally and expressing one's thoughts in approximations of standardized Englishes and forms of behavior that may be different from those of the Black immigrant youth. In addition, Black immigrant youth in the US have to navigate many influences in defining their own identity: their English languages and home cultures, their parents' expectations for academic success, understanding decolonizing perspectives, becoming part of an 'inclusive' multicultural society, "becoming Black" (Ibrahim, 1999) as often experienced differently from their Black American peers, and becoming Black as "Other" in the US racialized society.

In the research study that undergirds this book, the translanguaging assets of youth's *inonsans jan nwè* that emerge as well as the tensions and contradictions within which they are subsumed are explored through phenomenological interviews, Black youth's own experiences, and in their own words. I achieve this goal through in-depth analysis of the historical trajectories and students' multiliteracies across named languages/Englishes. In doing so, I acknowledge that tensions arise from the *intersectionality* of being bi- and multicultural, bi- and multilingual, as well as bi- and multiracial. These tensions also become visible as the immigrant students use their Englishes and other languages to cross different contexts symbolically, physically, virtually, and otherwise, while identifying as Black. To acknowledge these tensions, as Alim (2005) has shown, is to acknowledge that "Black youth possess a broad range of speech styles" and thus, to extend examinations of the ways in which Black language represents the "whole range of styles within speakers' linguistic repertoires" (p. 194). Furthermore, to engage in this examination is to respond to the question posed by Alim (2005): "*If the Black speech community possesses a range of styles that are suitable for all of its communicative needs, then why the coercion and imposition of White styles?*" [emphasis added] (p. 195).

Emerging under the broader umbrellas of sociocultural approaches to literacy (Street, 1995), critical literacy (Luke, 2018; Willis, 2023), and critical applied linguistics (Pennycook, 2001), the research study undergirding this book is therefore anchored theoretically and intersectionally using the lenses of (a) translanguaging, taken to represent Black students' use of their entire linguistic repertoire that reflects the multiliterate assets students present through language and raciosemiotic architecture via transracialization (Alim, 2004; Flores, 2020; García & Wei, 2014; New London Group, 1996; Smith, 2022d); (b) a decolonizing perspective based on "critical dialectic pluralism" (Onwuegbuzie & Frels, 2013) that includes attention to institutionally informed racialized realities as well as demonstrated strategies and struggles used to overcome challenges and forms of oppression in Black students' individual lives (see Dei, 2000); and (c) raciolinguistics as well as a raciolinguistic perspective signaling an understanding that Black language is intertwined with race, and race with language, requiring a focus on institutional norms to address colonial legacies (Alim, 2004, 2016; Rosa & Flores, 2017).

In keeping with the conceptual framework above, I problematize a primary focus on *academic literacy success* often devoid of flourishing that tends to characterize Black immigrant and transnational youth. I thus contribute to filling a gap in the field by painting a more holistic portrait of the literacies and translanguaging practices of Black Caribbean immigrant youth. Three questions guided the study of Black Caribbean immigrant youth's literacies that undergirds this book:

(1) How do Black Caribbean English-speaking immigrant youth describe their literacies as represented in their historical trajectories across in- and out-of-school settings?
(2) How do Black Caribbean English-speaking immigrant youth describe their translanguaging, accompanied by their transsemiotic practices, as represented in their historical trajectories across in- and out-of-school settings?
(3) In what ways are contested ideologies surrounding race, language, and migration reflected in Black Caribbean English-speaking immigrant youth's descriptions of their literacies through translanguaging, as accompanied by their transsemiotic practices?

An understanding of how Black immigrant youth leverage their multiliteracies through translanguaging to present their holistic literacies in the context of institutions and societies that function based on raciolinguistic and raciosemiotic ideologies will extend the literature that highlights the strengths presented by immigrant and transnational students of Color. At the same time, an emphasis on the raciolinguicized and often "schizophrenic institutional" (Smith et al., 2022, p. 78) realities that require such responses from students will draw attention to the need for restructuring education and societies in ways that foster "linguistic equanimity" (Alim, 2004, p. 195). This understanding will also add to the body of research that highlights how Black Caribbean students' literacies of migration function both within and beyond classrooms to create new imaginaries of what literacies look like when enacted holistically (Darvin & Norton, 2014; De Costa, 2014; Jiménez et al., 2009; McLean, 2010; Rubenstein-Ávila, 2007; Skerrett, 2012, 2020; Watson et al., 2014).

Constructs and Definitions

In this book, I choose to draw on my Black innocence – *inonsans jan nwè* – instantiating my St. Lucian French Creole heritage as an intentional part of my translanguaging and literate practices. I do this unapologetically as a Black Caribbean immigrant to present the Black immigrant literacies of Caribbean youth. As such, certain key terms central to this book are presented from their inception, in St. Lucian French Creole. This Creole is often considered as a less recognized 'variety of language' for the purpose of official schooling. However, much like more acceptable standardized forms such as French and English, it does legitimately convey notions about languaging of Black people in ways that reflect a distinct nuance associated with their "*racialized entanglements*" (Smith, 2022c; see also Pennycook, 2021). For the purpose of discussion in this book, the following constructs are operationalized as follows. In certain instances, I intentionally emphasize how named languages such as St. Lucian French Creole, French, and English variably portray the meaning embedded in these constructs.

(1) **Alien:** As recently as 2020, the term "alien" was used by the US government to refer to "an individual who is not a U.S. citizen or U.S. national" (Mattix, 2018). Aliens could become permanent residents or be naturalized as US citizens. According to the IRS (Mattix, 2018), "an alien [was someone] who entered the United States illegally without the proper authorization and documents, or who entered the United States legally and has since violated the terms of his or her visa or overstayed the time limit. An undocumented alien [was] deportable if apprehended."

(2) **Black Innocence:** Also known in St. Lucian French Creole as *"inonsans jan nwè,"* this term is used in this book to refer to the inherent brilliance of those racialized as Black by a failure to acknowledge *white gaze*, made visible in spaces where institutional expectation meets individual revelation via unapologetic diasporic transgressiveness (Davies, 1995) of Eurocentric norms. This innocence operates in all facets of society oblivious to and regardless of Eurocentric mechanisms operating to blind it and adeptly pursues "flourishing" (Keyes, 2002) based on a deeply entrenched commitment to life's purpose absolutely *sans attention* to white gaze.

(3) **Black Semiolingual Innocence:** The inherent brilliance in the literacies of the Black invoked by a failure to acknowledge *white gaze*, made visible through unapologetic semiolingual diasporic transgressiveness (Davies, 2013). This innocence operates oblivious to and regardless of Eurocentric mechanisms operating to blind it and adeptly leverages semiotics, with a specific focus on languaging, toward the goal of "flourishing" (Keyes, 2002) based on a deeply entrenched commitment to life's purpose *sans attention* to white gaze.

(4) **Englishes:** The term "Englishes" refers to the many different varieties of English that represent a plurality, variation, and change within the English language as a norm (Kachru, 1992). Englishes represent the interweaving of both standardized (e.g., Standard American English) and non-standardized (e.g., African American English) forms. I use '*non-standardized Englishes*' (e.g., African American Vernacular English, Jamaican Creole, Trinidadian English-lexicon Creole) here to refer to Englishes that do not adhere to what has been determined to be a 'Standard English' within a given context. Linguists refer to these variations as dialects, or New Englishes (Kirkpartrick & Deterding, 2011) and to their counterparts,

what I and others have labeled, *'standardized Englishes,'* as those that have been typically adopted for use in English literacy classrooms (e.g., Standard Jamaican English, Trinidadian Standard English, Standard American English).

(5) **Imaginaries:** A construct representing an imagining of "alternatives to development [that] summons a more substantive and non-linear understanding of human life and well-being – a bringing together of both material and non-material human needs" (Mahmud, 1999, p. 33). Mahmud (1999) has observed that "what is ultimately at stake is the transformation of the political, economic, and institutional regimes of truth production that have defined the era of development. This, in turn, requires changes in institutions and social relations, openness to various forms of knowledge and cultural manifestations, new styles of participation, and greater community autonomy over the production of norms and discourses" (p. 34). The notion of imaginaries represents such "construction [s] of collective imaginaries capable of reorienting social and political action" (Mahmud, 1999, p. 34).

(6) **Imajinè Inosan:** Informed by the notion of collective imaginaries (Mahmud, 1999), imajinè inosan functions as the Haitian Creole for *"imaginaries of innocence,"* also appearing in this book using the St. Lucian French Creole – *"entépwétasyon sosyal di inosans"* – and in English – *"imaginaries of innocence"* – representing envisioned pasts, presents, and futures as informed by the structure of Sankofa (Temple, 2010) that have been long-standing among people of Color and are intentionally invoked by the ability of the individual to function *sans attention* to whiteness. This functioning *sans* white gaze emerges alongside "the agenda of radical critique … [which] devises [a] means of liberating postcolonial societies from the imaginary of development and … [lessens] their dependence on the episteme of modernity" (Mahmud, 1999, p. 34). Imajinè inosan represents the "collective imaginaries capable of reorienting social and political action … to deploy non-reductionist and non-teleological notions of politics and economics, and, on the other hand, to facilitate participatory and democratizing potentials of … new social subjects" (p. 34). Imajinè inosan thus refers to "imagining alternatives to development [that] summons a more substantive and non-linear understanding of human life and well-being – a bringing together of both material and non-material human needs" *sans attention* to white gaze (Mahmud, 1999, p. 33).

(7) **Innocence:** Also "inonsans" in St. Lucian French Creole, innocence is taken to refer to the inherently imbued capacity of institutional-individual spaces created by Black students which operate legitimately *sans attention* to white gaze, juxtaposed against and disrupting the long-standing,

societally imposed "Black abstraction" that has for so long operated legally and otherwise to uphold an imagined "White innocence" (Ross, 1990). A defined marker of such innocence is a desire for flourishing in solidarity with others. Related terminologies such as "linguistic innocence" refer to the instantiation of such spaces through languaging and "Black linguistic innocence" to the capacity of Black students to reflect such instantiations.

(8) **Inonsans Jan Nwè:** St. Lucian French Creole for "*Black innocence*," which also appears in this book via French as "*innocence noire*" or via English as "*Black innocence*," "*inonsans jan nwè*" is an imaginary that liberates the mind, through "transcendent literacy" as proposed by Willis (2022), to consider the capacities including holistic languaging and literacies of Black children and youth – pre-white gaze – uninhibited and unassailed by the expectations of the colonizer.

(9) **Language Architecture:** Language architecture is the manipulation of language "for specific purposes" which frames students as "already understanding the relationship between language choice and meaning through the knowledge they have gained via socialization into the cultural and linguistic practices of their communities" (Flores, 2020, p. 25).

(10) **Languaging:** Languaging, for the purposes of this study, refers to inextricable links between students' language use and personhood (Cowley, 2017).

(11) **Language Ideology:** Language ideology, sometimes referred to as "beliefs" and "approaches" about language, represents the ideas, constructs, notions, and representations derived from individuals' social practices with language across multiple spheres, local and global (Razfar, 2012). Language ideology can be based on standardized language where it represents "a bias toward an abstract, idealized homogenous spoken language, ... imposed and maintained by dominant bloc institutions ... and drawn primarily from the spoken language of the upper middle class" (Lippi-Green, 1997, p. 64) or it may denote the opposite – ways of thinking about non-standardized language forms. Language ideology may also function bidirectionally where ways of thinking about language by one group impact ways of thinking about language by another group and vice versa (De Costa, 2010). An individual's ideology about language can be influenced by critical language awareness (CLA), which results when one is aware of the interplay between their use of language and the power associated with this use (Alim, 2005), by one's experience with linguistic discrimination (Tollefson, 2011) made visible in the implicit and explicit negative actions of others toward their use of language (Alim, 2005) and by linguistic profiling visible in the negative responses of others to one's auditory cues (Baugh, 2003).

(12) **Literacies:** Literacies refer to the multiple ways of making meaning from and with texts – multiliteracies – that are "deictic" (Leu et al., 2017, p. 1; New London Group, 1996), and reflect the use of multiple sources and successful navigation of meaning-making via the Internet (Leu et al., 2017).

(13) **Liminality:** Liminality is the variation in the transformative processes of those engaging third space characterized by a lack of certainty, willingness to be tentative, and surrender to compromise – based on the theory of hybridity (Bhabha, 1994).

(14) **Multiliteracies:** The notion of multiliteracies presumes that "metalanguages [are used] to describe and interpret the design elements of different modes of meaning" (New London Group, 1996, p. 83). Through these modes of meaning-making – tactile, gestural, spatial, visual, written, audio, linguistic, and synesthesia – youth negotiate a range of discourses by integrating "a variety of texts forms associated with information and multimedia technologies" (Kalantzis & Cope, 2012; New London Group, 1996, p. 61). Often used interchangeably with the term "new literacies," the notion of multiliteracies presumes that learners use a variety of techniques in various forms to infer meaning such as leveraging various semiotic resources to obtain information. These may include text messages, blogging, social networking websites, and listening to or reading information from electronic devices (Moss & Lapp, 2010).

(15) **Raciolinguistic Ideologies:** These are negative ways of thinking developed by language speakers (Flores & Rosa, 2015). Through these ideologies, the appropriation of imagined (or idealized) as well as actualized linguistic practices by racial populations based on a supposed standard English that is premised on a monoglossic language ideology does not constitute the sole basis used by others to determine the advancement of racial groups in our dominant system. The focus is on the white listener, how the language used by the racialized student is heard or interpreted by the white listening subject who "hears" or "interprets" from the dominant standardized English perspective (Flores & Rosa, 2015). Flores and Rosa (2015) observe that raciolinguistic ideology represents the privileging of "dominant white perspectives on the linguistic and cultural practices of racialized communities" regardless of the efforts of persons of Color to approximate the accepted language forms (pp. 150–151). This positioning, in turn, is used to construct racialized populations such as Latinos and Blacks in ways that are inferior and illegitimate, *regardless* of whether they use or attempt to use standardized linguistic (and English) practices.

(16) **A Raciolinguistic Perspective:** A raciolinguistic perspective addresses raciolinguistic ideology by articulating premises undergirding this ideology. Elements of a raciolinguistic perspective are "(i) historical and contemporary co-naturalizations of race and language as part of the colonial formation of modernity; (ii) perceptions of racial and linguistic difference; (iii) regimentations of racial and linguistic categories; (iv) racial and linguistic intersections and assemblages; and (v) the contestation of racial and linguistic power formations" (Rosa & Flores, 2017, p. 3).

(17) **Raciosemiotic Architecture:** Described in St. Lucian French Creole and presented in this book also as "*imaj ògannizasyon wapò ant sé diféwan was*," this term extends the notion of "language architecture" as proposed by Flores (2020) to illustrate how semiotics and multimodality are mediated by power relations, many of which are premised on the racialized structures that are encoded in what it means to make meaning with texts that are often nonlinguistic in nature. Students functioning as "*raciosemiotic architects*" "manipulat[e multiple modes] for specific purposes" (Flores, 2020, p. 25) while engaging racialization based on how they understand choice and meaning of multiple modalities to be related based on their socialization into cultural, linguistic, and racial community practices (see Smith, 2022d).

(18) **Semiolingual Innocence:** This term refers to the capacity of youth, no matter who they are, to fail to acknowledge or to leverage *white gaze* in its numerous forms in their semiotics as they do in their languaging, thus (re)inscribing their innate capacity through semiotics and languaging for flourishing through their holistic literacies. Semiolingual innocence operates based on a deeply entrenched commitment to life's purpose *sans attention* to (by Blacks, whites, or peoples of Color) or a leveraging of white gaze (by whites, Blacks, people of color, or people who 'pass as white'). Acknowledging the broad range of semiotics but also attending closely to languaging (i.e., hereafter *semiolingual*), the heuristic of semiolingual innocence is presented in this book as emerging from the literacies and languaging of Black immigrant youth. In turn, it is proposed as a pathway to reinscribe the innocence of all youth. Semiolingual innocence is presented as being characterized by eight mechanisms, each of which can be considered as an "*F*" of semiolingual innocence:

(a) **Flourishing:** Semiolingual innocence positions teaching for "*flourishing*" (Keyes, 2002) with translanguaging and transsemiotizing, discarding archaic notions of success (*Flourishing*).

(b) **Purpose:** Semiolingual innocence positions teaching solely for deeply entrenched *purpose* such that children and their parents hold the right to determine the codes undergirding E-languages and E-semiotics needed to foster life pursuits (*Flattening*).

(c) **Comfort:** Semiolingual innocence positions teaching for subconscious elicitation of emotion through immersion in *spaces of comfort* as a basis for cultivating "animation" (Orellana, 2015) via imagination through translanguaging and "transsemiotizing" (*Feeling*).
(d) **Expansion:** Semiolingual innocence positions teaching as an opportunity for leveraging metalinguistic, metacultural, metaracial, and metasemiotic understanding that expands 'monolingual,' 'monocultural,' and 'monoracial' as well as all repertoires (see Smith, 2022a, on transraciolinguistics) (*Fostering*).
(e) **Paradox:** Semiolingual innocence positions teaching to instantiate intentional paradoxical confrontations toward the cultivation of a "*both-and*" ethos, critical for emerging through the dialectic of 'oppressed' versus 'oppressor,' via flourishing (Freire, 1970/2000; Smith, 2013) (*Finessing*).
(f) **Originality:** Semiolingual innocence positions teaching to prioritize communicative capacities through translanguaging and transsemiotizing approaches to comprehension that preserve *originality of meaning* steeped in cultural indigeneity, regardless of the source (*Factualizing*).
(g) **Interdependence:** Semiolingual innocence positions teaching for intraracial and interracial interdependence, recognizing the shared humanity of all peoples (*Friending*).
(h) **Imagination:** Semiolingual innocence positions teaching for harnessing the imagination to solve local and global problems currently assailing the currents and futures of the world (*Facilitating*).

(19) **Semiotizing/Transsemiotizing/Translanguaging:** Translanguaging is used in this book to refer to the use of various E-languages embedded within the linguistic repertoire for meaning-making and transsemiotizing to the adept use of various elements of the semiotic repertoire for meaning-making. García and Wei (2014) advanced a holistic view of linguistic and semiotic resources, via translanguaging, where a "trans-semiotic system with many meaning-making signs, primarily linguistic ones … combine to make up a person's semiotic repertoire (p. 42)." The notion of transsemiotics, which draws from Halliday's (2013) proposition of "trans-semiotics," undergirds the construct as proposed by García and Wei and the development of the notion of the idea of 'trans-semiotizing' as dynamically coordinating a range of linguistic and semiotic resources (e.g., languages, gestures, facial expressions, sounds, visual images) to co-create meaning and thereby share and expand communicative repertoires (Lin, 2019). In this book, I adopt a "both-and" approach to translanguaging that draws from the ideological notion of an individual linguistic repertoire – I-languages (García & Kleyn, 2016; MacSwan, 2017; Smith,

2020a, 2020b, 2020c) – while also considering the *imposition of* external, abstract, and idealized systems – E-languages – during the process of translanguaging with one's linguistic repertoire (Cowley, 2017; King, 2017; MacSwan, 2017). This "both-and" approach transcends the prevailing and persistent oppressor vs. oppressed dynamic railed against by Paulo Freire (Freire, 1970/2000) from which he envisioned the emergence of "a new being: no longer oppressor nor longer oppressed, but human in the process of achieving freedom" (Freire, 1970/2000, p. 1). Similarly, I adopt a "both-and" approach to transsemiotizing that draws from the ideological notion of an individual semiotic repertoire – "*I-semiotics*" – while also considering the imposition of external abstract and idealized systems – E-semiotics – during the process of transsemiotizing with one's semiotic repertoire as is often visible through notions such as "raciosemiotics" (i.e., the influence of race on the coordination of semiotic resources; see Smalls, 2020).

(20) **Third Space:** Conceived of theoretically as a function of postcoloniality, "third space" denotes how oppositional positions or those that are binary come together to constitute merged dichotomies (Bhabha, 1994; Soja, 1996). Third space has been represented as an "in-between" hybrid space for language (Gutiérrez, 2008) where students' "first space" (home life and sociocultural experiences) comes into contact with a "second space" (school curriculum and discipline-specific language and learning) and functions as a site of boundary crossing across cultures and between a home language and the second language of school (Moje et al., 2004).

Significance

Attention to raciolinguistics (Alim, 2016) and its relationship to literacy practices continue to undergo significant global expansion in the past decade. From increasing foci on the relationship between race and language, language in literacy in countries such as Britain (e.g., Cushing, 2022, Cushing & Carter, 2022; Cushing & Snell 2022), and Finland (e.g., Mustonen, 2021), as well as the immigrant practices of Mongolians in Australia (e.g., Dovchin, 2019a) to languaging on the African continent (e.g., Vigouroux, 2017), in Korea (e.g., Park, 2022), in the US (e.g., Alim & Smitherman, 2012), and in the Canadian society (e.g., Ibrahim 1999; Shizha et al., 2020), the "twining" of race and language (Rosa & Flores, 2017) continues to be explored across populations of the *Majority World* (Pence & Marfo, 2008). These conversations function internationally as a response to a new wave of global racial reckoning spurred on, in part, by the viral video of the murder of George Floyd. For instance, many respond to long-standing descriptions of the implicit as well as explicit structure of racialization undergirding education such as *How the West Indian Child Is Made Educationally Subnormal in the British School System* by Bernard Coard, which featured filmmaker Steve McQueen's 2020 award-winning television series, *Small Axe* (Coard, 1971). In such responses, it is increasingly and vividly clear how racial injustice functions systemically and undeterred within institutions across the globe.

The emphasis of scholars on the interrelationship between race and language has, as a global project, placed the fields of literacy and language, squarely for what seems like the first time, in a dynamic where the pervasive sweeping of race under the proverbial rug is perhaps no longer a viable option. Operating as a stark reminder of the obscurity of repeated calls for a centering of race and racialization in literacy research (e.g., Willis, 1995, 2002, 2003, 2008, 2012, 2015, 2019), this emphasis has often been absent from widely disseminated publications such as the World Migration Report (e.g., McAuliffe & Khandria, 2020) and largely invisible in agendas such as that of the Organization for Economic Development (OECD). The seeming attempt to currently center race is visible in numerous associations' overt response to the call to undo centuries of harm to Black peoples. For instance, educational organizations such as the American Psychological Association (2021) have highlighted how the overlooking of racialization has caused undue harm to people of Color, and specifically Black peoples, apologizing for this history and outlining resolutions. Similarly, anthropological organizations such as the American Anthropological Association, through its Language and Social Justice Task Force, have recently produced a volume that synthesizes how patterns of communication are directly related to creating more just societies. By the same token, literacy, language, and educational organizations such as the Literacy Research Association (LRA), American Association of Applied Linguistics (AAAL), American Educational Research Association (AERA), National Council of Teachers of English (NCTE), and others increasingly point to the need to address racialized inequalities that function at the intersections of people's lives.

Looking back historically, it is evident that as early as 1961, the linguistic differences based on race – between Negroes and whites – have been a key area of study in countries such as the US. For instance, Barth (1961) described back then distinctions between the language of Blacks and whites. The author highlighted the ways in which languaging created status challenges associated with how Blacks perceived the self, their relationships with each other, and their relationships with whites. It was observed that a stark difference existed between how social experiences defined the meanings attached to words by Blacks as compared to whites. Extending this focus, Rickford and Rickford (1980/2015) later examined how gestures functioned differentially between Blacks and whites in the US. The authors pointed out, decades ago, that gestures functioned differently in the speech of American whites as compared to Blacks (see

Rickford & Rickford, 1980/2015). They documented how semiotic tools such as "cut[ing] the eyes" and "suck[ing] the teeth" are used routinely by Blacks in Caribbean countries, representations that I acknowledge are visible in spaces such as my homeland, St. Lucia. In turn, they illustrated that these were not reflected by white people, thereby creating a challenge for their understandings of the meanings of these gestures when white people experienced them. Referring to these as "African survivals," Rickford and Rickford (1980/2015) recognized the need to explore, more intently, the ways in which gestures such as these are distinctly representative of Blacks in America. The authors also highlighted how these gestures functioned across the Caribbean, Africa, and the US, laying the foundation for later research explorations.

The Black diasporic project of addressing racialization in language has since continued to grow for many decades, both implicitly and explicitly. It has operated though, very often, on the periphery of mainstream language and literacy research and instruction, a global project largely dominated by Eurocentric normative practice. For instance, following the *Students' Right to Their Own Language Resolution*, the National Council of Teachers of English (NCTE) Conference on College Composition and Communication copublished a landmark volume in 2008, edited by Deborah Holdstein, designed to broadly address languaging, African American Englishes, and the pedagogies of literacy needed to meet the needs of Black students and other students of Color in schools (*SRTOL*; Conference on College Composition and Communication, 1974). During the same period, scholars such as Gundaker (1998) were adamant in their challenging of monolithic notions of literate practice based on the languaging of Black peoples by documenting how creolization and vernacular language practices were used and leveraged across the US and the West Indies. Gundaker highlighted nuances present in the adept languaging of Black peoples across the diaspora, raising questions about dichotomies existing in our tendency to ascribe certain linguistic capacities to Black people (i.e., "inferiority") while overlooking their capacity for others (i.e., "superior" Eurocentric linguistic norms). Though significant and potentially paradigm-shifting for the field, scholarship such as this has largely remained on the sidelines of literacy research and instruction. This has occurred despite the persistence of authors to highlight the complex and adept languaging of Black peoples as opposed to an imposed monolithic conceptualization, and to characterize the racialization that operates at its center.

For Black Caribbean peoples, the often-peripheral functioning of the intricacies of languaging and race, made possible largely through notions such as Edward Said's Orientalism (Said, 1978) and Paulo Freire's invitation to transcend the "oppressor vs. oppressed" dynamic in education (Freire, 1970/2000), has operated primarily as a 'postcolonial' project. This postcolonial project remains visible in both the Majority World West Indian context (e.g., Bartlett, 2012; Bristol, 2012; Devonish & Carpenter, 2020; Thompson et al., 2011; Warrican, 2005) and also, globally, within Minority World countries such as the UK and the US. Joining scholars such as Cooper (2020), Ibrahim (1999, 2019), Nero (2001), and Skerrett (2006), who have drawn attention to differentiated pedagogies, experiences, and epistemologies necessary due to the languaging of Caribbean peoples in North America and in the US, and others such as Franklin (2013) and Wallace (2017a, 2017b, 2023), who have undertaken the broader and global centering of race in examining the responses of Black Caribbean peoples to educational systems in the UK, this book comes at a time when it is increasingly recognized that a failure to address the interrelationship of language and race in mainstream education, and literacy more specifically, represents, in effect, a moral intention to do harm (see Anya, 2016; Willis et al., 2022). We see a recognition of this failure in the documentation of the counseling needs of Caribbean students in the US that fosters healthy adjustment and the urgency of addressing linguistic diversity of immigrants as a determinant of healthcare (e.g., Morrison & Bryan, 2014; U.S. Department of Health and Human Services, 2022). We see it also in observations of the "twining" of language and race in the life of the Black immigrant for human "flourishing" (Keyes, 2002; Rosa & Flores, 2017; Smith et al., 2022) and comparative analyses of the role of race in the experiences of Black migrants across Britain, France, and the Netherlands and the US (Foner, 1985). Taken together, these acknowledgments represent an increasing intention to discuss variations offered in the literacies and languaging of Black immigrants that correspond to the need for moving beyond restricted pedagogies of schooling. They also demonstrate the commitment to instantiating novel imaginaries steeped in solidarity and community while locating the pervasively adverse response to such variations within their structural and foundational context, which is race.

Responding to this need, this book complements my current and previous research in the area of Black immigrant literacies and Englishes, which intersectionally revolves around race, language, and immigration (e.g., Smith, 2020a, 2020b, 2020c, 2022a, 2022b). The book uniquely extends current insights in the field of literacy by (a) centralizing race in conjunction with language to examine the literacy practices of Black Caribbean immigrant youth (Nalubega-Booker & Willis, 2020; Smith, 2019a); (b) using translanguaging and transsemiotics via a "both-and" model as a function of raciolinguistics, raciosemiotics, and a raciolinguistic perspective to clarify the multiliteracies of youth who are Black, immigrants from the Caribbean, and who use Englishes and associated semiotic resources (Alim, 2004, 2016; Alim et al., 2016; New London Group, 1996; Rosa & Flores, 2017; Smith, 2023a); (c) bridging gaps between notions such as "academic" and "invisible" literacies and between "academic" and "home" languages through examination of the "holistic literacies" of Black Caribbean immigrant youth (Smith, 2020b); (d) providing novel insights about how the constructs of race, language, and immigration intersect as a function of "transracialization" (Alim, 2016) and "transraciolinguistics" (Smith, 2022a) to broadly extend understandings of literacy in relation to racialized, and specifically, Black language speakers crossing boundaries; and (e) drawing upon a decolonizing interpretive lens to do so (Dei, 2000; Onwuegbuzie & Frels, 2013). More succinctly, the unique contribution of this book to the field can be found in its presentation of eight mechanisms to advance the holistic literacies of youth and in its promise of *semiolingual innocence*, described at length in Chapter 6.

Leading up to the insights in this book have been numerous collaborative endeavors undertaken with colleagues including symposia at the American Educational Research Association (AERA) conference such as the 2020 session, "Clarifying the Role of Race in the Literacies and Englishes of Black Immigrant Youth," undertaken in collaboration with Drs. Eliza Braden, Kisha Bryan, the late Benjamin (Benji) Chang, Bryan Hotchkins, Lydiah Kiramba, Michelle Knight-Manuel, and Vaughn Watson. Similarly, scholarship has been generated closely with colleagues to advance collaborations such as the 2021 AERA session "Critical Literacy for Racial Justice: Equity through Intersectionality," presented in conjunction with national and international scholars such as Drs. Joel Berends, Alecia Beymer, Awad Ibrahim, Gwendolyn McMillon, Vaughn Watson, Arlette Willis, and Rahat Zaidi. Also serving as a precursor to this book have been insights engaged in community with scholars racialized as Black in the US such as Drs. Allison Skerrett, Lakeya Omogun Lakeya Afolalu (Omogun), Cheryl A. McLean, Vaughn Watson, Michelle Knight-Manuel, Eurydice Bauer, Lenny Sanchez, S. Joel Warrican, Kisha Bryan, Lydiah Kiramba, James Alan Oloo, Kendra Nalubega-Booker, Arlette Willis, Eliza Braden, Ayanna Cooper, and Bryan Hotchkins in the 2020 *Teachers College Record (TCR)* guest-edited special issue titled, "Clarifying the Role of Race in the Literacies of Black Immigrant Youth." Other collaborative pathways through which this work has emerged have been discussions with Dr. Aria Razfar in advancing the centering of race in immigration through the 2022 *International Journal of Qualitative Studies (IQSE) in Education* special issue, "Algorithm of Love: Insights from Immigrant Literacies and Narratives," which highlighted scholarly insights from educators such as Drs. Eliza Braden, Gloria Boutte, Vaughn Watson, Bryan Hotchkins, Lenny Sanchez, Eurydice Bauer, and Rahat Zaidi. My in-depth discussions in community with Dr. Ramón Martínez as an LRA STAR Fellow, collaborations during the COVID-19 pandemic with scholars such as Drs. Arlette Willis and Gwendolyn McMillon undergirding the book *Affirming Black Students' Lives and Literacies: Bearing Witness*, and with Drs. Vaughn

Watson and Michelle Knight-Manuel underlying the forthcoming *Educating African Immigrant Youth*: *Schooling and Civic Engagement in K–12 Schools* have informed my evolving understandings as I came to this work. So did more recently completed collaborations with scholars such as Drs. Teresa Cremin, Natalia Kucirkova, and Diane Collier surrounding the guest-edited *Literacy* special issue, "Literacy for Social Justice: Charting Equitable Global and Local Practices" (2023) and with Drs. Vaughn Watson and Ayanna Brown surrounding the guest-edited *Research in the Teaching of English (RTE)* special issue, "Diasporic Tellings of Race, Literacies, Joys, and Geographies in the Lives of Black African Immigrant Youth" (forthcoming).

Extending insights explored thus far, *Literacies of Migration: Translanguaging Imaginaries of Innocence* paints a vivid portrait of Black Caribbean immigrant youth, whose Englishes are racialized, linguicized, and raciosemiotized even while their literacies are renegotiated across their countries of origin and the US. Evidence is presented of how they use their long-standing acumen with translanguaging to thrive as they draw from their unique individual linguistic repertoires – *translanguaging imaginaries of innocence*. In doing so, I offer an intricate view of how they reinscribe their *inonsans jan nwè*, reflecting an empowerment to knowingly engage with the tensions created between their attempts to draw from these repertoires and the ways in which external, idealized, and abstract systems work to impede, limit, and interrupt this process. By considering translanguaging as well as transsemiotizing for clarifying Black Caribbean immigrant literacies while also foregrounding race and racialized Englishes, I invite scholars, educators, teachers, and policymakers to create institutional mechanisms for empowering Black immigrant youth, their teachers, and their parents. Educational stakeholders are invited to do this given that students engage with tensions arising from translanguaging that rob them of what I describe as their *'linguistic innocence'* – known in French as *innocence linguistic* – the revelation of which may be entirely novel.

The lens of Black immigrant literacies as a basis for this book provides an avenue for challenging current dichotomous discourses regarding achievement that continue to pit *underperforming* African Americans against high achieving *model minority* Black immigrant youth from African countries, Caribbean countries, and beyond. Daring to disrupt the long-held and erroneous perception that to single out and discuss Black immigrants in the US is to somehow engage in divisive rhetoric, I challenge, instead, the idea that all Black immigrant youth as opposed to their racialized and immigrant US peers are *academic prodigies*. This myth often arises from the typical and meritocratic notion of these youth as *designer immigrants* or a *new model minority* who reflect *success*. In choosing to intentionally silence the invisibility of this Black population in the US which has functioned for so long under the guise of Black solidarity while subtly reinforcing the divisive goals of white supremacy, I show how racial discrimination occurs against the languaging and personhoods of Black immigrant youth in ways that are similar to their African American peers.

To achieve these goals, I draw partly from non-Eurocentric lenses which are increasingly needed to present decolonized research findings about people of Color. In doing so, I overtly meet, head-on, long-standing and increasing debates arising from such distinctions between Black immigrant and Black American youth and the promotion of raciolinguistic and raciosemiotic ideologies that affect the ability of these subpopulations to use their literacies of migration, in solidarity within racial groups, for mutual support. One such example is evident in the recent discussion surrounding the questions of Cynthia Enrivo's casting as Harriet Tubman given her lineage as a British actress of Nigerian (and not African American) descent (ABC News, 2020). Silencing the invisibility of these strained relations among Black subpopulations in the US while also acknowledging, with bravery, the heterogeneity within them, I encourage the field, by considering such examples as youth's voices in this book, to consider how a vision of holistic literacies can serve as a basis for understanding, examining, and leveraging the strengths reflected in Black Caribbean immigrant literacies.

Choosing to use the lens of Black immigrant literacies in this book can help to elicit information about Black immigrant youth's literacy practices and Englishes in their individual life's trajectories across their home countries and the US with the goal of helping them to acknowledge their Black innocence. Doing so can also allow them to identify their own process of negotiating tensions, as opposed to creating a standardized model that seeks to be representative of all Black immigrant youth. Through *Literacies of Migration*, I transdisciplinarily join, more broadly, scholars such as Bartlett et al. (2018), Cooper (2020), Dovchin (2020), Foner (1985), Fordham & Ogbu (1986), Ibrahim (1999, 2019), Kumi-Yeboah (2018), McLean (2010), Mwangi & English (2017), Nero (2006, 2014), Skerrett (2012, 2015), Skerrett & Omogun (2020), Suárez-Orozco & Suárez-Orozco (2009/2001), Wallace (2017a, 2017b, 2022), Waters et al. (2014), and Watson & Knight-Manuel (2017), among others, who have examined areas such as the Englishes, literacies, multiliteracies, cultures, acculturation processes, race, ethnicity, online literacy practices, digital literacies, and religious literacies of (Black) Black immigrant and transnational peoples and youth.

Through the nuanced decolonizing approach deployed, a portrait is painted of how Black immigrant youth use their self-determination to reclaim linguistic innocence and work towards imagined presents and futures even while simultaneously describing how institutional factors raciolinguistically and raciosemiotically influence their literacies. As a result of the engagement with these lenses, the fields of language and literacy are invited, with urgency, to extend a disruption of dichotomies long undergirding distinctions between the *academic* vs. *invisible* literacies of youth. The reader is invited to extend beyond tensions concerning such dichotomies regarding literacy and to focus instead on notions such as "language architecture" (Flores, 2020) and "raciosemiotic architecture" – "*imaj ògannizasyon wapò ant sé diféwan was*" (Smith, 2022d) as well as their affordances for understanding the multiliteracies of Black immigrant, and all youth. Making visible an awareness of instances where non-standardized and standardized Englishes and other semiotic resources of Black immigrant youth may be racialized, through language as well as *imaj ògannizasyon wapò ant sé diféwan was* (Smith, 2022d), this book extends the current scholarly focus regarding Black immigrants, Black immigrant youth, and their literacies, raising questions about how a raciolinguistic perspective potentially functions as a basis for more accurately representing the literacies and translanguaging of immigrant youth of Color in the US. Juxtaposing how youth's Englishes and literacies are negotiated through the lens of the white listening subject regardless of their efforts to persistently contest such ideologies against the reclamation of their lost translanguaging imaginaries, I empower those who work with Black youth and with all youth of Color, to dismantle and create institutional structures that reduce the burden imposed on *all* youth to navigate inescapable tensions surrounding languaging and semiotizing. By extension, exemplars from the "authentic narratives" – unsanitized stories presented in the voice of youth – allow for a reclaiming of the voices of Black peoples everywhere and throughout time (Smith, 2023b).

Much like Paulo Freire (1970/2000), whose broad challenge to the tendency in the educational enterprise to remain immersed in an oppressor vs. oppressed dynamic, as alluded to earlier, resulted in the envisioning of "a new being: no longer oppressor nor longer oppressed, but human in the process of achieving freedom" (Freire, 1970/2000, p. 1) emerging through the dialectic, the "both-and" (Smith, 2013) approach to translanguaging undergirding this book responds to the critical question posed by Alim (2005) with regards to raciolinguistics, which is:

By what processes are we all involved in the construction and maintenance of a "standard" language, and further, that the "standard" is somehow better, more intelligent, more appropriate, more important, etc. than other varieties? In other words, how, when and why are we all implicated in linguistic supremacy? (p. 194)

Extending this question posed by Alim (2005) I also ask, *In what ways are the literate repertoires of all, as are those of Black humans, restricted by the implications of linguistic and semiotic supremacy?* And also, *In what ways is linguistic and semiotic supremacy, as a function of being immigrant and Black, capable of illustrating the ways in which such supremacy, by default, handicaps all humans?* In doing so, I hope to liberate thinking about how Black immigrant literacies can serve as a vehicle for building solidarity within and across racial groups, many of whom have for so long erroneously believed that white supremacy works *only* against the interest of Blacks, Black immigrants, and of migrant people of Color. At the same time, I demonstrate how Black immigrant youth sustain their self-determination and thrive while simultaneously foregrounding the role of institutions in revamping raciolinguicized and raciosemiotized policies that come to bear on the literate and languaging repertoires of Black Caribbean immigrant youth.

Organization of the Book

To facilitate ease of reading, this book is organized into seven chapters. Chapter 1, the Introduction, provides an overview of the ideas undergirding the content presented across the book. The Introduction also includes definitions of key constructs used in the book and presents the organizing structure of the book. Chapter 2 presents the rationale for focusing on the lens of Black immigrant literacies as a basis for this book and provides the reader with an overview of the broad and long-standing body of research on language and literacy in the US that has emerged as a backdrop against which Black Caribbean languaging and literacies of migration are considered. Discussing the colonial imperatives across the Black diaspora influencing education and language use in Black immigrants' countries of origin that necessitate a legitimization of "Englishes" as languages, the chapter situates Afro-Caribbean languaging, Englishes, and literacies within its broader contexts by presenting a discussion of education, migration, and cultures while addressing the historical and contemporary educational landscape of Black people in the Caribbean. It also engages in a discussion of the historical and contemporary socio-educational landscape of Black immigrants in the US. Chapter 3 acknowledges the intertwined histories of Afro-Caribbean languaging, Englishes, and literacies across the Black diaspora. In doing so, the chapter attends to the long legacy of languaging emerging out of the Black race and reaching across the Black diaspora while also lamenting the *invented illiteracy* often imposed in the characterizations of Black peoples worldwide. Acknowledging the traditional lineage of '*Diaspora Literacy*' in making visible interconnections across Black peoples within and beyond the US, the chapter presents Caribbean Englishes, describing the languaging, Englishes, and literacies of English-speaking Afro-Caribbean students in the Caribbean and in the US. Calling for a silencing of the historical tradition of invented illiteracy used to characterize Black peoples across the diaspora and inviting a strengthening of accessible knowledges surrounding the rich literate and linguistic heritages they inherently possess, this chapter makes clear the broader transnational contexts influencing racialized translanguaging and transsemiotizing in Black immigrant literacies. Chapter 4 presents the conceptual framework for understanding the perspectives used as lenses to examine Black immigrant literacies in the book. The chapter discusses key elements of the theoretical framework: multiliteracies, translanguaging, raciolinguistics, language architecture, and raciosemiotic architecture. Together, the lenses of multiliteracies, translanguaging, a raciolinguistic perspective, language, and raciosemiotic architecture make it possible to examine the literacies of migration undergirding the translanguaging imaginaries of innocence of Black Caribbean youth. Chapter 5 provides the reader with a depiction of the methodology involved in conducting the study of Black immigrant youth's literacies undergirding this book. The chapter begins with my situatedness in the study as a Black immigrant and transnational single-parent-scholar-mother-educator. It then presents a description of the decolonizing interpretive research design steeped in *'critical dialectical pluralism'* used to examine the literacies of migration of Black Caribbean youth. The chapter presents the procedures undergirding interpretive analyses of the data as they relate to the multiliteracies, translanguaging practices, raciolinguistic and raciosemiotic ideologies in the lives of six Black Caribbean immigrant youth. Chapter 6 presents the findings that illustrate how the literacies of Black Caribbean immigrant youth are enacted. Based on these findings, the chapter discusses elements of the heuristic of *"semiolingual innocence,"* proposed to clarify understandings about how elements of multiliteracies, translanguaging, raciolinguistic ideologies, and raciosemiotic architecture – *imaj ògannizasyon wapò ant sé diféwan was* – intersect to clarify the literacies and translanguaging of the Black Caribbean immigrant youth. In turn, eight elements are presented, which characterize the heuristic, as mechanisms for reinscribing the semiolingual innocence of all youth. Chapter 7 synthesizes insights from the book and makes recommendations for researchers, teachers, administrators, and policymakers who wish to support Black Caribbean as well as Black Caribbean immigrant and transnational youth's holistic literacies via *"imaginaries of innocence"* – *"imajinè inosan"* or *"entépwétasyon sosyal di inosans"* – based on the role of these youth as language and raciosemiotic architects. In doing so, it invites the field to consider futuristic notions for enacting just presents such as *"liberatory Caribbean imaginaries"* that can instantiate our envisioning of the much needed "new beings" so aptly called for by Paulo Freire so long ago (Freire, 1970/2000). The chapter also invites a broader attention to translanguaging as it functions intralinguistically, often in Englishes, via the semiolingual repertoires of all youth.

A National and Global Imperative

Black immigrants currently account for about 9 percent of America's 42.4 million immigrants – a four-fold increase compared to the number of immigrants in 1980 and an estimated four million Black immigrants subsumed within the broader US immigrant population (Zong & Batalova, 2019). The

US Census Bureau (2013) projects that by 2060, 16.5 percent of US Blacks will be immigrants. These realities make it clear that understanding, addressing, and leveraging the literacies of this population is critical. The timeliness and relevance of this book are even more compelling considering what Portes (2019) refers to as American immigration policy that signals "the *end of compassion* [emphasis added] and the consequent loss of the country's unique moral stature in the world" (Portes, 2019, p. 2). Debates surrounding immigration, both nationally and globally, as well as national movements dedicated to the opposition of Blackness in the US (Dancy et al., 2018; Sexton, 2018) present evidence that immigration and race discourses both come to bear directly on Black immigrant youth and reinforce the dire need for mechanisms to support these youth and how they use their literacies to navigate inequities in and beyond classrooms. And *"immigrant of Color literacies"* (Smith, 2020b, p. 12) steeped in translanguaging imaginaries of innocence are becoming increasingly central to present and futuristic notions of overall well-being and thriving in a 'post-pandemic' world – *"flourishing"* (Keyes, 2002).

As Amanda Gorman observed in the now famous inaugural poem, "The Hill We Climb," *"We will not be turned around or interrupted by intimidation because we know our inaction and inertia will be the inheritance of the next generation, become the future"* (Gorman, 2021). Clarifying how *imaginaries of Inonsans Jan Nwè:* as articulated in the translanguaging and literate practices of Black immigrant youth in this book interrupts the temptation to indulge in inaction and inertia that threaten our collective futures. The discussions that follow will prove critical to instantiating *imagiscapes – imaginary landscapes –* of flourishing that support solidarity among Black populations and beyond.

2 Why *'New Model Minority'* Youth?
Understanding Black Immigrants in the United States

> When day comes, we ask ourselves, where can we find light in this never-ending shade?
> The loss we carry. A sea we must wade.
> We braved the belly of the beast.
> We've learned that quiet isn't always peace, and the norms and notions of what "just" is isn't always justice.
>
> Gorman, 2021

"*It felt like something out of a storybook*" [emphasis added], said Munya Chawawa, 27, a broadcaster and a satirist, who was a pundit during the BBC coverage that day. "I actually felt a bit tearful, seeing a foreign woman of color not only being accepted into the royal family but applauded by the masses filling the streets. It felt like I was part of a moment in history." Soon came headlines, however, commenting on Meghan's "exotic DNA," and how she was "(almost) straight outta Compton." A BBC presenter was fired for tweeting a picture of a chimpanzee and likening it to the couple's son, Archie. And Princess Michael of Kent – who is married to the queen's first cousin – wore a blackamoor brooch when she met Meghan for the first time.

Now that fairy tale is over, the message couldn't be clearer for high-schoolers.

"Even if you're rich and of a certain status, you're still black," Ogbuani said. "You're black first and foremost before you're rich." This has been a very rude awakening," said Ladapo, who studies economics and is president of her university's African-Caribbean Society. "*It reminded us that we shouldn't get too comfortable, and no matter how much we think we are accepted into society, we really aren't*" [emphasis added].

Excerpt from "Meghan Markle and British Racism: What Her Saga Says to Black Britons," Smith, 2020

The typically overlooked and invisible population of Black immigrant students in the US tend to be regarded as a *new model minority* and as *designer immigrants* (Kperogi, 2009; Simmons, 1999). Developed in 1966 to describe

Asian Americans, the term "model minority" has been used to refer to "groups that were at one time marginalized, educationally, economically and socially, but eventually rose up despite their many obstacles to become prosperous, admired and even emulated" (Kaba, 2008, p. 310). While scholars such as Kaba (2008) apply the model minority to Black (women) in a favorable light, others (e.g., Hartlep, 2012) assert that "the model minority discourse serve[s] as a rhetorical – social, political, and educational – device used to divide and conquer Blacks and Asians (as well as other non-White minorities) while maintaining the status quo" (p. 5), and therefore cannot be used to describe Blacks.

Black immigrant youth are thought to be a *new model minority* based on the view that they supposedly have the skills, goals, and interests that represent a higher aspiration than that of other immigrant, transnational (Kperogi, 2009; Simmons, 1999), and Black American peers (Watson & Knight-Manuel, 2017). For the purpose of this book, I use the term "new model minority" to refer to "a minority who is economically successful, has achieved that success by traditional, approved means ... is culturally assimilated ... and is silent about race and/or adhere[s] to the dominant racial ideology" (Reece, 2012, p. 25).

In undertaking the study undergirding this book, I acknowledge the underlying fragility of the notion of a *(new) model minority* when applied to students of Color, who supposedly reflect academic *success*. This fragility in students of Color is similar to the applicability of the term to Hmong American students (an ethnic group from China and Southeast Asia). For instance, Hmong Americans are said to successfully perform in ways that align with model minority norms when they help institutions "recruit 'diversity,' promote cultural events, and graduate from their programs despite academic struggles, ... achiev[ing] honorary whiteness" (Lee et al., 2017, p. 4). However, they are "blackened when they engage in student activism, demand curriculum inclusivity in schools, and request for meaningful inclusion in [the] campus decision-making process," signaling "resistance" based on "racialization [that] systematically silences and polices Hmong Americans to perform the model minority" (Lee et al., 2017, p. 4).

Aligned with Hartlep (2012), I problematize the notion of the term, *model minority*, or a *new model minority*, as applied to Black immigrant youth. My rationale – such a terminology is based on meritocracy and colorblindness (see Milner, 2012) and suggests to other underserved immigrant youth: *'If these Black youth can do so well despite their challenges with discrimination, language difference, and migration, then the rest of you minorities can do well too.'*

As the excerpts at the beginning of this chapter from high school youth in Britain, who regarded Meghan Markle as one of them who had 'done well,' show, the youth initially believed that Meghan had been accepted despite being a person of Color. They later experienced a rude awakening when they realized that despite being rich, accomplished, and joining what is considered to be a "royal family" based on society's standards, Meghan continued to be subjected to discrimination based on the color of her skin. This occurred in spite of her being phenotypically more representative of having what one might argue to be 'white skin' (i.e., appearing to be Caucasian) – *'white-passing.'* The students saw this discrimination portrayed in the double standards such as the *Daily Mail*'s story "about Prince William's wife, Catherine, Duchess of Cambridge, 'cradling her baby bump,' while Meghan was accused of 'pride' and 'vanity' for doing the same." They also saw it reflected in certain (white) British commentariat members' indications that allegations of racism against Meghan were overblown (Smith, 2020).

Like Meghan Markle, who, though 'successful' and from the higher echelons of society, was nonetheless regarded by Black youth as an immigrant of Color to Britain, *new model minority* perceptions of Black immigrant youth tend to hold because, in spaces such as the US, these youth have been described as reflecting considerably "better" academic performance than their African American counterparts (e.g., Anekwe, 2008; Duong et al., 2016; Farah, 2015; Freeman, 2016; Gilbert, 2008; Kumi-Yeboah & Smith, 2016; Mogaka, 2013; Nderu, 2005; Rong & Brown, 2007; Smith et al., 2019, 2022; Thomas et al., 2009; Waters et al., 2014; Wilson-Akubude, 2016). This perception has been visible for decades, with indications as far back as 2008 suggesting that "West Indians [as part of the Black immigrant population] had slightly better educational and occupational outcomes than their native African American, Puerto Rican, or Dominican peers, although performing [more poorly] than whites" (Waters et al., 2014, p. 373). Such perceptions have also persisted because Black immigrant students tend to come from countries where the official language spoken is English (Zong & Batalova, 2019) and thus tend to be often cast as 'proficient English speakers' despite their typical status as bilingual, multilingual, bidialectal, or multidialectal (e.g., Winer, 2006).

Going against typical indications of what was described as lower academic achievement in underrepresented students (e.g., African American, Hispanic) as compared to their dominant group peers (i.e., white: Ogbu, 2014; see Shockley, 2021, for an exception), Ogbu (1987, 2014) has contended that it is illogical to ascribe the 'success' of Black youth to cultural factors because underrepresented 'minority' groups that do perform better than their dominant group peers do not often share the same cultural backgrounds or experiences of these peers. He argued, based on global evidence regarding immigrant populations across countries and contexts, that a more reasonable explanation for this phenomenon is that underrepresented individuals (or "immigrant minorities" such as Black immigrant youth) who regard themselves as immigrants to a society tend to perform significantly better academically than those who consider themselves to be "indigenous minorities" of a former colonial subject. These "immigrant minorities," he claimed, a population to which Black immigrant youth tend to belong in the US, are taught to project a *cultural frame of reference* and an *identity* that allows them to simultaneously participate in the academic norms of the dominant group when they engage in schooling while also maintaining their own norms and identities that deviate from these practices when they are out of these academic spaces (Ogbu, 2014). Extending this argument further, Fordham and Ogbu (1986) developed the framework of "Fictive kinship" to explain the comparative underperformance of Black American students in the US, suggesting that Black youth feared being accused of "acting White" and thus socially and psychologically experienced a diminished effort which led to underachievement. While it is possible that some Black American as well as Black immigrant youth do deploy such strategies (we know now, based on the literature discussed later, that there is tremendous heterogeneity within and across sub-populations of Black youth), recent evidence, for example, explicitly challenges the notion of a seemingly monolithic population of "high-achieving" Black African and Caribbean immigrant youth in the US and by the same token, an "underachieving" Black American population.

Much like their Black American counterparts, many Black immigrant youth have been described as facing a significant number of challenges with academic performance (Ukpokodu, 2018). For instance, many dialect-speaking Caribbean students have been described as lacking 'proficiency' in the academic English language of the US based on differences in language structure, pronunciation, and vocabulary (Pratt-Johnson, 1993). Similarly, certain West African students have been shown not to have the language background and requisite English language skills for academic language and literacy in US classrooms (de Kleine, 2006). There is evidence that Black immigrant students are often assigned to English-as-a-second-language classes despite the official languages in their country being English and their familiarity with non-academic English (Obeng & Obeng, 2006). And they are often the target of linguicism, where power and privilege are differentially assigned to a version of the English language (i.e., SAE) that they do not speak (Agyepong, 2013; Awokoya, 2009; Nero, 2006; Skutnabb-Kangas, 1988). Black immigrant students also tend to be subjected to racialized language discrimination (Smith, 2019a) – which arises from raciolinguistic ideology (Alim et al., 2016; Rosa & Flores, 2017) where perceptions about privileged race and language function in tandem to delegitimize racialized speakers as they use English in the context of literacy teaching and learning within schools (Smith et al., 2018b, 2020).

In situations where the *academic* reading literacy of Black immigrants has been evaluated by international measures such as the Programme for

International Student Assessment (PISA), which largely informs policy (Michel, 2017), it has been found that Black immigrant youth, much like their Black American counterparts, have sometimes not been allowed to identify as bi-/multilingual or as bi-/multidialectal (de Kleine, 2006; Nero, 2006; Winer, 1993, 2006; Smith et al., 2018a, 2018b). Moreover, Smith et al. (2019) have shown, also from secondary analyses of PISA, that the *academic* reading literacy performance of Black immigrant youth, much like their African American counterparts in the US, falls below the PISA reading literacy average, despite the implied high-performing status reflected by these youth on the exam (see also Smith et al., 2022e). These indications suggest that long-established perceptions about the academic reading literacy of Black immigrant youth, as well as notions about their high achievement based on these perceptions, may be based on assessment results that do not accurately reflect youth's literacies. Findings from these studies also point to the need for a clearer and more holistic understandings of Black immigrant youth's literacy practices across home and school (Smith, 2016, 2017; Smith et al., 2018a). The discussion that follows responds in part to this need, framing Black immigrant literacies within the broader context of transnational and immigrant literacy research, followed by a presentation of the Black Caribbean educational and social realities within which Black Caribbean literacies are encapsulated, both in the context of the Caribbean and in the US.

Joining the Conversation on Immigrant and Transnational Literacies

The field of literacy has increasingly considered how youth enact literacies across borders. Among the frameworks and notions used to clarify how various populations of immigrant, migrant, and transnational youth use languaging and literacies to navigate their transition from their home countries to that of the US are:

(a) transnational and community literacies (e.g., Bajaj & Bartlett, 2017; De Costa, 2010; Jiménez et al., 2009, 2015; Skerrett, 2012, 2015; Taira, 2019);

(b) "do[ing] bilingualism" (García et al., 2015, p. 203);

(c) translanguaging (Daniel & Pacheco, 2016; García & Wei, 2014);

(d) transnational spaces (Horowitz, 2012; Rubinstein-Ávila, 2007; Smith & Murillo, 2012);

(e) transracialization, transliteracies (Alim, 2016; Stornaiuolo et al., 2017);

(f) continua of biliteracy (Hornberger, 2002);

(g) translingual Englishes, Global Englishes, World Englishes, Caribbean Englishes, transnational and language identity (Aponte, 2018; Darvin &

Norton, 2014; Dovchin, 2020; Galloway & Rose, 2015; Nero, 2001, 2014; Skerrett & Omogun, 2020; Smith, 2016, 2017);
(h) cosmopolitanism, language policy and ideology (Smith, 2019a; De Costa, 2010);
(i) positioning (Smith, 2019a; Yoon, 2012); and
(j) ideologies of authenticity, raciolinguistic ideology, a transraciolinguistic approach, racialized entanglements, transraciolinguistic justice, raciosemiotic architecture, institutional schizophrenia (Dovchin, 2020; Rosa, 2016; Smith, 2019a, 2020, 2022a, 2022b, 2022c, 2022d, 2022e).

The affordances of digital literacies (e.g., Darvin & Norton, 2014; Lam, 2013; McLean, 2010), identity (Compton-Lilly et al., 2017), cosmopolitanism (e.g., Campano & Ghiso, 2011; De Costa, 2010, 2014), culturally responsive pedagogy (Campano, 2007), and a third space (Gutiérrez, 2008), among numerous other frameworks, have also been used to clarify the literacies of youth from a myriad of backgrounds, some of whom are Caribbean, Chinese ("designer immigrants"), Mexican, Vietnamese, and Vietnamese American first- and second-generation immigrant youth (see also Smith, 2023a, for a discussion). Across these and other studies, scholars have demonstrated in varied, yet complementary ways, the assets that such youth present through literacy learning in a new context. For instance, in Skerrett's (2012) study of the changes experienced by a Mexican transnational youth in her language and literacy, she identified shifts in her participant, Vanesa, whose reading, writing, dance, and art illustrated her enactment of literacies across, in, and out-of-school contexts. Skerrett's (2012) description of this shift in language use, while also focusing on Vanesa's multiliterate repertoire, provided unique and novel insights into the process of knowledge-building experienced by this student as well as her emotional and attitudinal stance. Complementing the focus on multiliteracies highlighted by Skerrett (2012), McLean's (2010) findings about the literacies of a Caribbean American immigrant student, Zeek, revealed how the student drew from her repertoire of digital literacies to create, sustain, and leverage her multiple ethnic, gendered, and student identities.

Extending the emphasis on language shifts highlighted by Skerrett (2012) and of nuance across identities as reflected by McLean (2010), scholars have drawn from the lenses of cosmopolitanism, language ideology, identity and language policy (Campano & Ghiso, 2011; De Costa, 2010, 2014; Yoon, 2012) to illustrate how immigrant youth, some of whom are perceived as "designer immigrants," respond to English ideologies based on language policies to reflect global citizenship as well as navigate complexities in pursuing 'success.' Through Rubinstein-Ávila's (2007) scholarship on transnational spaces in the life of a Dominican Republican youth, for instance, it was clear that although the student, Yanira, reflected religious literacies, she was confused about the shifts needed in her language practices across her home country and the US context. Yanira used her linguistic repertoires to maintain emotional ties to her home country, yet privileged certain literate practices over others. The scholarship of Gutiérrez (2008) has further broadened such perspectives by illustrating how literacies of a migrant student, Ave, reflected embodied practices. These embodied practices intersected with language to influence how Ave and her peers develop imagined futures from shared present and past experiences as they engaged together in academic tasks via a third space.

In my recent scholarship (Smith, 2019a), which responds to the foregoing issues of inequity that affect the assets of immigrant youth, race was foregrounded to highlight the ways in which Jaeda, a Black Caribbean immigrant youth, was positioned by raciolinguistic ideology. This study showed how Jaeda used a *transraciolinguistic approach* to navigate visible shifts in her personhood based on conflicting notions resulting from a privileging of certain languaging and literacy practices across global and local spaces, as well as in and out of classroom and school contexts. Extending this notion of race in the literacies of immigrant youth (Smith et al., 2022), my colleagues and I have demonstrated how the racialized language practices and personhood of a Black immigrant adolescent were inextricably linked in her literacies (Cowley, 2017), reflecting what has been described as *"racialized languaging"* (Chow, 2014).

Based on the preceding body of work, calls have been made for transnational literacy curriculum that reflects multimodal elements which create spaces for emotions and attitudes arising from transnational experiences (Rubinstein-Ávila, 2007; Skerrett, 2012, 2015). This research has also emphasized the need for attending to motivating factors, contextual spaces, and intentions of youth that influence their use of digital literacies (Lam, 2013; McLean, 2010) as well as broader notions of their engagement with migration experiences beyond language and culture (Yoon, 2012). It has been shown that an understanding of literacies is needed which focuses on how students function across local and global spaces as opposed to clarifying them independently within each context (Rubinstein-Ávila, 2007). This scholarship has indicated that a (re)arranging of educational spaces is crucial if students are to leverage their literate repertoires effectively across cultures (Gutiérrez, 2008; Horowitz, 2012; Lizárraga & Gutiérrez, 2018; Smith & Murillo, 2012). It has also made visible the importance of patterns of communication undergirding literacies and languaging in sustaining students' transborder socialization and positioning and creating more just societies while highlighting how intergenerational familial practices are intertwined with language ideologies even as they are mediated by institutions of schooling (Lam & Warriner, 2012; Lee, 2021).

The current study on which this book is based extends such nuanced and timely insights through an exemplar of *Afro-Caribbean immigrant youth*. It connects the local to the global – an element of the *"Black immigrant literacies framework*" (see Smith, 2020b; see also Smith, 2023a) – by emphasizing the way in which the multiliteracies and translanguaging of students from an immigrant racialized population reflected monoglossic and raciolinguistic ideologies (see Nero, 2014; Rosa & Flores, 2017; Willis, 2018). At the same time, informed by "a raciolinguistic perspective" (Rosa & Flores, 2017) as mentioned earlier, I clarify roles of the institution in instantiating or eliminating these challenges while also highlighting the self-determination used by youth to transcend obstacles to reflect "success" as the art of *"flourishing"* – the experience of overall well-being (see Keyes, 2002, on *"flourishing"*; see Smith, 2019a, 2020b, on "a *transraciolinguistic approach*"). In doing so, I acknowledge that Black Caribbean immigrants and their literacies are not in any way monolithic, neither do the insights presented in this book singularly represent the vastly heterogenous literacies and languaging of Black immigrants across the globe. My focus on the Black Caribbean immigrants highlighted, and the use of the Black Caribbean immigrant lens, notwithstanding, allows for a better understanding of how intersections of race, language, and immigration function in the literacies and languaging of this unique population, and offers varying degrees of transferability to other similar populations and contexts.

Historical and Contemporary Educational Landscape of Black People in the Caribbean

An examination of the historical and contemporary educational landscape in the Caribbean reveals three key, though not (mutually) exclusive representations, characterizing the educational literature surrounding Black peoples in the Caribbean: *(a) historicity of coloniality and the pervasive effects of religion; (b) subsequent denial of racism and inclusivity sans race; and (c) an emerging and robust contemporary anti-racist stance.*

By "Caribbean" in this book, I refer to the island nations constituting the archipelago located in the Caribbean Sea. The Caribbean itself is also considered as a region that consists of the Caribbean Sea, its islands, and the surrounding coasts. The region is southeast of the Gulf of Mexico and the North American mainland, east of Central America, and north of South America. The Caribbean, long referred to as the West Indies because of the supposition that Christopher Columbus had traveled westward and stumbled upon isles in India (Oxford Reference, n.d.; Smith, 1978), but also historically acknowledged as part of the Americas, includes more than 7,000 islands; of those, 13 are independent island countries. Elsewhere, when I refer to the "English-speaking Caribbean," I am making reference to Caribbean countries formerly colonized by the British where English became the official language during the pre-independence era. Post-independence, many countries continued to use English as the de facto language for formal business transactions. Thus, the English-speaking Caribbean (i.e., Anglophone) region is used to denote these countries in which the de facto or official language is English.

The tendency to consider the English-speaking Caribbean as a consolidated group stems not only from colonial rule but also from the cross-historical, cross-linguistic, and cross-political commonalities that characterize these independent yet interconnected nations. Politically, a number of the English-speaking Caribbean nations gained independence within a similar time frame (1960–1980), specifically: Jamaica [1962], Trinidad [1962], Guyana [1966], Grenada [1974], Dominica [1978], St. Vincent [1979], and St. Lucia [1979] (Poddar & Johnson, 2005). And historically, commentary on the English-speaking Eastern Caribbean at the political, national, educational, and economic levels justified a holistic view of these countries (Armstrong & Campos, 2002; Brereton, 2004; Engerman, 1982; Lewis, 2004; Watts, 1990). For instance, speaking of the historical relationships among the countries' colonial backgrounds, language varieties, cultural contexts, and educational characteristics, Smith (1965) observed:

> It is clear that whatever the common patterns the British [Anglophone] West Indies share with other Caribbean territories, or with countries outside this Caribbean region, these British colonies nonetheless form a separate area for social research, on the ground of their present political relations as well as history. (Smith, 1965, p. 21)

For the purpose of this book, it is fitting to also group English-speaking Caribbean islands linguistically given that the nations also bear resemblance because "the West Indian Creole language situation as a whole" is based on similarity of speech, social structure, traditions, and institutions (Craig, 1974, p. 371). Similarly, there is merit in grouping them educationally given that the systems and policies across these countries were based on the academic structures of the colonial-era metropolis (i.e., from the 1800s onwards), resembling in many ways the current focus on didactic reading and writing (Simmons-McDonald, 2004).

Historicity of Coloniality and the Pervasive Effect of Religion

The historical tendency to examine the Caribbean educational enterprise from a colonial perspective is reflected across numerous West Indian works (e.g., Fanon, 1988; James, 1992; Jules, 2008; Sewell, 1978). This coloniality is often explored as a function of its link to Eurocentric imperial powers more broadly, and from its inception, as a mechanism linked to religiosity more specifically. These linkages, representing the fundamentally intertwined role of Eurocentrism and religion within institutions in the history of Caribbean educational systems, have occurred in ways that subvert Indigeneity and maintain the imperial project.

One such instance is visible in the recently vivid description of race, imperialism, and religion presented by Ryan Bachoo in Trinidad and Tobago. In this Caribbean country, the exercise of coloniality in the literate educational enterprise via the church was most often seen in the power yielded by the Roman Catholic religion and its historical linkage, as exercised across the Caribbean. The recently released documentary in which Bachoo presents this dynamic is titled, "Concordat: A Battle of Power, Race and Religion" (Bachoo, 2023). Bachoo illustrates how students in the Sacred Heart Girls' R.C. School in Trinidad and Tobago recite the first two decades of the rosary before their first class every morning after assembly and complete the five mysteries by reciting the final three decades after lunch (Bachoo, 2023). Bachoo explains that the practice of this prayer by the Roman Catholic school is based on an agreement between the Roman Catholic Church and the Government of Trinidad and Tobago that also allows Muslim as well as other religious schools to practice their own religious prayers.

The description of this agreement as a "Concordat" is based on its Latin origins, meaning, "an agreement between the Holy See, the Government of the Roman Catholic Church in Rome, and a Sovereign State" (Bachoo, 2023). As indicated by Bachoo, the document was "signed on Christmas Day 1960 between the Roman Catholic Church and the then Government of Trinidad and Tobago, and "would change the face of education in the independent nation for decades to come" (Bachoo, 2023). Bachoo also observes that the agreement, emerging from an eventual compromise between the then leadership of the country and the Roman Catholic Church, which had already taken on responsibility for educating the country's most vulnerable for at least two hundred years, signaled a truce rooted in politics, power, race, and religion and "would split [the Trinidadian] society for six decades." Dr. Claudius Fergus, Senior Lecturer of History at the University of the West Indies, "recall[ed] a showdown between church and state" and as Bachoo points out, at the time, Dr. Eric Williams, the then leader of Trinidad and Tobago, though "anti-clerical and opposed to denominational schools which he had stigmatized as a breeding ground of dis-unity," was well aware of the "towering figure" of Count Finbar Ryan, Archbishop in Trinidad and Tobago, with formidable "reach into the Vatican itself" and "the [direct] backing of the Papacy" (Bachoo, 2023). Citing Professor Emeritus Dr. Carl Campbell (Bachoo, 2023) to illustrate the reticence of Dr. Williams regards operations of church in relation to state, Bachoo (2023) points out in the documentary that:

[Dr. Eric Williams' regime reorganized the dual system] of church and state schools, since he was convinced that the churches had traditionally been supporters of the white colonial ruling class. His government reversed decisively the long established tradition, both in primary and secondary education, for the churches to build more schools and provide more new school places than the government.

Dr. Primnath Goopta explains in the documentary that Count Ryan had been startled by the response in Guyana, where "the majority of Guyanese schools in the 50's were owned and operated by the Catholic Church" (Bachoo, 2023). For instance, Count Ryan had seen the then leader of Guyana, Cheddy Jagan, fail to consider the interest of the Catholic church and other churches, and instead, nationally advocate for free education, a dynamic where, as Dr. Goopta observes, the "Catholic church [as the largest denomination] stood to lose the most" (Bachoo, 2023). As the documentary shows, Count Ryan wished to vehemently avoid a similar situation in Trinidad and Tobago. At the same time, as the documentary shows, though "personally [Dr. Williams] may have despised the Church, ... politically he needed it" (Bachoo, 2023). This dynamic thus served as the basis for the eventual "yielding of Dr. Eric Williams to the Roman Catholic Church [in the form of Count Finbar Ryan] on Christmas Day, 1960," and thus, a "bowing to the church's demands" in the signing of the Concordat by the then Education Minister, John Donaldson (Bachoo, 2023).

The larger countries of Guyana and Trinidad and tobago in the Caribbean were not the only ones to experience such impactful, yet varied degrees of connectivity as manifested between local governments and the Roman Catholic Church. Haiti, for example, a French-speaking territory, is another Caribbean country where, much like Trinidad and Tobago, the reach of the Roman Catholic Church was institutionalized, and remains largely visible. As François (2015) has observed, "since the signing of the Concordat of 1860 between the Vatican and Haitian State, Catholic congregational schools have borne the responsibility for educating the Haitian elites" (p. i). However, he notes that "these schools [were] a model of anti-Vodou and anti-Creole colonial school established within the framework of a French neocolonial project engineered by Gaspard Theodore Mollien to reconquer Haiti," an intention which goes contrary to the theory of hybridity advocated by Homi K. Bhabha that "acknowledges Vodou and Creole as two basic historical elements that would foster democratic learning spaces in the school context and empower the Haitian student" (François, 2015, p. 290). François (2015) explains that the "congregational schools prepared a type of subaltern, alienated, racist, autocratic, and violent elites that have always served the interests of the West while oppressing and marginalizing the Vodouists and Creole speaking Haitian masses," a situation where "total exclusion and marginalization of Haitian Creole and Vodou by Catholic school leaders" functioned as a form of "mis-education" (Woodson, 1933). Given the insights from these analyses, it is no surprise that Prou (2009) characterized the educational system in Haiti from 1979 to 2004 and continuing into the present day as being at a "critical juncture" (p. 29). La Réforme Bernard – the Bernard Reform – introduced in Haiti in 1982, included as a key element the introduction of

Kreyòl as an official language of instruction. However, this was complicated by challenges of implementing a controversial language-use policy in the educational system of Haiti which reflected complexities of the "historical, social, economic, and political contexts of Caribbean society" (Prou, 2009, p. 29). The result – a failure to recognize any major transformation despite the overhaul of education.

In St. Lucia, for instance, another Caribbean country (and the land of my birth), the influence of religion and the church were seen and felt with the arrival of Mico School missionaries in 1838 and the establishment of their educational enterprise for newly freed slaves across the country (St. Hilaire, 2007). In this country, which also reflects French heritage but where English functions as the official language, Mico-trained teachers were protestant English speakers who had been prepared in Mico Training Colleges and were unfamiliar with French Creole because it had not been spoken in their locales or was unknown. It was no surprise, then, that they rejected St. Lucian French Creole – a language spoken on the island alongside English – prohibiting its use, and in certain cases, physically punishing students who spoke it (Alleyne, 1961; Ramcharan-Crowley, 1961; St. Hilaire, 2007). At the time, the largely used St. Lucian French Creole had become synonymous with the Caribbean Creole, as Murdoch notes:

fed by the inscription of a double time of cross-cultural encounters, and an interpenetration of populations and practices originating both from the colonial metropole and from the African continent. As an inherently unstable category, it [Caribbean Creole] embodie[d] all the ambiguities and essentialisms of its origins in the colonial period. Indeed, in figuring either a European or an African subject, the term "Creole" [was] linked to displacements of place rather than race, and identifie[d] the descendants of any ethnic group born outside their country of origin. (Murdoch, 2009, p. 74)

Much like was seen in Haiti, the educational infiltration of the Mico missionaries in St. Lucia served only to eradicate St. Lucian French Creole while encouraging the European colonial language – English – in what was considered to be the educational, economic, and technological progress of developing nations (Ricento, 2000, p. 199; Smith & Kumi-Yeboah, 2015).

Looking across the Caribbean landscape, Dornan (2019) has described the linkages between religiosity and education in the Caribbean by exploring the role of Nonconformist missionaries, who, working with the British and Foreign School Society (BFSS), were a major part of providing elementary instruction to children who had been enslaved and emancipated in the nineteenth-century British West Indies. Drawing from the insights of untapped historical sources in the newly catalogued West Indian collection of the BFSS archives, Dornan highlights, historiographically, how pedagogical methods and practices were used by Nonconformist missionaries in the British

Caribbean, operating under the consolidated effects of the challenges of local context while grappling simultaneously with the intentions of the educational fervor of a global missionary.

What began as a religious mission would later become endemic to the 'postcolonial' educational enterprise, representative of what it means to experience learning in the Caribbean region – a fundamentally oppressive regime. Alluding to this oppression, De Lisle (2019) explains that while inclusion remains a desirable goal, particularly for descendants of formerly enslaved and colonized peoples, classroom environments in the Caribbean, such as many in Jamaica, "still reflect vestiges of that oppressive history, which continue to deprive many students of their agency and self-efficacy" and require a shift from teacher-centered approaches that disempower students to critical pedagogies that are empowering. And speaking of the need to address the resulting dysfunctionalism of education in the Caribbean context, Hickling-Hudson (2015) uses the image of pit latrines – *a toilet through which human feces are collected in a hole in the ground, used a long time ago by my family, and by many families in my village of St. Lucia as a child* – as a symbol for the condition of impoverished primary schools in poor countries of the Caribbean, to highlight the need for the 'ubuntu' philosophy as a response to educational inequity based on class. In Trinidad and Tobago, as is the case elsewhere in the Caribbean, the challenges posed by interrelationships of education and poverty with the political, economic, and the social dynamic are also highlighted as a key hindrance to the quality of student learning and of students' participation in mainstream education (De Lisle et al., 2017).

Subsequent Denial of Racism and Inclusivity sans Race

Coloniality, post-coloniality, and the historic link to religion, taken together, tend to often be characteristic of educational literature in the Caribbean. However, such discussions, though initially and vehemently indicative of the racialization of peoples of Color based on white supremacy in this context (see, for instance, Fanon, 1988; Mills, 1997), would later resonate with a rarity of attention to race, racism, racialization, or other representations of race, featuring instead a coloniality *sans* explicit attention to race. In fact, as Davies (2013) has observed, "some Caribbeans have claimed that there was or is no racism in the Caribbean while some have indicated that the United States is where they first encountered racism" and still others "say that Caribbean people do not experience racism in the United States in the same way as do African Americans" (p. 173). Pointing to the "international phenomenon" that is racism and how it "appears differently nuanced according to historical and cultural locations," as "a structural socioeconomic organizing system that creates a hierarchy in which race determines how individuals and communities are able to access resources and power," and also, "how they are located in systems from education to criminal justice, athletics to the entertainment industry," the observations by Davies (2013) raise questions about the contemporary tendency in the Caribbean to engage in discussions of postcolonialism *sans* explicit naming of and attention to race.

This questioning of the place of race in postcolonial discourse across the Caribbean is understandable considering that notions such as "third space" (Soja, 1996) instantiated by this discourse have often advanced a transcending of binaries through the merging of dichotomies, largely *sans* explicit naming and centering of race. Movement towards understandings of "third space," for instance, and in turn, "liminality" – *the variation in the transformative processes of those engaging third space characterized by a lack of certainty, willingness to be tentative, and surrender to compromise* – based on the theory of hybridity (Bhabha, 1994), have been central to a continued advocacy in the region for students' reliance of literacies of both their schools (i.e., second space) and communities (i.e., first space), on the one hand, and juxtaposed against a prescriptive reliance steeped in the privileging of certain named languages, on the other. Similar in some regard to but different from conceptions of transdisciplinarity based on quantum physics for multicultural education that touts the possibility of holding opposing viewpoints in mind at the same time for decision-making in diversity towards a 'new kind of education' (Nicolescu, 2010; Smith, 2013a, 2013b), "third space" and "liminality" have advanced significant understandings of how to engage the dialectic as a function of coloniality, but have also managed to do so largely *sans* a centering of race.

Engagement with post-coloniality that focuses on inclusion, though not centralizing race per se, is seen in recent research in the Caribbean that has called for this notion as a basis for education, deemed central to the empowerment of students (Bailey, 2019; Blackman & Conrad, 2017; Blackman et al. 2019; Martin-Kerr, 2019). For instance, in the book *Caribbean Discourse in Inclusive Education: Historical and Contemporary Issues*, Blackman and Conrad (2017) illustrate how earlier assertions and traditional notions of "inclusive education" omitted the "descendants of citizens of African-Caribbean origin in Britain, or of many black citizens in the United States" from being central to inclusive education discourse (Tomlinson, 2014, p. 96). The editors provide a premise for discussing emerging concepts of inclusive education surrounding student populations in the Caribbean context such as those previously excluded from certain examinations as well as allegedly underachieving males in Caribbean school systems (see Jennings, 2001). In keeping with the need for inclusive education to identify exclusive practices that position researchers and educators to interrupt thinking, reform practices, ideas, and their corresponding ideologies, the chapters presented in this book highlight a redistribution of the ways in which students in the Caribbean obtain access to learning and participate in opportunities available; in the recognition and value of differences that all students present in content, instruction, and assessment; and in the creation of spaces for non-mainstream students to have their needs in relation educational exclusion addressed. There is also a focus on problematizing the ways in which teachers respond to students' home vs. school languages during instruction; question misalignment between students' learning needs and high-stakes assessment systems; challenge the disregard of students' multiple identities that affect their social and academic experiences; highlight exclusivity in responding to orphanhood; call for reform in preparation for school leadership for inclusion; and examine factors inhibiting creativity in the process of meeting the goals of inclusive education. From the voices of youth who highlight their experiences with and perceptions of homosexuality and special education services to that of teachers concerning their anxieties for addressing the needs of diverse student populations, *Caribbean Discourse in Inclusive Education* paints a vivid portrait of the ways in which those who enact inclusive education in and beyond schools engage with issues that are used to exclude students from mainstream educational practices (Blackman & Conrad, 2017; Smith, 2019b).

Aligned with the redefinition of inclusive education as a function of post-coloniality that seeks to address how complexities are associated with the ways in which students are excluded, *Caribbean Discourse in Inclusive Education* vividly presents the insights of authors regarding "cultural injustices of misrecognition" among transgendered, gay, and lesbian students as well as "political injustices of misrepresentation" that persist with the learning disabled and those with attention deficit hyperactivity who are positioned on the margins of the educational system (Waitoller & Thorius, 2016, p. 368). In the case of the English-speaking Caribbean, as is shown in this book, policy development for inclusive education that merely addresses marginalized students is yet to be achieved and the authors' insights regarding these policies point to challenges that remain if these Caribbean nations are to inadequately incorporate notions of intersectionality into a working definition of inclusive education for their contexts. Scholars acknowledge, through powerful illustrations, the "historical justice claims of the inclusive education movement" in this previously colonized British English-speaking context, opening up the discussion for addressing notions of intersectionality within exclusion (Waitoller & Thorius, 2016, p. 368).

In keeping with the emphasis above, numerous scholars have illustrated how classroom environments in the Caribbean operate based on oppressive histories with a focus on (post-)coloniality notwithstanding a decentering of race. For instance, Bailey (2019), focusing on the experience of Jamaica, calls for critical pedagogy to be deployed by Caribbean educators as an intentional part of the decolonizing project. The avenue for doing so is constructivism, which, the author argues, can transform a colonially derived instructional culture as the basis for "potentially empowering students in the Anglophone Caribbean" (Bailey, 2019, p. 174). Millar and Warrican (2015), too, have examined how students in a Barbadian secondary school bridged existing divides between traditional and semiotic literacies in the context of a broader context in Barbados where students are perceived as disengaged from conventional literate practice, creating alarm on the part of those in the broader community. The authors' findings showed that students' engagement in literacies was manifested in many ways, creating the need for revisiting ideas about the nature of literacy and about redefining the roles that students and teachers are given in classrooms. With what may be regarded by some as a more forceful tenor, scholars such as Martin-Kerr (2019) have called for attention to seven manifestations of colonial consciousness as articulated by Barthes in addressing heterosexual normative practices in Jamaica and the influence on heteronormative ideologies. The criticality emerging from this research is echoed, if not further solidified, in Bristol's (2012) *Plantation Pedagogy: A Postcolonial and Global Perspective*, where primary school education in the twin-island Republic of Trinidad and Tobago is examined. Bristol addresses how current educational practices still reflect those from British colonial rule and the need for educational alternatives that are redemptive in nature, able to emancipate nationals from the remnants of slavery and colonial rule.

Long-standing and circular arguments regarding "student underachievement," visited and revisited very often in the Caribbean context, and mirroring with stark similarity, pervasive yet problematic discourses around 'underachievement' of African American students in the US (Smith et al., 2019, 2022; Warrican, 2021), echo the recurrence of post-coloniality in Caribbean contemporary educational research largely sans attention to race. Due to this dynamic, there appears to have been a failure to fully examine and adequately explain the foundational bases for what many view as 'impoverished academic performance' across the Caribbean. Often Eurocentrically driven, the analytical orientation to academic '*success*' of Caribbean children and youth, though widely unacknowledged, yields narratives that tend to allude to the "high underachievement in the Caribbean region" (Martin et al., 2017) yet fail to acknowledge the racialization undergirding motivations for seeking such 'success.' For instance, in the examination of 585 students' performance from five Jamaican schools, steeped in an expectancy-value framework and focused on their motivation, behavioral engagement, and academic achievement, the authors found that students' self-motivation was influenced by their motivation milieu and that the relationships between their motivation and academic achievement behavioral engagement was significantly mediated by their behavioral engagement.

In response to this conundrum, attention has been given, at least in part, to the need for decolonial conceptions to undergird examinations of achievement in the context of counternarratives that reflect the assets of Black Caribbean peoples. Reflecting such analyses are indications such as those that use the "opportunity gap explanatory framework" proposed by Dr. Richard Milner (Milner, 2012) to address the ways in which a focus on Caribbean student achievement obscures the importance of attending to opportunities denied. Drawing from this framework, my colleagues and I have shown how achievement narratives in the Caribbean, though often well-intentioned and seeking to extend beyond coloniality, tend to inadvertently reinforce it. We acknowledge this dynamic given that the systems used for teaching and assessing youth's educational practice remain steeped in curricula that themselves were designed to align with white Eurocentric norms (see Warrican et al., 2020). Specifically, in the released report "Factors That Influence Academic Performance of Students in the Caribbean: An Empirical Study," resulting from a collaboration undertaken with Dr. S. Joel Warrican, Professor of Literacy and Director of the Caribbean Educational Research Center at the University of the West Indies (UWI) in the Caribbean, and with other colleagues at the UWI, we examined evidence about student performance that can inform practice and add to the "knowledge of the conditions that facilitate or impede students' academic progress in the region" (Warrican et al., 2020, p. 1). Highlighting the colonial basis undergirding education in the Caribbean region, we used the "myth of meritocracy" as a key element in the "opportunity gap explanatory framework" (Milner, 2012) to explain in our conceptual framework, "both positive and negative aspects and realities of people, places, and policies in educational practice" and also, "systematically name what [we] observe and come to know inductively" (Milner, 2012, p. 699). Acknowledging that the educational context in the Caribbean functions as markedly different from that of contexts such as the US where the framework was developed, we nonetheless identified the myth of meritocracy as an operating and relevant heuristic for encapsulating the ways in which opportunities can be obscured for students in the Caribbean context. In this Caribbean report, we asserted that:

the myth of meritocracy suggests that when explaining educational outcomes, educators may be apt to embrace the idea that "their own, their parents, and their students' success and status have all been earned" such that any failure on the part of an individual in relation to educational outcomes "is solely a result of making bad choices and decisions" (Milner, 2012, p. 704). In doing so and while identifying achievement gaps, educators may misunderstand how factors such as socioeconomics interact with education even while they "appear to be more at ease, confident, and comfortable reflecting about, reading, and discussing how socioeconomics, particularly, resources related to wealth and poverty, influence educational disparities, inequities, outcomes, and opportunities" (Milner, 2012, p. 704). Individuals operating under the myth of meritocracy, for instance, might forget that they may have succeeded because of economic privilege, whether earned or unearned, and may presuppose that all individuals are presented with educational practices and opportunities that provide equal or equitable chances for success. Such a myth can function as a mechanism to explain how opportunities through teacher quality, teacher training, curriculum, the digital divide, wealth and income, health care, nutrition, and quality childcare all interact to affect achievement. (Irvine, 2010; Warrican et al., 2020, p. 3)

Our goal in attending to the myth of meritocracy as a function of decolonization designed to address the white gaze in our examination of academic achievement was meant to elucidate how this myth can potentially operate in Caribbean contexts, creating an obscuring of opportunities in discussions about achievement outcomes of youth. As recently shown, Eurocentric mechanisms function in the Caribbean educational context, implicitly undergirding literacy norms and how they function in student performance (Smith, 2020b). The examinations in the report are thus positioned as a way to consider opportunities in the form of factors such as school resources, technology, teacher quality, and curriculum which can help to more adequately identify and explore underlying institutionally informed patterns in achievement based on Eurocentric norms, deemed visible based on our findings in the Caribbean context. As we note, "in doing so, we hope to ultimately develop frameworks that explain achievement and opportunity which are steeped in the Caribbean educational experience and unique to the Caribbean region" (Warrican et al., 2020, p. 3). We expected also to extend beyond the tendency to describe Black peoples as broken and illiterate and to instead identify how institutional norms create structures or present obstacles designed to maintain a global project of white supremacy.

Such postcolonial approaches as those described above are continuingly called for and increasingly so in the Caribbean. This has been even more visibly the case since the murder of George Floyd in the US that lay bare the racialization often occurring overtly against Black peoples even as it functions silently and more or less acceptably under the radar within our colonially driven curricular heritage. The approaches are fundamental to disrupting notions of languaging steeped in hegemony and articulated as postcolonial heritage in the Caribbean. Delva (2019) observes how a failure to engage in this disruption in the Haitian context has seen the hegemonic role of French schools wreak havoc by inhibiting the education of its Haitian citizenry in an education system described as "struggling." Delva draws on research from Hebblethwaite (2012) to assert that French instruction in schools functions as a pedagogy responsible for the challenge in Haiti given that most students are described as 'monolingual' in French Creole. The author also draws from scholarship by Zéphir (2010) to highlight the exclusion of Creole culture as the culprit. Echoing Martiniquean psychiatrist and revolutionary Dr. Frantz

Fanon (Fanon, 1991/1961), Delva uses a colonialist perspective to make visible the project of educating Haitians, not to serve Haiti, but rather, in service of other 'developed' countries, creating a dynamic where Creole culture and Creole language are delegitimized in ways that require Haitian personhoods to dichotomize how they align with various parts of the self.

In many ways, Robertshaw (2018) presents an analysis that complements observations made by Delva, pointing to the juxtaposition of French functioning "historically [as] the country's exclusive language of virtually all written and official contexts, including education, government, and law" against Haitian Creole as the common language of all Haitians" (p. 4). Alluding to the calls for linguistic revolution in Haiti since its independence in 1804, Robertshaw describes the postcolonial project of introducing the peasant majority's monolingual Haitian Creole into the public sphere via the avenue of writers, intellectuals, and activists. Noting that the constitutional affordances received for Haitian Creole since 1987 did not abate the linguistic hegemony of French, Robertshaw asserts that Haitian literature such as Cric? Crac! (1901) by Georges Sylvain, where the celebrated adaptation of La Fontaine's fables is presented, functioned as a "compelling case for Creole's legitimacy" (Robertshaw, 2018, p. 4). He noted too that it operated as an avenue for challenging the lingering effects of colonization in Haiti, serving as a key challenge to the status quo often visible in the literature, politics, and society of Haiti.

As a noted exception to the focus on postcolonialism sans race in contemporary educational literature within the region, Windle and Muniz (2018), in their discussions of constructions of race in the neighboring Latin American country of Brazil, allude to racial resignification and resistance, highlighting the silencing of issues of race in Brazilian public education as a function of the international reach of race and as a reflection of its local transformation. The authors show how dominant discourses of racial democracy and mixing are situated to deny the possibility of a politicized Afro-Brazilian identity and illustrate how new social identities based on transnational circulation and hybrid identification are constructed in this context. Also working in Brazil, Uju Anya has examined how racialized identities emerge in this context as a function of second-language learning in the African American experience (Anya, 2016). Examining African American college students learning Portuguese in Afro-Brazilian communities and documenting how they learned to do and speak Blackness in Brazil, Anya has shown how Black Americans present their various selves in Portuguese through languaging, to reproduce or resist inequities and also clarified the racialized identities of Black students and how their investment in these communities influenced their as well as others' perceptions of their language learning success.

An Emerging, Contemporary, and Robust Anti-racist Stance

The focus on race in the neighboring Latin American context of Brazil signals what continues to be a gradually evolving yet marked recent departure in the English-speaking Caribbean from a tendency to foreground postcolonialism without an explicit naming of racialization in contemporary educational research. As Joseph (2012) observes, for at least some time, "a dynamic of a present-day avoidance of historical critique seems to have remained in the society, in part because of an enduring and potent ideology of whiteness" (p. 146). This recent departure, nonetheless, characterized by a push to intentionally name and center race, is visible, for instance, in examinations such as that conducted into the Nelson and Sons Royal Readers textbooks in Grenada, referred to by Joseph (2012) as colonial-era curriculum. Joseph's (2012) analysis of three stories in volume Royal Readers No. 4 demonstrates how the textbooks are used to communicate "several unstated and often unrecognized tenets of ideological whiteness, instilled by the colonial authorities to augment a project of subjugated and unquestioning acquiescence to their imperial power" (p. 146). As Joseph points out, the recognition of historical erasure in the textbooks is highlighted as a concern by research participants engaged in the study on this Caribbean island country where the research was conducted. It suggests a desire on the part of certain nationals to have supports for critically engaging with elements of their heritage.

Attending also to race from the perspective of comparative and international education in "South-South" migration (see Khan et al., 2022, for a problematization of such terms), Bartlett (2012) has examined the phenomenon where schooling is provided to youth of Haitian descent who are born in and live within the neighboring country of the Dominican Republic. Acknowledging the broader contextual challenges faced in accessing "basic education," Bartlett shows how "darker-skinned" Haitian boys, and more broadly, children and youth of Haitian descent in general, appear to be subjected to "intense verbal," and in certain cases, "physical abuse" (Bartlett, 2012, p. 393).

Even as an anti-racist stance surrounding educational research is seemingly resurfacing, but gradually, in the Caribbean context, a corresponding hesitance to make visible the racialization of Black Caribbean peoples in such research within the US has maintained a silent but firm grip on the American educational landscape. This hesitance, intentional or not, has historically rendered Caribbean peoples as often 'raceless' despite their immersion into an overt racially structured national and global landscape undergirded by a US Black-White binary steeped in white supremacy. I now explore some broad characterizations emerging from social and educational research surrounding the population of Black immigrants in the US as well as more specific representations of Black immigrant youth in this context that help to lay the groundwork for understanding subsequent examinations of the Englishes of Black Caribbean immigrant youth presented.

Historical and Contemporary Socio-Educational Landscape of Black Immigrants in the US

Black immigrants have a long history of entanglement with the peoples and spaces of the US, much of which has fundamentally affected, or been affected by, their educational pursuits, and thus their language. As far back as 1970, it is documented that West Indians constituted around 1 million and Africans approximately 76,500 of the 45 million "aliens" who migrated to the US (U.S. Department of Justice, 1970). Commensurate, then, with the influx of Black immigrants, were laws and quotas instituted by the US to curtail the influx of immigrants such as the Naturalization Act of 1790, which limited US citizenship to white immigrants; the Immigration Act of 1917, which barred people from British India, most of Southeast Asia, and most of the Middle East from migrating to the US; the Emergency Quota Act of 1921, which used a quota system based on nationality to overwhelmingly favor immigrants from Western Europe and exclude most immigrants from Asia and Africa; and the Immigration and Nationality Act of 1952, which was a revision of the quota-based system and allowed Asians to migrate legally to the US for the first time despite its continued discrimination against them (Migration Policy Institute, 2013; U.S. Department of State, n.d.).

Following the civil rights movement that resulted in the dismantling of "Jim Crow" via the Civil Rights Act of 1964 coupled with the Voting Rights Act of 1965, America would see a major disruption in the long-standing race-based immigration quota system signaled by the passing of the Immigration and Nationality Act of 1965, which gave priority to refugees, people with special skills, and those with family members living in the US, and banned discrimination - issuing immigrant visas based on "race, sex, nationality, place of birth, or place of residence," with several major exceptions (FitzGerald & Cook-Martín, 2015). Speaking of this Act signed into law by President Lyndon B. Johnson, the United States House of Representatives History, Art & Archives states:

Commonly known as the Hart–Celler Act after its two main sponsors – Senator Philip A. Hart of Michigan and Representative Emanuel Celler of New York – the law overhauled America's immigration system during a period of deep global instability. For decades, a federal quota system had severely restricted the number of people from outside Western Europe eligible to settle in the United States. Passed during the height of the Cold War, Hart–Celler erased America's longstanding policy of limiting immigration based on national origin. (para. 1)

The Archives acknowledge that "policymakers had vastly underestimated the number of immigrants who would take advantage of the family reunification clause" built into the act and that following Hart–Celler, "immigration jumped to nearly a half million people" with "only 20 percent [coming] from Europe" (para 1). It is no wonder that the Hart–Celler Act has been described as having "the most significant and direct effect on black immigration to the United States" (Bryce-Laporte, 1972).

The passing of the Immigration and Nationality Act of 1965 on the heels of the Civil Rights Act of 1964 saw the population of foreign-born Blacks significantly increase in the decades that followed. Kent (2007) notes that at the time, "the foreign-born black population rose nearly seven-fold between 1960 and 1980, and more than tripled between 1980 and 2005," an increase representing a significant shift in foreign Blacks as compared to all Blacks in America from 1 to 8 percent (p. 4). Among these, Jamaicans and Haitians were most largely represented from the Caribbean, and Ethiopians were the most largely represented from Africa. Following this Act, several additional immigration laws instituted in the decades that followed continued to facilitate a significant increase in the migration of Black immigrants to the US. Among these were the Immigration and Nationality Act Amendments of October 20, 1976, which "made it easier for foreigners to obtain visas to study, reunite with family, or market their skills"; the Refugee Act of March 17, 1980, which "fundamentally changed U.S. refugee policy to conform to UN protocol on refugees and provided for 500,000 visas annually," allowing for influx of refugees from countries with international and civil unrest such as Somalia, Ethiopia and Eritrea, Cuba and Haiti; the 1986 Immigration Reform and Control Act (IRCA), which allowed "undocumented immigrants living in the United States to apply for legal status"; and the 1990 Immigration Act, which "increased the number of immigrants admitted on the basis of skills for U.S. jobs," introducing the "diversity visa lottery to admit immigrants from countries not well-represented among the U.S. immigrant population" (Kent, 2007, p. 6).

Requirements across immigration laws such as those described above, though significantly varied prior to, and following, the landmark Hart–Celler Act, have implicitly, as well as explicitly, set the stage for what would later come to represent a large degree of variation in the educational characterization of Black immigrants in the US. From "highly-skilled" requirements such as the diversity visa programs that tended to attract "well-educated" immigrants and the temporary non-immigrant student visas secured by international students to the often-acknowledged "strong educational background of the newcomers from Africa" who were shown in 2005 to have "more impressive education credentials than Caribbean blacks, African Americans, and non-Hispanic whites" (Kent, 2007, pp. 7–9), the educational attainment of Black immigrants has repeatedly drawn interest if not marked scrutiny and even scorn. Kent (2007) notes, "the difficulty, high costs, and lengthy distance Africans faced to enter the United States favored immigrants with exceptional ability and persistence" (p. 7).

This dynamic, coupled with the burgeoning increase in Black immigrants following the Hart–Celler Act, would see a situation unfold in the US where this population was not only increasingly represented but also perceived largely based on educational attainment. Consider, for instance, trends in population growth of Black immigrants in the past five decades. The vast majority of the Black immigrant population in the US as of 2022 originated from the African continent and from the Caribbean, with the Caribbean remaining the region which functions as the largest origin for Black immigrants and Africa accounting for the most rapid growth (Tamir, 2021). Together, as Tamir (2021) observes, "these two regions accounted for 88% of all Black foreign-born people in the U.S. in 2019" and specifically:

Between 2000 and 2019, the Black African immigrant population grew 246%, from about 600,000 to 2.0 million. As a result, people of African origin now make up 42% of the country's foreign-born Black population, up from just 23% in 2000. Still, the Caribbean remains the most common region of birth for U.S. Black immigrants. Just under half of the foreign-born Black population was born in this region (46%). (Tamir, 2021)

Among the countries most largely represented in Black immigrant origins as of 2022 are Jamaica (760,000), Haiti (700,000), Nigeria (390,000), Ethiopia (260,000) Dominican Republic (210,000), Ghana (190,000), Trinidad and Tobago (170,000), Kenya (130,000), Guyana (120,000), and Somalia (110,000). Notably, Jamaica and Haiti have remained the top countries of origin for Black immigrants since 2000, representing almost four-in-ten (39 percent) Black immigrants. Nonetheless, an observed decline was noted in 2019 with their collective share of Black immigrants decreasing to 31 percent as Nigeria and Ethiopia were identified as the top birthplaces for Black African immigrants to the US in 2019. As of 2019, one-in-ten Black people in the US are immigrants (i.e., first-generation/foreign-born) and a significant part of the Black American population have been identified as having recent immigrant connections such that "they were born in the U.S. and have at least one foreign-born parent." It is projected that the Black immigrant population will "account for roughly a third of the U.S. Black population's growth through 2060" (Tamir, 2021).

Coupled with specifications of immigration law, many of which require "highly-skilled" or "educated" personnel, it is easy to see how the increasing and varied population dynamics of Black immigrants has positioned this population as one largely judged based on educational attainment in the US, a dynamic which has, in turn, come to dominate the narrative that *is* Black immigration. As of the Pew Research Center's findings in 2022, "a growing share of Black immigrants [in the US] have a college degree or higher" and "between 2000 and 2019, the share of Black immigrants with at least a bachelor's degree has increased faster than among other populations" under analysis. The Pew Research Center observes that "nearly a third of Black immigrants ages 25 and older (31%) had at least a bachelor's degree in 2019, up from 21% in 2000," a "10 percentage point increase [that] was larger than the increase among the Black U.S.-born population (8 points), the entire U.S.-born population (9 points) and the entire immigrant population (9 points)" (Tamir, 2021). In addition, Black immigrants are said to "earn college degrees at a similar rate to all U.S. immigrants (31% vs. 33% among those 25 and older in 2019)." Representations such as these, visible across the mediasphere, and percolating within and across educational communities, can be said to be responsible for what often becomes a largely lopsided view of who the Black immigrant is, and the educational supports deemed useful, necessary, and significant for this population across the US academy, colleges, and schools.

Against this contextual and historical backdrop, it becomes possible to understand the following key nuanced yet varied, and even sometimes contradictory, representations that often characterize the educational experiences and characteristics of Black immigrants in the US, characterizations presented here as narratives of: (a) invisibility, (b) achievement, (c) ethnicity and culture vs. race, (d) peer relations, and (e) possibility. I refer to these key representations as 'narratives' given that they function as the storying of Black immigrants in education that is often painted in and beyond the academic literature and by which Black Caribbean immigrant youth tend to be framed in the US.

Narratives of Invisibility

In the book *Erasing Invisibility, Inequity, and Social Injustice of Africans in the Diaspora and the Continent*, which explores the state and "experience of African education both on the continent and in the diaspora," Drs. Omiunota Ukpokodu and Peter Otiato Ojiambo introduce the edited volume with a call for "visibility . . . to the scholarship on Africa and African immigrants and their contributions to the academe" (Ukpokodu & Ojiambo, 2017, p. xix). Noting that "negative images and narratives about Africa as the 'Dark Continent' remain prevalent," the authors lament that "little is known about [African] experiences and the contributions they make toward the advancement of their communities, particularly, the challenges and issues they face in the larger society and institutions of learning." While it may be said perhaps that Afro-Caribbean immigrants in the US often do not have such negative connotations attached to their personhoods as do their Black peers who migrate from the African continent, given that the category of "African American" most often recognized in education tends to function as one within which all Black peoples in the US are subsumed, there remains an invisibility and obscurity of the Black immigrant at large, whether achieved by intention or not, that operates pervasively across and is endemically intertwined with a glaring resistance to address the unique needs of this rapidly growing population of children and youth in US education. Whether accompanied, in part, by the erroneous notion that to isolate Black immigrants as a sub-population whose needs are addressed is somehow representative of divisiveness (discussed later), or the insistence that their implied status as 'model minorities' supposedly reduces their need for supports and for "affirmative action" even as they experience "institutional schizophrenic" responses that tout them as capable while their personhoods are rejected, emotionally, physically, psychologically, and otherwise erased (Smith et al., 2022), the glaring invisibility of Black immigrants in US education persists (Louis et al., 2017; Smith, 2020b).

Arguably, a multiplicity of meanings is embedded in the notion of "invisibility" as relates to race relations in America, as has been addressed by Dr. Constance Sutton and highlighted by Dr. Roy Simon Bryce-Laporte. Bryce-Laporte, a Black sociologist from the Republic of Panama with dual citizenship in Panama and America, responsible for establishing one of the first departments of African American studies in the US and who led Black studies at Yale University, introduced a paradigmatic shift in the concentration of Black research on voluntary Black immigrants, extending the then focus which had primarily been on Black peoples brought unwilling to the US as slaves.

Bryce-Laporte used the term "invisibility" to mean that "much of black presence and black problems go unattended in the larger society" (Bryce-Laporte, 1972, p. 54). This notion of invisibility, as pointed out by Bryce-Laporte, existed alongside other notions such as those that present "the visibility of blacks vis-à-vis whites" as the key basis for the "racial problems in the United States" (Bryce-Laporte, 1972, p. 54). He explained that "black immigrants could be said to suffer double invisibility as immigrants and black immigrants or double visibility as blacks in the eyes of whites and as foreigners in the eyes of native-born blacks," a conundrum that undergirds the nuanced conceptions of "invisibility" in this book as experienced by this population whose failure to be recognized is simultaneously juxtaposed against the acknowledged "double invisibility" imposed in the Black-White racial context of the US (Bryce-Laporte, 1972, p. 31). He explained:

On one hand, as blacks, [the demands of Black immigrants] and protests as a constituent group have been responded to with the same disregard shown by the larger society and its leaders towards efforts of native American blacks to reshape the society to meet their particular needs and cultural orientation. On the other hand, while black foreigners (and their progenies) have held a disproportionately high number of leadership and successful positions and have exercised significant influence in black life in this country, their cultural impact as foreigners has generally been ignored or has merely been given lip service in the larger spheres of American life. On the national level, they suffer double invisibility, in fact – as blacks and as black foreigners. (Bryce-Laporte, 1972, p. 31)

It is no surprise, then, that in an interview with *The Times*, Bryce-Laporte once observed, "If there is a forgotten or overlooked fact of black history, it is migration." He explained that "black immigrants are perhaps the least visible but most articulate and active of America's ethnic constituencies, yet no place has truly been given to black immigrants" (Martin, 2012, p. 22; see also Alim & Smitherman, 2020, on "raciolinguistic exceptionalism" for a problematization of the notion of the 'articulate' Black). Thus, recognizing the presence of Black immigrants in America from its earliest inception, Bryce-Laporte observed:

> what is important and established is that blacks came to Virginia, Florida, Arizona, New Mexico, and so on "before the Mayflower" – to borrow the phrase of black historian and journalist, Lerone Bennett (1961). Technically speaking, then, members of all races now residing in this country (perhaps only with exception of the Amerindians) were originally immigrants and, accordingly, blacks constitute one of the earliest immigrant groups in the United States or on the larger American continent. (Bryce-Laporte, 1972, p. 31)

Acknowledging notwithstanding, a noted exception to, and complicating the statement above considering that descendants of Black people brought to the US as slaves are not immigrants (i.e., African Americans) – Bryce-Laporte (1972) indicated over five decades ago that the latter population has tended to be the focal point of comparison for the Black immigrant's accomplishments, rather than the larger, foreign-born and native-born populations of the country. Indeed, the lament of invisibility on the part of the Black immigrant has been entrenched pervasively in what Bryce-Laporte (1972) describes as America's reticence "to encourage a study of black immigrants *from within its ranks* [emphasis added] compared to the works being produced on other minorities, including the mostly American black community" (p. 32). Dodoo observed in 1997 that Black immigrants in the US were considerably less researched in comparison to Hispanic and Asian immigrants, noting that when this population was indeed examined, the focus tended to be on studies of the socio-economic condition of Black immigrants to the US (Butcher, 1994; Dodoo, 1991, 1997; Kalmijn, 1996; Model, 1991, 1995), on comparing American and immigrant Blacks with a representation of immigrant Blacks as a homogenous population (Chiswick, 1979; Dodoo, 1991), or on one sub-population as a primary focus – Black Caribbean immigrants vs. African immigrants (Butcher, 1994; Kalmijn, 1996; Model, 1991, 1995).

Thus, even as there has been possibility for making visible the narratives of Black immigrants in the US, it is not often that a sufficient acknowledgment of the heterogeneity within has been recognized or that this has been framed sufficiently within the broader immigration discourse. Ghong et al. (2010) have described the demographic variation of populations from the continent of Africa that undergird Black immigration. They explain that the diversity presented by Black immigrants from Africa is embedded in the experiences of individuals who may originate from its north or south, reflect phenotypical variations that range from "White" to "Black," represent linguistic variations that range from Anglophone to Francophone, and that reflect varied socioeconomic realities. The authors address the tendency of teachers in schools to engage with new African immigrants as 'African Americans,' a dynamic that causes their multilingual capacities and cultural histories to be overlooked. In turn, they highlight the frustration of African parents who are often made responsible for educating teachers about their children and outline culturally responsive practices that teachers can use to address these concerns. Similarly, Allen et al. (2012) have responded to anti-immigration discourses in ways that highlight the often-elusive knowledges steeped in West African immigrants' culture and indigeneity by positioning the assets of this population in the US classroom. The authors have used culturally relevant theory to both challenge invisibility and stereotypical notions of Africans and demonstrate the heterogeneity of Black immigrants, inviting a focus on Black immigrant youth's "hybrid identities, indigenous knowledges, and enactments of cultural competence and socio-political consciousness within curriculum" (Allen et al., 2012, pp. 1, 13).

Extending this focus, Kiramba et al. (2020) have called for a recognition of the multilingual and multicultural resources brought by African students to US classrooms. In their study of the cross-cultural educational experiences of thirty Black African immigrant youth in US schools, the authors draw from culturally sustaining pedagogies (Paris & Alim, 2014) to describe how participants struggled with cultural and linguistic differences, the stereotypical tropes and marginalization imposed on them in the school environment, and low expectations from teachers even while they worked to adjust to practices of school in the system, which invite teachers and educators to teach in ways that acknowledge African immigrants. Similarly, Malcolm and Mendoza (2014) have described how Afro-Caribbean international students "often become engrossed in a complex racial and ethnic dialogue wherein they are thrust into homogenous categorizations forcing them to negotiate their Afro-Caribbean self with identities perceived by others such as African American, first- and second-generation Caribbean immigrant, African, and Latin American," observing a tendency to "homogenize ACIS [Afro-Caribbean international students] [that] overlooks their experiences and development [so that their issues] become essentially invisible for administrations and in the literature on student identity development" (p. 595). The authors call for a disruption of the homogenized discourse on ACIS, a label potentially also denoting certain Black Caribbean immigrant youth.

In response, and extending the focus to Black immigrant educators, my colleagues and I have made visible the learning of five 'vernacular-speaking' Afro-Caribbean educators about their multilingual and multicultural awareness upon their migration to the US (Smith et al., 2020). Our findings showed that the Black immigrant educators learned about their awareness of language and culture as they modified their intonation, the content of their messages, their facial expressions, decided to speak or to be silent, and identified concerns about language in their home countries about which they were previously unaware. We observed that reflexivity was critical to the educators' learning about their multilingual awareness and about the specific sources that helped them to navigate cultural incongruence, which proved critical to learning about their multicultural awareness. The study showed that the educators developed "transnational linguistic fluidity" as they demonstrated awareness through learning, challenging prevailing assumptions that because they are immigrant, multilingual, and Black, they are naturally predisposed to reflect awareness of language and culture.

Narratives of Achievement

Though often made invisible in the US system as compared to their foreign-born immigrant and native-born Black counterparts, it is often the case that when Black immigrants are indeed the focus of educational research, there is a tendency to focus on their achievement as a defining characteristic of how they 'measure up,' very often, against their African American peers as relates to the broader dominant norms based largely on white student performance in this system.

One such example is seen in the research of Gilbert (2008), who, acknowledging the tendency of African immigrants to be subsumed within the African American population, tested the long-standing Cultural-Ecological Theory of School Performance advanced by Ogbu and Simons (1998) that Black immigrant students academically outperform their non-immigrant counterparts and that differences in achievement can be attributed to educational commitments that are stronger in Black immigrants than in other families. Using the Progress in International Reading Literacy Study of 2001 (PIRLS), a large-scale international survey and reading assessment involving fourth grade students from thirty-five countries, including the US, as the basis for their examination, the scholar tested four hypotheses, namely, that Black immigrant students have "more receptive attitudes toward reading," a "more positive reading self-concept," "a higher level of reading literacy," and that "the relationship of immigrant status to reading perceptions and literacy persists after including selected predictors" (Gilbert, 2008, p. vii). Gender as well as immigration were key considerations undergirding these comparisons. Findings from the study showed no difference in the attitudes to reading or in reading self-concept among immigrant and non-immigrant students. While the performance of second-generation immigrant boys was greater than that of non-immigrant and foreign-born immigrant boys in reading literacy, there appeared to be no difference found among girls. Moreover, for girls, certain sociocultural predictors such as number of books in the home and length of US residence, appeared to reflect a relatively stronger relationship to reading self-concept than was reflected by immigrant status. Together, these findings highlighted the need for addressing gender and generational status as well as sociocultural factors influencing Black immigrant students' academic perceptions and performance in US schools. They are corroborated also by findings from studies examining the relationships of social identity, academic identity, and college-going aspirations of Black immigrant students in relation to their native-born peers which show distinctions across ethnicity and generational status with regards to how Black students reflect perceptions of their social identities on their academic motivation (Mwangi & English, 2017).

Addressing the notion of generational status among Black immigrants and other peers while acknowledging the heterogeneity existing within this group, Obinna (2016) has comparatively examined the academic performance of Black immigrants as relates to African Americans as well as Asian and Hispanic students of comparable immigrant generation. The study intended to undertake a more comprehensive understanding of Black immigrant students by considering how they performed on standardized tests, their grade point averages (GPAs), and with regards to college enrolment as related to peers. Using data from the Educational Longitudinal Survey of high school sophomores conducted by the 2002 and 2006 National Center for Education Statistics (NCES), the study showed that "while second-generation blacks outperform[ed] the native-born generation on standardized tests, this [did] not extend to GPA or college enrolment," raising questions about the tendency to draw conclusions about the achievement of Black immigrant students that overlook the nuance surrounding factors such as generational difference.

Responding to the calls for more in-depth understandings of sociocultural factors affecting Black immigrant achievement, and also addressing the long-standing 'racialized elephant in the room' as relates to African American and Black immigrant populations in education discourse, my colleagues and I (Smith et al., 2019) have used the "opportunity gap explanatory framework" advanced by Milner (2012) to challenge 'underperformance' vs. 'outperformance' narratives often appearing in the characterization of US Black immigrants in relation to their African American peers (admittedly acknowledging that there is increasing conflation between identification as 'immigrant' and as 'American'). Much like Gilbert (2008), but focusing on a different data set, we examined a corpus of data from the 2012 Programme for International Student Assessment (PISA) with a focus on self-identification of language use and its influence on PISA reading literacy performance. Pointing to the findings, which indicated that Black immigrant students' literacy performance, though higher than that of African Americans, was lower than the average performance set by the OECD as acceptable, we highlight that it is more important to engage in discourse about opportunities denied to Black immigrants *as well as* to their African American peers than it is to merely focus on comparative achievement, as reflected by their capacity to meet a Eurocentric standard of literate practice that has not, by its very intention and design, been developed to capture the nuances and assets brought by *all* Black students to the languaging table (Smith et al., 2019; see also Smith, 2022e).

Ngo (2008) appears to express similar notions in addressing how the experiences of immigrant youth and families in schools and the society of the US have been positioned in ways that are represented largely as a juxtaposition of immigrant cultures against that of the dominant US culture. The author argues that US schools and society have been conceptualized primarily as conflicts between immigrant cultures and dominant US culture, challenging the structuring of immigrants' experiences, cultures, and identities as "unchanging and fixed in time" and advancing a view of culture and identity which is "constructed within the double movement of discourse and representation" (Ngo, 2008, p. 4). Ngo describes how such stark dominant representations may result in understandings of immigrant youth identities that are simplistic in nature and may also obscure understandings of the emerging and novel identities of immigrant youth. This nuanced portrait called for understanding how Black racial identity functions for certain American and Nigerian youth and has been captured by scholars such as Onyewuenyi (2018) who complicate existing achievement discourses by acknowledging the complexities involved in comparing achievement within the Black population. Such an intraracial emphasis is reflected also in research examining Black immigrant college youth (Daoud et al., 2018).

The constantly evolving heterogeneity of experience highlighted among Black immigrant youth (e.g., Ngo, 2008; Onyewuenyi, 2018; Smith et al., 2019) mirrors that from a mixed-methods examination by Clayton and Zusho (2016) which observed how "personal, cognitive, contextual, and sociocultural factors are important determinants of Jamaican undergraduate students' academic motivation" and that "sociocultural (e.g., familial, economic, religious) factors" played a critical role in impacting this motivation. Together, these authors show that the tendency to use 'achievement gap' connotations, as reflected in examinations such as those that portray Black immigrant students as 'outperforming' their Latino/a peers (Patel et al., 2016), can potentially obscure the need for acknowledging assets brought by immigrant students of Color to languaging, and also, possibly result in an emphasis on deficits of students as opposed to opportunities denied by a system primed to disregard their assets. Such connotations, scholars observe, can also inadvertently further deepen the rift between Black immigrant and African American populations by suggesting explanations for achievement such as differentiated investments of

Black Caribbean immigrant parents in their children's education as opposed to that of African American parents even while failing to center the ways in which systemic engagement (or lack thereof) of schools and the US society with the latter population differs from that offered to the former (Pinder et al., 2014). In fact, as Onyewuenyi (2018) has shown, "when care is taken to compare groups that are equivalent in parent education, Black Americans perform as well as Nigerians" (p. 6).

Arguably, while these connotations may possibly present explanations about achievement that are steeped in clarifying what Calzada et al. (2015) explore as the "immigrant paradox," where certain Black young students from immigrant families supposedly perform 'better' than their non-immigrant Black peers, the sustained focus on students and overlooked emphasis on the tendency of schools, curricular, and societal practices to honor certain forms of achievement over others in and beyond US schools persists. Admittedly, there remains a long-standing call for disaggregation of Black student data by institutions (e.g., Smith et al., 2019; Ukpokodu, 2018; Waters et al., 2014), which remains critical to identifying the heterogenous needs of Black students in ways that can allow teachers, schools, districts, and the broader society to provide adequate supports to this population. As Patel et al. (2016) indicate, understanding sociocontextual stressors possibly affecting student achievement is necessary for accurate discussions of their performance that reflect their "full academic potential" (p. 121). A discussion of this full potential, as put forward by scholars such as Dávila (2015) in her examination of two young African immigrant women English learners' perspectives on reading, and literacy more broadly, in relation to motivation and identity, would allow for students' full linguistic repertoires (García & Wei, 2014) to be visible as they engage with reading in classrooms and developing a sense of belonging in the US community.

The need for problematizing achievement narratives becomes even more critical given the aforementioned notion of the 'model minority' which tends to accompany Black immigrants in the US and continues to function as a divisive mechanism that inhibits solidarity across Black communities. This trope is, in turn, manipulated by systems within contexts such as the US, and also in the UK where it has been alluded to as "the culture trap" (Wallace, 2023) to advance divide-and-conquer politics while maintaining the status quo. Responding to how "African immigrants in the U.S. have been headlined as America's 'new model minority,'" Ukpokodu's (2018) examination of aggregated and disaggregated data designed to weigh the claim that African immigrant students demonstrate educational achievement and excellence that is 'superior' to that of their peers finds no evidence. In addition to acknowledging the limited research on the educational performance of African immigrant students in US K–12 schools, Ukpokodu asserts that the "notion of a 'model minority' attributed to African immigrants is disingenuous and a disservice to [African immigrant students]" in the US, urgently calling for an "overhauling" of data collecting and reporting systems, the debunking of the ascription of "model minority" to this population, and much like Calzada et al. (2015) and Daoud et al. (2018), for a disaggregation of data for Black immigrant students. This debunking of the notion of African immigrant youth as a "New Model Minority" is similarly advanced by Onyewuenyi (2018), in comparisons of Nigerian and African American high school youth, who points out "no indication of an 'immigrant advantage' in grades for Nigerian youth relative to Black American youth" (p. 5).

Notably, these findings stand in stark contrast to "evidence confirming the model minority hypothesis" as represented by a historical portrayal of West Indian immigrants' socioeconomic advantages to native-born Blacks found in examinations of the depiction of first-wave West Indian immigrants to the US in Black print culture (Tillery & Chresfield, 2012). Such was the sentiment articulated in the early twentieth-century content analyses of four newspapers widely circulated across the Black community between 1910 and 1940 and later, post the Hart–Celler Immigration Act passed in 1965, following which a huge wave of Black immigrants became residents in the US. For instance, Dodoo (1997) has shown, using data from the 1990 Census of Population, how the comparative distinctions in earnings attainment of male African immigrants, their Caribbean-born counterparts, and native-born African Americans positioned Africans as earning more than both Caribbean immigrants and native-born Blacks despite the fact that "controlling for relevant earnings-related endowments erase[d] the African advantage, and elevate[d] Caribbean earnings above those of the other two groups" (p. 527). Acknowledging claims of immigrant superiority advanced by scholars such as Reid (1939) and Sowell (1978) even while recognizing conflicting evidence (Kalmijn, 1996; Model, 1995), Dodoo asserted that indeed there existed "a belief in some academic circles, as well as among the broader American public, that Caribbean immigrants generally outearn[ed] native-born blacks in America" (Harrison, 1992; Waters, 1994). Highlighting potential sources of confusion about the variations touted regarding progress of foreign-born populations in relation to their native-born peers, Dodoo confirmed, at the time, that a Caribbean "advantage" did exist in earnings of Black immigrants but that this was limited to British Caribbean immigrants and based on occupation but not on earnings. Operating from the basis of "occupational earnings," Dodoo asserted the presence of a "Caribbean occupational advantage" on the part of Black immigrants from this region, arguing that this understandably explained the perceived belief that West Indians educationally 'outperformed' American Blacks. At the same time, the author surmised, it was acknowledged that Africans, who were shown then to have an earnings disadvantage (Butcher, 1994) and an occupational disadvantage largely based on discrimination as respectively compared to their African American peers, appeared to be absent from such discussions, a perplexing indication considering their then status as "one of, if not the most highly educated of all immigrant groups" (Dodoo, 1997, p. 529) in the US (Butcher, 1994; Katende, 1995).

Given these indications steeped in socioeconomics, and the corresponding foundational role of the key construct of "socioeconomic status" (SES) as a basis for conducting educational research in the US, it is no surprise that such broader discourses, though largely peripheral to the educational research enterprise, have tended to function as a key determinant of how the often-homogenized population of Black immigrant students would later come to be perceived and engaged *with*, or *not*, whether considered independently or which are largely subsumed within the broader Black population across colleges, universities, and schools.

Narratives of Ethnicity and Culture vs. Race

The tendency to advance rhetoric concerning Black immigrants that remains steeped in notions of "achievement," much of which is informed by accompanying homogenizing conceptions of a "model minority," have a deep-rooted history in the tendency to utilize terms such as "ethnicity" and "culture" versus "race" in the educational and other literature on Black immigrants in the US. This practice, which bears a startling resemblance to the 'postcolonial' discourse sans explicit naming of race in the English-speaking Caribbean, stands in stark contrast to the normative practice of explicitly naming racialization in 'African American' educational research. Such discourse, as Pierre (2004) has observed, became obvious in social science post the landmark Hart–Celler Act of 1965 in the US, and "employ[ed] the concept of 'ethnicity' in ways that reinforce the racialist myth of Black (American) cultural inferiority" (pp. 141, 150). Pierre (2004) contends that the "discursive use of Black immigrant 'ethnic' and 'cultural distinctiveness,' while admittedly reflecting an important recognition of the heterogeneity of the US Black populations, is in fact predicated upon a repackaged 'culture of poverty' discourse that serves to reaffirm the overarching racial order" (pp. 141, 144). In showing how current discourses of "ethnic distinctiveness" serve to perpetuate "a form of racism under a theory that denies the relevance of race while it continuously recodes the biological notions of race as 'culture,'" Pierre (2004) makes the case that "Black immigrant distinctiveness" as presented "through the prism of the cultural narratives of ethnicity, allows for the perpetuation of a 'cultural racism' that adversely affects all Blacks" in the US (pp. 141, 144). Calling for a rejection of "ethnicity theory" as currently conceptualized, the author invites a grounding of theories of Black distinctiveness within analyses that capture how power relations and ongoing practices function as a project of racial subjugation.

Such calls, if applied to studies such as the one used by my colleagues and me to examine culturally and linguistically diverse African immigrant students attending public urban middle and high schools in the US, would require an extension beyond merely "pedagogical, linguistic, and curricular variation struggles in the classroom; transitional contextual challenges; cultural mismatch; miscommunication, and stereotypes" identified in the experiences of this student population to *necessarily* locate the urban youth's uses of "familial, navigational and aspirational capital" as a basis for resisting stereotypical assumptions and "develop[ing] resilient skills necessary to navigate the inherent challenges" in the racialized structures of the US schooling system responsible for the perpetuation of these challenges (Kiramba et al., 2021, p. 43). In doing so, the distinctiveness of the challenges faced by the African students would also be subject to analyses grounded in the logics of racial subjugation by which the US system continues to operate.

A problematization of ethnicity and culture narratives concurrently with a centering of race in the experiences of Black immigrants as called for by Pierre (2004) is visible in the presentation of lived experience such as that described by Dr. Pierre Orelus, a Haitian scholar and educator. Orelus (2012) presents his immigrant story as one that illuminates politics in the country of origin versus the country of destination and is situated strategically within the broader sociopolitical, linguistic, and racial context of the US. There, immigrants, as Orelus (2012) notes, and "particularly immigrants of color, have faced many challenges" (p. 19). The problematization of ethnicity and culture is visible also in writings such as "Constructing Black Selves" where the 'assimilation' of Black immigrants from Jamaica, Cuba, Haiti, the Dominican Republic, and other island nations in the Caribbean after the huge wave of immigration made possible by the 1965 Hart–Celler Immigration Reform Act is discussed with a view to clarifying both race and ethnicity in the social and cultural context of the US (McGill, 2005). It is further mirrored in emerging discourses of cosmopolitanism and culture that rely on intersections of post-coloniality, ethnicity, and race to challenge a long-standing "utopianism of colorblind universalism," thereby arguing for the "persistence of 'race' and racialized thinking in lived experience" (Luczak et al., 2019, p. 5).

In alignment with such discourses, I have used a raciolinguistic perspective to complicate the notion of World Englishes (Kachru, 1992; Rosa & Flores, 2017) in examining how Black immigrant educators from one African country and from countries in the English-speaking Caribbean approximated certain standardized Englishes after their migration to the US. The study identified sources of English (il)legitimacy to which educators were subjected as others reacted negatively to their accents, race, communication, and vocabulary and highlighted how "cultural incongruence and confusion led educators to (re)claim their English legitimacy and to leverage pedagogical approaches regarding tone, expectation, delivery, and linguistic content and context" (Smith, 2020a, p. 106). Demonstrating how educators reflected 'a transraciolinguistic approach' through metalinguistic, metaracial, and metacultural understanding as a function of repositioning institutional norms and "(re)establishing legitimacy of their standardized Englishes as Black speakers in the U.S. academy" (Smith, 2020a, p. 106), I illustrated the burden imposed on Black immigrants and all Black populations and populations of Color, whose linguistic practices require such a challenge to present their personhoods legitimately in US contexts, classrooms, and the academy.

This taking up and centering of "race" as an intentional element of the discussions of Black immigrant literacies and more recently, as a basis for exploring hegemonic practices undergirding explorations of discourses undergirding how their educational achievement is characterized, represents a shift to privilege narratives of complexity over those that appear to simplify representations of immigrant peoples and youth, as called for by Ngo (2008). For instance, in the examination of African immigrant youth's identities, Awokoya (2009) considers how family, school, and peer groups influence students' racial and ethnic identities, attending closely to institutional and societal expectations imposed on students in relation to "what it means to be African, Nigerian, African American, and Black" (p. 9). Awokoya (2009) argues that these expectations "dramatically shift across contexts" and "significantly confound the racial and ethnic identity constructions and negotiations for these youth," creating the possibility for African immigrants' educational needs to be better understood by US educational systems (p. 3).

Such possibilities are visible in studies conducted by scholars such as Braden (2020) who have demonstrated how racialized experiences specifically, and cultural experiences generally, both work in tandem to affect how African immigrant students engage with schooling in the US. Braden explored, through an after-school critical literacy workshop with one Black immigrant family from Senegal where relationships were built among parents, students, and educators, how these were based on such understandings in ways that enable teachers to have more nuanced understandings about Black immigrants while at the same time, enhancing students' well-being. Her findings showed that the critical literacy workshop enabled the family to prepare their children to anticipate the challenges of the racialized society of the US and allowed all to recognize how transnational literacies functioned importantly to help build children's racial and heritage knowledge. She also demonstrated how spaces for conversation were possible through children's use of literature and film, allowing the family to share with other parents, how racial injustices operated within the US society, the colorism deployed by teachers in the classroom, as well as the value of African heritage pride. According to Braden (2020), the study helped to affirm the "Black thinking" of the Black immigrant family as well as their "sociopolitical consciousness," allowing them to "articulate their feelings about racist acts and violence and the need for African heritage pride" (pp. 2, 20), and reiterating the importance of integrating information about movements such as #BlackLivesMatter in literacy curriculum.

The possibilities highlighted by Awokoya (2009) are also visible in studies that illustrate the value of Afrocentric practices for teachers in ways that affirm the Black racial identities of African immigrants such as Yandi, a second-generation immigrant child, whose complexities as presented by her culture are often overlooked in US schools (Braden et al., 2020). They extend research by scholars such as my colleague and I (Kumi-Yeboah & Smith, 2016) who have focused on enhancing Black immigrants' critical multicultural education through class discussions, social media and technology, non-educational practices, and cultural and language. They also challenge the field to complicate findings from studies such as those conducted into the cultural learning of Afro-Caribbean immigrant teacher educators, demonstrating how their experiences with teachers in the US enabled them to develop "knowledge beyond practice in their learning to know, do, be and live together with others" (Smith, 2018, p. 263), and which show that their learning reflected "the processes of observation, reflection, awareness, requesting student feedback in the moment, and the passing of time that resulted in adjustment to their body language, changes in their expectations of students, a modification in their communication, code-switching, and sensitivity" (p. 263).

Peer Relations

With a complexifying of achievement narratives that address conceptions of 'model minority' status among Black immigrants and that disrupt the often obscured racialization of their personhoods in US research, there have become increasing opportunities to examine peer relations and interactions among Black immigrants and their African American populations, a site of contestation that, as repeatedly mentioned previously, continues to be manifested in contemporary society (e.g., Smith, 2013). Among studies exploring this dynamic have been research by scholars such as Stuesse et al. (2017) which, recognizing perceptions of the tensions that persist in relations between immigrants and African Americans, highlight how the ongoing efforts to interpersonally connect these populations have significantly increased in the US. Using seventy-five interviews conducted with individuals in charge of such initiatives and based on a review of fifty-plus pedagogical resources developed and used in this process, the authors classify and assess these programs to illustrate successes and shortcomings by drawing from an "anti-racist, African

Americanist framework" steeped in what they refer to as the "standpoint of [the] black figure, crouched on the ground as others pluck fruit off the tree of opportunity" (Steinberg, 2005, p. 43). Their findings show that while there are successes recognized in the form of spaces created for interaction and for engaging in shared analyses of differences across racial subgroups and while transformative effects of these programs are visible both intrapersonally and interpersonally, there are opportunities for addressing what they describe as "immigrant-centricity" in the emerging relationships and for engaging immigrants in conversations regarding how they "relate to Whiteness, Black Blackness, and racial hierarchies in the United States and in their countries of origin" (Stuesse et al., 2017, p. 245).

Deviating partially from African Americans as the focal point of comparison and addressing assertions concerning the obsolete nature of race as a defining feature of American life and intergroup relations, Thornton et al. (2017) have used the National Survey of American Life data to explore interethnic attitudes among African Americans and Black Caribbeans in relation to African immigrants. Findings illustrate the nuances among Black sub-populations in the US, pointing out the similarities in African Americans and Black Caribbeans' feelings of closeness to Africans. Highlighting that Black Caribbeans who were younger males, experienced more financial strain, were residents in the northeast, and immigrants migrating eleven years prior to the study, especially reported more closeness to Africans. The authors point out that African American males appeared to be the only group reporting specific feelings of closeness.

The emergence of challenges for engaging immigrants in what are seen as efforts to advance intergroup relations among Black immigrants and their African American peers is viewed by certain scholars as an issue of "Americanization" (Thornton et al., 2017). Extending beyond the typically explored Black ethnic divides between African American and Black Caribbean populations (Thornton et al., 2017), Okonofua thus positions African immigrants and African Americans at the center of engaging the "contestation of Blackness" in the US by highlighting how the schisms created between these two populations and the conflicts and tensions sustained benefit other racial categories. Locating the key source of the persisting dissonance across the complex interactions among whites, African immigrants, and African Americans, squarely in white racial framing, a theory of "manipulative deflection" is advanced that describes how "powerless groups unable to effectively challenge the forces that oppress them, attack people like themselves" (Okonofua, 2013, p. 1). In this theory, Okonofua (2013) argues fundamentally that "it is the subjective experience of deprivation that diminishes the construction of a holistic Black identity and produces confusion and conflict among Blacks in the United States" (pp. 1, 10).

Such constructions of racial framing that seek to place the burden for intergroup relations squarely at the feet of the systems traditionally responsible for advancing white supremacist ways of being, whether inadvertently or not, appear to inform efforts to consider specifically how broader societal tensions among Black immigrants and their African American peers are manifested in schools. For instance, my colleagues and I have recently explored the relationships of Black immigrant youth with teachers and peers as part of a study focused on teachers' cultural awareness of Black immigrants and on the pedagogical strategies implemented by these teachers as they worked to support the academic success of Black immigrant youth in US urban schools (Kumi-Yeboah et al., 2020). Through the lens of culturally responsive teaching, we demonstrated how students' bi-cultural identity complicated responses of teachers and peers to them as well as expectations of them in the US society. Specifically, Irizarry and Cohen (2019) have also illustrated, using data from the Early Childhood Longitudinal Study – Kindergarten Class of 1998–1999, how race, ethnicity, and immigration status intersect to influence teacher ratings by exploring how teachers vary in their ratings of academic ability across four conventional racial/ethnic groups and thirteen racialized subgroups. Findings from the study showed that Black first-graders, regardless of whether they were Black American or Black immigrants, appeared to receive lower ratings in language and literacy. This presented a stark contrast to ratings of Asian first-graders who were rated more highly in math, a practice influenced by teachers' tendency to generally rate students more highly if they had East Asian or Southeast Asian backgrounds. Of significant import is the authors' assertion that teachers demonstrate perceptions of student academic behavior as reflected by the study that potentially explain why Black Americans tended to receive lower language and literacy ratings and why Southeast Asian and East Asian immigrants tend to reflect higher math ratings.

Extending this focus at the high school level, scholars such as Agyepong (2019), working through critical ethnography, have elucidated the experiences of Black West African immigrant students as well as non-immigrant students, using postcolonial theory in conjunction with notions of anti-Blackness, to explore how perceptions of Blackness and Africanness influence the ways that teachers, guidance counsellors, and peers treat this immigrant student population in two New York public high schools. Mirroring calls for attending to institutional as well as individual realities reinforced by a raciolinguistic perspective (Rosa & Flores, 2017), the study allowed for examinations of how African immigrant students make sense of the treatment and perception received by institutional actors in relation to their identity as well as the ways in which the context of the school affects the challenges and affordances experienced by African immigrant students. Findings from the study showed that the school contexts influenced how Blackness and Africanness were perceived and understood, with each school reflecting variations in terms of perceptions about who is considered Black and the factors responsible for a person being Black. In turn, echoing scholars such as McLean (2020) and Skerrett and Omogun (2020), each school reflected variations in how Black immigrant and non-immigrant students were treated, pointing to the heterogeneity and complexity identified previously in the literature regarding the racial category of Blackness. Agyepong (2019) further simultaneously points to the privilege as well as struggle that socially and academically characterizes African students' Black and African identities, drawing attention to the notion that model minority perceptions of African immigrant students by teachers, counsellors, and peers at both schools did not necessarily align with the grade point averages of African immigrant students. Acknowledging this paradox and lack of evidence, Agyepong (2019) notwithstanding, recognizes that touting Africans as model minorities was used across both schools to denigrate their African American and Latinx peers in ways that "[complicate] yet maintain dominant racial ideologies and structures (i.e., Whiteness on top, Blackness on the bottom) in the U.S." (p. ii).

"Narratives of Possibility"

Contentions characterizing the positioning of Black immigrant populations, and students more specifically, in educational discourse and beyond, have persisted alongside the continued emerge of asset-based narratives – "narratives of possibility" (Watson et al., 2022) – constructed to illustrate how Black African immigrants and Black Caribbean immigrants, the two major, yet heterogenous Black immigrant sub-populations in the US, possess a myriad of assets. Among these are studies such as the recent (re)framing of pedagogies of loss in popular media narratives of African immigrant communities. Working as a response to sociologist Dr. April Gordon's description of a "new diaspora of black Africans to the U.S." (p. 84), Watson et al. (2022) use Afrocentric praxis (King & Swartz, 2016) in conjunction with BlackCrit to challenge deficit framings that emphasize "what a student, family or community is lacking" and articulate instead, "how the cultural and linguistic strengths of African immigrant communities are named (or not named) in popular-media narratives of African immigrant communities" to differently locate a "pedagogy of love" (p. 588). The authors point to eldering and communal responsibility, to language as a colonial modality of loss, and to "speculative seeing" as a function of a pedagogy of love, in enabling the shift from deficit- to asset-based perspectives of African immigrant youth (Watson et al., 2022, p. 588).

In related literature, Watson and Knight-Manuel (2020) have worked with African Indigenous, and with African, Black, and Chicana/Latina, feminisms to undertaken attempts to "humanize the Black immigrant body" by examining the interplay of popularized narratives of immigrant youth and young adults as well as their Diasporic literacy practices. Exploring "embodied Diaspora literacies as affirming and extending presences and absences of Black immigrant bodies across two contexts: an after-school African Club, and a qualitative inquiry of civic learning and action-taking of immigrant youth and young adults from West African countries," Watson and Knight-Manuel show how the humanity of Black immigrant youth and young adults is intertwined with their embodied Diaspora literacy practices. Through the use of "Diasporic tellings, an intentional naming and humanizing research approach" that draws from the words of Chinua Achebe, the Nigerian author who reflected on the urgency of a global "balance of stories," the authors "theorize humanizing the Black immigrant body as a vibrant, necessary research and teaching stance to recognize the humanity of Black immigrant youth who daily negotiate and render visible their language and literacy practices" that "comprise the coalescing of Black immigrant bodies, discursive perspectives, and material artifacts of teaching and learning, and their racialized, social, and educational experiences across contexts of schools and communities" (Watson & Knight-Manuel, 2020, p. 2).

The articulation of "Diasporic tellings" by Watson and Knight-Manuel above that intends to humanize Black immigrant youth emerges from their earlier research which used an interdisciplinary framework centering a Sankofan approach to examine how social processes have been presented to describe African immigrant students' navigation of their identities and civic engagement as a function of their heritage practices and their Indigenous knowledges (Watson & Knight-Manuel, 2017). Findings from this earlier examination identified a need to disrupt three key representations of inequalities affecting African immigrant youth's educational experiences of immigrant youth, namely, the homogenizing notions that present monolithic conceptions of West Africa and of the West African countries of immigrant youth, deficit understandings of the identities and the heterogeneity characterizing Black immigrant youth from West African countries living in the US, and unidimensional views of the civic engagement of these youth. These indications focused specifically on African immigrant students, and reflect in part, as has been illustrated in this chapter thus far, broader discourses surrounding Black immigrants across the US educational spectrum and in the American society at large (see also Watson et al., in press). They point to recurring themes that are repeatedly brought to bear on the narratives emerging more broadly across the Black immigrant population in the US and locate sources for such representations across a broad range of social, historical, socioeconomic, geographic, and other locales. In doing so, they inform the increasing emergence of intersectional (Crenshaw, 2021) lenses that function as the basis for reflecting the numerous possibilities across the Black immigrant population as reflected by their assets.

The identification of literate possibility is also visible in growing efforts that have intersectionally highlighted the linguistic and literate legitimacy of Black immigrant populations in the US. It can be seen in research such as the scholarship of Park (2017) designed to examine how three high school-aged refugee youth from Africa manipulated and leveraged languages and discourses in the US context by drawing from ethnographic data, the analysis of which was steeped in sociocultural theories of language. Intersectionally engaging the social, religious, as well as the linguistic, the study disrupts limited perceptions of African Muslims who, though facing multilayered challenges that create a unique conundrum for students in US, present multilingual practices and complex identities which illuminate how "refugee youths experience school in their new land, and how they see themselves and others" (Park, 2017, p. 2). Similarly, depictions of literate possibility are visible in Burkhard (2021), whose examinations of the adult ESL Somalian student Naima – a former refugee turned American citizen in the US – illustrate intersectionally how racial, religious, and gendered biases coalesced to affect her experiences in an ESL course and, in turn, influenced how she understood herself as a learner. The findings also showed the importance of aligning pedagogies in classrooms to address intersectionally oriented marginalization as occurred in the case of Naima based on race, ethnicity, gender, religion, and language.

A key element increasingly emphasized in the intersectional focus on Black immigrant populations that signals a willingness to explore possibility, and which forms a foundational basis for the explorations in this book, is the longstanding representation of Black immigrant linguistic richness in the US. Though historically largely denied and/or silenced as a basis for legitimate research even while the racialized languaging of Black Americans has been explored though largely discarded, there continue to be new waves of frameworks designed to accommodate the heterogeneity of Black language as a function of Black migration, immigration, and transnationality. Such is the case in research presented by Milu (2021) that explores the raciolinguistic experiences of African immigrants in high school classrooms with a view to advancing transnational Black language pedagogies that allow for the more feasible emergence of Black immigrant students' linguistic repertoires in the US. It is also the case in calls for embracing translingualism as advanced by Kigamwa and Ndemanu (2017) and for countering anti-Black racism in world language teacher preparation (Austin, 2022). Specifically, Kigamwa and Ndemanu (2017) point to the broad array of indigenous and European languages that characterize people from the African continent and that have informed variations in Englishes across countries in Africa as well as the accents that individuals present. Highlighting translingualism developed by

Africans as a function of generational status, the medium of instruction in the countries from which they originate, length of time during which they were exposed to "standard English," age of migration to the US, and response to social expectations for English speaking based on American norms, Kigwama and Ndemanu (2017) address intersectionality in the Englishes of African immigrants by equally considering how historical, socioecological, and linguistic realities are presented in the speech of African immigrants while also attending to the influence on their personhoods across country of origin and country of destination.

Aligned with such indications of literate possibility, Dávila (2019) has illustrated the need to shift away from "learning discrete language skills in one language" to "supporting complex language and content learning fluidly across languages and content areas in ways that affirm students' identities and new learning" (p. 634) in working with Black immigrant youth. Her findings were based on examinations of the language practices and learning experiences of ten adolescent multilingual immigrant and refugee English Learners (ELs) from the Democratic Republic of the Congo (DRC) and extend her earlier research that intersectionally explored English learners' perspectives on reading, and literacy, motivation, by examining the identities of two young African immigrant women in an urban high school in the US southeast. In this earlier research, Dávila (2015) illustrated, through a focus on gender, immigration, and school performance, that although the students were learning to read in what is considered to be an abstract 'new language,' they "were simultaneously developing literacy in their first languages through autonomous reading practices, including reading native-language texts, and on-line news sources" (p. 646).

Mirroring the versatility of Black immigrant youth with languaging, Kiramba and Oloo (2020) have illustrated how one Ghanaian-born youth's multilingual abilities were made visible as she engaged with identities ascribed to her while also resisting impositions on her literate capacity in the midwestern US. The authors' examinations align with the critical policy analysis undertaken by Nalubega-Booker and Willis (2020), using critical race theory, to examine the implementation and practice of second-language/bilingual laws and policies in the state of Illinois via the lens of one Ugandan immigrant and her first-person reflection of her lived experiences. Findings from this examination, which reflects the institutional as well as individual approach to raciolinguistic analyses as called for by Rosa and Flores (2017) in "a raciolinguistic perspective," showed a lack of alignment between the discourse and rhetoric surrounding second-language/bilingual laws and policies on federal, state, and local levels and the practices implemented 'on the ground' in school districts and classrooms (see Nalubega-Booker, in press). Nalubega-Booker and Willis explain how this missing coherence between broader discourses and classroom practice functioned as a mechanism for delimiting the access of one Ugandan

African immigrant student to what is regarded as mainstream language and linguistic education and also placed inhibitions on her access to other academic opportunities.

Now that the broader context within which Afro-Caribbean immigrant students and their literacies are positioned historically, racially, comparatively, linguistically, socially, economically, and contemporarily across the Caribbean and the US is more fundamentally clear, I end this chapter with a call for centering Blackness in immigration, which forms the basis for my segue into the crux of this book – racialized translanguaging in Caribbean Englishes and the accompanying broader transsemiotizing of Black Caribbean immigrant youth.

Centering Blackness in Immigration to Illuminate Sites of Possibilities

Seven years ago, in the special issue titled, "The Diverse Immigrant Student Experience: What Does It Mean for Teaching?" Dr. Carola Suárez-Orozco, Professor in Residence at the Harvard Graduate School of Education and Director of the Immigration Initiative at Harvard University, articulated "an eclectic array of approaches to a pressing topic – How should educators consider the diversity of immigrant student experiences?" (Suárez-Orozco, 2017, p. 1). In this article, she invoked a question posed by Dr. A. Lynn Goodwin, Vice Dean and Professor of Education at Teachers College, Columbia University, nearly a decade and a half prior to her publication of the special issue, concerning the "adequacy of teacher preparation vis-à-vis immigrant children," and the lingering reticence to "do the right thing" (Goodwin, 2002, p. 156; Suárez-Orozco, 2017, p. 1). The question of doing the right thing for immigrant children and youth, as suggested by the foregoing discussion, is complicated by the epistemologically charged discussion surrounding the knowledges of immigrant peoples – a discussion which invites considerations surrounding what it means *to do the right thing* by asking "for whom and by whom" (Smith, 2023a, p. 14).

In this special issue by Suárez-Orozco (2017), Blackness and immigration are highlighted by Dr. Awad Ibrahim, Air Canada Professor in Anti-Racism at the University of Ottawa and author of one of the Forewords to this book, as a function of "becoming Black" in the Canadian context where "the imposed binary of race [was considered to be] less extreme [then] than in the US context," a contrast to the US locale where "Blackness is [considered as] unidimensional and immediately imposed on newcomers" (p. 523), and a dynamic which reminds us of the stark differences in how immigration populations are racialized as Black in the US. This phenomenon, signaled by the deliberate taking of the life of George Floyd, a Black American, in broad daylight, is visible in statistics such as Black immigrants being six times more likely to spend time in isolation (Franco et al., 2020) and in reports indicating that Black immigrants represent over 10 percent of immigrants in removal proceedings in the US between 2003 and 2015 despite constituting less than 6 percent of the undocumented immigrant population.

Suárez-Orozco (2017) proposed in the special issue the use of an ecological framework (Bronfenbrenner & Morris, 2006) and a "risk and resilience model" as two complementary conceptual models to "make sense of the experiences of immigrant or refugee students" (p. 525). Presenting the Bronfenbrennerian perspective, she described how "students' opportunities are shaped by the interrelated contexts in which they are embedded with important implications for educational and well-being outcomes" and using the "risk and resilience" perspective, she offered that "immigrant students are remarkably resilient and bring their own agency and assets to their lives" thus requiring attention to "social context, family-level variables, and child-level factors in considering outcomes that can either add to risk or serve to buffer it" (Suárez-Orozco, 2017, p. 526). Admittedly, the presence of immigrant resilience and agency is incredibly useful at the individual level and provides a context for considering opportunities in their interrelated contexts. Yet, without a centering of race, it is possible that such an individual approach may not, perhaps, as Rosa and Flores (2017) point out, ultimately and sufficiently equip schools, colleges, universities, and other institutions to urgently identify and address potential blind spots that do exist in US systems largely undergirded by white supremacy.

The persisting presence of such blind spots (Ghabra, 2022), though often largely obscured, ignored, circumvented, or made invisible in educational research, for so many decades, can be seen when acknowledged, in how they are manifested as part of the US justice system where over 40 percent of the families in ICE detention as of 2022 were Haitian migrants, a rate identified as "54% higher than the rate for other immigrants in detention" (RAICES, 2020, para. 3). The blind spots are also visible where bail bonds are significantly higher for Haitian immigrants, leading the Refugee and Immigrant Center for Education and Legal Services in the US (RAICES) to proclaim that "freedom is more expensive for Black Immigrants" (RAICES, 2020, para. 3). They are seen in statistics indicating that "although 7% of non-citizens in the U.S. are Black, they make up a full 20% of those facing deportation on criminal grounds" even in the absence of "evidence that Black immigrants commit crime at greater rates than other immigrants or U.S-citizens" (Morgan-Trostle & Zheng, 2016). And they are visible in statistics which indicate that Black immigrants face the highest asylum rejection rates, with Haitians, Jamaicans, and Somalians at the top of the list (RAICES, 2020). When considered in the context of a justice system, which, much like that of education, affects the entire trajectory of a child's or adult's life, intentional efforts to address blind spots in the lives of Black immigrant populations within schools can no longer wait (Ghabra, 2022).

In alignment with my colleagues and I who call for racial justice in literacy research (LRA, 2016; Willis & Smith, 2021; Willis et al., 2021), the blind spots systemically existing amid an almost raceless approach to immigration in literacy research stir up an urgency of collective imagination (Mahmud, 1999) and action that defy a long-standing rhetoric designed to protect the interests of dominant rule. In the acknowledgment by Suárez-Orozco (2017) of "the vast minimization of the damaging legacy of slavery" and the "prevailing narrative of the curriculum of [that] era" (p. 527), we see a dire need to identify the ways in which complementary frameworks such as the ecological framework and risk and resilience model invite a centering of race as a basis for disrupting normative practices like these that are inextricably bound within the lives of the Black immigrant.

Even for the most resilient youth, as articulated by Suárez-Orozco (2017) in her response to the circumstances surrounding immigrants in US schools and to the stereotypes typically associated with certain ethnicities that lead to "only the most resilient of students remain[ing] engaged" and to "immigrant students from families who do not share the culture of the teachers who teach them [to be] particularly susceptible to negative expectations and poor outcomes" (pp. 528–529), overlooking racialization and a consideration of its underlying effects as a basis for considering how certain immigrants may be significantly and unduly affected by its intricacies as a function of language in schools raises questions about the potential of these and other institutions to "do the right thing" (Goodwin, 2002, p. 156). While articulated "promising practices for all students" based on the literature from the research examined (Suárez-Orozco, 2017, p. 529) suggests that schools continue to implement reforms founded on "progressive multicultural education"; use "interdisciplinary, project-based, and student-centered approaches to curriculum and instruction were central to teaching and learning across the schools"; "create curricula that are relevant to the lives of their diverse students"; utilize "decentralized pedagogical strategies designed to place the student at the center of learning and to deliver content while moving away from traditional teacher lectures for at least part of the time"; seek "multiple strategies to assess their students and ways to prepare them for high-stakes testing"; "implement some kinds of academic supports to help students be successful"; and place "particular focus on the postsecondary school experience" (p. 529), the foregoing body of research raises questions about how Eurocentric norms tend to undergird even progressive approaches to multicultural education and which, in turn, remain steeped in centuries of curricula 'innovation' that operate to maintain the "white gaze" (Morrison, 2020). In considering the positioning of promising practices for all students presented, the poignant words of Dr. Ofelia García and colleagues in "Rejecting Abyssal Thinking in the Language and Education of Racialized Bilinguals: A Manifesto" vividly come to mind:

We are a group of scholars who have worked in language education for years. We are situated within two of the most powerful and interconnected English language empires – the United States and Great Britain. The lenses we have used for our work have been different, but the objective of our work has been the same: to center the experiences and knowledges of racialized bilinguals, their language, and their education. By racialized bilinguals we mean people who, as a result of long processes of domination and colonization, have been positioned as inferior in racial and linguistic terms. We hold that much of the scholarship on language education has been tainted by what the Portuguese decolonial philosopher Boaventura de Sousa Santos (2007) has called "abyssal thinking." This hegemonic thinking creates a line establishing that which is considered "civil society," and declares as nonexistent those colonized knowledges and lifeways positioned on the other side of the line, thus relegating them to an existential abyss. Our critique of abyssal thinking aims to unsettle European colonialism's division of populations into superior "civilized" races and inferior "uncivilized" [ones]; and it aims to challenge too the insidious legacies of these colonial logics in the contemporary world (Quijano, 1991, 1993, 2000). We point to how the colonial logics stemming from abyssal thinking have been so well established that they are not readily apparent. (García et al., 2021, p. 203)

In considering the authors' rejection of the type of "abyssal thinking" that "erases the existence of counter-hegemonic knowledges and lifeways, adopting instead the 'from the inside out' perspective that is required for thinking constructively about the language and education of racialized bilinguals," it may be possible to see why promising practices for immigrants that center Eurocentric ways of knowing inadvertently reinforce the very frames against which immigrants of Color, and particularly Black immigrant populations, including youth, are forced to contend. Much like the authors use their "deep personal experience and extensive field-work research" to "challenge prevailing assumptions about language, bilingualism, and education that are based on raciolinguistic ideologies with roots in colonialism" (García et al., 2021) and as has been called for in a disrupting transnational literacies that have for so long decentered race across the educational enterprise (Smith, 2020b; Smith et al., 2023), it seems critical if not exigent to flip a script for "promise" that remains focused on preparing students to "*succeed*" based on "high-stakes testing" and Eurocentric measures of success given the broadening mental health pandemic assailing students in US schools and persisting across the globe where one-in-six US youth aged six to seventeen experience a mental health disorder each year (NAMI, 2022). These statistics, which show that "more than a third (37%) of high school students reported they experienced poor mental health during the COVID-19 pandemic, and 44% reported they persistently felt sad or hopeless during the past year" as of 2021, and which were already reflecting a growing challenge prior to the COVID-19 pandemic, reiterate the numerous calls for rethinking schooling for immigrants of Color, and in general as we know it in the US. The indications that "over a third (36%) of students said they experienced racism before or during the COVID-19 pandemic [with the] highest levels ... reported among Asian students (64%) and among Black students and students of multiple races (both 55%)" further call attention to the growing failure of schools to address threats to Black immigrant students and other youth of Color in the absence of a clear focus on race (Centers for Disease Control and Prevention, 2022).

Highlighted practices more tailored for immigrant students as shown by Suárez-Orozco (2017), admittedly, at first glance, often seem potentially useful to educators and scholars because they mirror a literature base that has, for the most part, catered to norms set for language and literacy learning that are steeped in admirable "best practices" though often framed by deficit notions of what students who migrate to the US often can and cannot do. For instance, practices justified for meeting the needs of newcomer students and second-language learners are designed to ease their negotiation of the cultural transition and their learning of a new language such as "help[ing] newcomer youth negotiate cultural transitions" and "adjust to their new environs" but do not provide opportunities for these students to teach their peers about knowledge they bring. Similarly, practices are designed to often support "gaps in interrupted schooling and literacy" and provide "systematic second-language acquisition policies and practices" but can be largely based on assumptions about learning that often position students as lacking knowledge of language and of the world. By the same token, the intent to provide second-language learners (SLLs) with support "to simultaneously build content knowledge" in addition to developing oral communicative proficiency in the language of their new country" is undertaken because "many of them enter school with low academic-language proficiency skills" – a dichotomy for determining proficiency that Flores (2020) and others have condemned, invoking instead "language architecture," a notion mirrored conceptually by constructs such as "already-present literacies" (Watson, 2018) and "language brokering" (Orellana & García, 2014) as mechanisms for foregrounding the assets of youth. Beyond the above, the practice of encouraging students "to use their first language to help them learn the second language, even if teachers or other students do not understand their mother tongue" has for decades been challenged by García and colleagues whose propositions about translanguaging resist and reject the 'abyssal thinking' that instantiates the demarcation between named languages in ways that obscure the recognition of students' full linguistic repertoires (García et al., 2021, p. 531).

As illustrated in the body of research presented on Black immigrants thus far, positioning schools, systems, and societies as having "great potential" to be "sites of possibilities" (Fine & Jaffe-Walter, 2007) for "immigrant children and youth's constructive immersion in the new culture and society" and specifically for youth racialized as Black, immigrant, and transnational will necessitate an interruption to normalcy as we know it, one that extends well beyond the *'promising'* and *'best'* practices for an imaginary 'immigrant' of the past. The embedded interconnections of language, race, coloniality, across decades both in and beyond the English-speaking Caribbean have created a situation for Black Caribbean immigrant youth where racialization embedded covertly within the structures of literacy and languaging in their home countries becomes overtly revealed in the manifestations of expectations for their use in racialized US society. The positioning of Black immigrants and transnationals as model minorities who 'do better' than their African American peers, educationally, economically, or otherwise does not help, nor does the tendency to be characterized in terms of culture and ethnicity but not race.

As the literature shows, upon migration, Black immigrant youth join a US society perplexed by contradictions of who they are expected to be, particularly depending on how their "Blackness" and their "languaging" as well as "literacies" are perceived. In a US society where pernicious tensions exist in navigating how they are perceived by African immigrants, African American peers, white populations, and others, they tend to be regarded often and only based on if and how they "*succeed*" but can be positioned to reflect much more if approached from the perspective of possibility (Watson et al., 2022). When viewed as having "holistic literacies" (Smith 2023), they can be seen as humans who (wish to) flourish – who bring literacies and languaging that hold vast opportunities.

As Amanda Gorman aptly suggests in the quote that begins this chapter, the quest to "find light" is often accompanied by acknowledging that "quiet isn't always peace" and "norms and notions of what 'just' is isn't always justice" (Gorman, 2021). In the case of Black immigrant youth, the silent panacea has been all but peace and the burgeoning roar of inequity all but justice. To function as sites of possibilities, schools, colleges, universities, institutions, and societies, as García and colleagues suggest, will need to resist the urge to forge efforts to return to a pervasive mediocrity of normalcy that defies students' aspiration to purpose. Instead, they will need to insist on the cultivation of novel imaginaries of opportunity, such as translanguaging imaginaries of innocence, that can persist, at long last, in a breakthrough. This breakthrough will indelibly manage to unmask at last the knowledges that immigrant students of Color, and specifically Black immigrant students, bring into a present of schooling, breaking at the seams from centuries of a failed yet incessant longing for *'success'*, and grounded in a white supremacy with "material advantage" as the bottom line (Mills, 1997, p. 33). Only then can we see the desire for a furtherance of human transnational flourishing steeped in inherent purpose.

3 Afro-Caribbean Languaging, Englishes, and Literacies of Migration across the Black Diaspora
Unmasking the Fallacy of Invented Illiteracy

> And yet the dawn is ours before we knew it.
> Somehow we do it.
>
> Gorman, 2021

Situating Afro-Caribbean Languaging, Englishes, and Literacies of Migration: Education, Migration, and Cultures across the Black Diaspora

Any legitimate situating of Afro-Caribbean languaging, Englishes, and "literacies of migration" (Capstick, 2016) – "mediated through both alternative and Native modalities beyond the normative cognitive process of textual decoding and encoding preferred in school" (Baquedano-López & Gong, 2022, p. 29) – is incomplete absent sufficient attention to its interrelationships with Black peoples across the broader African diaspora. This situatedness makes visible the legitimate histories of African ancestral heritage in languaging across the Black diaspora despite a historical tendency to deny or to overlook such existence – spurring on a fallacy of *invented illiteracy*. Bernal (2020) addresses the persistent denial, for instance, that the Greek language has borrowed from Ancient Egyptian and West Semitic, observing that nineteenth-century philologists were markedly opposed to the possibility and highlighting the acknowledgment that contemporary archaeologists now believe there was close contact among East Mediterranean people in the Bronze and Early Iron ages. Documenting the significant linguistic influence of Ancient Egyptian and West Semitic on the Greek language, Bernal (2020) shows that more than half of the Greek language fails to be accounted for by the influence of the Indo-European. This was no surprise as Charles Mills points out, given that traditionally, "European thought in general, developed within the framework of the Racial Contract and, as a rule, took it for granted" (Mills, 1997, p. 27).

Reticence such as the above that fails to acknowledge the contributions of Ancient Egyptian and West Semitic to Indo-European languages is steeped in the substantial lingering effects of colonialism, and specifically, colonial ideologies of race, which, as Heller and McElhinny (2017) note in their examination of linguistic intimacy across five continents, as guided by the lens of Edward Said, remain visible in the imperialist agenda that used the project of schooling to target Black and Indigenous bodies. Though largely focusing on colonialization and less on an explicit naming of race per se, Brown (2000) concurs, highlighting that in Africa, a continent where the majority of Black bodies were targeted, the impact of colonization on education appears not to have been reduced since independence and continues to significantly affect developmental outcomes across the continent. Taken to refer to "the policy or practice of acquiring full or partial political control over another country, occupying it with settlers, and exploiting it economically," Nwanosike and Onyije (2011, p. 41) have described how colonialism emerged as a function of industrialist and economic needs in Europe, bolstered by capitalist agendas desirous of the resources of then colonies to maximize profits, and propagated through education. Similarly, though less focused on race per se, and more on coloniality, Nwanosike and Onyije (2011) describe the role of education in this dynamic as a two-edged sword, having been the primary mechanism through which colonialism was propagated and then, also becoming the key avenue for continued attempts at its abolition. Mfum-Mensah's (2005) discussion of education in the African country of Ghana is a stark example of this conundrum. On the one hand, as Shizha (2013) observes, the curricula used in schools largely still reflect colonial education from previous rule and disregard pre-colonial African voices, which centered knowledge steeped in indigenous cultures, despite decades since the independence of African countries. On the other hand, as in many other formerly colonized nations, 'alternative primary education' programs such as the Shepherd School Program in rural northern Ghanaian agri-pastoral communities are beginning to rely on the 'first' language of children as the medium of instruction based on conceptions of post-coloniality (Mfum-Mensah, 2005; see García & Wei, 2014, for a problematization of this notion of named language as well as Smith & Warrican, 2021, and Smith et al., 2022, for a raciolinguistic problematization of the reliance on "cognitivist" notions in language as the basis for determining student 'success').

Scholars such as King (2015) and King and Chetty (2014) have captured the sociolinguistic nuance underlying such tensions that exist in the South African context, focusing on "codeswitching" in bilingual classrooms within this locale. Such efforts, which are applauded as opportunities for reclaiming sub-Saharan Africa's indigenous knowledges, are at the same time viewed as a challenge because of the possibilities that indigenous discourses pose to traditionally held knowledges of 'school' (Shizha, 2013). They exist alongside commensurate initiatives to internationalize language, for instance, such as Esperanto in the nineteenth century as a vehicle for world peace, which failed to be actualized in ways that resulted in equality and an undoing of colonial harm. Emerging out of the rationale that an international language could be one that everyone masters and thus reduce inequality, such initiatives may have underestimated the role of linguistic ideologies and their interrelationship to race in the colonial dynamic (Alim, 2016; Alim & Smitherman, 2020), undergirding transnational markets of 'whiteness' (see Christie & McKinney, 2017; see also Richardson & Stroud, 2021).

Given this tenuous global history, any situating of Afro-Caribbean languaging in its global context must be one that attends as closely to colonialization as it does to the placement of an explicit naming of race at the center of the latter. As Mills (1997) observes in discussions of *The Racial Contract*:

> White supremacy was a generally assumed and accepted state of affairs in the United States as well as in Europe's empires! ... But statements of such frankness are rare or nonexistent in mainstream white opinion today, which generally seeks to rewrite the past so as to deny or minimize the obvious fact of global white domination. (Mills, 1997, p. 27)

Such global logics as described above, which make visible the legacy of languaging left by the colonial enterprise, have historically been invoked in studies of language by scholars such as Dr. Geneva Smitherman (see Milu, 2021). As outlined in discussions such as those presented by Dr. Esther Milu, this invocation makes clear how "White, middle-class English is treated as the dominant and standard variety and placed at the top of the language hierarchy ... marginaliz[ing] all other languages, including English varieties" (Milu, 2021, p. 417). Milu continues:

> The focus on English fails to account for how other imperial languages of Europe, like Spanish, Portuguese, and French, have historically contributed to a racist and oppressive "sociolinguistic order" globally, particularly in formerly colonized Afro-Diasporic contexts. For example, in the US, Spanish, Portuguese, and French are viewed as marginalized given the focus of English dominance. Yet, for some transnational and immigrant Black students, these are, in fact, languages of the colonizer. The focus on the US local context and English linguistic hegemony might not raise transnational and immigrant African students' critical consciousness about how their African Indigenous languages have historically been marginalized by European languages. (Milu, 2021, p. 417)

Acknowledging the limitations of a focus on English and Englishes, notwithstanding, we see historically, as well as more recently, nonetheless, that these global logics have also been invoked in studies of literacy and the English language arts by Dr. Arlette Willis, Professor of Literacy at the University of Illinois Urbana-Champaign and recipient of the Literacy Research Association (LRA) 2022 Oscar S. Causey Award. This was accomplished in part in her proposition of "transcendent literacy," a notion that she conceptualized based on her description of the life of Omar ibn Said. In her 2022 LRA Oscar S. Causey address, Willis (2022) paints a portrait of "Omar ibn Said's life as informed by African cultures, ethnicities, histories, languages, and literacies in the Senegambia region" and juxtaposes this against "the history of Black literacy access in the US" (para. 1; see Willis, 2023, for a full depiction of the life of Omar ibn Said). She shows, using the autobiography of Omar ibn Said, how he "stealthily applies sophisticated literacy skills to contest living under anti-Black racism and chattel enslavement through his rhetorical and strategic use of Quranic surahs and verses." Her analytical observations reveal that the early translations and interpretations of the autobiography of Omar ibn Said, as written by white men who were English-dominant and literate in ancient Arabic as "filtered through Eurocentrism and White supremacy, failed to discern Omar ibn Said's proclamation of his humanity and bold condemnation of chattel enslavement." On the contrary, she notes that "scholars with expertise in African history and Islam, valorize[d] his resilience as an African Muslim who remained faithful to Islam under anti-Black racism, the horrors of chattel enslavement, and attempts at Christian conversion." Willis offers the autobiography as one which

> dismantles prevailing assumptions about people of African descent as sub-human, without culture, history, intellect, language, or literacy. It also revolutionizes what we know about the history of literacy in the US; provides authenticated knowledge of literacy among people of African descent; exposes the pervasiveness of White supremacy; and unveils the roots of deliberate anti-Black literacy laws, policies, and practices, historically and contemporaneously. (Willis, 2022, para. 1)

She argues that "to create an equitable approach to literacy, we must begin with authenticated knowledge to transcend the past and present" (para. 1).

In considering the call from Willis to begin with authenticated knowledge for *transcendent literacy*, it is possible to see how this knowledge has been taken up differentially in the (de)legitimization of Black languaging across the diaspora. The "authenticated knowledge of literacy among people of African descent," as called for by Willis, has a long history of being documented and made visible to the world at large. Volumes such as *The SAGE Handbook of African American Education*, which focuses on leadership, historical, current, and critical issues relating to African Americans (e.g., Tillman, 2009) and books such as *Perspectives on American English* (Dillard, 1980) exist concurrently with emerging national and international narratives that challenge explicitly the role of linguistic hegemony in the fabric of the US educational and literacy enterprise and the 'postcolonial' global project at large (Pihama & Lee-Morgan, 2019; Sedlacek et al., 2023). Moreover, mechanisms such as a "global language of blackness" have been called for in this globalization project of (de)legitimization through languaging as a function of racialization to address the "misrecognition of black subjects as sub-human" (Givens, 2016, pp. 1, 4). From explorations that consider "imperial logics and practices tying the US South to the larger project of colonial domination in the Caribbean and Latin America" in reexaminations of Black transnationalism and diaspora from the position of corporate plantation laborers in the "global black south" (see Khan et al., 2022, for a complication of the term "Global South"), to examinations that consider the resulting social struggles accompanying the 1954 *Brown v. Board of Education* decision in the US (McInnis, 2019), evidence abounds to show how attempts at legitimization coupled with a paradoxically corresponding insistent delegitimization of "authenticated knowledge" (WIllis, 2022), among people of African descent operate perpetually in a dialectic, posing an impediment to transcendent literacy.

Take, for instance, the US, a country that many Afro-Caribbean people call home, and the context which forms a primary basis for the study undergirding this book, a responsive praxis, among other mechanisms, and its corresponding conceptual bases described as revolutionary and often used for accessing and reclaiming authenticated knowledge of peoples of African descent, is "Critical Studyin'" (King, 2006, 2021). King proposed Critical Studyin' as a praxis (King, 1995a, 1995b, 1997) steeped conceptually in Diaspora Literacy (culturally informed knowledge) and Heritage Knowledge (group memory) as a key mechanism for reclaiming the authenticated knowledge of people of African descent across the diaspora. Coined by and emerging from the writings of African and Caribbean literature, Dr. Vèvè A. Clark, a scholar of African American dance history and African diaspora theater, the term "Diaspora Literacy" finds its roots in analyses of the identity quest of Afro-Caribbean women in postcolonial West Africa and has functioned historically as central to the movement, concept, and pedagogy of "Black Studies" (King, 2021). And the term "diaspora," though coined originally as a label used to describe "scattered colonies of exiled Jews outside of Palestine ... has come to mean the forced migration of other groups as well – most prominently, the dispersion of Africans throughout the Americas after the slave trade" (Wilentz, 1992, p. 385). This term, emerging to represent how people with various elements of shared cultures become dispersed across locations that tend to be hostile, has thus created a reflection of traditional influences alongside cultural reflections indicative of a simultaneous attempt to cope with the impositions of the dominant society within which they are immersed.

King (2021) describes the conceptual tool, Diaspora Literacy, as "knowledge making" and also, "the ability to 'read' various cultural signs as continuities in African-descended people's experience," and then later, as "a narrator's or reader's ability to understand and/or interpret the multilayered meanings of stories, words, and other folk sayings within any given African diaspora community." With regards to the conceptual tool of Heritage Knowledge, King (2021) asserts that this knowledge functions as the basis for "collective cultural agency" where it represents "group memory" operating as "a repository or heritable legacy that makes a feeling of belonging, peoplehood, and communal solidarity as an outcome of education possible." Similar in orientation to *transcendent literacy*, Diaspora Literacy aims to place the Black perspective, and not the dominant oppressive system, at the center of working towards liberation. Diaspora Literacy – because it seeks to center the reading of African diasporic communities, and Heritage Knowledge – because it emphasizes the collective – both function as key mechanisms for generating, preserving, and making visible the authenticated knowledge of peoples of African descent across the diaspora.

Decades ago, King (1992) made visible the usefulness of Diaspora Literacy for engaging in identification of covert omissions and for revealing the accurate understandings of the knowledges of people of African descent that remained excluded from classroom textbooks in California. Advancing the goals of the "deciphering practice" of Black Studies, the beginning of which was marked by the reestablished link between theory and practice as well as intellectual work and activism (Davies, 2013), King's discussions of Diaspora Literacy acknowledged how textbooks used in classrooms included discussions of slavery but, at the same time, failed to reflect the ways in which specific symbols of cultural heritage needed to be read in order to authentically represent the lives of people of African descent in Africa and in the New World. Since then, the viability of Diaspora Literacy for revitalizing Indigenous African knowledges has made it central to generating authenticated knowledge and its vision for engendering solidarity to allow for a collective envisioning of Black people *sans "white gaze"* (Morrison, 2020).

Efforts to help Black people reclaim how they learned to know, do, be, and live together with others based on their African Indigenous knowledges through Diaspora and Heritage Literacy is steeped often in feminism, spirituality, and the connection to soul survival (Boutte et al., 2017; Dillard, 2012a). Critical Studyin' as a praxis has offered pathways for the development of critical sociohistorical knowledge necessary for Black people to explore how race and racism function in Black history. Such was the case with a world history teacher who allowed for the generation of critical sociohistorical knowledge that affirmed Afro-Latin humanity with consideration to both Afro-Latinxs and Afro-Latin Americans to broaden notions of Black education. Another instance was observed where "Critical Studyin'" in literacy provided an avenue to introduce students and their teachers in a predominantly Black school to the study of freedom (Fisher, 2005) using spoken word poetry and allowing for access to Diaspora Literacy and Heritage Knowledge (Fisher, 2006). Fisher (2003a) has also explored spoken word and poetry venues in the Black community as a basis for developing Black students' identities and literacy practice. She refers to such communities as African Diaspora Participatory Literacy Communities (ADPLCs), with some characterized by the use of open mic poetry that recreates the feeling of community which was a part of jazz clubs and literary circles during the Harlem Renaissance. Fisher describes ADPLCs as created and largely supported by people of African descent beyond school and work and argues that these communities allow for the blending of spoken and written literate practices and therefore dismantle dichotomies that tend to persist conceptually and pedagogically in reading and writing (Fisher, 2003b, 2006).

In certain instances where racial violence is addressed and racialization centered to address anti-Black violence in the US, African Diaspora Literacy has been used in conjunction with Afrocentric praxis to operationalize notions such as revolutionary love as juxtaposed against "fake love" (Johnson et al., 2019). Afrocentrism also has been used in conjunction with Critical Race Theory and Black Critical Theory via a Sankofa methodology to disrupt colonization in early childhood curricula and engender positive linguistic, gendered, racial identities as well as a sense of community and self-love (Wynter-Hoyte & Smith, 2020). Afrocentric methods via Diaspora Literacy have been visible via duo Afronography where Africana/Black Studies scholarship is used to interrogate and assess opportunities provided by selected online audiovisual and text resources for education about Africa, to affirm African Diaspora Literacy consciousness, solidify connectedness to Africa, and help African American students identify with Africa and the African Renaissance (Baker & King, 2022). For preservice teachers, Black history knowledge has been leveraged, via a Black history framework that drew intersectionally from Diaspora Literacy, historical consciousness, and Black critical race theory, to function as a tool for improving how teachers approach instruction by asking them to write Black history narratives that reveal their interpretations of Black history, disclosing both their critical and uncritical Black history knowledge (King, 2019). And in situations where scholars intended to address what were identified as "negative, deficit perceptions of all associated with Africa including themselves" held by Afro-Caribbean American students, Dillard's teaching Black students how to "(re)member" (Dillard, 2012a) as part of African Diaspora Literacy has been used with Sankofa-based African Diaspora Content, to identify how African-descended high school students' experiences influenced their perception of Africa, the African diaspora, and themselves as African descendants.

The intention of Diaspora Literacy and Heritage Knowledge to center the Black person's knowledges – and thus the Afro-Caribbean – as opposed to the oppressor's unjust impositions are aligned with the goals of "authenticated knowledge" in *transcendent literacy* (Willis, 2022). They allow for an extension beyond the white gaze as is called for explicitly in the projection of languaging as superseding its primarily relegated role in response to racialization. However, the extension of the notion of authenticated knowledge as well as its nuance as a function of transcendent literacy seems to also be simultaneously invoked when it asks that race and racialization extend beyond the individual and be made central to the systematic and institutional attempt to generate and legitimize authentic knowledge undergirding literacies even while it seeks to call for a transcension of their roles as *the* basis for literate legitimization. In doing so, authenticated knowledge recognizes what I will later posit as the "*innocent*" status of languaging functioning as a legacy of people of African descent before the white gaze, and thus, (re)inscribes the *linguistic, and semiolingual innocence* (also defined and discussed later) of all Black people who legitimately leveraged it then. In turn, unlike Diaspora Literacy which appears to locate a "(re)membering" (Dillard, 2012a) or a '(re)finding' of Blackness, "Afrocentricity," or "Indigeneity" beyond the historical or contemporary *Black languager*, whoever this may be, "transcendent literacy" seems to imply that no matter who the person of African or other descent is, they *already* possess their own authenticated knowledge, and thus, their legitimate representation of literateness – no matter how Black or otherwise it is perceived to be – thereby eliminating its reliance on an external entity through which it must be defined. In other words, in the context of the Afro-Caribbean transitioning as a foreign-born *to*, or as the descendant of a foreign-born *in*, the US, transcendent literacy appears to allow these individuals, like all individuals of African descent across the diaspora, the capacity to generate and to inscribe their inherent claim to authenticated knowledge regardless of their positioning as Africans in Africa *or* as descendants of slaves in the New World and irrespective of their positioning in time. Transcendent literacy appears to imbue this *innocent* status on all people of African descent who leverage language in their legitimate Blackness, challenging them to do so completely oblivious to how whiteness positions them, that is, *sans white gaze*.

The call by Willis (2022) for authenticated knowledge via transcendent literacy is visible in numerous efforts of Afro-Caribbean and other peoples of African descent across the diaspora to reflect how their knowledges function legitimately through language. For instance, in the New Negro, Indigenist, and Négritude movements of the 1920s and 1930s, a germination evolved, born of nationalism and transnationality alongside a distancing from the Eurocentric white gaze as the basis for creating Black writing, and what Clark (2009) refers to as a writing of "regional, ethnic, and peasant experiences into existence" (p. 9). It should be noted here that around this same time, in 1914,

Europe held a grand total of roughly 85 percent of the earth as colonies, protectorates, dependencies, dominions, and commonwealths. No other associated set of colonies in history was as large, none so totally dominated, none so unequal in power to the Western metropolis. (Cited in Mills, 1997, p. 29)

As such, white supremacy, it must be noted, required literate peoples to function as illiterates to support global economic domination.

The consequently justifiable "epistemological break away" in Caribbean writing therefore, that emerged from the Francophone Antilles, the Anglophone emigrant Caribbean, and Native Central/Hispanic Caribbean, though not operating entirely sans white gaze, according to Clark (2009), appeared to signify "protest directed against cultural repression on the one hand and racial self-hatred on the other" (p. 9). It would become the foundation of contemporary Afro-American, Caribbean, and African literary scholarship. Such is the image painted in works such as *Praisesong for the Widow* by Paule Marshall (1983) where the Black, middle-aged, middle-class widow, Avey Johnson, embarks on a cruise with friends to the Caribbean only to later abandon them in search of an unexpected and beautiful adventure that connects her to her long-lost culture. It is also the imaginary presented in accounts such as by Dr. Carole Boyce Davies who uses experiential knowledge and theory from her childhood journey in Trinidad and Tobago and across communities in Nigeria, Brazil, England, and the US, to intersectionally paint a picture of the complexity of Caribbean culture and space as influenced by migration across the Americas and mediated by sexuality, gender, and race (Davies, 2013). And it is the representation offered in "international" discussions and twenty-first-century global matters undergirding the social and cultural issues that characterize Caribbean education and schooling across islands of the Greater and Lesser Antilles (Blair & Williams, 2021).

To understand the use of Englishes for examining the literacies and language practices of Black Caribbean immigrants presented as juxtaposed against the broader contexts thus described, I now present conceptions of World Englishes, Global Englishes, and Caribbean Englishes, cross-circle Englishes, before subsequently discussing pre-established conceptions concerning the Englishes and literacies of Black Caribbean immigrant youth in the Caribbean and in the US (see Smith, 2016, 2017, 2020b, for previous discussions).

Caribbean Englishes across the Black Diaspora

"Englishes" in this work is used to refer to the many different varieties of English that represent a plurality, variation, and change within the English language as a norm (Kachru, 1992). Englishes represent the interweaving of both standardized (e.g., Standard American English) and non-standardized (e.g., African American English) forms. I use '*non-standardized Englishes*' (e.g., African American Vernacular English, Jamaican Creole, Trinidadian English-lexicon Creole) here to refer to Englishes that do not adhere to what has been determined to be a 'Standard English' within a given context although it is sometimes the case that certain non-standardized Englishes are codified. Linguists refer to such variations as dialects, or New Englishes (Kirkpartrick & Deterding, 2011) and to their counterparts, what I and others have labeled *'standardized Englishes'*, as those that have been *typically* adopted for use in English literacy classrooms (e.g., Standard Jamaican English, Trinidadian Standard English, Standard American English).

I use the term "Englishes" and not "dialects of English" in this work, as I do elsewhere in my scholarship, because the notion of a dialect naturally evokes linguicism and raciolinguistic ideology from the white (and often, Black and brown) listening subject. I assert that this natural reaction that inadvertently involves linguicized and raciolinguistic assumptions about Black youth's languages (see Viesca, 2013) appears to obstruct a dialogue with the white listening subject (a position often adopted by people of Color) (see Smith, 2019a, 2020a) about the possibilities and potential of English *dialects* as languages in and of themselves. By presenting dialects as legitimate languages, I work towards legitimizing linguistic practices of Black immigrant youth, who are naturally Othered by their *"dialectal"* status, a practice geared towards advancing invented illiteracy for material advantage and thus bolstering white supremacy.

World Englishes

"World Englishes," conceptualized in certain instances as Global Englishes (e.g., Galloway & Rose, 2015), is based on the idea that three concentric circles, inclusive of 'inner,' 'outer,' and 'expanding,' explain the ways in which Englishes are used across the globe (Kachru, 1992). The 'inner circle' of Englishes involves those Englishes predominantly spoken in Anglo-Saxon countries such as the US, Australia, and Canada; the 'outer circle' describes Englishes often seen in countries colonized by Britain such as Bangladesh, India, and those in the Caribbean; and the 'expanding circle' represents Englishes learned as a foreign language in countries such as China, Indonesia, and Nepal (Kachru, 1992). In this "three-circle" model, Englishes are said to be based on national identity. However, offering evolving notions concerning these Englishes, Mahboob and Szenes (2010) observe:

the new varieties of English, especially outer circle Englishes, are spoken by people who live in countries that were strongly influenced by British administrative and colonial policies and these policies have influenced how and what Englishes are used there. For example, during the British colonial period, indentured servants were recruited from India and moved to parts of South and East Africa, the Caribbean Islands, South East Asia (e.g. Malaysia) and the Pacific Islands (e.g. Fiji). The descendents of these people speak a variety of English that is quite distinct from the other Englishes spoken in their countries. So, we find that users of Malaysian English who are of an Indian origin speak a different English from those of Chinese or Malay origin. Similarly, South African Englishes include South African Indian Englishes, South African Black Englishes, and South African White Englishes – and all of these have their own sub-varieties that are influenced by a large variety of first languages. Thus, using country-based names for these Englishes does not do justice to the rich diversity of Englishes used within these countries. (Mahboob & Szenes, 2010, p. 581)

In this observation, we see a subtle indication of the economically induced advantage invoked where Minority World peoples of the 'inner circle' could more readily lay claim to Englishes that allowed for 'success' as compared to their Majority World counterparts. Others who have critiqued the model in more recent times observe that it does not consider the use of Englishes that extend beyond geography and national identity (Canagarajah & Ben Said, 2011), which is often the case with online spaces where numerous Englishes are used fluidly across national and geographical contexts. And scholars such as Dovchin (2020), in considering Englishes as a function of migration, much like I have proposed in "cross-circle Englishes" with a focus on centering race (Smith, 2020b), have examined their translingual nature as well as ideologies of authenticity and race that undergird their instantiation across boundaries – "translingual Englishes" (for tangential discussions, see Blommaert, 2007; Canagarajah, 2013; Lee & Alvarez, 2020; Mesthrie, 2019).

Caribbean Englishes

As part of the World Englishes model, Caribbean Englishes (CEs), also defined as dialects of English, operate along an English/Creole continuum, and are also sometimes referred to by natives of the Caribbean as simply "English" (Carrington, 1992). CEs function as 'outer circle' Englishes and may be standardized (e.g., Bahamian Standardized English) or non-standardized (e.g., Trinidadian English Creole). Standardized CEs, defined as the closest to standardized Englishes (i.e., similar to Standardized American Englishes), are often referred to as 'The Queen's English,' or also simply, 'English.' Non-standardized CEs, on the other hand, commonly referred to as dialects of English, are denoted as 'Creoles,' or 'patois' (Carrington, 1992).

Dr. Shondel Nero, Professor of Language Education in the Department of Teaching and Learning in the Steinhardt School of Culture, Education, and Human Development at New York University, has described the historical uniqueness of and challenge for CEs as part of World Englishes, stating that "within the world Englishes paradigm, CE has been seen as somewhat unique" (Nero, 2006, p. 503). She notes that the late Dr. Braj Kachru, former Indian-American linguist and professor at the University of Illinois Urbana-Champaign, also acknowledged "the challenge of placing CE, partly because this variety has evolved in ways quite unlike any of those in the three traditional concentric circles of English" (Nero, 2006, p. 503). According to Kachru (1992):

countries such as South Africa or Jamaica are difficult to place within the concentric circles. In terms of the English-using populations and the functions of English, their situations are rather complex. (Kachru, 1992, p. 362)

Nero goes on to explain that

the Caribbean closely approximates the Outer Circle because of its history of British colonization, except that in the Outer Circle countries, which are mostly in Asia and Africa, there is a more clear-cut bilingual or multilingual population. In the Anglophone Caribbean, because Creole has not been publicly recognized or accepted as a language in its own right, there is no widespread popular perception of bilingualism per se (even though linguists and folklorists assert the autonomous status of the Creole language). Thus, the linguistic situation in the region may be characterized as bidialectal, where the majority of the population move back and forth along the creole continuum engaging in what LePage and Tabouret-Keller (1985) call "acts of identity," that is to say, revealing through their use of language both their personal identity and sense of social and ethnic solidarity and difference. (Nero, 2006, p. 503)

This explanation serves as a rationale for the historical presence of CE as part of the research on Pidgins and Creoles, which has since transitioned such that CE is now reflected in research typically known as the family of World Englishes (Nero, 2006).

In the context of the Anglophone Caribbean, when CEs tend to be researched, there is evidence that Caribbean multilingual teachers who function as teachers of Black Caribbean youth before migration are typically speakers of both standardized and non-standardized CEs and sometimes engage in self-marginalization by privileging standardized over non-standardized Englishes (Milson-Whyte, 2014). In a forthcoming chapter, I have collaborated with Dr. S. Joel Warrican to illustrate how these teachers, having become educators, navigate raciolinguistic ideological tensions in these Englishes across their Caribbean nation states and that of the US (Warrican & Smith, in press). In this chapter, the data undergirding which were part of a larger research study funded by the Texas Tech University Scholarship Catalyst Project (2019), we drew from "cross-circle Englishes" (Smith, 2020b), "a raciolinguistic perspective" (Rosa & Flores, 2017), and "a transraciolinguistic approach" (Smith, 2022b) to acknowledge what we refer to as raciolinguistic markers characterizing the reported experiences of the educators. These markers – *"rejection, distortion, oblivion, commission, omission, and misrepresentation"* – as reflected by educators who were once teachers were based on the rich insights into institutional and individual tensions emerging from ideologies of their Englishes. Analyzing similarities and differences present at the institutional and local levels in the racialization of Englishes across transnational contexts of the US and the Anglophone Caribbean, we characterized the raciolinguistic markers identified as follows:

- **Rejection:** Refusing to accept the self unless it approximates language norms of the White listening subject;
- **Distortion:** Claiming not to want to use language associated with the White listening subject while still simultaneously and intentionally seeking its approval;
- **Oblivion:** Choosing to use the English language aligned with expectation for approximations of language associated with the White listening subject;
- **Commission:** Enacting language norms of the White listening subject validated by the institution as the sole pathway to opportunity;
- **Omission:** Missing opportunities to learn institutional attempts to redefine linguistic norms that align with one's personhood because they deviate from previously and widely accepted White listening subject norms;
- **Misrepresentation:** Presupposing that the racialized structures undergirding language and power in society necessarily allow for simplistic individual decision-making process with language(s).

(Warrican & Smith, in press)

In presenting these markers, we offered rich insights into the institutional and individual tensions emerging from ideologies of Englishes in the practices of former teachers and current educators that inform how many Black Caribbean youth in the English-speaking Caribbean are socialized into the use of language.

Whether it is because of the "Pidgin/Creole" naming or the transition to being characterized as Caribbean Englishes, these raciolinguistic tensions manifested by English speakers in the English-speaking Caribbean have largely gone unnamed and are often explicitly unexplored as a function of race. For instance, when addressed in the Caribbean context, Caribbean Englishes tend to be described as being particularly visible in the English-speaking Caribbean where Standard English functions as a dominant and official language despite the bidialectal, bilingual, and multilingual nature of countries. In this region where heteroglossia functions societally as the norm, Caribbean nationals speak many non-standardized Englishes, including thirty-five Creoles and fifteen indigenous languages (Simmons-McDonald, 2006; Voice, 2011). Often, it is acknowledged that students possess predominantly non-standardized English linguistic backgrounds (Warrican, 2009; Winer, 2006) and English-related Creoles and vernaculars have been said to interfere with their literacy performance (Bogle, 1997; Craig, 1974; Miller, 1989). For instance, in 2009, it was lamented that Caribbean bidialectal youth performed poorly on national measures of literacy and in other subject areas such that 21 percent of the candidates sitting the Caribbean Secondary Education Certification (CSEC) examinations achieved passing grades in five or more subject areas (e.g., math, English language arts, science, history, and social studies). Similarly, there is often deep consternation about indications such as those which indicate that 52 percent of students in 2009 either did not pass any CSEC subject or received passing grades in just one subject area (Jules, 2010). Admittedly, it is these measures that serve as pathways to economic advancement signaling what many view as 'success.'

Deviating from the developed tendency to explore language and culture in the Caribbean with limited if not complete lack of attention to an explicit naming and centering of race over the past few decades, Dr. Hubert Devonish, Professor Emeritus of Linguistics in the Jamaican Language Unit within the Department of Language, Linguistics and Philosophy at the University of the West Indies, Mona, Jamaica, working in collaboration with Dr. Karen Carpenter, senior lecturer at the same university, focus in their recent book, *Language, Race and the Global Jamaican*, on centering race in the discourse of the majority Black nation of Jamaica. The authors operate at the interstices of racialization and sociolinguistics to juxtapose the tendency of the systems in Jamaica to rely on white ideological framings even while its people globally have managed to become representative of intersectionally based cultural norms that allow the culture, race, and language of Jamaica to be known by the world, largely through its music and "dialect." Choosing to locate this contemporary dynamic within its colonially based history while also acknowledging, through naming, the explicit ways in which Jamaica emerged socially based on race, via conceptions of "colorism" – *white, brown, and black* – Devonish and Carpenter (2020) rightfully locate the tensions undergirding the Jamaican enterprise of languaging in its raciolinguistically determined foundation.

The decision to return to a contemporary and more overt naming of race in the description of Caribbean Englishes as presented above can be juxtaposed against the tendency in the US – where the Black immigrants under study in this book function – to historically explicitly attach connotations of Blackness or whiteness to Englishes such as those that often operate on the periphery of Eurocentrically driven systems (e.g., "dialects": Southern White English, Black English) in contrast to corresponding variations of standardized languages (e.g., Mainstream American English) that tend to be revered. For instance, Englishes that have been thought not to conform to white Eurocentric norms in the US have been overwhelmingly accepted and referred to as "Black English" or as "Southern White English" (complicating intraracial distinctions undergirding raciolinguistics discussed elsewhere: Smith, 2020b), while their contemporaries in the Caribbean region, often described as "Creole," "Plantation Creole," "dialects," or "vernaculars," have tended not to be so race-named in educational or other discourse.

In fact, in discussing the "Black English" of the US, formerly referred to as "Early Black English" or "Plantation Creole" (Birmingham, 2015), though it is shown to be closely related to "varieties spoken in the West Indies," to West African languages, and to gestures such as "cut-eye" and "suck-teeth" that exist in the Caribbean (Rickford & Rickford, 2015; see also Cameron, 2018), linguistic variations reflected by the latter contexts tend to supposedly lose the raciolinguistic connotations typically applied in the US context given the neutralization preferred in their naming. This occurs also in situations where Englishes are used by the Afro-Seminole population who have relations to Gullah speakers of Georgia, South Carolina's coast, and the Sea Islands, and whose languaging – Creole English – though on the periphery, fails to assume explicit connotations of Blackness in its naming. Such is the case despite the presence of the latter in the sociolinguistic context and its relationship to Englishes visible elsewhere in the US (e.g., Hughes, Seminole, Okfuskee and Okmulgee counties in Oklahoma, potentially Florida) and in the Caribbean island of the Bahamas (Hancock, 2015). And it is seen in discussions where Englishes and languages native to West Africa that reflect similar variety tend to be referred to as "Creoles" (e.g., Yoruba), much like those in the Caribbean that historically tended to be characterized as Atlantic Creoles (Holm, 2015; see also Winford, 2003, 2019).

Languaging, Englishes, and Literacies of English-Speaking Afro-Caribbean Students

Representations such as the above, of contemporary research on CEs operating largely *sans* attention to race, are especially prevalent in the body of research concentrated on students in what has been historically known the Anglophone Caribbean – *Anguilla, The Bahamas, Barbados, Belize, Bermuda, The British Virgin Islands, The Cayman Islands, Jamaica, Trinidad and Tobago, Turks & Caicos, Guyana, Grenada, Dominica, St. Lucia, St. Vincent, and the Grenadines.* Moreover, they have been advanced largely at the nexus of coloniality where concurrently unnamed sites of contestation steeped in raciolinguistic ideologies are spurred on by white supremacy. This is visible, for instance, in the exploration of the linguistic challenges of those often referred to as 'bidialectal' students (see Smith & Warrican, 2021, for a theoretical problematization of this term) as they receive literacy instruction and are assessed in the Caribbean.

In one such study focused on Jamaican learners, the English dialect has been considered as a function of literacy instruction. Researchers used an intervention to enhance first and second grade students' language awareness and self-concept, improve their Jamaican (English-based) Creole (JC) and Standard Jamaican English (SJE) literacy skills, and enable them to develop mastery of material taught in the content areas (Bilingual Education Project [BEP]; Devonish & Carpenter, 2007). Results from the Jamaican intervention indicated that with the exception of monolingual speakers of JC, first and second grade students encountered difficulty with bilingual delivery (i.e., JC, SJE) (Devonish & Carpenter, 2007). And in a study conducted by Warrican (2006) focused on participants in the third year of high school where high school students engaged in read-alouds, discussion, and silent reading of informational and fictional texts, findings reflected that students lacked interest in reading, maintained negative attitudes to reading, and engaged in self-deprecating behaviors. These behaviors counteracted efforts to enhance feelings of self-efficacy in reading and in other academic forms (Warrican, 2006). Responding to such indications, 'dialect' variation in the literacies and languaging of high school students has been explored by Millar and Warrican (2015), as discussed earlier, using an action research study designed to create a third space for bridging gaps between traditional and semiotic literacies and between students' home English varieties and the Standard English language used in Barbadian classrooms. Findings from the study showed that the students engaged in literate activities that drew from their home Englishes in numerous ways as their roles and that of their teachers were redefined.

Studies concerning Caribbean 'bidialectal' learners' literacy have also examined their informal writing as well as oral literacy and formal literacy assessment. For instance, students from grades one to six in Jamaica were administered phonics tests with an emphasis on the nature and production of sound patterns, literacy, phonetics, phonics, and their ability to discriminate between consonant clusters based on variations characterized by SJE and JC (Lacoste, 2007; Mitchell, 2007). Findings reflected students' tendencies to read below grade level and to possess knowledge of very few letter sounds (Mitchell, 2007). Operating in the same raciolinguistic context of Jamaica, Lacoste (2007) found that primary grade speakers and readers tended to attach known JC sound systems to words requiring SJE structures, increasing proficiency with articulation and gestures of cluster patterns after engaging in repetition. And working in collaborations with colleagues to explore the literacies of students in Trinidad and Tobago, we have located the challenges often associated with literacies of Caribbean non-standardized English-speaking students in the colonial legacies of the islands, arguing that this is why students continue to be administered literacy assessments that do not take into account their non-standardized English language use (Smith et al., 2018a). In keeping with the broad-based research corpus that has advanced language and literacy research in the Caribbean *sans* explicit attention to race, our study nonetheless observed that this practice reinforces a privileging of Standard English as a language of assessment in literacy and devalues certain World Englishes. We examined how Trinidadian 'bidialectal' adolescent youth self-identified linguistically on the 2009 Programme for International Student Assessment (PISA) literacy assessment, demonstrating the relationship to their reading, math, and science literacy performance as self-identified 'native' English and 'non-native' English-speaking students. Our findings showed that a "majority of students self-identified as [Standard] English speakers despite the predominant use of nonstandardized Englishes in their country as well as large and significant differences between 'self-identifying native' and 'self-identifying non-native' speakers of English, with higher mean scores for the former group in all three assessed areas of literacy as measured in English" (Smith et al., 2018a, p. 2). Based on these findings, we surmised that "self-identifying native English speakers performed significantly below the PISA 2009 OECD mean of 500 and reflected a high degree of volatility in performance," suggesting the need for "closer attention to the pervasive role of colonialism in the dominance of Standard English in multilingual testing," "attention to bidialectal students' performativity in World Englishes that challenge normative Standard English literacy proficiency," and "assumptions steeped in colonialism that underlie Standard English literacy testing on the PISA international measure [to] be revisited if bidialectal adolescent learners are to be accurately represented on these measures in much the same manner as their monolingual and Standard English speaking counterparts" (Smith et al., 2018a, p. 2).

Across the board, the challenges above faced by Caribbean youth arise in a context where Caribbean English (CE) speakers often self-identify as 'Standard' English speakers and lay claim to what is perceived as the (standard) language despite the deviation of their non-standardized English variety from this imagined 'Standard' English (Nero, 2006; Smith et al., 2018a, 2022). As Nero (2006) asserted, speaking of Caribbean students in the US, "I have found that, generally, Anglophone Caribbean students will list *only* English as their home language on the form, as opposed to, say, an Indian student who might list Gujarati and English, or even Gujarati alone" (p. 505). Nero explains:

Caribbean students' self-ascribed public linguistic identity with English *only* often reinforces a dual impulse in the minds of their American teachers. On the one hand, teachers might project a high level of receptive and especially productive competence in standardized English on them, and then penalize them if their work does not evidence such competence, especially in writing. On the other hand, teachers might assume that their Caribbean students' accented English is not "real" English because it "sounds" different than the teachers' or, worse, because the CE speaker is likely non-European and an immigrant, and so they approach and evaluate the students' English as not merely different but deficient. (Nero, 2006, p. 505)

Yet, inadvertently, CE speakers maintain an ongoing shift between the denigration and celebration of their non-Standard English varieties, reflecting what has been referred to as "attitudinal schizophrenia" (Kachru & Nelson, 2001). Nero (2006) explains that this occurs partly due to the question of their linguistic identity, which she describes as "complex" (p. 503). As shown by Nero:

While speech at the basilectal level is typically denigrated because of its association with low socio-economic status and lack of education, the basilect and especially the mesolect are often used to assert "true" Caribbean identity in informal and private domains. (Nero, 2006, p. 503)

This, she explains, creates the "attitudinal schizophrenia" identified above where "there is a contradictory impulse of simultaneously denigrating and celebrating the vernacular" (Nero, 2006, p. 504).

Nero's explanation provides a basis for understanding why, "at school, and in other formal and public domains both in the Caribbean and elsewhere, most CE speakers identify with English, and more importantly, think of themselves as native speakers of English" (Nero, 2006, p. 504). It also clarifies why educators in the Caribbean tend not to be challenged by and understand CE-speaking students because "they too are mostly from the local community" and why "in many cases, the first challenge to CE speakers' identification with, and use of, English is when they enter school or college in North America or England where standardized American and British varieties of English are privileged" (Nero, 2006, p. 504). Winer (2006) echoes Nero's assertions, arguing that in many ways, CE speakers' Standard English ideology leads them to be intentional about using Standard English in formal settings because it promises upward mobility and social status, but they simultaneously treasure their local non-standardized English varieties in informal contexts as symbols of national identity (St-Hilaire, 2011). For example, a CE speaker from Trinidad might use Trinidad Standard English when speaking with friends during a structured indoor class session at school but revert to the Trinidadian English Creole when speaking with the same individuals during an unstructured outdoor session at church (see Smith et al., 2018b).

It is such a conundrum that led to the consensus in Creole linguistics for Creole research to address speakers' development of literacies – goals articulated by the Ministers of Education within the Caribbean Community (CARICOM) and in turn, advanced via a position paper from their 1993 Barbuda conference. Unsurprisingly, these goals expressed the need to cultivate pride of students in their home language even while competence in the official language of "Standard English" was maintained (Bryan, 1997). Explored in a Caribbean context where migration would later be heavily examined via literacy through songs, poems, plays, films, and novels, much like it was in the African American cultural context, and leading to works such as that of Claude McKay, a Jamaican-born and prominent figure in the Harlem Renaissance who became "the signature writer of the Caribbean encounter with the United States" (Davies, 2013), issues surrounding the English Creoles of the Caribbean thus became intertwined with migration.

Afro-Caribbean Immigrant Literacies and Englishes in the US

When Caribbean English speakers migrate from spaces where their "outer circle Englishes" are used to contexts such as the US where "inner circle Englishes" operate largely based on race – a dynamic now described as "cross-circle Englishes" (Smith, 2020b) – they are forced to reconsider the ways in which they have previously used Englishes as well as the discrimination that they have leveraged against non-standardized Englishes (i.e., long referred to as "dialects") which become inferiorly treated in academic settings (Smith et al., 2018b). Admittedly, though almost historically overlooked in American sociolinguistics, where, as illustrated earlier, a focus on race as a social variable undergirding linguistic behavioral patterns has tended to be often focused on 'African American English' and its comparisons to 'Standard American English' as spoken by whites (e.g., Bailey, 2001; Cukor-Avila, 2001; Myhill & Ash, 1986; Rickford, 1985; Wolfram, 1971), the emergence of an emphasis on Afro-Caribbean immigrant literacies and Englishes in the US functions in part as a basis for early language research, but also, as a response to calls such as those from Spears (1988), Winer and Jack (1997), and Nero (2001) for "more complex analysis of the interaction between race and language" (Blake & Shousterman, 2010). Repeatedly highlighted in the "sorely underestimated social and linguistic heterogeneity of the black population in the US, which need[ed] to be considered in studies of the language of black speakers" (Blake & Shousterman, 2010, p. 35), the understudied literacy and linguistic repertoires of Caribbean speakers in the US reveal an initially gradual but increasingly robust engagement with the complexities reflected by Black immigrant children and youth, across generations, ethnicities, Englishes, and socioeconomic conditions.

One of the earliest examinations into the literacies of Black Caribbean immigrant students which focuses on race in the US was undertaken by Dr. Annette Henry, Professor in the Department of Language and Literacy Education and cross-appointed to the Institute for Race, Gender, Sexuality and Social Justice at the University of British Columbia. Henry's scholarship examines race, class, language, gender, and culture in sociocultural contexts of teaching and learning in the lives of Black students, Black oral histories, and Black women teachers' practice in Canada, the US, and the Caribbean. In her early study, Henry (1998) used a weekly reading/writing/discussion workshop where she leveraged engaging texts to provide culturally and gender-relevant topics to eight Caribbean girls labeled "limited English proficient" (LEP), most of whom were from the island country of Jamaica, and who "were constantly *reading* the world and yearning for spaces to read, write, and speak themselves into the curriculum" (Henry, 1998, p. 188). Through their reading of the *Diary of Latoya Hunter: My First Year in Junior High* (Hunter, 1992), a text written by a young Jamaican girl in New York, and through the responses via a journal to parts of Latoya's diary, Henry intended that the text would be connected to the girls' lives. Speaking in her findings from the study of how Black girls "come to voice" (hooks, 1994) and of the "transgressive speech" (Davies, 1995) of Black women that functions as a challenge to oppression, Henry (1998) stated:

I was working with young women caught in the mix and borrowing from both cultures who wanted to become "Americans" but spoke a language devalued in American classrooms. They were insecure expressing themselves orally and in writing, unacquainted with the kinds of "liberal" inquiry-based teaching/learning situations advocated in American schools. Living in the fold of old wounds also evoked a linguistic history that had negative educational consequences. Moreover, as adolescent girls, they were struggling with personal and family issues. (Henry, 1998, p. 186)

Henry acknowledged, based on existing scholarship (McNerney, 1978; Sutcliffe, 1992), that "perceived pronunciation or grammatical errors in American English may be perfect Caribbean Creole" (Henry, 1998, p. 243) and that at least, as far back as 1995, "Caribbean Creoles [were] often devalued in educational settings where standard English is the reputed norm" (p. 237). Henry's study also led to a rethinking of the curriculum as she learned about issues related to the lives of the students such as sexual activity as part of childhood and teenage experiences. In response, she showed them *Just Another Girl on the IRT*, a film by Harris (1993), who, according to Redding and Brownsworth (1997), was the first Black woman to have her film released by a major distributor. Highlighting responses of the students to the film, Henry shared:

The girls were enthused about the themes raised by this film which, due to time constraints, I had to show in half-hour segments. Arriving at our weekly sessions, video under my arm, I would try to do the "teacherly" things such as "recap," or pose some guiding questions before viewing it. They were bursting with eagerness to watch the video. "Me nah wan' talk'bout it. Let's see it, noh!" exclaimed Inara, looking at me with the video under my arm. "It's the bomb!" shrieked Dorne. (Henry, 1998, p. 187)

Henry observed that students' responses reflected their "grappling with a new sociocultural context," pointing out that they "had developed a psychological resistance to written English" as the "master discourse" (Davies, 1995) and "underscoring a colonialist linguistic imposition of the English language in Caribbean life" (Henry, 1998, p. 187). She illustrated how this occurred with one of the Caribbean students, a fourteen-year-old referred to as Kay, who had been referred to as a "non-reader" by her teacher and who had migrated from Jamaica to the US at the age of eleven. Henry pointed out the possibility of the master discourse being present, explaining that although the student could identify letters of the alphabet as a migrant to the US, and also words such as "to" and "but," her behaviors presented a paradox where she seemed to fear yet yearn at the same time, the practice of "successful reading." According to Henry, this was reflected in the student's tendency to borrow books from the library but allow them to "pile up in her locker" as well as in her occasional resistance to reading/writing activities. Henry shared, from one of the students, Tamisha, that "This group is good ... because sometimes you want to ask your mother things, but you just can't and we learn things here" and, upon completion of the study, from another student, Alice, a fourteen-year-old Belizean, "Well, like before, if I talk to someone – [I learned] like, don't be afraid. Like what's on your mind, you could just tell somebody what's on your mind. And don't keep it in." Henry's conclusion, alluding to her invoking the film *Daughters of the Dust*, which represents Black women caught between two cultures, reflected back then, how the students with whom she was engaged were challenged to deal with issues steeped in the psychological, political, and social, often creating a dynamic where they may not have "participate[d] fully in literacy activities, yet [may have been] bursting to read, write, and engage in discussions" (Henry, 1998, p. 188).

Also approaching the dynamic of Caribbean Englishes of immigrant students in the US and explicitly addressing race, but from a slightly different perspective, was Dr. Shondel Nero, whose ground-breaking research, as alluded to earlier, has functioned as a stimulus for investigations of Caribbean Englishes. Nero has conducted decades-long examinations into the large-scale and ongoing migration of Anglophone Caribbean natives to North America, focusing often and particularly on the city of New York (Nero, 2006). Observing the influx of CE-speaking students in schools and colleges of the US and Canada, Nero (2006) describes the dynamic where students, much like those from Trinidad and Tobago, who identified themselves as "Standard English" speaking, present Englishes in the US context that tend to be misunderstood by the North American population at large. Admittedly, she locates this bone of contention within the long-standing question of whether "English-based Creoles" should be regarded as "dialects of English" or as "separate languages" (Nero, 2006, p. 502). Her argument, mirroring debates in Jamaica that questioned the treatment of "speech varieties" in society as belonging to the same language when different, and in the acknowledgment of the political and not merely linguistic question, reflected indications by Mufwene (2001, 2004) of the "insidious naming tradition" which separates languages and dialects that have less to do inherently with the varieties themselves than with "who [was] setting the [language naming] norms" (Nero, 2006, p. 502). In particular, Mufwene (2001) described the phenomenon of linking race and language, which, though long established in the scholarship of numerous scholars of Color (e.g., Alim, 2004), has suddenly become more visible across multiple fields. Mufwene stated:

the naming practice of new Englishes has to do more with the racial identity of those who speak them than with how these varieties developed and the extent of their structural deviations. It has little to do with how mutually intelligible they are. (Mufwene, 2001, p. 107)

Nero's allusion to this naming practice, which has persisted for a long time, among "Caribbean and other linguists" as a "debate about whether to consider

English-based Creoles dialects of English or separate languages" is bolstered by her radical insertion of race in the CE-speaking dynamic, pointing to the fact that teachers who encounter CE speakers face a challenge given three key assumptions often made in US and UK classrooms. The assumptions are the idea that a supposedly "native speaker" is linked to race or ethnicity; the supposed monolithic nature of English; and the positioning of only standardized English as "English" (Nero, 2006, p. 504). Steeped in this explicit intertwining of race and language and in a challenge to the Eurocentric frames existing to define languaging, Nero describes how the tensions experienced by CE-speaking students, emerging from this site of linguistic contestation in the Caribbean as they crossed borders into the racially divided North American context, create a situation where they are compelled to revisit how they make assumptions about English, about who owns English, and about their identities in relation to language. Speaking then of this dynamic, Nero asserted:

The average Caribbean person is not even aware that these academic debates on language vs. dialect exist; they only encounter them when they are forced to consider movements such as those in Jamaica to make Creole an official language, or when they come to school in North America and are placed in an ESL class because their English "sounds" or "looks" nonnative; hence, the assumption that their home language is other than English. (Nero, 2006, p. 503)

Nero went on to state:

This social construction of race as inherently implicated in linguistic identity and in claims of language authority has direct implications for how teachers view and assess Caribbean students' language and, by extension, how the students view and assess themselves. (Nero, 2006, p. 504)

These assertions have largely informed recent discussions that question the naming practices ascribed not only to these Englishes as "dialects" but also to all dialects of the largely Majority World population. Specifically, in articulating our position on this notion, S. Joel Warrican and I have made the bold assertion that

the field of education, and society in general, has maintained the privilege and power associated with the numerous advantageous elements of bi/multilingualism as a characteristic of the white speaking subject even while decrying, subverting, denying, and disregarding the corresponding evidence available regarding the simultaneous legitimacy, advantage, and resourcefulness available in the bi/multilingualism of the racialized object. (Smith & Warrican, 2021, p. 2)

Our rationale for doing so was steeped in

the clear indication that dialects and the people who speak them tend to be designated as inferior, particularly when these individuals constitute racialized populations, further exacerbat[ing] the need to address how such terminologies unapologetically sanction the "languagelessness" of speakers and "position colonized subjects as incapable of communicating legitimately in any language" (Rosa, 2016; Rosa & Flores, 2017, p. 4). (Smith & Warrican, 2021, p. 2)

Ultimately, our premise was that "sanctioning language usage as *'dialects'* erases personhood" (Smith & Warrican, 2021, p. 2). We argued that "the prescribed illegitimacy by the *white subject* and the equally and inadvertently accepted inferiority on the part of the racialized *object* [i.e., via 'white gaze'; see Morrison, 2020; see also Flores & Rosa, 2015], have been shown to largely be unassociated with white users of *dialects*" (Smith & Warrican, 2021, p. 2).

In turn, we urged the field, in the treatment of CE speakers, as with their 'dialect-speaking' counterparts across the world both in practice and research, to deviate from the label 'dialect' and instead utilize the term 'bilingual users of Englishes' or in other cases, 'multilingual uses of Englishes' (B/MUE). Arguing that the "responsibility for the burden that youth and individuals bear based on a co-naturalization of language and race" functions as "an institutional or societal, but not an individual, responsibility" in line with Rosa and Flores (2017), we made the case that "*bidialectalism*, on the basis of its inherent linguistic variation and not its rule-governing or structure, represents a *natural category*" and that

including *dialects* and named *languages* operating in tandem along a language continuum based on *linguistic distance* and *recognition*, inadvertently reifies raciolinguistic and monoglossic ideologies based on cognitivist norms that sustain the *bidialectal* burden even as they instantiate the notion of a *prototypical bilingual* as far removed from being *bidialectal* (i.e., a person who uses regularly two prototypical languages and masters both on high levels of proficiency). (Smith & Warrican, 2021, p. 14)

Conceptually, we used this argument that targets deeply embedded cognitivist perspectives in language teaching and research to propose the naming of B/MUE students even as we raise questions about notions of a *language* versus a *dialect*, namely, *By whom is language designated a dialect? For whom, in what context, and to what end?*

Much like Alim (2004) observed in his early depiction of the relationship between race and language, and Rosa and Flores (2017) later articulated in a raciolinguistic perspective, the call for institutions to shoulder the responsibility of how race and language position students to which we respond above remains a legitimate one. Nero (2006) has lamented the ways in which schools have functioned as "chief culprits in perpetuating the notion that only proficiency in the standardized prescriptivist grammar of English privileged in school, especially evidenced in essayist literacy, counts as 'real English' with grammar functioning as the supposed 'shibboleth in school'" (p. 505). She observed back then that "while teachers might be tolerant of diversity in pronunciation or lexicon, they are less so of grammar, which reflects the attitude in the society at large" and mirroring the plight of the African American student population in the US, she stated:

> To the extent that a Caribbean student does not display proficiency in standardized grammar or displays a *different* grammar, particularly in writing, she or he will be considered as not knowing how to write, or worse, not knowing English at all. (Nero, 2006, p. 505)

In turn, using examples of features of CE which were potential sources for misunderstanding in American classrooms, Nero made the argument for shifting paradigmatic approaches to how students are placed, assessed, and how their language develops. Among the features that Nero describes are "presumed understanding based on surface level linguistic familiarity" which, as clarified by Palmer (1996), causes "speakers from different backgrounds [to] draw on different conceptualizations when communicating with each other," regardless of their use of the same language (i.e., English). For teachers of CE-speaking students with whom Nero worked, it was clear that the assumption was made that cultural conceptualizations undergirding Englishes in the US also undergird Englishes in the Caribbean contexts from which the students migrated when this was not the case. Nero also identified "accent" as another source of potential understanding but only when the accents functioned "at the extreme ends of the spectrum" such as the placement of stress on various syllables in words by CE speakers as opposed to North American speakers. She pointed to disproportionately negative responses to CE pronunciation and to writing, particularly because of a heavy focus on "Standard English" grammar at the time of the study, in schools.

Unlike some who argue for the placement of CE-speaking students in English as a Second Language (ESL) classrooms, albeit in Caribbean classrooms (e.g., Devonish, 1986), Nero proposed then that Caribbean students in the US not be placed in such an ESL context. She maintained that their receptive as well as oral English skills were much more advanced than that of the "traditional ESL student" (e.g., Spanish or Chinese speakers) and that their English-speaking self-identification would potentially create a challenge for their motivation to learn English when presented to them as learning a "second" language. Clachar (2003) has supported this cautious approach to having Caribbean Creole English (CCE) speakers subsumed within the 'generic' population of 'ESL learners' given that comparisons of Creole English-speaking students and ESL students show distinct challenges in the writing of learners of standard English as a second dialect versus that of ESL learners. Evidence presented by Clachar indicates that doing so may mask complex differences among these learners as relates to challenges in literacy such as communicative patterns in the speech communities across these populations. For instance, Clachar (2004) has shown that:

The structure of discourse in Creole cultures as well as the ramifications of an oral tradition were shown to have an effect on the Creole-speaking subjects' tendency to draw on conjunctions and clause-linking strategies typical of registers of spoken discourse in their academic expository writing. On the contrary, the ESL subjects, from a literate tradition, exhibited fewer challenges than their Creole-speaking counterparts with respect to the transfer of the speech conjunctive system into the registers of written academic discourse. (Clachar, 2004, p. 1828)

Clachar's discussion of the variations across communities reinforces the need for attention to how social and cultural patterns shape the communicative repertoires of students in the Creole speech community and in turn, how these communicative repertoires are represented in the 'academic expository writing' of Caribbean Creole-speaking students. It also points to the ways in which institutional expectations for 'academic expository writing' become imposed on Creole-speaking students whose grappling with 'unfamiliar registers of academic expository prose' tend to be prioritized over their capacity to leverage, via translanguaging, their linguistic and semiotic repertoires in ways that advance the arguments or intentions of their writing. Reinforcing the need to complicate conceptions of the 'native speaker/nonnative speaker' dichotomy and disrupt ESL/English dichotomies as made visible by CCE, Clachar's indications extend earlier discussions by Nero (2000) of the linguistic context of the Anglophone Caribbean which highlights how certain features of CCE operate in distinctly different ways from features of Standard American English in North American schools (Nero, 2000).

They also raise questions about the persistently deficit positioning of speakers of Englishes whose linguistic repertoires are often historically placed on the periphery of the US linguistic enterprise (e.g., African American speakers). This dynamic, I have argued, "not only fail[s] to meet the needs of non-standardized English speakers but also place[s] our monolingual speakers at risk" (Smith, 2016, p. 194). Observing that the refusal of national policy to address language in ways that "not only [place] linguistically diverse speakers as deficient and in need of fixing but also [position] their monolingual counterparts (who lack this diversity) as necessarily privileged and proficient" compromises US citizens' literacies for effective communication, I have invited an urgency in national policy that "moves[s] from an approach to multilingualism that is dichotomous, based only on standardized monolingual language norms, [to one that] instead adopt[s] a translingual language approach that bridges gaps between the monolingual and the multilingual population" (Smith, 2016, p. 194).

The contentions above reinforce the arguably insistent calls by Nero (2006) for the placement of CE-speaking students in mainstream classrooms "with teachers who have been trained in linguistic diversity, including world Englishes, through ongoing staff development" and whose training should include becoming familiar with (1) Caribbean culture, beyond what Winer calls the "sun and fun" exotic view of the Caribbean; (2) prototypical features of CE; and (3) speech community discourse norms, including nonverbal communication (e.g., direct eye contact with the teacher or an adult is considered rude in Caribbean schools, which is very different from American schools). (Nero, 2006, p. 508)

Recommending the hiring of Caribbean teachers in North American classrooms as a strategy for addressing the needs of CE-speaking students and citing her own practices as an educator of New York City teachers, Nero suggested that students be asked to clarify when communication was impeded by pronunciation, grammar, or vocabulary features; the dialect features and speech of students' writing be used to discuss 'appropriateness' of various genres; alternative forms of assessments adapted for various Englishes be used; students write and share their stories in their Englishes as well as the Englishes of the classroom; literature used in class reflect Englishes and writers who use various Englishes; among other strategies.

The recommendations proposed by Nero for CE speakers have informed attention paid elsewhere to the needs of Caribbean Creole individuals from Anglophone/English-speaking, Francophone/French-speaking, Hispanophone/Spanish-speaking, and Néerlandophone/Dutch-speaking cultures and particularly to pedagogical strategies such as code-meshing and translingualism that reduce stigma, support students' linguistic identity development, and foster pride in the 'Creoles' of Anglophone Caribbean English speakers (Milson-Whyte, 2018). They have also been extended in recent scholarship in ways that reflect Nero's earlier calls for a focus on the connections between race as language in the CEs of Caribbean speakers in the US. For instance, heeding such calls, as alluded to earlier (Smith, 2019a), I have shown that increasing evidence confirms that multilingual and multiethnic English-speaking students face challenges with Englishes and English literacies when they migrate between their home countries and the US. These challenges, faced by immigrant and transnational students, involve their dialects, accents, and communication styles, which lead them to question their capacity to speak English appropriately and grapple with what it means to be successful users of English literacy. Although examinations of these students' Englishes and literacies often centralize language, it is not often that race and language are equally foregrounded to illustrate the effects of both elements in the literate practices of these youth, many of whom are students of Color. Drawing on positioning theory to describe how a Black immigrant English-speaking adolescent – Jaeda – underwent shifts in her experiences that (re)positioned her as a literate user of Englishes, I illustrated how the individual and global analyses recommended by "a raciolinguistic perspective" (Rosa & Flores, 2017) reflected Jaeda's development of a transraciolinguistic approach that allowed her to persist with a sense of agency (Smith, 2019a).

Extending this scholarship in the *Teachers College Record* special issue/ yearbook "Clarifying the Role of Race in the Literacies of Black Immigrant Youth" (Smith, 2020b), I have called for a centralizing of race in research that examines the Englishes and literacies of the largely invisible population of Black immigrant youth in the US. My rationale for this argument was based largely on the increasingly divisive rhetoric surrounding Black immigrants and Black Americans, exacerbated by current racial tensions and further amplified amidst a politicized landscape and COVID-19. This rhetoric, I observed, has continuously erupted from often implicit and negative connotations associated with Black immigrants as a "new model minority" when compared with their "underperforming" Black American counterparts and evolved into the use of dichotomous intraracial ideologies that continue to pit one subgroup against the other. Beyond this, I argued, race continues to be present as a key part of conversations in the Englishes and literacies of Black American students. And notions of race and racism, as seen through constructs such as "critical race theory" (Crenshaw et al., 1995), "racial literacy" (Sealey-Ruiz, 2021), "linguistic racism" (Calvet, 1974), and "a raciolinguistic perspective" (Rosa & Flores, 2017), remain central to conversations about how Black Americans' language and literacy use is understood and evaluated in US schools.

Pointing out that we know little about how Black immigrant literacies and Englishes reflect racial tensions that affect literacy instruction and assessment because data surrounding their academic performance across the US, more often than not, remains subsumed within the data of Black students overall, and illustrating that immigrants of Color are nonetheless often subjected to linguistic and racial discrimination faced by Black American counterparts, I asked the question *Why is an understanding of race and racism not central to the distinct, varied, and unique Englishes and literacies of Black immigrant youth?* As Charles Mills concurs, "Race is made to seem marginal when in fact race has been central" (Mills, 1997, p. 54). To address this gap in the field, I examined affordances from the lenses of diaspora literacy, transnational literacy, and racial literacy, which hold promise for understanding how to foreground race in the literacies of predominantly English-speaking Black immigrant youth. I demonstrated how each of these lenses, as applied to the literacies of the invisible population of Black youth, allows for partial understandings regarding these students' enactment of literacies based on their Englishes and semiotic resources.

In turn, I illustrated how these lenses can work together to clarify the role of race in Black immigrant literacies. Based on these discussions, I presented the framework of "*Black immigrant literacies*" (Smith, 2020b, 2023a) to assist researchers, practitioners, and parents who wish to better understand and support Black immigrant youth. I also invited researchers who work with populations that include such youth to consider how race, when central to research and teaching surrounding the literacies and Englishes of these youth, can provide opportunities for them to thrive beyond their perceptions as "academic prodigies" while also facilitating relationships with their Black American peers. I invited teachers also to consider ways of viewing Black immigrant literacies that foster a sense of community between these youth and their Black American peers as well as ways of engaging their literacies in classrooms that allow them to demonstrate how they function as language architects beyond performance on literacy assessments. And I urged parents to provide spaces beyond school contexts where Black immigrant youth can use their literacies for social adjustment. My practical intent for the framework as a basis for addressing the needs of Black Caribbean immigrant students in classrooms and schools, and extended at length in *Black Immigrant Literacies: Intersections of Race, Language, and Culture in the Classroom* (Smith, 2023a), was that schools, teachers, the dominant population, institutions, and society at large would gain further insights into some of the complexities and nuances that exist within the Black population and be cognizant of these nuances when engaging with Black immigrant youth.

In the aforementioned special issue, Skerrett and Omogun (2020) respond to this call above, undertaking an examination of the language and literacy practices and experiences of Black immigrant and Black transnational and immigrant youth of Caribbean origin who call the US home. The authors intended to examine similarities, differences, and nuances present in the language and literacy practices and experiences of students. Their discussions indicate that both Black immigrant and Black transnational youth reflect literacies in the form of reading, writing, the performing arts, and digital literacies. Specifically, they point out how youth use their literacy and language practices to deconstruct Blackness as a monolithic racial category, reflecting a myriad of ethnoracial identities and micro-cultural practices as they maintained ties to their countries of origins as well as to the 'destination' country of the US. In turn, they highlight the importance of allowing these students to have opportunities to evolve in their identities developed across nations so that they can adequately consolidate these identities through their languages and literacies. The authors later extend their focus to Haiti, acknowledging Black immigrant youth as an understudied demographic, and exploring, through a textual analysis of the novel *American Street* (Zoboi, 2017), how a Black Haitian immigrant youth constructs her identity in the US (Omogun & Skerrett, 2021). Through their analysis, the authors illustrate how the student resisted raciolinguistic ideologies and relied on her Haitian "faith literacies" as well as her multiliterate practices to (re)construct her identity. They in turn invite research that clarifies the complexities involved in how Black immigrant youth negotiate their identity within countries of destination, pointing to the potential of textual analyses as a basis for such knowledge and for informing pedagogy.

McLean, too, has further articulated the complexities of this dynamic in the aforementioned special issue "Clarifying the Role of Race in the Literacies of

Black Immigrant Youth" (Smith, 2020b), justifying the need to center race in CEs and literacies by conducting a meta-analysis of Black Caribbean immigrant adolescents, and illustrating how their multimodal and digital literacy practices functioned as a response to the "Black" racial category. In this analysis of five Black Caribbean immigrant adolescents, she illustrates how they responded to the racialized category "Black" and constructed their multimodal and digital literacy practices, using data snapshots to demonstrate how issues of race pointed to the dialogic ways in which youth leveraged their literacy practices while being Black and immigrant even as they confronted dominant representations of race that often negated their cultural identities. Her research showed that the students invested in "emotional identity work" when talking about how they experienced race with a reflection of pride and sometimes shame, but also resilience. In doing so, McLean highlights the conflicting sense of national pride experienced by the Black Caribbean youth, on the one hand, and their racial prejudice and feelings of a lack of worthiness, on the other. She shows too how self-worth for the students was intertwined with the racialization of labels steeped in the identities of being "Black" and "immigrant" as they used tools and spaces as sites of resilience to (re)frame their identities.

Warrican (2020), likewise responding to the call in the above special issue, has shown how moral licensing intersects with raciolinguistic ideologies to define the identities of Black immigrant youth and their resulting academic achievement. Presenting moral licensing as "people pointing to some act that is considered good to justify or excuse behavior that they recognize to be bad or immoral," Warrican (2020) observed that "moral licensing is a psychological phenomenon that allowed, for example, slave owners to feel virtuous when they claimed that they treated their slaves well, feeding, clothing and sheltering them in ways that others did not, while overlooking the fact that they were depriving these kept individuals of their freedom" (p. 8) and thus, explains in part why immigrants are treated the way they are in countries such as the US. Warrican stated:

The application of moral licensing to excuse certain behaviors may be a deliberate and public act, but sometimes it is subconscious. There is no doubt that there are those who are aware of how doing a moral act can allow them to get away with future immoral actions, and they may use this awareness to their advantage. Others may stumble into this advantage, recognize its benefits and decide to utilize it while disregarding the fact that they are performing immoral actions. The benefits of immorality, through moral licensing, seem more compelling to such persons than continuing on a path of moral deeds. (Warrican, 2020, p. 8)

He further argued that:

It is possible that the level of ignorance relating to Black immigrants' identities is what causes members of the dominant group to react with outrage when they see any sign of protest and resistance in response to their actions. Perhaps resistance is unexpected because, as the theory of moral licensing suggests, these Black immigrant youth, now and later as adults, should be grateful for an America that welcomed them after their "unfulfilling" lives in their home countries. (Warrican, 2020, p. 15)

Based on these assertions, he calls for a renewed focus on extending beyond "basic service[es]" in schools as relates to Black immigrants in the US where the "act of providing only a basic service may fall into the realm of moral credits [such that] some policymakers or even teachers believe that it is their only obligation to Black immigrant youth after the state has done the good and noble deed of allowing them into the country" (Warrican, 2020, p. 17). Warrican (2020) observed that "while providing such a basic service is necessary and may appease the consciences of the dominant group and might even pander to their notion of moral credits, overall it is not sufficient," calling for a "greater good" that "foster[s] an environment where Black immigrant students feel safe to participate fully in class, which could ultimately lead to increased academic success" (p. 17).

It is increasing engagement with these complexities occurring across intersections in the lives of Black Caribbean immigrant students and youth that led me to articulate how a transraciolinguistic approach might function as a tool for teachers in literacy and English language classrooms (Smith, 2022b). In articulating this vision for Black Caribbean immigrant students *in The Reading Teacher*, I argue that this student population increasingly uses literacies to cross boundaries, locally, virtually, geographically, willingly, and involuntarily (i.e., as refugees) while possessing versatile linguistic backgrounds that allow them to effectively navigate new school and life worlds. Highlighting also that many students who cross boundaries are students of Color who wrestle with what it means to critically read the word and the world (Freire & Macedo, 1987) even as they grapple with racialization, I reiterate that at the intersection of students' border-crossing, languaging, and racialization are opportunities for understanding how teachers can center race by identifying and leveraging literate assets that immigrant and transnational students of Color use to make meaning in and beyond classrooms. Extending earlier discussions used to conceptualize a transraciolinguistic approach, I presented this approach as an intersectional and critical tool for attending to racialized language while also addressing border-crossing in students' literacy practice. Among the tools highlighted to do so are *"Creating Storylines with the 3 M's,"* which are metalinguistic, metacultural, and metaracial understanding and can be used to foster a transraciolinguistic approach with immigrant/transnational racialized youth, as well as *"Revisiting Literacy and English Language Arts Standards with the 3 M's,"* which can be used to foster a transraciolinguistic approach for all youth (Smith, 2022b; see also Smith, 2023a).

These practical insights complement mixed-methods scholarship undertaken with colleagues which has problematized the notion of Black immigrant youth being designated as high achieving or as a new model minority when comparing their literate 'success' with that of their Black American peers (Smith et al., 2022). Drawing from ideological and autonomous views regarding literacies while recognizing notions such as languaging informed by personhood, monoglossic norms, heteroglossic perspectives, and raciolinguistic ideologies, which come to bear on the literacies of Black immigrant youth, we examined Black immigrant literacy from both qualitative and quantitative paradigms.

Quantitative findings revealed that "native English-speaking" (see Cook, 2015, for a problematization of this term) Black immigrant youth had significantly higher scores on reading literacy than native English-speaking Black American youth on the PISA. Notwithstanding, as has been previously shown, Black immigrant students performed below the PISA average despite indications of outperforming Black American peers. Among all Black students in 2009, 'native English speakers' outperformed 'non-native English speakers.' However, superior reading literacy performance among native English speakers was not as obvious in 2015 as was observed in 2009. We also showed that in the iteration of the PISA 2015 reading literacy assessment, "non-native English speakers" outperformed native English speakers among Black immigrants, whereas native English speakers had higher scores than non-native English speakers on reading literacy among Black Americans.

Qualitative findings showed that (a) literate success in one Black immigrant youth's (i.e., D'Arcy) literacy practices was influenced by multilingualism as both an asset and a deficit, (b) dialectal difference was perceived as language interference and as binary (i.e., legitimate vs. non-legitimate), (c) there was persistent unacceptability of D'Arcy's language, accent, and certain literacies across home and school, (d) expectations about D'Arcy's racial literate identity remained steeped in assumptions regarding racialized language and raciolinguistic ideology, and (e) teacher interventions revealed tensions across (racio) linguistic ideologies. We observed from this study that:

> The schizophrenic institutional norms that sanctioned D'Arcy's supposed academic literate success allowed her to eventually gain access to a university, even while inadvertently reifying ideologies and their corresponding delegitimized perceptions of her literacies. These norms created, through the white gaze, a repeated and persistent rejection of her authentic literacies when she attempted to comply with acceptable linguistic norms as a racialized subject. (Smith et al., 2022, p. 20)

Through this study, we invited researchers to consider how social adjustment (Alegría et al., 2017) and resilience (or a lack thereof) are directly linked to literate practices that may function as part of (racialized) languaging. We also called for attention to research on embodiment that allows for examination of how these constructs intersect with the health, affect, and well-being of Black (immigrant) youth, particularly in the wake of social isolation and health disparities exacerbated by COVID-19 and given the recent unrest accompanying the racialization of Black and (im)migrant people across the globe.

The study functioned as a mechanism to disrupt practical notions of what it means for youth, Black immigrant or otherwise, to reflect success in literacy by problematizing the ways in which Black immigrant students seemingly escape the label of underperformer (ascribed to their African American and certain immigrant peers) even while being subjected to raciolinguistic and monoglossic ideologies based on institutional norms that delegitimize their personhood, linguistic repertoires, and literacies, creating potential challenges for their well-being. As we showed in the case of D'Arcy, she remained racialized, and her authentic literacy practices were overlooked and excluded from literacy classrooms and in social spaces beyond schools, even while institutional systems eventually rewarded her with acceptance to a university as an indicator of literate success.

We asked, *How valuable is it for D'Arcy to be successful with literacy if she is isolated and feels unable to find a sense of belonging in academic and social spaces of a university (and by extension, the society)?* In turn, we called for theoretical examinations of nuanced illustrations of racialized languaging that allow for individual (as opposed to broad and shared) understandings of immigrant youth of Color who each bring unique literate trajectories to bear on their social adjustment during migration.

Such elucidations have since formed the basis for imaginaries that can be developed to articulate what the future of linguistics might look like through the lens of Black immigrant literacies. In providing one such instantiation, I have shared how the framework of Black immigrant literacies, derived largely from the experiences of Black Caribbean immigrant youth, can function as a prism for creating a futuristic world steeped in "transraciolinguistic justice" as we prepare for what will become a largely virtual landscape of the impending future via attention to "global metaverse," "civic," "legal," and relational futures" (Smith, 2022a, p. 112). Acknowledging that the world continues to experience the recent wave of racial reckoning and its associated backlash, I have urged the field of applied linguistics to renew efforts through which language functions as an avenue for redemption and restoration of humanity and of the world. Citing the role of racialization in the language-related challenges faced nationally and globally that have spurred on a wave of examinations which extend beyond a focus on the intellect and that increasingly allow for a simultaneous grappling with what it means to advance language solutions that equally center human sensitivity and the body, I have pointed to the effects of racism on language use by immigrants, including immigrants of Color, many of whom are often introduced into the US as "languageless" (Rosa, 2016) And observing that we operate now on the verge of an imminent global metaverse within which the world will soon largely exist, I espoused provocative questions about the degree to which language, and racialized language, will continue to function as the primary mechanism for operating in a future world order. I drew from the Black immigrant experience in the US to demonstrate why the future of applied linguistics in a global metaverse must be concerned with "transraciolinguistic justice" that (1) creates opportunities beyond racialized language as a function of the imminent global metaverse, (2) disrupts the racialization of language for relegating citizenship based on national norms as a function of civic engagement, and (3) dismantles racialized language and borders that hold up the exclusion of "foreignness" to transform the relational experience.

The impending reality of a global metaverse, I asserted, lays flat distinctions among migrants while also introducing a plethora of spaces where racialized language further functions as subtext in a non-material world which calls for a (re)thinking of what it will mean to instruct, assess, plan for, and preserve languages in a soon to be, predominantly, virtual global existence. Civic and legal engagement in a global metaverse, I showed, can potentially transcend racialized language, allowing for the disruption of perceptions that advocate a lack of connectivity of diverse human publics across national and global borders. Relational healing through a focus on transraciolinguistic justice in a global metaverse, I illustrated, represents an opportunity to restore the brokenness of the oppressed and cultivate opportunities for building bridges across diverse realities, critical to the abandonment of centuries, and the introduction, of an era of peace. I concluded that to the degree that the field of applied linguistics is prepared to engage transraciolinguistic justice, will determine, in large part, the extent to which it adjusts to a largely virtual world.

Unmasking an Economically Induced Fallacy: Invented Illiteracy across the Black Diaspora

In the beginning of this chapter, we were invited to journey in part with Dr. Arlette Willis, who has undertaken an impeccable analysis of Omar ibn Said's writings as an impetus to challenge the long-standing characterization of invented illiteracy typically ascribed to Black peoples worldwide. The analyses conducted by Willis are steeped in "primary and secondary sources beyond histories of literacy in the US" as well as "scholars of African history and literacy, Islam, and the transatlantic slave industry" and used to present the notion of a "transcendent approach to literacy" (Waldron et al., 2023). Speaking of the etymology of transcendence, Willis observes:

I begin with the etymology of transcendence, a word whose origins in the West are found in English, French, and Latin. The concept also exists in Fulani, the native language of Omar ibn Said, as I learned from a former student, Dr. Maimouna Abdoulaye Barro. She is a native speaker of Fulani (known as Pulaar in Senegal), and her ancestors are from the same village as Omar ibn Said, Baroobe Jakel. She states, in Pulaar, the concept has philosophical and spiritual/metaphysical connotations: dunn-daari (n) transcendence, and dunndolinde (v) transcend (personal communication, February 8, 2023). Across languages, transcendence means to go beyond or exceed normal boundaries. (Willis, 2022, p. 18)

This undertaking by Willis to demonstrate a transcendent approach to literacy delineates a need for respecting the humanity of each person, provides access to literacy as a human right, acknowledges literacy as a global construct, and produces what she refers to as "authenticated knowledge" (Willis, 2022).

Willis states:

The brief philosophically rich autobiography [of Omar ibn Said] conveys his value systems, ways of knowing, and ways of being, as he wrests power from his enslavers. He declares that he is human – equally human to his enslavers – possessing culture, gender, intellect, language(s), morals, and religion: Defying White supremacy. (Willis, 2022, p. 67)

In this illustration of a transcendent approach to literacy, Willis poignantly illustrates how

writing in Ancient Arabic, [Omar ibn Said] offers a glimpse into his life and uses Qur'anic allusions to shield his understanding about his life in the US ... [and] continues to speak to us, reminding the world that millions of African enslaved people were literate centuries before enslavement: Telling our truth and reclaiming our history and literacy from erasure. (Willis, 2022, p. 67)

It is such an undertaking that this chapter extends, making clear the presence of past literate lives as a foundation for painting the presents and futures of Black peoples across the globe. As I have previously asked: *What happens when the Black Majority World is repeatedly described as illiterate? And how has the idea of a globally illiterate Black population functioned as the basis for relentlessly relegating Blackness as broken, as devalued, as a basis for disregard?* (Smith, 2023a).

Even though Black people in spaces such as the US, Africa, and the Caribbean are often described as illiterate, this depiction is inaccurate as it is often based only on a definition of literacy as defined by Eurocentric norms – norms designed to foster a feigned 'success' steeped in what Dr. Charles Mills has referred to as "European economic domination" (Mills, 1997, p. 31). In other words, this domination has perpetually operated at the foundation of the established structure of white privilege. It is not surprising, then, that these norms were determined not to take into account what Black people often do effectively with literacy every day to flourish. Acknowledging such, it might be surmised, as articulated succinctly in Dr. Eric Williams' *Capitalism and Slavery*, would not have been profitable considering that it was African slavery which "helped to make the industrial revolution possible" (Williams, cited in

Mills, 1997, p. 34). This especially seems to be the case considering the following: Black people worldwide have managed to leverage their unique literate capacities to somehow survive the horrors of slavery, apartheid, and modern-day racism; yet their capacity for using literacies daily based on Afrocentric practice is often significantly overlooked in favor of an emphasis on 'illiteracies' guided by Eurocentric norms. While 'basic' literacy as determined by European norms might indeed be a critical part of any person's individual literate repertoire, there is a fallacy in the insistence that Black peoples are illiterate based on literacy tests designed to further a 'success' steeped in material and economic advantage as part of a global project of white supremacy.

The overlooked capacity of the literacies of Blacks seems to be especially poignant given the return to hate characterizing US 'ground-zero' states such as Florida where a symbolic, and now evolving literal, ban on Blackness accompanies what seems to be a rigid return to Eurocentric colonial norms that appear to threaten democracy even as they tempt the world at large to reimagine a not-too-recent reality governed by centuries of horror cast as a supposed 'benefit of slavery.' Moreover, the prevailing notion of the illiteracy of Black people in countries such as the US continues to be bolstered by the divisive rhetoric of 'African Americans' as underperforming even as Black African and other Black peoples are positioned as *Model Majorities*.

Those who advance this rhetoric are adamant that the illiteracy of Black people, a term often used to characterize populations in the Majority World, is a travesty, and one that must be addressed at all costs. They cite statistics such as those advanced by the 2019 report from the National Center for Education Statistics in the US with data from 2012 and 2014 indicating that 23 percent of Black adults in the country reflect low literacy, compared to 35 percent of white adults and 34 percent of Hispanic adults. And they lament statistics such as those from the US Department of Education, National Assessment of Educational Progress (NAEP), that 84 percent of Black students lack proficiency in mathematics and 85 percent lack proficiency in reading skills. Nuancing this argument, there are those who point out with horror that 72 percent of the world's illiterates are in Africa even while others observe that a 'high literate rate' in the Caribbean has not translated into an educational panacea. Yet, contrary to being "defective in a way that requires external intervention to be redeemed (insofar, that is, as redemption is possible)" (Mills, 1997, p. 42), Black people often know inherently what they are trying to do with languaging as Black individuals use literacies largely based on the impact that they wish to have on their audience. For people racialized as Black who language, the words of Amanda Gorman ring true: "And yet the dawn is ours before we knew it. Somehow we do it" (Gorman, 2021).

As I have shown thus far, there is obsolete futility in attempting to reduce and prescribe Black people's capacity for literacy to reductive and prescriptive notions steeped in what we determine to be 'basic' English literacy. Rather, we must avoid assumptions and seek understandings of Black students' goals for living purposeful literate lives as individuals and in families, communities, and societies, demonstrating to them from the time they enter school, institutions, and society, that they have power to use various syntactic structures across the numerous Englishes, languages, and literacies they possess for desired communication, effect, and impact (Edwards & Smith, 2023; Edwards et al., 2023). At the same time, it must be recognized that the global project of racialization of language has operated in large part to bolster economic gain, requiring at the very core of industrialization a subjugation of the languaging and personhoods of those who have inherently sustained it.

Perhaps, then, I assert at this juncture that the long-standing question isn't *How can we solve illiteracy for Black peoples in particular or for any peoples in general?* when the premise of this challenge is the direct result of a Eurocentrism determined to obliterate peoples through English languaging and literacy for economic advantage. Rather, it becomes: *How do we present a full and accurate portrait of the exceptional literacy of Black peoples – one that recognizes what they can do when preoccupied with an insistence on what they cannot?* (Smith, 2023a). *And how do we disrupt a pursuit of global economic gain that is designed at its core to subjugate based on race while feigning provision of success?* This, I contend, is the impetus for presenting holistic literacies from the lives of Black immigrant people – signaling students' *translanguaging imaginaries of innocence*, not for what is perceived as success but rather, for flourishing.

4 Conceptualizing Translanguaging in Black Immigrant Literacies

Multiliteracies, Raciolinguistics, Language and Raciosemiotic Architecture

> Somehow we've weathered and witnessed
> a nation that isn't broken,
> but simply unfinished.
> We the successors of a country and a time
> where a skinny Black girl
> descended from slaves and raised by a single mother
> can dream of becoming president
> only to find herself reciting for one.
>
> Gorman, 2021

Historicizing Translanguaging and Multiliteracies

Before translanguaging became a concept that the Majority World had to fight for, it was deeply entrenched in our ancestral histories. Even as the fields of literacy, language, TESOL, second language, applied linguistics, and bilingual education wrestle with reclaiming translanguaging as a construct that schools and institutions must acknowledge, billions of people across the world, as they have done for centuries, have daily drawn legitimately from their entire individual linguistic repertoires to make meaning of their life pursuits in the world. To be clear, translanguaging as often espoused in Minority World circles and literature is not new, nor is the notion that people of Color, and all peoples, for centuries, have daily drawn from their holistic linguistic repertoires, despite the need to now reiterate its centrality or the many attempts to reinscribe its legitimacy in schools of the now. In fact, as Willis (2022) implies in her adept historicizing of the life of Omar ibn Said of African descent (see Chapter 3), before the colonizer came and imposed ways of knowing, being, learning to live with, and doing, people translanguaged daily.

This willingness to vaguely acknowledge, while simultaneously rendering into obscurity the historical and largely pervasive and legitimate norms of the Majority World before the European colonizer, has been recently characterized by Pavlenko (2022) as "historic amnesia." Drawing from and illustrating how "the millennia-long history of institutional multilingualism reveals that the claims of the uniqueness of today's 'multilingual challenge' are patently false, deeply ignorant and utterly absurd" and urging an unseeing of multilingualism through the mere "keyhole of the 19th century Western European nation-states, 20th century labor migrations and their 21st century 'superdiverse' outcomes" (Pavlenko, 2022, p. 33), Pavlenko shows just how "the history of multilingualism is often told from the perspective of ideologically monolingual – or bilingual – nation-states because that's where many influential scholars reside" (p. 34). The author assets:

> The Whig history of progress from 'circumstantial' multilingualism of yesteryear to 'superdiversity' of the present-day is a self-serving enterprise that reinforces the established academic hierarchy and allows its adepts to 'defend' and 'celebrate' immigrant multilingualism and to brand their own work as new, superior and distinct (for analysis, see Pavlenko, 2019). The non-history also benefits the field at large by giving it a compelling raison d'être – exceptionality of today's 'multilingual challenge.' (Pavlenko, 2022, p. 34)

Pavlenko's description of this dynamic is very often seen in the use of terminologies such as "translanguaging" and "new literacies," which are brought forward as supposedly novel constructs in their conceptualization and application for the purpose of mainstream Minority World schooling, but which, in practice, as illustrated by scholars such as Alim (2004) and so many others, have long since been leveraged for centuries in the formerly flourishing Indigenous systems and nations of the largely adept multilingual peoples (of Color) of a precolonial Majority World.

Much like translanguaging, the notion of novelty often inadvertently summoned for decades in renderings of 'multiliteracies' (New London Group, 1996) suggests a tendency to suffer from 'historic amnesia' (Pavlenko, 2022) that has obscured the multimodal heritage of our ancestral pasts, creating a supposition that we must "[trace] progress from the rigid national language paradigms [of the past] to the unbridled diversity of our [current] world" (Pavlenko, 2022, p. 5). This historically amnesiac reality has necessitated reminders that notions such as 'new literacies,' 'multiliteracies,' and 'digital literacies' are not new, and thus, only persist as necessary conceptual reinstantiations because of the global project of white supremacy borne along by Eurocentric schooling. This schooling, in turn, perpetuates the need to consider the *re*inscribing of multimodality and its 'new' ways of meaning-making through language and other semiotic tools as ancestral heritages, historically and perpetually offered by Majority World Blacks and other peoples of Color across the globe.

In doing so, the presentation of the lenses of multiliteracies and translanguaging for examining Black immigrant youth discussed in this chapter align with García et al.'s (2021) invitation to reject "abyssal thinking in the language and education of racialized bilinguals" and in turn, highlight how multilingual practices of the Global Majority, for centuries, have relied on meaning-making through multimodality. Working in concert with '*a raciolinguistic perspective*' (Rosa & Flores, 2017) to elucidate the translanguaging and transraciolinguistic practices of Black immigrant youth (Smith, 2020a, 2020b, 2020c, 2022b), these lenses make visible the language and raciosemiotic architecture (Flores, 2020; Smith, 2022d) of these youth as well as the need for reclamation of the long-standing capacity emerging from multimodal assets used globally by youth that are often relegated to obscurity by a project of racialization of language undergirding literacy classrooms.

As alluded to earlier, Willis (2022) has recently described the criticality of acknowledging Black life in precolonial history using the case of and demonstrating in the life of Omar ibn Said. Her notion of "authenticated knowledge" in literacy research (see Chapter 3) must begin again to inform what schools do and how learning occurs in institutions via "transcendent literacy" (Willis, 2022). I concur and assert that centering racialization to resurrect translanguaging and multiliteracies as a thing of the past is critical to acknowledging the historicity of these Majority World constructs in current examinations surrounding the presents of all youth.

Theorizing Multiliteracies, Raciolinguistics, and Translanguaging

Acknowledging the historicizing presented, and as implied thus far, the study undergirding this book is thus broadly situated under the umbrellas of critical literacy (Luke, 2018) and critical applied linguistics (Pennycook, 2001). Critical literacy from its inception has emphasized the ability of students to read both the word and the world (Freire & Macedo, 1987). For critical applied linguists, critical literacy has come to mean recognizing the need to always "question the status of the critical, to open up the debate, and to admit that nothing is certain or safe" (Pennycook, 2001, p. 176). Guided by the question "What is the status of the critical in the concept and the project of 'critical literacy?'" (Lippi-Green, 1997, p. 24), critical literacy for critical applied linguists is concerned with using critical literacy as a mechanism for

> throwing the very project of critical applied linguistics into disarray, or at least into history, because it means now that we can work, strategically, from the outset with a politicized understanding of applied linguistics, with the view that any applied linguistics worth the name (and worth working with and struggling for worth spending time on) ... is always already political and, moreover, an instrument and a resource for change, for challenging and changing the wor(l)d. (Pennycook, 2001, p. 176)

Operating within this broader framework where *raciolinguistic epistemologies* require attention to "When and what is knowledge as defined by people of Color?" (Smith, 2023a), the study documented in this book draws from the intersectional lenses of multiliteracies, raciolinguistics, and translanguaging to examine the literacies of Black immigrant youth. I now discuss the premises for drawing from these lenses as well as present the interrelationships among them.

From Academic and Invisible Literacy to (Multi)literacies

Competing tensions have been known to exist between the autonomous skills-based (i.e., prescriptive) (Paris, 2005) and ideological (i.e., authentic) (Street, 1995) perspectives of literacy. Those who advocate for an autonomous literacy perspective focus largely on foundational skills needed for reading and writing where language is viewed as a system, proficiency is emphasized, and 'constrained' skills valued (Canagarajah, 2006; Paris, 2005). This perspective appears to privilege *academic literacy* – "the ability to communicate competently in an academic discourse community," to read, evaluate information, present, debate, and create knowledge "through both speaking and writing" (Wingate, 2018, p. 350). Through this process, literacies are emphasized that involve "engaging with, producing, and talking about texts that have currency in primary, secondary, and postsecondary education" (Morrell, 2002, p. 72). Despite being characterized as "never anyone's mother tongue, even for the privileged classes," under an autonomous skills-based perspective (Street, 1995), *academic literacy* functions as an expectation for every student within specific academic discourse communities (Wingate, 2015, p. 11).

Such communities in the US, many of which are governed by what Flores (2013) refers to as monoglossic ideology, tend to privilege what is known as academic language – often thought of as specialized "content-specific vocabulary and complex sentence structures" (Flores, 2020). Academic discourse communities also often privilege just one language – English (e.g., Smith, 2016; Wiley, 2014) and have also been shown to prefer just *one* form of standardized English – Standard American English (SAE) – while inadvertently excluding other standardized[2] English linguistic repertoires (e.g., Jamaican Standard English, Trinidadian Standard English) (Smith, 2020b). In doing so, monoglossic ideologies that govern *academic literacy* teaching go against what Dr. Ofelia Garcìa has described as a heteroglossic perspective (Garcìa, 2009) – one that affords students the linguistic flexibility to easily manipulate English dialects (both standardized and non-standardized) as well as their other home languages when they engage in *academic literacy* practices.

The privileging of monoglossic ideology (Wiley, 2014) over the heteroglossic norm (García, 2009) that governs youth's enactments of their literacies within academic discourse communities in the US poses an increasing challenge to evaluating what many perceive as the '*academic literacy success*' of students from a range of diverse populations (Brooks, 2015; Curry, 2004; de los Ríos & Seltzer, 2017; Peercy 2011; Razfar, 2012; Smith, 2016, 2019). As previous research has shown, youth continue to struggle with *academic literacy success* while their invisible literacies (discussed later) remain overlooked as they are sometimes (in)advertently discouraged from leveraging these "funds of knowledge" (Moll et al., 2005; see also Kiramba, 2017) in literacy classrooms. Many of these youth are dialect speakers, English and bilingual learners, or international or immigrant students, and therefore, also find themselves challenged by the monoglossic standardized English norms of academic literacy despite possessing a versatility with language that a heteroglossic norm provides (e.g., Brooks, 2015; Darvin & Norton, 2014; De Costa, 2014; Dyson, 2003; Jiménez et al., 2009; Lam, 2000; McLean, 2010; Nero, 2014; Rubinstein-Ávila, 2007; Skerrett, 2012; Smith, 2016; Watson et al., 2014).

In contrast to academic literacy, those aligned with an ideological notion of literacy believe that literate practice must be situated within its social and cultural contexts to be adequately understood and addressed (Street, 1995). Based on this perspective, certain scholars have repeatedly shown that students' home languages predict as well as operate alongside their academic success and their literacy learning in schools (e.g., August et al., 2009; Bauer et al., 2017; Gort, 2012; Mislevy & Durán, 2014; Siegel, 1997; Sireci & Faulkner-Bond, 2015; Skutnabb-Kangas, 2013; Solano-Flores et al., 2002). In an ideological notion of literacy, students leverage linguistic repertoires with which they are familiar in the home that allow them to be more adept with what Hamel (2006) refers to as *"invisible literacy"* – the informal and functional knowledge and skills put into practice across home and school contexts. Unlike the limitations posed by the monoglossic standardized American English norm underlying academic literacy instruction in schools, the *invisible literacy* practices leveraged by students via an ideological perspective allow them to draw from their home languages and dialects in ways that emphasize a heteroglossic norm (Flores, 2013; García, 2009; Smith, 2016, 2019; see also Ivanic et al., 2009, on *vernacular literacies*). Yet, though critical to students' academic literacy development, it has been shown that limited opportunities are available for youth to draw from their *invisible literacies* (Kiramba, 2017) in schools. Students also often fail to receive sufficient academic literacy support (Lea & Street, 1998) and there is often the understanding that their home languages draw from "non-academic language," which, in comparison to academic language, is "less specialized and less complex" (Flores, 2020, p. 23).

Discrepancies resulting from long-standing tensions between autonomous and ideological perspectives of literacy often position the literacies of youth in ways that either emphasize the "funds of knowledge" they bring from the home (i.e., ideological) or their literate performance on standardized literacy assessments (i.e., autonomous). For Black immigrants who are typically regarded as "model minority" youth, these tensions seem even more visible when their *academic language* and literacy practices are thought to be privileged and their *invisible literacies* and *home languages* overlooked. While standardized literacy assessments that draw from supposed academic language and literacies are thought to all too often reflect standardized language norms privileged by schools (i.e., autonomous) (Canagarajah, 2006), Flores (2020) has recently observed that if students are perceived as language architects who "manipulate language for specific purposes" (p. 25), the tensions that persist regarding their academic and home languages can be reconciled.

I assert that such reconciliation is possible also across *academic* and *invisible literacies* when students are considered as having the capacity to make decisions about language use and make meaning with text or signs based on context. Like Flores (2020), I agree that it is possible for students' supposed unfamiliarity with the norms of school texts to be simply one with which they must be taught to bring their "already-present literacies" (Watson, 2018) to bear in school contexts. Considering Black immigrant *new model minority* youth as language architects frames students as "already understanding the relationship between language choice and meaning through the knowledge that they have gained via socialization into the cultural and linguistic practices of their communities" (p. 4). In other words, such a perspective repositions Black immigrant youth's *academic success* as their learned ability to use language architecting already deployed in the home in ways that allow them to navigate (un)familiar expectations of school. From this perspective, the focus of research is therefore not to determine if and how Black immigrant youth possess *academic* literacies that are more pronounced than their *invisible* literacies. Rather, research can instead consider how they effectively leverage their holistic literate repertoire across home and school contexts in ways that meet demands across these contexts. This proposition is not new. In fact, it is aligned with Rampton's (1985) historical critique of "the putative home/school language divide" (p. 188) presented in discussions of British Asian speakers of English, which challenged the misguided notion that students largely spoke English at school while they primarily used their mother tongue at home.

Such an approach to researching youth's literacies is consistent with the notion of multiliteracies, which presumes that "metalanguages [are used] to describe and interpret the design elements of different modes of meaning" (New London Group, 1996, p. 83). Through these modes of meaning-making – tactile, gestural, spatial, visual, written, audio, linguistic, and synesthesia – youth negotiate a range of discourses by integrating "a variety of texts forms associated with information and multimedia technologies" (Kalantzis & Cope, 2012; New London Group, 1996, p. 61). Often used interchangeably with the term "new literacies," the notion of multiliteracies presumes that learners use a variety of techniques in various forms to infer meaning, such as leveraging various semiotic resources to obtain information. These techniques may include text messages, blogging, social networking websites, and listening to or reading information from electronic devices (Moss & Lapp, 2010). Transcending the dichotomies inherent in an *'invisible-academic literacies'* dynamic for Black immigrant youth cast as a "new model minority," the conception of multiliteracies allows for a holistic view of student literacy practices – *'holistic literacies'* (Smith, 2023a).

This holistic view is visible in scholarship that has advanced notions of "transliteracies" which reflects how writing as well as other modes of literacy are used by bi/multilingual students to determine when and where they might use certain codes (Orellana, 2015). For Orellana, the concept of "transliteracies" refers to literacy practices that cut across modalities and languages. She has illustrated, in her scholarship, how multilingual youth transitioned across languages and literacies, reflecting opportunities to demonstrate a richness of metalinguistic awareness, much like Jaeda (discussed in Chapter 3) did with metalinguistic understanding in her contestation of raciolinguistic ideologies as a Black Caribbean immigrant and transnational youth (Smith, 2019a). This holistic view is also explored in how youth's multiliterate practices evolve as a function of space and place invoked through their writing, the social and physical setting of a music school, and the locale of a city (Watson & Beymer, 2019), elucidating how youth's multiliteracies as social practice, via "praisesongs of place," are used to construct tributes to their city and represent community strengths. It is visible also in the recent research on Black Caribbean immigrant youth which acknowledges how multimodal and digital literacies intersect with students' racial identities to reflect tensions in how they grapple with the racialized category "Black" as they negotiate their identities (McLean, 2020). McLean (2020) describes how, in the case of Black Caribbean immigrant youth, part of this newcomer experience involves negotiating what "race" and "blackness" mean in terms of their academic, social, and personal lives. These negotiations occur often as an evolving process that functions very differently for each Black immigrant youth and child.

Monoglossia, Heteroglossia, and Raciolinguistics

Black immigrant youth – perceived as a *new model minority* primarily originating from Africa and the Caribbean – often possess linguistic repertoires that can be standardized or non-standardized, and are based on a *heteroglossic language perspective*, one that views multilingualism (instead of monolingualism) as the norm (i.e., ideological) (García, 2009). As discussed earlier, despite this language variation, academic institutions often sanction what is regarded as the prescriptive academic literacy of these youth as the basis for *success*. This focus, in turn, often privileges hegemonic language practices based on *monoglossic language ideology* (García, 2009) in US schools that favor "standard" over "non-standard," "native" over "non-native," and "official" over "unofficial" languages (Shohamy, 2006, p. 2). It also reinforces translingual discrimination where inequalities based on transnational migrants' specific linguistic and communicative repertoires are (il)legitimized by national norms (Steele et al., 2022). Flores (2020) has shown that the privileging of hegemonic practices is visible in the dichotomies created and maintained between a supposed academic vs. non-academic language distinction premised on "monoglossic and raciolinguistic ideolog[ies] that frames the home language practices of racialized communities as inherently deficient" (Flores, 2020, p. 24; Flores & Rosa, 2015; Rosa, 2016). Such ways of thinking – raciolinguistic ideologies – operate such that they cause the "linguistic practices of racialized populations [to be] systematically stigmatized regardless of the extent to which these practices might seem to correspond to standardized norms" (Rosa & Flores, 2017, p. 3).

Joining long-standing debates about linguistic discrimination (e.g., Labov, 1969; Rickford, 2006; Rickford & Rickford, 1995; Siegel, 2012; Skutnabb-Kangas, 1988; Smitherman, 1977; Thompson et al., 2011), politics (e.g., Willis & Harris, 2000), and race (e.g., Willis, 2002), much of which are informed by Critical Race Theory (Cabrera, 2018), Rosa (2016) has described how raciolinguistic ideologies influence negative ways of thinking developed about, and by, language users, many of whom are *new model minority* Black immigrant youth who leverage standardized and non-standardized Englishes. He explains that a *monoglossic language ideology* which privileges "dominant white perspectives on the linguistic and cultural practices of racialized communities" (Rosa, 2016, pp. 150–151) is leveraged in ways that cause racialized populations, many of whom are Black and Latino, to feel inferior and illegitimate even when they try to approximate standardized linguistic (and English) practices. What is not acknowledged, however, is that this appropriation of imagined (or idealized), as well as actualized linguistic practices by racial populations based on a supposed standard English that is premised on a monoglossic language ideology, does not constitute the sole basis used by others to determine the advancement of racial groups in our dominant system.

From the perspective of raciolinguistic ideology, the focus is on the white listener, how the language used by the racialized student is interpreted or heard by the white listening subject who "hears," "interprets" from the dominant standardized English perspective (Flores & Rosa, 2015) – performing what I describe as the *"white audit"* (see also Ramjattan, 2019, 2023). Flores and Rosa (2015) observe that raciolinguistic ideology represents the privileging of "dominant white perspectives" (pp. 150–151), invoking the "white gaze" (Morrison, 2020; in the context of this work, *white audit*). This positioning (see Smith, 2019a), in turn, is used to construct racialized populations such as Latinos and Blacks in ways that are inferior and illegitimate, *regardless* of whether they use or attempt to use standardized linguistic (and English) practices. Challenging the notion that youth of Color (e.g., "new model minority" Black immigrant youth) can make progress or show "literate success" in an academic system where they *adequately* appropriate standardized language practices, Rosa (2016) asserts that a raciolinguistic perspective is critical if we are to dismantle the meritocratic myth that "access to [linguistic] codes of power and the ability to use these codes will somehow enable racialized populations to overcome the white supremacy that permeates U.S. society" (p. 166).

A raciolinguistic perspective, functioning as a response to raciolinguistic ideology, shows how foundational forms of governance in society have co-naturalized discourses of race and language to negatively represent the literate abilities of racialized populations (Rosa & Flores, 2017; see Smith, 2019a, 2020b; Smith et al., 2022, for applications of the construct). Through this process, historical and contemporary societal forms of governance use ways of thinking steeped in the link between race and language to inform who benefits from academic systems of schooling. From this perspective, conceptions of Englishes – whether World, Caribbean, or West African – do not operate in a vacuum independent of the racial categorization of their speakers. Flores and Rosa (2015), in their description of how such ideologies affect perceptions of those who use these Englishes (as is the case with African American English speakers), explain that Standard English is incorrectly perceived as an "objective linguistic category" such that when it is spoken by various racial populations, it naturally affords them access to mainstream educational opportunities and the advantages that its curriculum provides. For the Black immigrants in this study, white supremacy is thus entailed in their leveraging of Standard English, which is bolstered by the "white gaze" – or more applicably, *white audit*. Specifically, Black immigrant youth's reading of the world becomes framed by hegemonic whiteness, "the systemic and cultural means by which White supremacy is continually reproduced" (Cabrera, 2018). In such a dynamic, "cultural and discursive practices ... serve to naturalize unequal social relations along the color line" functioning in a "superstructure of White supremacy" that attributes value to whiteness "as a privileged, dominant, and frequently invisible social identity" (Cabrera, 2018, p. 223; see also Braden, 2020). As Black youth leverage their Englishes, as immigrants, they are forced to reconcile with expectations of white supremacy for these Englishes. Though seemingly invisible but nonetheless covertly present in their home countries, these expectations regarding Englishes for Black immigrant youth become clearly enacted through the white gaze and *white audit*, as race joins immigration at the table of hegemonic whiteness in the US.

Elements established as central to a raciolinguistic perspective are "(i) historical and contemporary co-naturalizations of race and language as part of the colonial formation of modernity; (ii) perceptions of racial and linguistic difference; (iii) regimentations of racial and linguistic categories; (iv) racial and linguistic intersections and assemblages; and (v) the contestation of racial and linguistic power formations" (Rosa & Flores, 2017, p. 3). The *first* element emphasizes the focus on colonial histories, highlighting the ways in which projected European subjects and the languages of these subjects have been deemed superior to racialized non-European 'objects' and to the linguistic repertoires developed by these objects. The *second* element focuses on the ways that perceptions of racialized language derive from the privileging of white listeners as superior, both at the individual as well as organizational and institutional levels, resulting in practices such as linguistic profiling. The *third* element highlights how relationships are developed between linguistic and racial forms – "twining" – such that together, they hold certain cultural values. The *fourth* component notes the significance of centralizing race as a unit of analysis beyond the US context and as equally important as constructs such as class, gender, ethnicity in examinations of the co-naturalization of race and language for furthering research on intersectionality. The *fifth* component reiterates the need to shift the focus away from how racialized populations modify their linguistic practices and instead to equally identify the ways in which dominant white perspectives are complicit in reifying colonial practices that use co-naturalization of race and language to dominate academic and other institutions.

The concept of raciolinguistics has been outlined and taken up in research within and beyond the US across examinations such as those represented in Alim and Smitherman (2020). In these explorations, researchers have used the notion of raciolinguistics, for instance, to examine constructs such as how "mixed race" and "mixed language" function in the context of the imperial, observing the importance of distinguishing the tendency to focus on the "who" and "what" of "mixedness" to how judgments are made about these persons in the colonial enterprise via paradigms of mixedness described as immiscibility, absorption, blend, and end (Reyes, 2020). Another such examination, conducted in the Caribbean context of Cuba, illustrates how the time-spaces of coloniality – "chronotopes" – reproduce racial orders in spaces designated as "postcolonial", through the functions of racing bodies and performances via semiotics in ways that can often preserve or erase these racializing signs as highlighted in the Africanization embedded in Cuban religion and folklore (Wirtz, 2020). Others have explored how raciolinguistics works in discursive practice to reinforce immigration violations as illegal via the racializing notion of "immigrant illegality" – a construct which creates perceptions of fear in relation to undocumented migrants by connecting the notion of an "illegal alien" with people who are largely Mexican and Central American, who come from the south of the US border (Dick, 2020), and which has significant implications for racialization of Black documented and undocumented immigrants in the US (Sheares, 2022). This reality is made visible in the fact that Black non-citizens in the US account for 20 percent of those facing deportation on criminal grounds even though only 7 percent of non-citizens in the US are Black (Raff, 2017), and that deportation rates for criminal grounds in 2013 was 76 percent for Black immigrants compared with 45 percent overall (Morgan-Trostle & Zheng, 2016).

Raciolinguistics as taken up in Black immigration has been used to explain notions of racial becoming where immigrants "become Black" (Ibrahim, 2019). Ibrahim explains that this process occurs as immigrants who migrate to North America or to Canada engage with Blackness as a product of its multicultural, multiethnic, and multilingual characterizations, which raises questions in their minds about how their Blackness fits into the broader context of North American Blackness. In considering immigration as a function of Blackness, Alim (2020) has proposed also the idea of transracialization based on analyses of Barack Obama's discursive moves and an autoethnography of his own raciolinguistic practices. Alim describes transracialization as a process where racial identities shift across contexts and during specific interactions and argues for the notion of the "transracial subject" to "transgress" how border crossing is steeped in ways of being that define what it means to "race" personhood. Much like Freire (1970/2000) calls for transcending of the long-held oppressor vs. oppressed dynamic and invokes imaginaries that signal the emergence of "a new being" who is "no longer oppressor" nor "oppressed" (p. 1), and Willis (2022) calls for transcendent literacy as a return to inscribing the literate humanities of people of Color pre-white gaze – representations of precolonial culture that colonialism wished to destroy (Fanon, 1988, p. 31) – even while acknowledging racialization as the basis for this, Alim guards against a call for discarding race as it is known and instead proposes "transracial politics" which simultaneously requires a subversion of racial categorization while maintaining it (Alim, 2016). In doing so, becoming raced as Black immigrants in the US makes visible how the sense of self undergoes perpetual construction in a dialogue that remains always subjected to power relations, implicit or explicit (Du Bois, 1903/1999).

Emerging through thinking with the notion of transracialization as a construct of raciolinguistics and based on the notion of transdisciplinarity as steeped in quantum physics is "a transraciolinguistic approach" (Smith, 2013, 2019a). The prefix "trans-" refers to that which is simultaneously "between," "across," and "beyond" (see Nicolescu, 2010, and Smith, 2013a, on transdisciplinarity for multicultural education). Taken together, "trans-" and "raciolinguistics" is therefore "transraciolinguistics." As the above implies,

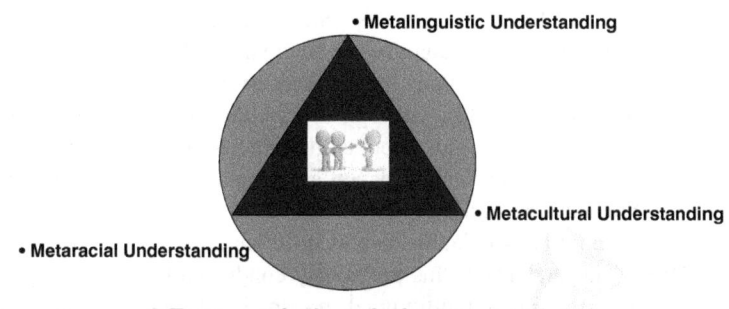

- Metalinguistic Understanding
- Metacultural Understanding
- Metaracial Understanding

A Transraciolinguistic Approach

Figure 4.1 A transraciolinguistic approach
Source: Central illustration courtesy of AlexanderMas/Stock/Getty Images Plus

transraciolinguistics represents what is simultaneously between, across, and beyond various representations of raciolinguistics. A transraciolinguistic approach emerged from a previously conducted research study, which focused on the language, culture/ethnicity, and race of Black Caribbean immigrant and transnational youth (Smith, 2019a). The youth used language differently in what was experienced as the novel culture of the US after migrating from their home countries and as they navigated differences in their interactions with others (Smith, 2019a).

Reflecting a transraciolinguistic approach, the Black Caribbean immigrant students simultaneously engaged in thinking about their thinking about race (i.e., metaracial), thinking about their thinking about culture (i.e., metacultural), and thinking about their thinking about language (i.e., metalinguistic) in their interrelationships with diverse others (Smith, 2019a). The students used "metalinguistic, metaracial, and metacultural understanding of their experiences with race and language, and by extension, culture [ethnicity], to determine how to function effectively within non/academic settings in ways that did not completely sacrifice" who they were as persons (i.e., personhood, Cowley, 2017; see also Smith, 2019a) (see Figure 4.1 for an illustration of a transraciolinguistic approach).

Through metaracial understanding, the students thought about their thoughts about race including how "Englishes" (i.e., more than one English) (Kachru, 1992) and other languages "are racialized and largely socially constituted" (Smith, 2020a, p. 139; Martinot, 2003). Through metalinguistic understanding, they thought about their thoughts about language (see Herdina & Jessner, 2002; Zaidi, 2021), becoming aware of and controlling linguistic elements that they used, including how and why they flexibly chose Englishes and other languages for different purposes (Smith, 2020a). They also engaged in meaning-making as they analyzed individual words and phrases of language that helped to "intensify their literacy acquisition and enrich their experience [s]" (Zaidi, 2021, p. 282). Through metacultural understanding, the students thought about their thoughts about culture, including acknowledging how race and Englishes or other languages are associated with certain cultural ways of being. Metacultural understanding enabled the students to recognize how to transcend cultural associations across different contexts (see Sharifian, 2013).

One of the students in this previously conducted research study was Jaeda (pseudonym), a Black multilingual, transnational (and later, immigrant) student of Jamaican heritage. Like her Black multilingual Caribbean immigrant peers, Jaeda felt comfortable sharing with me – a Black Caribbean immigrant single-parent-scholar-mother-educator and former teacher –her experiences as we interacted over time during my engagement with the students as an advisor for their Caribbean organization (see Chapter 3 and Smith, 2022b, for details of the study). A transraciolinguistic approach was visible as Jaeda reflected metalinguistic understanding. She did so by refusing to let her language, including Englishes, be labeled as inferior or illegitimate because of how others caused her to feel about her use of Englishes (see Smith, 2019a).

Jaeda also reflected metaracial understanding as she realized that being Black as an African, being Black as an American, and being Black as a Caribbean person meant different things to different people in the US (i.e., metaracial understanding). And she reflected metacultural understanding as she recognized how the cultures of the Caribbean and the US had different expectations regarding how race and language worked together for her as an immigrant Black person. This caused her to go beyond the limitations of others' negative constructions of her based on intersections between her Englishes and race to develop a sense of agency with these Englishes in literate practice (Smith, 2019a; see also Smith, 2020a). In doing so, Jaeda recognized and changed her ways of using various Englishes across boundaries to meet demands across different contexts.

Figure 4.1, which illustrates a transraciolinguistic approach, presents two individuals on the left and one individual on the right. The two individuals on the left physically represent racialized students of Color who use metalinguistic, metaracial, and metacultural understanding to navigate literate practices in their interactions with others in the context of institutionally and societally imposed realities. They also symbolically represent the racialized linguistic and broader semiotic resources that are entangled with or operate beyond these students as a function of the institutional and societal contexts in which they exist and which may position students along an inferior-superior spectrum. Similarly, the individual on the right represents a student from the dominant group (racialized as white or otherwise) who is also able to adopt and leverage such understandings with racialized students while affected by institutional expectations. This individual also symbolically represents the linguistic and broader semiotic resources that are entangled with or operate beyond them as a function of the context in which they exist and which may position the student along an inferior-superior spectrum. The permeable equilateral triangle aptly denotes the transraciolinguistic space where students simultaneously use these three forms of understanding (i.e., metalinguistic, metaracial, metacultural) in interaction with each other and are impacted by institutionally informed realities. The broad permeable circle within which the triangle is located acknowledges that other forms of understanding (i.e., metagendered, metareligious, metaeconomic) exist across institutions and the society that influence how racialized and non-racialized students together make meaning through their many interactions with text and with the world.

In acknowledging what Bhabha (1994) describes as "interstices" – the imposition of neither here nor there that characterizes margins or demarcations between spaces – which are made sustainable through the crossing of borders as well as the interactions and contestations that accompany these, transraciolinguistics instantiates a deviation from focusing merely on persons per se as highlighted by a raciolinguistic perspective (Rosa & Flores, 2017), and signals, in part, attention to how 'third space' begets relationships between and among (non-)racialized people and systems in ways that allow students to flourish or their personhoods to perish. In doing so, a transraciolinguistic approach suggests that dismantling the binaries of power as intentionally sought through conceptions such as "third space" (Soja, 1996) requires at its core a naming of race as *the* central source of power imbalance systematically undergirding a myriad of structures, normative expectations, and institutions across the global landscape (see Alim 2004, 2016; see also Rosa & Flores, 2017).

Contrary to the supposedly hierarchically neutral imaginary invoked by "third space" where "first" and "second" spaces are viewed as sites of ongoing contestation, but also acknowledging the permeable borders or interstices that exist and where differences undergo consistent deconstruction and reconstruction that it evokes, transraciolinguistics seeks not only to redefine "third space" (Soja, 1996) as a transcending of binaries through the merging of dichotomies but to also intentionally locate named binaries in conversation with each other across multiple levels of reality (Smith, 2013a). Transraciolinguistics seeks to do so by naming *race* as the undergirding impetus for mediating binary crossings of third space. In this process, transraciolinguistics predisposes a conversation around dichotomies as a spatial imaginary primarily functioning *between and among* (and not merely within) people and systems and capable of operating on multiple levels of reality (Smith, 2013; Smith et al., 2017). In turn, it leads to a consistent questioning of the degree to which white supremacy and the privileging of Eurocentric norms sit quite often at the table of third space. Transraciolinguistics thus invokes but also extends beyond the Du Boisian notion of double consciousness that positions the fate of American consciousness as dependent on the evolving relationships and dialogue emerging across subjectivities of the minority and where two separate but intertwined forms of consciousness exist, and thus, moves beyond the Hegelian notion of the master-slave dialectic (Du Bois, 1903/1999).

Translanguaging and Transsemiotizing with Englishes

Considering the argument to engage yet transcend racialized positioning and to also extend beyond dichotomies surrounding the academic and invisible literacy practices of Black immigrant youth, translanguaging via a multiliteracies approach, when recognized as a long-standing inheritance of the Majority World, can be crucial to understanding how these youth engage daily in literacy practices based on the Englishes and broader semiotic resources that they possess (Smith, 2020b).

The research on translanguaging to date represents debate with regards to its conceptualization as an ideological and practical construct (e.g., García & Kleyn, 2016; King, 2015; MacSwan, 2017; Poza, 2017). In the work of García and Kleyn (2016), translanguaging de-emphasizes the monolingual norms inherent in an additive notion of language learning that focuses on a number of linguistic systems operating concurrently with each other. From the perspective of García and Kleyn (2016), translanguaging has instead emphasized the bilingual or multilingual speaker as possessing one composite, individual language created from the intersecting cognitive and linguistic interactions within the speaker in a given moment. This leads to what García and Kleyn (2016) have described as "one linguistic and cognitive behavior" (p. 13). In this approach, named languages are regarded as socially constructed and are therefore said to have no linguistic reality, creating multilingual language practices and multilingual identities that are part of a dynamic process (García & Kleyn, 2016). The speaker (and not society) possesses the power to consistently make decisions about how to leverage linguistic and other multimodal resources for transformation (Kleyn & García, 2019). In this perspective, the use of such resources is misaligned (more often than not) with the structural realities and abstract confines of societally determined idealistic named languages (Kleyn & García, 2019).

A partially contrasting view presents a multilingual perspective of translanguaging via an "integrated model of multilingualism" based on the assertion that individuals each reflect varied mental grammars in the shared "idealized" languages that they leverage *even while also* drawing from a linguistic repertoire that is authentically unique to the individual (MacSwan, 2017). This view stems from (a) the notion that there are structural variations of language that are external to the individual and are based on rules of grammar reflected by many who speak what is societally referred to as a language (i.e., E-language), which leads speakers of multiple languages or language registers to adhere to certain structural rules of the grammars of each language that they possess; and (b) the indication that any individual who leverages multiple languages, or dialects, or even just variations of language in general (i.e., monolinguals) develops from birth a unique way of using language – linguistic repertoire – given the social environment in which he or she functions (i.e., I-language), which leads speakers of any language (monolingual or multilingual) to use language socially based on this distinct repertoire (MacSwan, 2017).

Though reflecting contrasting views, in part, translanguaging as conceived by MacSwan (2017) functions similarly to García and Kleyn's (2016) notion on the basis that individuals do have a unitary linguistic repertoire that is based on their actual I-language (and not an idealized) use of language. Where MacSwan (2017) deviates from the approach put forward by García and Kleyn (2016) is on the notion that (a) linguistic repertoires functioning at the internal level differ significantly from the mental grammars functioning at the external level that govern the language use of a bilingual/multilinguals/monolinguals; and that (b) this differentiated and shared grammatical structure used to govern language (i.e., E-languages) cannot therefore be unitary. Cowley (2017) agrees that such external structures do exist and are particularly useful for analysis of language but maintains that they are less emphasized in the notion of languaging, from which translanguaging is derived. Thus, while translanguaging for García and Kleyn (2016), as well as colleagues (e.g., Otheguy et al., 2015), represents a unitary language system from which bilinguals draw their uses of language in ways that do not reflect differentiated linguistic or cognitive behaviors, for MacSwan (2017), this unitary system functions at the level of I-languages where the user engages in languaging in ways that align with the individual's linguistic repertoires (I-languages). In turn, MacSwan asserts, I-languages (or an individual linguistic repertoire) cannot exist in the absence of E-languages where the user knowingly or unknowingly draws from specific and shared linguistic grammars that align with the languaging process in action.

Put simply, MacSwan (2017) argues that in the absence of E-languages, despite their abstract and idealized nature, long-standing attempts to justify the notion of individual linguistic repertoires (I-languages), which present a contrast to structural systems (E-languages) that have and do continue to influence how students deploy grammatical structures of named languages, are all futile. Extending beyond this argument, King (2017) asserts that a theoretical vs. practical distinction should determine how translanguaging is considered. He notes, in line with Cowley (2017) and MacSwan (2017), that theoretical and research examinations of translanguaging are possible only when E-languages are considered to be a part of what multilingual students do.

Nonetheless, King also observes that in practical settings such as the classroom, school, and society where teachers and students engage in discourse, it is best to adopt a notion of I-languages where all interlocutors draw from their individual linguistic repertoires. The ideological (i.e., social and political) vs. practical (i.e., structural/grammatical) distinctions presented here regarding translanguaging suggest that it provides an opportunity to consider an individual's uses of I-languages (ideologically) *and* E-languages (structurally) regardless of the (lack or presence of) variation within language presented by individual speakers. Ideologically speaking, therefore, and in keeping with García and Kleyn (2016), translanguaging affords a lens to consider how individuals' leverage I-languages (MacSwan, 2017) as speakers operating across contested political, racial, and social contexts where colonization and stigmatization of language influence a speaker's decisions about language use.

For instance, through translanguaging theory, we can examine an African American Language (AAL) speaker who draws from his or her linguistic repertoire (which may include gesture, humor, dress, posture, etc.) to make choices about vernacular uses of English and standardized approximations of Englishes while she engages in translanguaging practices in much the same way as a speaker would with the standardized languages, Spanish and English. And based on the foregoing assertions, we can also explore an American monolingual speaker of English who draws from his or her linguistic repertoire (which again may include gesture, humor, dress, posture, etc.) to make choices about how they will use variations of the English language in a board meeting vs. a sports bar, or who might intermingle variations of language from their linguistic repertoires in either setting. We might also examine how a Kenyan speaker of Swahili draws from their dialects of English while using both Swahili and an approximation of standardized English (which may include gesture, humor, dress, posture, etc.) in a fifth grade classroom. By the same token, from a structural perspective, it is possible to consider how a speaker translanguages as they draw from discrete mental grammars (i.e., E-languages) (MacSwan, 2017) of their standardized and non-standardized Englishes controlled as bilinguals/multilinguals or as "monolinguals" to make choices about the use of these grammars based on the needs of varied contexts. These indications allow for a consideration also of E-semiotics and I-semiotics, mirroring the E-language and I-language distinctions presented.

In light of the above, for the purpose of clarifying Black immigrant literacies while also foregrounding race and racialized languaging, and considering the capacity to transcend it, the ideological perspectives of translanguaging and transsemiotics can serve as a concrete base. Specifically, by way of its focus on I-languages (MacSwan, 2017) (i.e., individual linguistic repertoires: García & Kleyn, 2016; MacSwan, 2017) and I-semiotics, translanguaging allows for the examination of Black immigrant uses of Englishes and semiotics in ways that ideologically reflect notions of being Black, being immigrant, and engaging in racialized languaging and semiotizing. Not only can this application be useful for providing clarification about such users' literacies, but it also proves to be critical as a means of extending conceptions of literacy to include racialized immigrants' literate practice. Such an approach further highlights how theories of translanguaging and transsemiotizing might be extended conceptually with regards to what this notion means for racialized users of language who enact literacies.

Beyond this, the simultaneous focus on E-languages (MacSwan, 2017) afforded by translanguaging and transsemiotizing allows for the examination of shared elements of grammatical structure for various named standardized enactments of the English language (e.g., Trinidadian Standard English) and for its non-standardized uses (e.g., Jamaican Creole English) as well as for E-semiotics. This examination can facilitate an understanding of users' "E-languaging" (*my modification*) and E-semiotics as mediated by their distinct and unique "I-languaging" (*my modification*) and I-semiotizing during their enactment of literacy practices. Such understandings can in turn be particularly useful for clarifying how literacies emerge based on the Englishes of Black immigrant youth, and specifically those coming from predominantly English spaces such as the English-speaking Caribbean. Such clarifications are critical given the newly ascribed status of these youth as *Black* (i.e., racialization), their newly imposed status as "aliens," "resident aliens," or "non-resident aliens" (i.e., the terminology ascribed to *immigrants* to the US), and their immediate categorization as *racialized users* of English whose status as "native-speaking" English speaker is questioned for the first time.

As individuals migrating from English-speaking territories in the Caribbean who initially "become" but also continue to engage in a process of "becoming Black" (Ibrahim, 2019; see Smith et al., 2022) while using literacy in the context of the US, translanguaging via this lens provides an opportunity to consider what happens when Black immigrant youth draw from their *individual linguistic and semiotic repertoires* (i.e., through I-languaging and I-semiotics) to use literacy in a novel context where race and the color of the Black body are foregrounded as opposed to the original context of 'home' in the English-speaking Caribbean where a majority of the population are often people of Color.

This opportunity through translanguaging and transsemiotics is especially critical given that the linguistic repertoires of such Black immigrant youth reflect nuances that, as indicated earlier, can help to understand shifts in race, immigration, and status as speakers of Englishes. As previous research has shown, in the US (and elsewhere), many Black immigrants are for the first time exposed to being overtly described as Black (Ibrahim, 2019; Nero, 2006; Smith, 2019a). Being Black while drawing from linguistic repertoires that reflect intralinguistic variation – between and across named standardized and non-standardized Englishes operating as part of English-speaking students' linguistic repertoires (Smith, 2018) – often creates a situation where the "linguistic practices of racialized populations are systematically stigmatized regardless of the extent to which these practices might seem to correspond to standardized norms" (Rosa & Flores, 2017, p. 3). Such racialized functioning of Englishes, based on raciolinguistic and broader raciosemiotic ideologies that privilege a dominant white perspective as the legitimate basis from which to judge the linguistic practices of racialized communities (Flores & Rosa, 2015), is one with which Black immigrants are also asked to wrestle as they function as language architects (Flores, 2020) of their Englishes to leverage literacy practices given the predominantly English-speaking context from which they come.

In other words, while grappling with the identity shift around being Black and "becoming Black," such immigrants from English-speaking contexts are also faced with challenges while drawing from linguistic repertoires where their status as legitimate speakers of English is challenged (Nero, 2006; Smith, 2018, 2019). This directly influences what they do with literacy and how they rethink its use. Beyond this, as individuals who are also acquiring an "alien" (i.e., immigrant) status as Black speakers of Englishes in the US and whose role as language architects of their Englishes and enactment of their literacies is further impacted by becoming "immigrant," they must also attend to the varied ways in which they enact their literacies (gesturally, through clothing, via humor, and otherwise). Such attention is critical as they determine how to thrive in a system and increasingly politicized context steeped in raciolinguistic ideology (Rosa & Flores, 2017) where being immigrant and Black, using racialized Englishes, and speaking with what is regarded as a foreign English accent are in constant opposition to the deployment of their unique and individual linguistic repertoires. But it is also crucial if institutions and society are to consider how to adjust expectations and norms that reduce the burdens imposed based on these tensions.

So what does it look like for researchers to foreground race when using translanguaging and transsemiotizing as a lens for studying the multiliteracies of Black immigrant youth? In transcending the ensuing dichotomous tensions that persist both with regards to translanguaging for Black understanding immigrant literacies, I adopt a "both-and" approach (Smith, 2016, 2023a), drawing from the far-reaching and transformative contributions of Paulo Freire in *Pedagogy of the Oppressed* (Freire, 1970/ 2000), which has long since called for a transcending of the prevailing and persistent historically determined oppressor vs. oppressed dynamic (Freire, 1970/ 2000, p. 1). This approach is partially aligned with García and Kleyn (2016) and emphasizes the notion of individual linguistic repertoires from which youth draw as they engage in translanguaging. Yet, given the inescapable tensions within which people function as they draw from these repertoires while navigating a world where systems continue to be imposed via named languages, I am also cognizant of the value of a translanguaging model such as that presented by MacSwan (2017). A "both-and" approach to translanguaging and transsemiotics is also steeped in transracialization as offered by Alim (2016), which allows for situating examinations of (Black immigrant) youth's translanguaging and transsemiotizing practices in their realistic and contested racialized contexts even while seeking to *also* understand how institutions foster their agency and support a design of their futures through mediating, engaging, processing, and negotiating tensions in their literacies as a function of, yet beyond, race. The allowance of a "both-and" approach for "a new being" to emerge through historical shackles and the dialectic, neither as oppressor nor oppressed (Freire, 1970/ 2000), functions as the basis for ensuing liberatory imaginaries of innocence via languaging of personhoods.

Ideologically, based on this premise, and using the intersecting lenses presented, I intended to examine how students engage tensions created between their unique individual linguistic repertoires *and the imposition of* external, abstract, and idealized systems during the process of translanguaging and transsemiotizing. As a researcher seeking to examine Black immigrant literacies through translanguaging and transsemiotizing while foregrounding race, the following elements steeped in I-languaging and I-semiotics, that is, deployment of standardized and non-standardized Englishes and other semiotic resources represented in tandem with linguistic repertoires of Black youth across contexts, allowed for consideration of the following: (a) the ways in which Black immigrant youth draw from and alternate their uses of multiple Englishes when the Englishes deployed (verbally, gesturally, in writing, through humor, etc.) are racialized; (b) what Black immigrant youth say about their choices regarding how multiple Englishes are leveraged (verbally, gesturally, in writing, through humor, etc.) when asked about racialized language; and (c) how Black immigrant youth's literacies reflect their choices to manipulate multiple Englishes (verbally, gesturally, in writing, through humor, etc.) across racialized contexts.

And structurally, as a researcher working to examine Black immigrant literacies through translanguaging while centralizing race, the following elements steeped in E-languaging and E-semiotics, that is, deploying shared mental grammars reflected in the standardized and non-standardized Englishes and semiotics represented by Black youth across contexts, allowed for consideration of the following: (a) the ways in which Black immigrant youth who orally or verbally produce a sentence such as the following with varied named Englishes reflect grammatical structures of multiple Englishes: *What me did tell she when me say not to go by da sea was that she would get hurt if she did*, pointing to how the student and institution engage agentively together around such structures that racialize youth's Englishes (verbally, gesturally, in writing, through humor, etc.) as Black immigrant youth; (b) the ways in which Black immigrant youth who reflect varied Englishes and their phonologies (verbally, gesturally, in writing, through humor, etc.) respond when such structures are racialized by others with whom they interact; and (c) the ways in which Black immigrant youth's literacies reflect decisions to alternate their uses of grammatical structures and phonologies (verbally, gesturally, in writing, through humor, etc.) based on the racialized and non-racialized contexts across which they function.

Attending to how racialization impacts the multiple modalities that students of Color leverage, this dynamic extends the notion of "language architecture" as proposed by Flores (2019) to illustrate how semiotics and multimodality are mediated by power relations, many of which are premised on the racialized structures that are encoded in what it means to make meaning with texts that are often non-linguistic in nature. Students functioning as *"raciosemiotic architects"* "manipulat[e multiple modes] for specific purposes" (Flores, 2020, p. 25) while engaging racialization based on how they understand choice and meaning of multiple modalities to be related given their socialization into cultural, linguistic, and racial community practices– thus "raciosemiotic architecture" (see Smith, 2022d). Through raciosemiotic architecture there are opportunities for engaging students' multiple modes of meaning-making for particular purposes while centering the often-invisible racialization of these modes based on how students make meaning through multiple modalities across cultural, linguistic, and racial communities (Smith, 2022e, 2023).

In taking this approach, steeped in notions of oppression as "neither-nor" and transracialization as subversion but also maintenance of race (Alim, 2016; Freire, 1970/2000), translanguaging via a both-and approach as instantiated in this conceptual framework serves as a lens for examining tensions arising from how Black immigrant youth draw from their I-languaging and I-semiotics (i.e., via individual semiolingual repertoires) while enacting literacies. It also facilitates examination of the shared mental grammars they draw upon based in institutional and societal expectations while using their Englishes (E-languaging and E-semiotics). Despite being often defined in relation to bilingual or multilingual speakers who largely reflect standardized (e.g., English, Spanish, French, German) as opposed to non-standardized (e.g., African American Vernacular English) language varieties, this approach to examining translanguaging and transsemiotizing can help to conceptualize the ways in which (Black immigrant) bidialectal youth (as do other multilingual groups) operate as individuals *and* as part of linguistic and semiotic societies, who reflect their Englishes and semiotic resources through their literacies.

This proposition can provide insights about the role of translanguaging and transsemiotizing as tools for the social, cultural, and emotional adjustment of Black Caribbean English-speaking immigrant youth. Depicting Black youth's E-languaging and E-semiotics can clarify how teachers might best support students' individual and unique processes of negotiating tensions between the differentiated grammatical structures that youth leverage *and* ideological responses to their Englishes that inhibit or foster a sense of agency crucial to their ability to thrive based on their individual semiolingual repertoires. Examining the literacies of these youth using such an approach to translanguaging and transsemiotics can empower teachers to help students navigate "institutional schizophrenia" (Smith et al., 2022). They can do so as they face its inescapable tensions using their translanguaging capacities in a world where they must continue to engage with idealized language systems even while their Englishes are racialized (see Smith, 2019a; see also Bartlett et al., 2018). A graphic depiction that presents an example of such an approach to researching Black immigrant youth's literacies is presented in Figure 5.1 (see Chapter 5 and Smith, 2020b).

Applying the notion of translanguaging and transsemiotizing to Black immigrant youth who speak English dialects (i.e., Englishes) as well as standardized forms of English also means that it becomes possible to use this notion to examine how heteroglossic and monoglossic norms operate as opposing forces in the multiliteracies of these youth (Smith, 2020b). This advancement has since found justification in the recent acknowledgment by García (2022) of the potential for merging translanguaging with Global (World) Englishes (in language and literacy teaching), a discussion mirroring the notion of *translanguaging with Englishes* (Smith, 2022a) as presented through the lens of Black immigrant literacies (Smith, 2020b). For instance, García (2022) has since reflexively posed questions for rethinking how notions of translanguaging may have potential for elucidating the linguistic repertoires of English-speaking peoples who manifest intralinguistic variations as a key part of their languaging:

What would happen, one wonders, if the concepts learned in these contributions regarding GELT [Global English Language Teaching] and translanguaging were put together? I wonder, for example, why my scholarship on translanguaging has not benefited from the theoretical and methodological advances supported by the CERFCV [Common European Framework of Reference for Languages Companion Volume: Council of Europe, 2020], and most especially the lenses of interaction and mediation. I wonder why in my own scholarship I continue to talk about English, about Spanish, and have not offered Englishes and Spanishes as an alternative. What does the naming of Englishes and Spanishes advance? What does it hide? Are Englishes and Spanishes also social constructs like English and Spanish? Does it advance the conversation or do we regress by picking these terms up?" (García, 2022, p. 6)

She has also since asked questions such as:

> I also wonder why GELT does not pay more attention to students' plurilingualism. GELT may emerge from a plurilingual framework, but it seems to be English-focused, despite its naming of the activity as Englishes. Has GELT given any thought to how bilingualism and multilingualism works in the minds and lives of racialized bilingual speakers? Without translanguaging, the object of study in GELT remains a language, albeit the borders have expanded to include what were thought of as varieties of English. And yet, without GELT, translanguaging in the teaching of English seems to be simply the recognition that the students are plurilingual and come from bilingual racialized communities. (García, 2022, p. 6)

Maintaining in the selfsame narrative that "without GELT translanguaging does not offer the English teaching profession a way to think beyond named languages in the ways that students make sense of language, and the ways in which they interact in language," García (2022) seems to suggest that

> by putting [GELT] and translanguaging along each other ... [it is possible to] show the language education profession how to truly ensure that English language practices are owned by the many bilingual/multilingual communities that dream of English being part of their repertoire. For all of us to own Englishes, language education must blend a translanguaging paradigm with that of World Englishes Language Teaching, ensuring that speakers can leverage their own practices in interactions, and that others listen to them with intent and purpose that value their languaging, however different this may be. (García, 2022, pp. 6–7)

I concur, and align with Canagarajah (2011), who insists that "acts of translanguaging are not elicited by teachers through conscious pedagogical strategies; they are produced unbidden" (p. 401). Such is the case in scholarship by Orellana (2015) who examined the translanguaging practices of immigrant children and showed how the codes and practices of language in the lives of translingual children are fluid, and not fixed or separate. Illustrating how immigrant children make transitions effortlessly between multiple languages, Orellana established that linguistic practices of this population reflect flexibility, adaptability, and versatility. Focusing on notions of multilingualism that often describe students as possessing two or more named languages, Orellana (2015) established, based on her scholarship with immigrant students, that translanguaging "encapsulates many different kinds of hybrid language practices" (p. 105). In doing so, she clarified how translanguaging was often made visible in students' collective practices as well as their personal interactions, when others encouraged them to leverage the communicative toolkits they possessed to cross borders, both linguistic and cultural, even as they resisted linguistic hegemony and creatively made use of the linguistic reservoirs that they possessed. As Dr. Suresh Canagarajah, Edwin Erle Sparks Professor of Applied Linguistics, English, and Asian Studies at Pennsylvania State University, did with a 'native' Arabic speaker

(Canagarajah, 2011), I examine Black immigrant youth's literacies through the lens of translanguaging in the study undergirding this book, with a view to providing insights into how Black immigrant youth navigated ideologies of race, language, and migration, as they relied on their role as language and semiotic architects to reflect their *holistic literacies* (Smith, 2023a).

Racializing Translanguaging and Transsemiotizing

In this chapter, I have presented the conceptual framework that undergirds the study functioning as the basis for this book. This framework, serving as a mechanism for analyzing data in the study, presents translanguaging and transsemiotizing as lenses in conjunction with multiliteracies and a raciolinguistic perspective, for clarifying how the Englishes and semiotics of Black Caribbean immigrants undergirded their literacies as a function of language and raciosemiotic architecture in their transgression of raciolinguistic and raciosemiotic ideologies. The foregoing discussion illustrates what is often perceived as the competing tensions between "*invisible/authentic*" and "*academic*" literacy practices while also highlighting distinctions often presented between "*home*" and "*academic*" language, all of which are subject to raciolinguistic and monoglossic language ideologies when deployed in the Englishes of youth.

The use of multiliteracies, such as through music and praisesongs of place by Watson and Beymer (2019), to represent the strengths of youth, as articulated earlier in this discussion, invites undiluted notions of translanguaging, which are often difficult to aspire to in institutions of schooling dedicated to traditional labels. For instance, one such situation in which the challenge for translanguaging arises is the call for its enactment through "disciplinary literacies." In and of itself, disciplinary literacies is a conception that often maintains distinctions between those literacies which represent more traditionally accepted forms of knowledge (e.g., mathematics, science, social studies) and their counterparts that largely do not (e.g., music, art, physical education). As an example, Stewart et al. (2022) show "translingual disciplinary literacies" as a pathway to creating equitable language environments based on analyses of data from high school teachers that made visible their heteroglossic language ideologies and enactment of these literacies presented as a challenge to monoglossic standards and linguistically oppressive systems. While admittedly well-intentioned and capable of disrupting mainstream norms, translanguaging practices of youth such as those presented by Watson and Beymer are traditionally not often considered as central to "*disciplinary worthiness*" as those inherent in "privileged disciplines," and thus, in and of itself, the notion of 'disciplinary literacy,' though largely accepted in the field of literacy for decades, can often mirror "academic language" and "academic literacy" discourses, inadvertently signaling an intentional return to Eurocentric white gaze and *white audit* as a basis for translanguaging, the very conceptions overtly posing a challenge to the liberatory power of the latter (García et al., 2021).

Inviting a critical stance that preserves 'old' literacies from well-intentioned approaches which may often inadvertently signal an epistemological and ideological return to white gaze as a basis for youth's literacies, and disrupting home-school, invisible-academic dichotomies in which descriptions of youth's literacies tend to be steeped, the lens of multiliteracies used to undergird the study presented facilitates an understanding of how youth draw from linguistic and semiotic resources to make meaning through their literacies while simultaneously challenging institutionally designed raciolinguistic literate labels and practices that have worked for so long to maintain multiliterate practice as peripheral to the educational enterprise. Invoking Amanda Gorman's commentary with which this chapter begins, as indicative of the hopefulness necessary amid such pervasive tensions, we see nonetheless, that arising from this dynamic: "somehow we've weathered and witnessed a nation that isn't broken, but simply unfinished" (Gorman, 2021). Alluding to the linguistic and semiotic capacity that Gorman exudes in the face of her racialization within the US, much like the Black immigrant and transnational youth under study in this book, her multiliteracies that summon race yet transcend it make possible the confession, "We the successors of a country and a time where a skinny Black girl descended from slaves and raised by a single mother can dream of becoming president only to find herself reciting for one."

A raciolinguistic perspective as applied to multiliteracies thus serves here as a lens to reconcile tensions undergirding youth's lives by examining the literacies of "new model minority" Black immigrants and how they use their roles as language and raciosemiotic architects to make meaning as racialized persons through linguistic and semiotic resources while also foregrounding a focus on the role of the institution in dismantling raciolinguistic hierarchies during this process. In doing so, it is possible to explore how transracialization functions as a basis for subverting race while also maintaining it (Alim, 2016), becoming visible in the literacies of Black immigrant youth. Problematizing the ways in which raciolinguistic and raciosemiotic ideologies affect Black youth is consistent with the challenge to the term *new model minority*, as applied to Black youth, given that both constructs draw from a meritocratic myth (see Smith et al., 2022). Moreover, centralizing race, as called for by Willis (2018), and removing it from the periphery of discussions related to the literacy practices of immigrant and *new model minority* youth of Color, serves as a way to describe how youth reflect agency in response to racialized language and semiotics. Adopting this lens also allows for a focus on institutional change which is central to a raciolinguistic perspective (Rosa & Flores, 2017; see also Smith, 2020b; Smith, et al., 2022).

5 Methodologically Examining Black Immigrant Literacies

A (Decolonizing) Interpretive Analytical Design

> And so we lift our gaze, not to what stands between us, but what stands before us.
> We close the divide because we know to put our future first, we must first put our differences aside.
> We lay down our arms so we can reach out our arms to one another.
> We seek harm to none and harmony for all.
> Let the globe, if nothing else, say this is true.
> That even as we grieved, we grew.
> That even as we hurt, we hoped.
> That even as we tired, we tried.
> That we'll forever be tied together, victorious. Not because we will never again know defeat, but because we will never again sow division.
>
> Gorman, 2021

Coming to This Inquiry

I came to write this book about the literate lives of Black immigrant students during my experience as a faculty advisor with responsibility for Caribbean students in a Caribbean student organization. As a Black-immigrant-transnational-single-parent-mother-scholar-educator in a large public predominantly white institution in the southwest US where I worked, I had assumed the role of guiding students in this Caribbean student organization. When I first entered the university, the organization had been dormant and therefore, Caribbean students had no formal space on the campus within which to create or find affinity. Upon realizing this challenge, I worked with the appropriate university division, with a co-advisor, and with designated Caribbean youth to revive the then-dormant organization. Focusing on revising the constitution, developing a system for governance, instituting structures for monthly meetings, and registering the organization, the youth and I got the organization 'back up and running.' Functioning initially as co-advisor for the organization, I met with the designated student leadership monthly to plan ongoing meetings, organize functions that were often culturally focused, and to discuss the ways in which they were engaging with other organizations on the campus and in the community to advance the mission of the organization.

I developed a close connection with the Caribbean students and over time, recognized they were challenged without a physical space that they could call their own. Up until the end of our first year together, they had provided very insightful comments about how the university might work to better facilitate students of Color, given the limited numbers currently in attendance. I thought then about how useful it would be to use the ongoing insights from their recommendations about how they wished to be supported as Black youth, to enhance the spaces in which they functioned within and beyond the university. It was during this time that the Caribbean youth, many of them newcomers to the US, accepted my invitation to be part of a research project designed to better understand their cultural, linguistic, and social challenges within and beyond the university setting as immigrant students of Color. Upon receiving approval of IRB2016-88, I invited students to voluntarily consent if they were willing to be a part of the study. Many of the students already had a rapport with me as co-advisor of the organization at the time of the study, and therefore, they felt comfortable letting me know if they were unable to join. I reassured them that there was no requirement on their part and enlisted only students who were willing and enthusiastic about becoming part of the research. Those who signed up initially but were unable or unwilling to continue the study were allowed to discontinue and reassured that there were no repercussions.

By the time the study ended, I had become the advisor for this Caribbean student organization, supporting students with monthly meetings and cultural functions, providing guidance on an individual basis, and facilitating their progression towards program completion and graduation. My role as an advisor and researcher in this space was therefore one where I drew from my experiences as a Black immigrant, transnational mother, and as a scholar-educator to provide cultural support, academic advice, and advocacy.

Insider Knowledge and Experience

As a Black immigrant literacy educator, I bring to this work my experience with immigrant and transnational as well as American students and educators in the US, and my experience as a former teacher in the Eastern Caribbean. My shared understandings of the ways in which racial, linguistic, and cultural expectations are imposed on Black immigrants to the US as well as my evolving understanding of these phenomena through my research on Black languaging in the Caribbean are also brought to bear on this work. My focus on the racialized language and on tensions arising from various expectations regarding the literacies of Black immigrant youth is informed anecdotally by a phenomenon with which certain members the Black immigrant community are familiar – the tendency to prioritize exceptional academic performance at the expense of what are often perceived as non-academic experiences – but, which, as shown in the literature, has not been sufficiently explored to date (see Ukpokodu, 2018). At the same time, my illuminated understandings of who Black immigrants are as Black peoples have largely come to be clarified in large part as contextualized by the relationships between Black immigrants and African Americans, Africans, as well as other Black peoples and peoples of Color in and beyond the US.

As a "well-meaning" former Caribbean teacher in Trinidad and Tobago and in St. Lucia, I was all too familiar with how this tendency manifested itself in West Indian classrooms. After all, I had spent much of my time in the West Indies, after being trained in my early years of teaching to view the "[nonstandardized] language of the Black child ... as something to eradicate" in schools (Alim, 2005, p. 187) even while being taught its value as a cultural exercise. Like the high school teacher with whom Alim (2005) worked ethnographically in Philadelphia's schools, after years of teaching multilingual, multiracial, and multicultural children in the Caribbean, I was led to a similar conclusion with my students as the one she presents: "I have to say it's kind of disheartening because despite *all* that time that's been spent focusing on grammar [with my students], like, I don't really see it having helped enormously" (Alim, 2005, p. 187). Like this teacher, I was "disheartened" and "saddened" by the "lack of results" that I had hoped for in my efforts to somehow "improve" the language of Black and other Caribbean children (Alim, 2005, p. 187). And as Alim (2005) observes when he states, "what teachers like this one are probably not aware of is how they are enacting whiteness and subscribing to an ideology of linguistic supremacy within a system of daily cultural combat" (p. 187), I was completely oblivious then to how my intention to uphold what I believed was "Standard English" as the "Holy Grail of Language" represented my complicity in preserving linguistic hegemony. Much like Alim (2005) described the language of Black students at this school as "the thing that teachers at Haven High 'combat the most' and the project of 'eradicat[ing] the language pattern' of Black students as 'one of the few goals'" that this teacher had had for multiple years (p. 187), I too held similar perspectives as a Black Caribbean teacher in the predominantly Black schools of the Eastern Caribbean. In fact, it was my dissonance surrounding the significant effort to improve languaging and its stark misalignment with the test results of many of my Caribbean students that led me on the journey beyond the West Indian shores in search of answers.

As the mother of a first-generation Black immigrant adolescent at the time of this study, and as a friend of many mothers whose children are also first-generation Black immigrants or Black nationals of/from the English-speaking Caribbean and Africa, I had seen the premium placed on the "academic" literacies of youth. This caused me to wonder about the ways in which the authentic literacies of these youth, steeped in languaging based on their

Englishes, via what Alim (2005) has presented as their Black raciolinguistic styleshifting (see Baugh, 1983; Labov, 1972; Rickford & McNair-Knox, 1994, for earlier discussions undergirding this construct), can also be foregrounded in schools. My emphasis on translational research that addresses the cultural and linguistic responsiveness of teachers, many of whom work with Black immigrant youth, had revealed anecdotally and in research studies that many still struggle to determine how to respond to the literacies of Black immigrant youth and to the nuances presented by the unique experiences they bring to literacy classrooms. My learning also about Blackness as a person and as a scholar exploring racialization in literacy and language, though arguably much more recently, had been informed largely by my constant engagement with African American, African, Caribbean, Latinx, Asian American, and other sister scholars concerning Black Liberation Theology (Calhoun-Brown, 1999; Lincoln & Mamiya, 1990; Phelps, 2000; Willis et al., 2022), Black Feminism (Collins, 2000; Crenshaw, 1991), Critical Race Theory (Bell, 1995; Crenshaw et al., 1995; Delgado & Stefancic, 2001), and the Black Radical Tradition (Robinson, 2000). Immersed in this learning, I came to be more cognizant of why and how Black immigrants were racialized as Black peoples in the US in ways that informed institutional and individual responses to their literacies. Wishing to understand this dynamic better, I saw this undertaking as a way to further provide clarity about this dynamic for myself, teachers, and for researchers (see Ibrahim, 1999, 2019, 2020, for previous discussions). Doing this, I thought, could potentially extend pathways that support stakeholders as well as administrators, educators, and policymakers who work with Black immigrants in US schools.

Beyond the above, my decision to write this book is also inspired by my deeply personal experience as a "foreign-born," "international," and "immigrant" student and scholar as defined by the nation-state via the United States Citizenship and Immigration Services (USCIS). As an *'immigrant'* to the US, I was first considered by the USCIS as an *"alien,"* that is, "not a U.S. citizen or U.S. national." I was designated a *"nonimmigrant,"* "granted the right to reside temporarily in the United States" (Mattix, 2018). Functioning as an "alien" and "nonimmigrant" student, I followed the necessary rules and guidelines required to avoid "violating my status" as I did not want to fall "out of status" (Mattix, 2018). To transcend beyond my "alien" status, I, like so many others, had to be "granted the right by the USCIS to reside permanently in the United States and to work without restrictions in the United States" (Mattix, 2018). This right was determined based on my "job skills," because, as per the USCIS, "an alien who has the right combination of skills, education, and/or work experience, and is otherwise eligible, may be able to live permanently in the United States" (Mattix, 2018). Remaining *"in status"* as an alien and *"nonimmigrant,"* as well as being able to prove that I had the aforementioned skills as an *"immigrant,"* would translate into my eligibility to become a "Lawful Permanent Resident (LPR)" (Mattix, 2018).

Looking back now, it is easy to see how my transition through the system based on the descriptors above, and as a student and educator moving from *'alien'* and *'nonimmigrant'* status to *'immigrant'* and *'lawful permanent resident,'* depended largely on what many might view as the meritocratic elements of being a *'new model minority.'* As the chair of my dissertation, Dr. Jenifer Jasinski Schneider, will attest, being one who held an unfailing and long-standing belief in my *Black semiolingual innocence* as an emerging Black immigrant scholar (discussed later), reinforced by her insistence on advocating unapologetically for preservation of my *semiolingual transgressiveness* – with care despite raciolinguistic norms in the academy – I came to learn a lot about the raciolinguistic ideologies embedded in immigration laws used in the US and even more so, about how to avoid breaking these laws. In doing so, as one of Alim's (2005) research informants discussed earlier rightly observed, I operated then from the perspective that, *"If you livin in the White man's world, you gotta play by the White man's rules. At least as long as they runnin shit"* (p. 195).

Thus, every time my student visa neared expiration, I experienced tremendous anxiety about what would happen if my daughter and I were deported, and for the duration of my studies in the US, I avoided traveling back home because of the fear of not being able to return. Yes, many of my non-immigrant peers at the time indicated that they had nonetheless done this with little challenge, but others had stories that caused me to privilege caution over the desire to be with my family, all of whom had remained in the Caribbean with the exception of my daughter. In fact, my decision not to travel back home during my studies was in large part based on the fact that I knew I would need to improve my life to provide my daughter with economic, social, educational, and global opportunities that I did not have as a child and had struggled to secure as an adult – as my Gen Z daughter would say, *securing that bag*. If I went home and could not get back to the US so that I could complete my studies, I knew I would spend a lot of time trying to *'make ends meet'* for the rest of my life and thus my persistence as an immigrant was tied to an imagined economic freedom. I therefore made the difficult choice to avoid any situation where I might jeopardize my *"nonimmigrant status"* even while sacrificing the visits to my family. I determined that providing my daughter with a future better than mine would have to be a priority. Now that I think back on it, I was also too poor at the time to purchase a ticket to the Caribbean and refused to ask my parents who had already sacrificed so much to try to send me one.

While I am now aware of the repercussions of the sacrifices I made then, and though it is easy to wonder about what life would have been like had I remained with my family, I have accepted that it is easier for scholars to theorize about the importance of remaining with family in reality than it is to constantly wonder, as a person, in the full range of the world's reality, about the source of '*one's daily bread*.' And so, my story as an '*immigrant*' to the US was one that evolved through sacrifice, compassion with self, and a constant self-monitoring of my actions through the lens of the USCIS, understanding fully why parents often want their children to 'learn English for success' even while I also recognize why children need to flourish beyond simply 'doing school well' much like I did as a Black Caribbean child and as I eventually encouraged my Black Caribbean immigrant daughter to do as a parent in the US. For me, in keeping with a *both-and* approach and functioning on multiple levels of reality, these seemingly opposing viewpoints could both be true at the same time.

Until I emerged out of my '*nonimmigrant status*,' with a solid spiritual conviction that managed to sustain me throughout this time, I did not realize just how much being an '*immigrant*' had cost me, socially, emotionally, and culturally. And so, my '*immigrant*' story that emerged out of self-determination borne out through the decision to persist against all odds towards an elusive 'success' as an "*alien*" is one that, to me, seems central to this work. While I am not every '*immigrant*' – no two Black immigrants share the exact experiences – there are some common realities that we face, as I have come to learn anecdotally and through my research over the years. Just as I thought daily of the future of my daughter, and of the futures of my nieces and nephews that it took me years to be able to see (I didn't visit when they were young), other (Black) immigrants too persist in the US and elsewhere against insurmountable odds. And their immigrant children and youth make choices daily about how they will craft their "*immigrant of Color literacies*" (Smith, 2020b, p. 12).

As a scholar and educator of literacy, the story that I often tell in my research about how I come to my scholarship does not often include the nuanced, heartfelt, and personal confessions presented above. In fact, my many initial attempts to tell any story were largely unaccepted, overtly rejected, and misunderstood for years post-dissertation even while being gleaned for their innovations in the US academy (Smith, 2013a, 2013b, 2016). Much of this gleaning, of course, went unnoticed on my part due to my Black '*semiolingual innocence*' (discussed later). Attempts to include my international and immigrant story via what seemed to be unrecognized and transgressive Black languaging, just a decade ago – before autoethnographies, the telling of self, and the invitation of migrant Blackness from what is often lauded and referred to as the "Global South" (see Khan et al., 2022, for a problematization of this term) became what appears to now be the norm – were met largely with derision, scorn, and 'white gaze' rejection. This '*raciolinguicism*' steeped largely in overt justification undergirded by the subtlety of moral licensing (Warrican, 2020) was leveraged at large by many editors and reviewers of seemingly legitimate journals in the academy. Looking back now, I can see how my personal stories, told via Black languaging, were perhaps novel to the 'white listening subject' (Rosa & Flores, 2017) in the US. It was no wonder then that they were often disregarded in my proposed '*scholarship*' because they seemed too '*grand*,' '*far-reaching*,' '*personal*,' or because they were considered as having no supporting '*evidence*.' Yet, they were integral then, as they remain now, to painting a portrait of how my transnational Blackness functions integrally to my research, even as I operate in close proximity to whiteness and its privilege as a largely light-brown skinned immigrant professor transgressing English and language norms in the US. Despite my entanglement, these stories have allowed me to pose a significant challenge to long-standing Eurocentric dominance intertwined with American nationalism that has for so long been endemic to the fields of languaging and literacy.

It was no surprise that it took a Black scholar who himself was a Caribbean national to initially advocate for an explicit reinscribing of my Black *semiolingual innocence* – an innocence that the US academy repeatedly threatened to strip from my personhood as I 'became Black' (Ibrahim, 1999), 'became immigrant,' and 'became a "non-native English speaker"' (Smith, 2022a; see Cook, 2015, for a complication of the term "native speaker"). Contrary to the long-standing belief by the chair of my dissertation to whom I referred earlier – a white woman – that there was nothing wrong with my languaging, written or spoken, I had been repeatedly told by white as well as Black and other scholars of Color that these personal insights were not '*academic enough*' to be included as part of my writing, never mind what a few described as my adept weaving of the emotional through the intellectual enterprise. My writing was also too bold, too complex, lacking nuance, or insufficiently organized for the white and otherwise American audience. I have come to understand now that it is the "*semiolingual transgressiveness*" (discussed later) of transcendent literacy (Willis, 2022) that operates *sans attention* to "white gaze" (Morrison, 2020) which creates such a terror for receiving languaging that dares to operate in its inherent human innocence. In other words, this is what it looks like when Black languaging dares to function with zero attention to white gaze. Much like *Black Panther* and *Black Panther: Wakanda Forever*, and the advocacy of the Black Panther political movement, this Black semiolingual innocence that I presented, much to my dismay, was one that the academy wished to obscure, make invisible, and erase. I saw it often when professors who were white attempted to make me believe my languaging or personhood as a Black immigrant was better than that of Black Americans while at the same time felt threatened by its power. I saw it when professors who were people of Color failed to acknowledge it, to legitimize it, to advocate for it. And I saw it when colleagues who were people of Color adamantly and unapologetically gave voice to it, unafraid enough of its consequences to propel me to free it.

I chose a decolonizing lens in this study to allow me to reinscribe my Black semiolingual innocence in much the same way that it formed the basis for elucidating the notion of *innocence linguistic* as a fixture in Black immigrant and all Black lives. I choose here, deliberately, to stand for a moment, with my truth, and to retrieve, relieve, and retrace those nuances in my past as an 'immigrant,' transnational, and as Black, because this process is critical to reconciling my *'selves'* through my scholarship, something that I do not often get to do. I thus brought to the current study and to the associated analyses my past personal experiences as well as my thoughts about diversity, language, and race based on the ways in which I understood these concepts to first work in isolation, and later, in tandem. For instance, much like the literature that points to Black immigrants' recognition of how linguicism also serves to sideline Englishes only upon arrival to the US (Nero, 2006), I too was initially oblivious to the idea of what it truly meant to be Black and to dare to have such a skin color in a white world until I migrated to America.

In contrast, I had previously been well-aware of the ways in which (standardized) English as well as English and French dialects (e.g., non- and standardized Englishes often unaccepted formally in and beyond US academia and schools) were positioned alongside each other as they wrestled for power and privilege in my home country (see Milson-Whyte, 2014). And I had been aware of the effects of colorism instantiated by the tendency of individuals in the Caribbean to reflect a phenotypical preference for my 'light skin' and the 'light skin' of others over our 'darker-skinned' counterparts, a distinction that I have also seen in the US considering the tone of my dark-skinned daughter in comparison to mine. Yet, this did not change the fact that I was startled and continue to grapple with the ways in which others respond to my standardized English in the US. Moreover, it has taken me a while, *and I mean, years*, to realize that much of the negative reaction that I faced during my initial stay in the US, as well as much of what I continue to battle with in terms of a questioning of my capacity to be as "productive" and "legitimate" as a Black scholar – whatever that means – had and continues to have a lot to do with the color of my Black skin. In doing so, I acknowledge too that the challenges I have faced in learning about how whiteness (Alim, 2005) is used to construct me despite my clear and inherent legitimacy for architectural languaging and literacies as a Black speaker, educator, and scholar – *semiolingual innocence* – while they are perspectives from which I can never completely detach, have repeatedly been transcended as I repeatedly and unapologetically transgress academic norms. I will admit that I have faced some disillusionment, at times, because I often realize that I cannot somehow return to the days before I 'ate the fruit,' as it were, when I was but a *'mere'* educator in the Caribbean and during my early days in the US (whatever this means). Nonetheless, while I have come to terms with the fact that what others will always see and hear *first* when they encounter me in the US is this – 'a Black immigrant'– I am now also aware that my life in the US, and prior, in the Caribbean as a human, much like many of my Black sisters, brothers, others, has repeatedly included moments where I am transported through *imajinè inosan* (discussed later) that portend the creativity inherent in the possibilities made visible by transcendent literacy (Willis, 2022).

As a human and as a scholar undertaking this work who brought these *imaginaries of innocence* to bear on my interactions, I was interested in broadly understanding how Black immigrant students reflected literacies as inherent to them and not in comparison to their white counterparts (see Smith et al., 2019). Given the tendency of qualitative research to provide understandings that are unique, complex, multilayered, and nuanced, I decided to also use a qualitative approach to this examination. For me, insights from the qualitative study presented would provide a more holistic understanding of the literacies of Black immigrant youth. Besides, my previous and collaborative analyses of Black youth's literacies using quantitative methods pointed to the need for qualitative insights that could extend findings from this recent scholarship. I anticipated that drawing from a qualitative paradigm via a decolonizing interpretive lens with which to consider Black immigrant literacies and Black immigrant youth as individuals could provide the field with additional clarity surrounding the ways in which students' needs can be better addressed. For me, being able to support Black immigrant youth, their peers, parents, their teachers, administrators, and educators, in ways that I wish my daughter and I had been supported when we grappled with the novelty of the US, represented a critical avenue for advocacy. Even so, I have now evolved further in my understanding that what is needed within a decolonizing perspective is a dismantling of long-standing dichotomies that separate approaches used to understand local, global, and complex realities (Alim, 2005; Freire, 1970/2000; Smith, 2013), and which allow for a transgressiveness (see hooks, 1994) with methods such as the "critical dialectical pluralism" approach as advocated by Onwuegbuzie and Frels (2013). For me, this evolution has allowed for impartial intentionality in my working in solidarity with all Black peoples across the globe, no matter who they might be.

A Decolonizing Interpretive Approach for Examining Black Immigrant Literacies

Methodologically, I draw partially from a "decolonizing interpretive research design" (see Darder, 2015; Dei, 2000) that functions as a "deeply subaltern form of qualitative research practice; one which seeks to formidably challenge and disrupt the one-dimensional Eurocentric epistemicides prevalent in traditional theories of schooling and society" (Darder, 2015, p. 64; Paraskeva, 2011). As proposed in my call for "raciolinguistic epistemologies" that allow for the emergence of the Majority World's knowledges as a project of racialized language, I suggest that the long-standing epistemological question *"When and what is knowledge?"* (Crotty, 1998, p. 46) might now become, *"When and what is literacy knowledge as considered by whom?"* (Smith, 2023a).

Aware of Westernized individualistic notions regarding knowledge that often remain unchallenged in an interpretive design (Cohen et al., 2011), I embraced the philosophy of Ubuntu – "I am because we are; we are because I am" (Chilisa & Ntseane, 2010, p. 619) – to adopt a humanist approach that reflects respect and compassion while emphasizing human dignity and support for community (Lituchy & Michaud, 2016). In doing so, I give precedence to the collective social (i.e., Indigenous) while honoring the individual (i.e., Western European) (Getty, 2010; Ibrahima & Mattaini, 2019). Acknowledging that most of my scholarship thus far and the scholarship on which my work is premised utilizes 'Western' methodologies where evidence of knowledge is gained from hearing, sight, smell, taste, and touch, I challenge the notion that 'non-Western' ways of knowing, rooted in the contextual and historical or in aesthetics, revelation, and spirituality such as those that come to us by the gods or spirits, should be disregarded in my legitimate understandings of how I, as Black woman, come to know the world and how Black children and youth read it (Ibrahima & Mattaini, 2019; Matsinhe, 2007; see also Willis et al., 2022). After all, I credit the revelatory Spirit of God with an understanding of how to craft the truths here revealed.

At the same time, my goal in centering non-Western ways of knowing does not dismantle the insights of Eurocentric ways of knowing that I have come to rely upon for most of my scholarly and formerly student life. In fact, as I observed recently (Smith, 2022e), I am entangled with them racially and they with me – "racialized entanglements" – and therefore they are intricately intertwined with my personhood. Thus, in line with Dei (2000), I am interested in what a "hybridity of knowledges" (p. 113) can bring to the proverbial table when allowing "different bodies of knowledge" to "continually influence each other" by reflecting the "dynamism of all knowledge systems" (p. 113). For me, this dynamic is visible in my supposed mastery of standardized English steeped in Eurocentric norms that now permit me to interrogate how these 'Western' norms inadvertently create and rely on monolithic perspectives of knowledge in my privileged position of proximity to whiteness.

This dialectical perspective to knowledge via a decolonizing approach acknowledges the following key principles, all of which undergird my analytical framework (discussed later): (a) reflecting a search for knowledge framed by ideologies that are never neutral; (b) understanding that research practices tend to operate in ways that protect the status quo and create hegemonies; (c) critiquing and recreating reality by naming and addressing norms of power that create asymmetry; (d) using research practices that challenge hegemonic practices and create possibilities based on evolving ways of reading the world; (e) using research undertaken to influence change in practice for those who are most vulnerable; (f) promoting a humanizing dialectical process that extends beyond subject/object framings in research, critical to engaging researchers and the people with whom they work in constant and democratic dialogue (Darder, 2015). The dialectical perspective on which I rely in part has been further advanced through constructs such as "critical dialectical pluralism" that advocate conducting "research wherein an egalitarian society is promoted and sustained for the purpose of advancing both universalistic theoretical knowledge and local practical knowledge, and to conduct culturally progressive research" (Onwuegbuzie & Frels, 2013, p. 9). Specifically, drawing from certain elements of this critical dialectical pluralistic approach, the research study undergirding this book emerged through interaction with participants, as guided by Onwuegbuzie and Frels (2013), allowing the latter to have a

co-equal say in what phenomenon should be studied; how research should be conducted to study this phenomenon; which methods should be used; which findings are valid, acceptable, and meaningful. (Onwuegbuzie and Frels, 2013, p. 9)

I agree with Dei (2000) when he states that the "'Indigenous' is never lost" as I have maintained a reliance on 'non-Western' ways of knowing even while laboring daily as a Black immigrant researcher and educator within and across transnational 'Westernized' contexts and frameworks (p. 113). My work within this dynamic that has emphasized epistemologies, ontologies, and axiologies, often at odds with what my spirit tells me is morally right, human, and humanely acceptable, as well as aesthetically appropriate for Black youth, is what has brought me to this point: one where I feel morally compelled to allow for an interplay between these Westernized philosophies of professional worlds and the non-Western ways of knowing and doing grounded in ancestral spirit, revelation, and soul (Dillard, 2012b) that have consistently been a part of my personal life. Williams (2016) acknowledges this interplay when he describes how postcolonial literatures of the Caribbean "reduce the scope of indigenous knowledge and oral tradition ... [and] at the same time" allow for "the development of [a] 'critique of colonial rule'" (p. 107). Much like the notion of Freire's (1970/2000) dialectic where the wish is for the human to emerge as neither oppressed nor as oppressor, and Alim's (2016) notion of transracialization as one where racial categorization simultaneously requires subversion and maintenance, Williams (2016) shows how Caribbean writers thematically worked in the 1930s to interweave "their unique and composite identity in and through literary and non-literary writings" as a pathway to "self-consciousness and an awareness of colonial exploitation" even while "positivist ideas ... from Europe enter[ed] the cultural and intellectual discourses of island societies of the Caribbean region through colonial schools and ... [and religious] organizations" (p. 107). Aware of the long-standing potential for power and coercion to minimize the developing double consciousness of immigrants becoming Black and minorized in such a dialectic interplay (Du Bois, 1903/1999), my inescapable immersion in these processes as a being and scholar often inadvertently co-opted by *colonized intellectualism* (Fanon, 1961/1991) nonethelewss symbolized my epistemological entry to this work.

Questions Guiding the Inquiry

Acknowledging gaps in the field as well as operating through problematization (Alvesson & Sandberg, 2011) of literacies and translanguaging for Black immigrant youth as discussed earlier, I asked three questions to guide this study of youth's literacies:

(1) How do Black Caribbean English-speaking immigrant youth describe their literacies as represented in their historical trajectories across in- and out-of-school settings?
(2) How do Black Caribbean English-speaking immigrant youth describe their translanguaging, accompanied by their broader transsemiotic practices, as represented in their historical trajectories across in- and out-of-school settings?
(3) In what ways are contested ideologies surrounding race, language, and migration reflected in Black Caribbean English-speaking immigrant youth's descriptions of their literacies through translanguaging, as accompanied by their broader transsemiotic practices?

Towards a (Decolonizing) Interpretive Analytical Framework

Guided by the questions above and informed, in part, by a decolonizing interpretive research design (Darder, 2015; Dei, 2000), I move towards a "(decolonizing) interpretive analytical framework," to recreate the futures of Black immigrant youth. I place the word *decolonizing* in parentheses to signal my partial reliance on this perspective while *also* inadvertently drawing from Westernized frames. This integrated framework reflective of Westernized and non-Western lenses foregrounds the dialectic critical to acknowledging the interplay between decolonizing methods that highlight non-Western Eurocentric epistemologies about Black youth *and* hegemonic Westernized perspectives that consistently pit 'ill-equipped,' 'inadequate,' 'incapable,' and 'underperforming' Black American youth against their 'academically successful,' 'new model minority' Black immigrant counterparts. I use this "(decolonizing) interpretive analytical framework" to accomplish that goal by examining socially constructed Westernized realities, epistemologies, and axiologies steeped in hegemonic Westernized ways of viewing Black youth while simultaneously interrogating these notions through the *contextual knowledge, historical values* (i.e., past, present, future), and *insider realities* of non-Westernized thought (Smith et al., 2022). In turn, I identify strategies useful for Black youth's self-determination by focusing on efforts leveraged by these youth to overcome obstacles with literacies, as well as strategies [that can be] deployed by institutions, or not, to support them. Table 5.1 (available at www.cambridge.org/LiteraciesofMigration) presents an overview and an example of the analytical framework used to examine the literacies of six Black immigrant youth in this book.

Participants

Eight students signed the consent forms as part of the broader study (IRB2016-88) undertaken while I worked in the Caribbean student organization at a southwestern university in the US. Six youth were purposefully selected who became part of this work. Data sources as part of this broader study included demographic questionnaires about students' backgrounds, in-depth semi-structured individual interviews (Seidman, 2012), personal journaling (Tuckett & Stewart, 2004), and focus-group interviews (Krueger & Casey, 2009) on the part of the students about their experiences. I chose to focus here on the in-depth semi-structured individual interviews as these data were primarily concerned with students' descriptions about their Englishes, literacies, and linguistic practices for the duration of the study.

As part of the interpretive approach used in this work, the six purposefully sampled youth – Asha, Earsline, Fred, Jermaine, Melody, and Nickler (pseudonyms) – from the English-speaking Caribbean functioned as primary participants. They originated from the Bahamas and Jamaica and all spoke the non-standardized as well as standardized Englishes of those countries.

To align with the decolonizing interpretive approach employed, twelve educators functioned as secondary informants in this study. The educators involved six US immigrants from Jamaica, Trinidad and Tobago, the Bahamas, and St. Lucia, and six educators who functioned as literacy educators, administrators, nationals and residents of Barbados, Jamaica, St. Lucia, and Trinidad and Tobago in the English-speaking Caribbean.

Focal

Focal participants were purposefully selected as immigrants to the US who had lived in the US for at least zero to five years at the time of the study. The participants were all nineteen-year-old Bahamian immigrant youth who spoke non-standardized and standardized Englishes. With the exception of Melody, all students originated from the Bahamas in the English-speaking Caribbean. Asha had lived the US as a student for the duration of one year at the time of the study. She had previously visited the US numerous times since she was six weeks old and had spent three weeks in Washington, DC, as part of a global youth leadership program before she migrated to the US. During her first year in the US, she spent her entire summer in the Bahamas. Asha indicated that she spoke Bahamian Creolized English and Bahamian Standard English. Earsline had spent one semester in the US as a student at the time of the study. She had previously visited Florida multiple times before she migrated to the US. Earsline was soft-spoken but a member of several student organizations and vice president on the executive board of the Caribbean student organization of which we were a part. She indicated that she spoke Bahamian Creolized English and Bahamian Standard English.

Fred was confident, vocal, energetic, an athlete, a member of several student organizations, and president of the executive board of the Caribbean student organization of which we were a part. Fred indicated that he spoke Jamaican Creolized English and Standard American English. Jermaine was a Bahamian student who had lived in the US for two years at the time of the study. He was calm, confident, and shared that he spoke Bahamian Creolized English and Bahamian Standard English. Melody was a female Jamaican American who had moved back and forth between Jamaica and the US until middle schools, and since middle school had assumed primary residence in the US. She was soft-spoken yet firm and confident. Melody served as the secretary of the student organization of which we were a part, studying business management and Spanish, and explained that she spoke Jamaican Creolized English and Standard American English. Nickler was a vivacious and energetic female who had lived in the US for one year at the time of the study. She had close friendships with Melody, Asha, and Earsline, and was supportive of the initiatives that they organized as part of the Caribbean student organization. She shared that she spoke Bahamian Creolized English and Bahamian Standard English.

Non-focal

Non-focal or secondary participants functioning as informants were educators who had been purposefully selected for two studies that I had previously conducted.

In ones of these studies, I had focused on participants who were Black foreign-born nationals (i.e., first-generation) and who had migrated to the US from the Bahamas, Ghana, Jamaica, St. Lucia, and Trinidad, or who had lived in the English-speaking Caribbean. The immigrant educators who were part of this group had also been selected previously based on their experiences visiting, living, and teaching in colleges of education in the US for at least two years and given their use of at least one standardized (e.g., Jamaican Standard) and one non-standardized (e.g., Jamaican Creolized) English. Participants had each completed bachelor's and master's degrees by the time of this study. They had also been either enrolled in or had completed doctoral degrees in the areas of mathematics, early childhood, counseling, higher education, social studies, and literacy education. Each participant had taught at the primary (i.e., elementary), high school, and/or university level before assuming positions as educators in their colleges within US higher education. Overall, the participants had each taught for a total of at least ten years, and at the time of the study, three of them served as Graduate Teaching Associates, three others as Assistant Professors, and one as a newly tenured Associate Professor. Selecting participants from a range of countries with varied standardized and non-standardized Englishes, across areas of expertise, and who functioned at multiple levels (i.e., Graduate Teaching Associate, Assistant Professor, Associate Professor) in higher education allowed for a representation of results that considered a myriad of factors.

In the other study that I had previously conducted, the data from which also served as a basis for informing insider knowledge in the current work, the participants were Caribbean nationals who had been selected based on their experiences living as residents in the Caribbean with leadership and administrative roles as literacy teacher educators at teacher-preparation institutions and universities in St. Lucia, Barbados, Jamaica, and Trinidad and Tobago. They were all focused on literacy or English language arts in their practice, were responsible for teacher candidates, had oversight as varying administrators in the tertiary system of education in the Caribbean, and were purposefully selected because five of them held administrative roles. In large part, they helped to determine if and how teacher candidates matriculated through the educational system as a function of the Englishes and literacies that they had been able to master.

Data Sources

To analyze data from the current study that emerged from students in the Caribbean student organization, and in line with the interpretive design partially relied upon here, I drew from in-depth semi-structured interviews of primary participants *and also* from those of informants who served as secondary participants.

The use of interviews for this study is based primarily on the notion that in-depth phenomenological interviews function as a superior mechanism for gathering data about people in society (Becker & Geer, 1957; Trow, 1957) and the indication that interviews prove to be by far the most reasonable means to gather information about participants' "subjective understandings" (Schutz, 1967) and perceptions (van Manen, 1990). Interviews with primary participants were designed to elicit information about Black Caribbean immigrant youth's literacy practices and Englishes in their life's trajectories across their home countries in the Caribbean and the US. In line with the decolonizing interpretive design partially relied upon in this work, in-depth semi-structured interviews previously conducted with secondary participants were also used to understand the uses of Englishes and the ideologies underlying them as used by Black educators who had migrated to the US and as Black educators using Englishes in the English-speaking Caribbean.

Primary

The initial interview protocol used with primary participants contained twenty-one questions. Each interview lasted approximately one hour. Questions elicited information concerning acculturation (Carola Suárez-Orozco, personal communication, February 20, 2015); intra-linguistic discrimination within language, speech (Wee, 2005), and ethnic (Schwartz et al., 2010) communities; intra-linguistic discrimination as an interpersonal (between individuals or groups) construct (Wright & Bougie, 2007); and language as a proxy for discrimination based on race (Johnson, 2005). Examples of prompts in this protocol included: *Tell me all about when you first came to the US*; *Tell me about the languages and dialects you use in your home country and the US. How do you use these languages and dialects?*; *What languages do you use in the US?*; *How do others respond when you speak your English vernacular or dialect in your home country and the US?*; and *How do you feel about communicating verbally and in writing here in the US and in your home country?* The second interview protocol was developed after all initial interviews had been completed and was designed to probe further the information provided by participants in the first round of interviews.

Secondary

As alluded to earlier, I relied secondarily on the data of two additional studies in which I had previously focused on the Englishes of Black educators in the Caribbean and Black immigrant educators in the US. These studies, approved via IRB #2019–599 at a southwestern university and IRB #PRO6857 at a midwestern university, were selected as a means of obtaining secondary data because of the focus on decolonizing methods deployed in this work. In the decolonizing interpretive analytical framework chosen for the current analysis, there is a need to draw upon the historical values (i.e., past, present, future), contextual knowledges, and insider realities that frame the responses gathered in data collected from Black immigrant student participants (see Table 5.1; see Smith et al., 2022; and also Darder, 2015). By choosing to draw secondarily from these studies, I provide an opportunity to use 'non-Westernized' decolonizing methods as a basis for interrogating 'Westernized' ways of knowing in the responses of Black immigrant youth.

For each of the aforementioned studies, individual in-depth semi-structured interviews were conducted with each participant face-to-face, via phone conference, or via Zoom conference. Interviews were based on protocols, each containing twenty-one questions that ranged from broad educational experiences in the home country for Caribbean nationals, to specific experiences with language and Englishes across home and US contexts and classrooms for immigrants residing in the US. Artifacts enabled the participants to remember certain events and were thus encouraged for their interviews. Questions guiding these interviews were developed carefully based on findings from previous research concerning the standardized and non-standardized Englishes of immigrant educators with an intent to understand how these educators used their standardized Englishes as well as challenges faced. Examples of questions posed included: *What was the first time (if any) that you noticed a unique difference in the way you spoke English and the way Americans speak English in the US? Describe an experience of this kind*; *Describe the challenges you faced with English as well as the parts of your experience that you have enjoyed (if any)*; and *How important is it for you to sound like a British or American speaker of English in interactions with colleagues/students/others?*

Relying on these data allowed for a holistic understanding of participants' experiences as steeped in their backgrounds as individuals, teachers, students, scholars, and educators. Since certain secondary participants served as educators in their colleges while enrolled as doctoral students in the US before eventually obtaining their doctoral degrees, several referred, in their interviews, to experiences that they had as doctoral students, but which also coincided with their then roles as educators. Moreover, given that discussions in the interviews of these educators sometimes focused on the experience of being an immigrant in general, in some cases participants made reference to their uses of Englishes prior to becoming educators in their colleges that were central to how they constructed their understandings about the overall experience of being an immigrant educator in the US.

Procedures

I relied on an adapted version of Seidman's (2012) three-interview series to conduct individual interviews with participants.

Primary Data

Each participant engaged in two in-depth semi-structured phenomenological interviews with me face-to-face in my office at the university where I worked. The first interview was focused on (i) participants' life histories and (ii) details of the experience of using Englishes including affordances as well as language discrimination faced by the Black immigrant youth. Given the requirements of Seidman's interview model, interview protocols for the second interview were based on participants' responses in the first interview; drafted after participant responses to the first interview had been obtained; and forwarded (after an IRB amendment) to participants prior to the subsequent round of interviews. Each interview session lasted approximately one hour. The second interview was conducted four weeks after the first to allow for transcription and for drafting of the questions for the second interview. This process was required because the second interview protocol was dependent on the findings derived from the first. This second interview focused on participants' reflection on the meaning of the experience (Seidman, 2012) of using Englishes, language discrimination, and cultural adjustment through Englishes, and lasted for a total of approximately one hour.

Secondary Data

Each participant engaged in individual in-depth semi-structured interviews with me, face-to-face, via phone conference, or via Zoom conference. I followed the same procedures for these interviews conducted with primary participants as described above.

Analysis

I engaged in a two-dimensional level of analysis. First, in line with the "(decolonizing) analytical framework" (see Table 5.1) developed and based on a "decolonizing interpretive research" design (Darder, 2015; Dei, 2000), I engaged first in interpretive analysis of primary participant data, which were transcribed and prepared for analysis after interviews had all been completed. Through this process, I came to understand the realities, knowledge, and values attached to the primary participants' ways of viewing and using Englishes and literacies, the ideologies affecting their perceptions and use of these Englishes and broader semiotics, and the affordances that enabled them to persist towards a sense of agency and self-determination (Fanon, 1961/1991). I relied upon the theoretical framework in which multiliteracies, raciolinguistic, and translanguaging intersected to inform my inductive and deductive analysis of primary participant data.

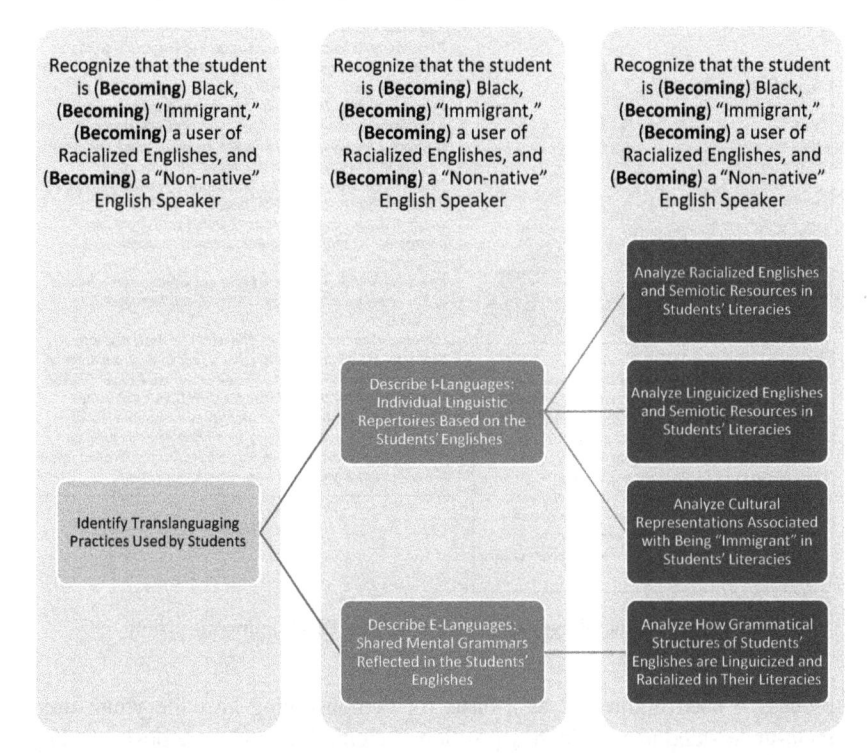

Figure 5.1 Translanguaging via an integrated model of multilingualism for clarifying Black immigrant literacies

Using Table 5.1, I engaged in inductive analyses via open coding (Charmaz, 2006) of these data through the iterative process of identifying in vivo codes, aligning them with excerpts from the data. Through constant-comparative analysis (Charmaz, 2006), I revisited codes and then identified and described constructs across each theoretical framework related to a given code (see Table 5.1 for an example of this process). Also using Table 5.1, I engaged in deductive analysis of the data by seeking to determine which elements of multiliteracies, raciolinguistic, and translanguaging frameworks were being reflected in the data. To address multiliteracies in this process, I focused on identifying the ways in which youth described their literacies as premised on traditional reading and writing (i.e., linguistic mode) as well as multimodality more broadly (i.e., by drawing from broader semiotic resources). To address translanguaging in this process, I used Figure 5.1 as a basis for identifying when youth alluded to E-languages and I-languages as a basis for their languaging (see Smith, 2020c). To address raciolinguistic ideologies in this

Speech Act – Conversations and interactions between Jaeda, her teachers, and her peers.

Storyline – Duality
Those who speak Standardized American English (or standardized language) are accepted. Those who do not speak it are not. If Jaeda wants to be accepted, she must speak Standardized English. When she does, she may or may not be accepted by members of her Black race. Speaking Standardized American English is not what gets Jaeda social acceptance because it also requires her speaking and behaving in ways that are sanctioned or approved by various members of her Black race.

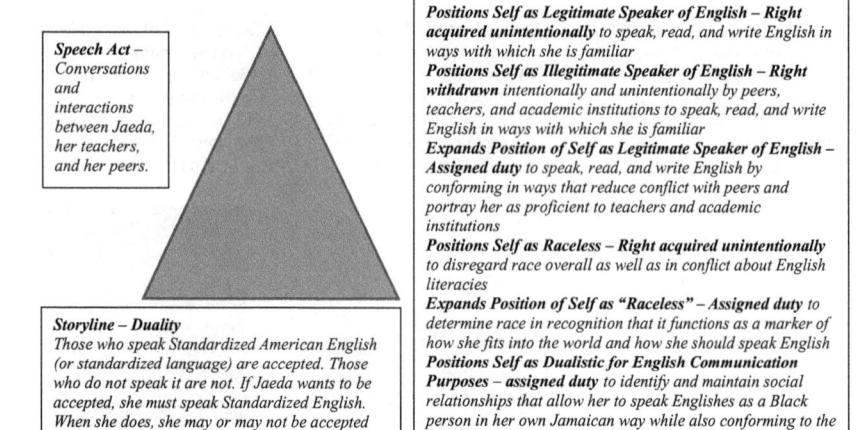

Positions Self as Legitimate Speaker of English – Right acquired unintentionally to speak, read, and write English in ways with which she is familiar
Positions Self as Illegitimate Speaker of English – Right withdrawn intentionally and unintentionally by peers, teachers, and academic institutions to speak, read, and write English in ways with which she is familiar
Expands Position of Self as Legitimate Speaker of English – Assigned duty to speak, read, and write English by conforming in ways that reduce conflict with peers and portray her as proficient to teachers and academic institutions
Positions Self as Raceless – Right acquired unintentionally to disregard race overall as well as in conflict about English literacies
Expands Position of Self as "Raceless" – Assigned duty to determine race in recognition that it functions as a marker of how she fits into the world and how she should speak English
Positions Self as Dualistic for English Communication Purposes – assigned duty to identify and maintain social relationships that allow her to speak Englishes as a Black person in her own Jamaican way while also conforming to the Englishes required in and by academic institutions

Figure 5.2 Raciolinguistic positioning of a Black immigrant youth

process, I used Figure 5.2 as a basis for demonstrating how the youth used meta-understandings while they positioned themselves and were positioned by others who functioned as listening subjects (Smith, 2019a), careful to indicate how white supremacy, through the white gaze and *white audit*, influenced the immigrant and transnational students as they leveraged their Englishes while forced to reconcile with expectations of white supremacy in their translanguaging and transsemiotizing. Subsequently, I revisited codes and then identified and described constructs across each theoretical framework related to a given code (see Table 5.1, rows 5, 6, 7, etc., for an example of this process).

As a Black immigrant-educator-scholar with insider knowledge about the use of Englishes in an English-speaking Caribbean context as well as in the US, I honored my ability to bring both an etic and emic lens (Charmaz, 2006) to this process as part of a (decolonizing) interpretive framework. In the final step of this process, I grouped similar codes into categories and labeled these categories in ways that would highlight the nuances evident across interpretive and (decolonizing) interpretive insights. When there was similarity across three or more categories, I grouped these and presented them in the findings as a theme.

My second step, in line with the "(decolonizing) analytical framework" (see Table 5.1), involved engaging in decolonizing interpretive analysis of secondary participant (i.e., informant) data. Through this process, I identified the broader contextual knowledges, historical values, and insider realities from secondary participants' responses about using Englishes in the US and the Caribbean that suggested how and why raciolinguistic and monoglossic ideologies framed responses presented by the Black immigrant youth. In this way, I engaged the dialectic between interpretive analysis premised on Westernized ways of knowing while also giving credence to decolonizing interpretive analysis based on non-Western approaches to finding "truth." That notwithstanding, I was curtailed in my capacity to present full descriptions of informant insider accounts due to space limitations and thus, provide only brief insights of the vast and broad knowledges of the secondary participants in this book. See Table 5.1 for an overview of this process.

Credibility, Verisimilitude, Transferability

Through member-checking, participants reviewed my narration of the findings (Lincoln & Guba, 1985) and concurred that they were comfortable with my representations of their thoughts and feelings (Merriam, 2009). In presenting detailed reports concerning how the study was conducted (Maxwell, 2013), maintaining reflexivity (Janesick, 2010), and through the use of multiple data sources (Merriam, 2009), I preserved credibility of the study. Credibility and trustworthiness were further addressed by ensuring that epistemological perspectives – such as knowledge as social construction – undergirded analysis, interpretation, and presentation of data through narratives, both from an interpretive and a (decolonizing) interpretive perspective (Darder, 2015; Dei, 2000). Member-checking with participants ensured that I was true to their narratives, helping to preserve visibility of the process of analysis, and supported credibility through the use of "thick" and "rich description" via participant voices. This process, in turn, contributed to external validity and to transferability to similar individuals and contexts, helping to foster representativeness (Charmaz, 2006) as I make my process visible (Table 5.1) to those who may wish to gauge transferability or to replicate the study.

Aware of the multiple perspectives within both Westernized and non-Westernized approaches to research, wary of essentialization, and wishing to maintain trustworthiness as well as credibility of the analyses in this overall work (Charmaz, 2006), I solicited the feedback of five external reviewers who also functioned as scholars and educators at "research intensive" universities to listen to my arguments about the conceptual, theoretical, and methodological perspectives being presented as well as assumptions undergirding my research. They were each invited to orally share their insights as I made notations to the evolving interpretations. One of these colleagues was a Black Caribbean linguistically diverse scholar in language and literacy studies, and the other, a Black Caribbean scholar in higher education. The third was a Black linguistically diverse American scholar with expertise in literacy studies and the fourth, a Latinx scholar, who held expertise in applied linguistics. The fifth was a white monolingual American scholar in literacy and language studies. These reviewers examined my descriptions of my process of data analysis from an etic as well as an emic perspective to determine whether they agreed with my designations as I transitioned from raw data to themes and provided feedback concerning coherence of the overall manuscript based on their understanding of questions guiding this work. Their insights allowed for revisitation of analyses to be more representative of the data and to reflect the dialectic ingrained in participant stories, creating opportunities, as Amanda Gorman observes, for lifting the gaze, "not to what stands between us, but what stands before us." They served as a mechanism to close "the divide because we know to put our future first, we must first put our differences aside" (Gorman, 2021). Through an invitation of the voices of populations functioning as 'insiders' as well as 'outsiders' to the "authentic narratives" (Smith, 2023a) presented of Black immigrant and transnational youth, provision was thus made for the symbolic laying "down" of "arms" so peoples across races, nationalities, ethnicities, and so on, "can reach out" their "arms to one another," seeking "harm to none and harmony for all" and recognizing we can "forever be tied together, victorious."

Notwithstanding measures taken as described above, I acknowledge a limitation such that certain participants' voices, for example, that of Asha and Fanus, tended to be represented more forcefully and more often across the findings than that of other youth given space limitations as well as the salience of their data excerpts to the cross-cutting categories' themes.

6 Translanguaging Imaginaries of Innocence
A Holistic Portrait of the Literacies of Black Caribbean Immigrant Youth

> When day comes, we step out of the shade of flame and unafraid.
> The new dawn balloons as we free it.
> There is always light. If only we're brave enough to see it. If only we're brave enough to be it.
>
> Gorman, 2021

In 2015, Kan Kan Riddim released the song "Phenomenal," written and sang by Trinidadian and Tobagonian Soca artist Rodney "Benjai" LeBlanc, and produced by AdvoKit Productions. The song included the following lyrics:

> Soca does give meh meh powers
> Make me jump and fete fi hours
> Soca does give meh meh powers
> Drink meh rum and share with others
> Fete fi hours, soca powers
> Is a wonderful feeling
> Share with others
> All my brothers
> All my sisters
> Today we making we name
>
> We partying sun or rain
> We doh care what the people say
> Once the music hit meh veins
> So much powers ah cyah explain
> Until ah cool again, when the father take me away
> All wey meh friends will say
> ***I'm Phenomenal***
> ***I'm Phenomenal***
> ***I'm Phenomenal***
> ***I'm Phenomenal***
>
> Soca does give meh meh powers
> Turn me into masqueraders
> Soca does give meh meh powers
> Draw me straight in different colors
> Masqueraders, we get powers

> Is a wonderful feeling
> On stage together holding me banners
> With different colors
> We crossing the stage
>
> Kan Kan Riddim, 2015

The allusion to being "phenomenal" invoked by Soca artist Benjai in this song, written by Rodney Le Blanc, is semiotically expressed in the corresponding music video set against the backdrop of the never-ending ocean, inscribing phenomenality through multimodal representations to Black peoples across a broad range of life spheres. *Graduates, construction worker, dancers, office workers, lawyers, pilots, nurses, mothers, doctors, dancers, mothers* – peoples illustrated first based on their professional expertise but who then come together collectively as "brothers and sisters" – all join in the joy of masquerading, feeling, drinking, fete-ing, and partying, as is the way of the Caribbean spirit. Capturing the notion of "flourishing" (Keyes, 2002) that requires a wellness of the whole being through this vividly painted imaginary that juxtaposes the joys of living freely as co-existent with the pursuit of purpose, it is fitting that the song "Phenomenal" functions as the entry point to this chapter, through which I paint a holistic portrait of the literacies of Black Caribbean immigrant and transnational youth.

Specifically, I present findings from interpretive analyses of the data as they relate to the multiliteracies and translanguaging practices engaged in by six Black Caribbean English-speaking youth across their Bahamian and Jamaican Caribbean home countries and the US. I contextualize these findings within (decolonizing) interpretive analyses that clarify the raciolinguistic and *raciosemiotic ideologies* informing students' multiliteracies and translanguaging practices. In doing so, this chapter shows how the literacies of Black immigrant youth are enacted holistically by adeptly illustrating the languaging and semiotizing associated with and the ideologies influencing these literacies. Based on the findings, I present and discuss *semiolingual innocence* as a necessary heuristic for understanding how elements of multiliteracies and *translanguaging* practices as well as raciolinguistic and raciosemiotic ideologies intersected to clarify the literacies leveraged by Black Caribbean youth. In turn, through semiolingual innocence emerging from *transracialization* of the *enmigwé nwè* as an analytical prism, I invite a reinscribing of the innocence of Black youth, whose ancestors have for centuries leveraged semiolingually, *sans white gaze*, their multiliteracies for agentively reading and writing themselves into the world.

To accomplish the above, I first present findings from my (decolonizing) interpretive analyses to illustrate the ways in which "holistic literacies" (Smith, 2023a) were manifested in the lives of six Black youth with origins in the Bahamas and Jamaica in the English-speaking Caribbean, whose stories formed a basis for the study undergirding this book. In doing so, I rely on "rich" and "thick" descriptions (Lincoln & Guba, 1985) from the Black Caribbean youth whom I came to know as a *Black scholar-mother* during my time with them in the Caribbean Student Association. My intentionality in presenting the authentic voices of Black Caribbean youth is based on what I have previously described as the *raciolinguistic erasure* of their holistic voices from academic books, journals, articles, and materials which typically insist that the data from their lives be truncated and analyzed into oblivion in ways that result in a fragmented understanding of the youth. Based on these unsanitized "authentic narratives" (Smith, 2023a) of the Black Caribbean immigrant youth steeped in the notion of "critical dialectical pluralism" (Onwuegbuzie & Frels, 2013), I then show how the holistic literacies of the Black Caribbean youth became visible as they functioned as immigrants in the US. Following this, I demonstrate how holistic literacies were leveraged across the US and Caribbean in the lives of these youth. Based on these depictions, I engage in a naming of the holistic literacies that emerged from these analyses, and in turn, articulate a framework of *semiolingual innocence* as the basis for expanding the reach of translanguaging and transsemiotizing to all in schools, through attention to its role in and beyond Englishes as part of students' linguistic and broader semiotic repertoires.

Holistic Literacies of Black Youth in the English-Speaking Caribbean

Growing up as children racialized as Black in Jamaica and the Bahamas for the Caribbean youth who functioned as primary participants in the study undergirding this book, meant (a) a reliance on 'broken Englishes'; (b) paradoxical acceptance of Englishes both at home and at school; and (c) overt de/legitimization of Englishes.

Reliance on 'Broken Englishes' in the Bahamas and in Jamaica

Asha described her Bahamian English as 'broken' and associated this brokenness with intergenerational heritage. She explained how oral literacy in the Bahamas is different from Standard American English orthography providing examples such as the transposition of "w" for "v" and the use of "irl" in "oi" words such as "boil," "oil," and "toilet." She shared:

Mostly [in the Bahamas], I just use English but it's broken English so a lot of people switch "v's" with "w's" so instead of saying "what" they'd say "vat," ummm, I dunno, but Bahamians don't say like "oil" or "boil," they put "irl" in it so like ... "toirlet" instead of "toilet," they switch it.

Asha's metalinguistic understanding (Smith, 2019a) allowed her to recognize the variations in standardized structures of the named languages that she possessed and how these variations translated into individuals 'sounding' different based on phonetic juxtapositions of letters and their sounds across Englishes in her linguistic repertoire. The raciolinguistic ideologies (Rosa & Flores, 2017) undergirding phonics and phonemic notions in Asha's Englishes appeared to be aligned with the insistence on the E-language, Bahamian Creolized English, as "broken" and another E-language, Bahamian Standard English, as supposedly aspirational based on white listening subject norms (Rosa & Flores, 2017). In doing so, she seemed comfortable approximating orthographies steeped in what those in her Bahamian schools and society believe is a certain privileged E-language – *standardized English as the better one.* Asha's perceptions of racialized language were thus derived from the privileging of white listeners as superior, both at the individual as well as organizational and institutional levels, resulting in an occasional rejection of Bahamian Creolized English as part of her linguistic repertoire. Activating her self-determination, Asha in turn reflected a distancing of her personhood from linguistic markers in Bahamian Creolized English that signaled perceived inferiority based on the white listening subject's association of this language to deficit. She said:

I don't say it [like that, with the "v" for "w"] but my grandparents really say it a lot. The older people [speak it more] and have stronger dialects than we do but I still understand them when they say it.

Much like Asha, Melody described her Jamaican Creolized English as "broken." She shared:

My mom's from Jamaica. She's Jamaican. Her accent is Jamaican English. She lived like twenty years in England, nineteen years in Jamaica. But the thing is me and my sister, we have language problems because my mom had a very thick accent like her family, so we started talking Patois all the time, all the time, so then we had to take English as a second language classes all the way up to middle school. Basically, like I feel I was speaking English [in elementary school], but you know, Jamaican, broken Jamaican; kids bullied me and my sister all the time. I would like, go home, cry about it because no one understands what I was saying.

And later she stated, alluding again to "brokenness":

Yes, but back to my mom, now she hates sounding Jamaican. She became a proper person. She's very proper. She reads a lot and I think that is kind of changing her. She reads all the time and so, she carries herself at high level and she wants me to meet that level. She doesn't want me to speak down at this level [where I use Jamaican Creolized English]. She always wants me to learn different languages. She put her money aside for me to go back to China. She wants me to be fluent in Mandarin. I am working on language all the time because she wants me to speak Spanish and Mandarin at the same time. She knows Spanish, French, and something else. So now she pronounces her words; you'll never hear her speak like, broken [Jamaican English]; but you also hear the [Jamaican] accent. She sounds more American [now] but she still has problems with saying some difficult words. When I'm at home I speak totally different with the same [Jamaican] accent like my mom. Immediately. I can turn [my American accent] off and turn it on. I got used to that. So, when I'm at home, I am totally comfortable.

Complicating this dynamic, Fanus prepositioned himself in terms of a binary when he described being unable to use proper English well in writing, sharing:

We speak predominantly broken English. So, we chop off words. So, a key word in Bahamas I think is "Bey" B-E-Y. So, I don't know someone, I don't know their name. I say "Bey, come here." There're a lot of phrases like you say back home that most people in Bahamas can understand. [Or, I might point to] a series of boxes, [and I could] say, "Could you give me a wibe?" W-I-B-E. Yes. And that's predominantly, I wouldn't say, spoken among adults, but it's [also] spoken among kids ... My primary school, the standard British English. I myself personally had a hard time with proper English on paper, but I could speak clearly versus on paper because it's slang, I would spell words wrong. I can't. I would always find myself messing it up.

When Fanus said, "I myself personally had a hard time with proper English on paper" but also acknowledged that he was capable of using oral language clearly despite speaking "predominantly broken English," the metalinguistic understanding (Smith, 2019a) demonstrated by Fanus allowed him to position himself in a way that reflected a view of himself as able to use the language he believed was expected of him in speaking – a certain imagined version of Standard English – but only partly able to meet these expectations in writing. The binary introduced by E-languages in his individual linguistic repertoire that allowed his literacies to both cause Fanus to feel capable, and also *not*, seemed aligned to the invisible though rigidly imposed expectations for speech in the Caribbean classroom by the white listening subject (Rosa & Flores, 2017). This binary was also reflected in expectations for writing based largely on cognitivist conceptions (Berthele, 2020) designed by Eurocentric norms to undergird what should function as approximations of language by people of Color. Together, these requirements of Fanus formed the bases by which he judged himself, determining in turn how he legitimized his personhood or not, based on his literacies as expressed through his "written proficiency," and his speech across the E-languages of Bahamian Creolized English and Bahamian Standard English in the Bahamian context.

Jermaine too described himself as using two E-languages across his linguistic repertoire, with the 'unbroken' English designated as "proper." He shared:

For the most part, I speak English and like Patois. In the Bahamas, we say "she" and "he" instead of "her" and "him" then we say "her" instead of saying "she." "I will tell she about this." I guess the way we pronounce words. Instead of going to the store, we might say "I gahing to the store." So one common thing is on some of the smaller [Bahamian] islands, people pronounce their "v" as a "w" and their "w" as a "v." I lived in the city. There's really two major cities. Nassau, which is the capital, and then

Freeport. I lived in Freeport. I guess I grew up with my grandparents. My grandmother she was born and raised in the Bahamas. She spoke proper English. She still have the accent and everything, it's just that she was very proper. Dialect is everywhere [back home].

Everybody speak like that. It's not that she spoke proper English but if she had to come to America, she wouldn't have to change the way she speak too much because you could understand her when she speak.

Based on indications from Asha, Melody, Fanus, and Jermaine, the institution of schooling, as well as the home and society at large, worked together to reinforce the raciolinguistic ideologies that told them that one named language (Bahamian Creolized English, Jamaican Creolized English) was inferior to the other (Bahamian Standard English, Jamaican Standard) and that caused them to refer to their inferiorly positioned Englishes as "broken" or to their superiorly positioned Englishes as "proper." This was intensified by their placement in either ESL classes, which was the case with Melody, or the support they were provided with tutoring, which was the case with Jermaine, who explained, "It was easier [for me to adjust in the US] because I was in athletics. I had tutoring if I needed it. I always had the resources. I was in track and field and I still am."

Paradoxical Acceptance of Languages at Home and at School in the Bahamas

In addition to perceived brokenness of certain Englishes in their repertoires, growing up as Black children in the Caribbean for certain youth participants meant learning that their named languages – Creolized and Standard Englishes – were differentially but both accepted, based on contradictory expectations within the home and also the school. One of these students, whose literacies reflected such paradoxical acceptance, was Asha. Asha used her oral and written literacies both at home and at school in accordance with paradoxical literate norms. As a child, Asha appeared to accept expectations of her languaging by the white listening subject (Rosa & Flores, 2017) for Bahamian Standardized English, an E-language, only because she had the opportunity to use her Bahamian Englishes with her mother even while her dad rejected them. She shared:

For me growing up, actually, my dad did not encourage me using dialect. I went to a private school, and he said, "I did not pay $1,500 three times a year for you to talk this way." Like he was really big on me speaking properly all the time. I dunno [how I felt], I didn' really care 'cuz I could switch with my mom. My mom lets me [use Bahamian Creole] but my dad didn't really encourage it. So my dad doesn't really come in when I talk to my mom, but the thing is, about that, he switches, 'cuz he's from a different island [in the Bahamas], he's from Acklins so he grew up there and they have like a separate accent used sort of, where they use dialect, it's a bit different, it's worse. And I love when he switches into it so I don't understand why he didn't really encourage us to use it, but I love when he does. He gets very proper [though] when he goes out. Sometimes he puts on a little English accent, he's really proper [in situations like this] all the time.

As a child, Asha was thrilled to hear her father use the Bahamian Creolized English from his homeland island in the Bahamas which seemed largely different from the English used in the Bahamian island where she lived with her family. She enjoyed that this E-language was very different from the Bahamian Standardized English and his use of this language in his individual linguistic repertoire presented him to Asha in a very different light. The tone in her voice when she said she "love[d]" it when he did that conveyed an emotive response inspired by her father's use of the E-language that she seemed to wish for.

Asha's metalinguistic understanding (Smith, 2019a) was used to reflect a subtle awareness of how her feeling of joy was connected to the E-language that her father restricted from her linguistic repertoire and which she was able to experience because it was allowed by her mother. The restrictions imposed by her father, operating dualistically in nature at home, functioned similarly in contradiction across the primary and secondary schools that Asha attended. She shared:

I think in the [Bahamas] it depends on the school [what language they use]. Definitely my school was called Queen's College so it was really big with the British and with the former rule by the British, so I think they really care about how we speak because we are a representation of the school. [But] most public schools in the Bahamas do not care. As long as you write in Standard English, they don't care how you speak.

Asha had attended a private school, as she stated, and the norms there were very different from that of public schools:

I went to a private [high] school. Most of our teachers now are from England in my school. [The school goes] to England to recruit teachers for our school, or I had a lot of Jamaican teachers so maybe that's why the girl [that I mentioned earlier who asked me if I was Jamaican] thought I was Jamaican. So I speak the way I do because of that. I know when I was young too, because I had a British teacher, I had a British accent for like a year, before I switched back to a Bahamian teacher.

In these indications, reflecting the individual-to-global analyses called for by Rosa and Flores (2017) in a raciolinguistic perspective, white listening subject norms differentially influenced Asha's use of E-languages in her linguistic repertoire at home and at school. Even as a youth, she adeptly connected these norms to colonization by the British as was outlined by a raciolinguistic perspective, implicitly observing the co-naturalization of race and language even though she does not explicitly name race – "*racelessness*" (Rosa & Flores, 2017). As Rosa and Flores (2017) have outlined in a raciolinguistic perspective, a focus on colonial histories highlights the ways in which projected European subjects and the languages of these subjects have been deemed superior to racialized non-European 'objects' and to the linguistic repertoires developed by these objects. In Asha's experience, this dynamic was reflected as Bahamian and British teachers imposed expectations for the leveraging of her linguistic repertoire in ways that privileged structures of phonetics, grammar, and phonics of one E-language over another.

Asha's approach to self-determination occurred such that she attributed the way she used language – *'properly'* – to her father's as well as her teachers' imposition of white listening subject norms in the home and school, stating, "My dad's way of using language definitely impacted how I use [language]. It's why my accent isn't so strong," and, speaking of her teachers' use of Englishes, she shared, "So I speak the way I do because of that." Being a child in elementary school emerging into a teenager when she had these experiences, her father's and teachers' requirements for her languaging appeared to take precedence over what she should want for herself, causing Asha to seemingly relinquish autonomy over her individual linguistic repertoire (García & Wei, 2014) to her father who had paid for her tuition in high school and who needed her to "speak properly all the time." The institutions of home and that of school in the Bahamas were in turn positioned by Asha in ways that reflected, at least in part, their reliance on raciolinguistic ideologies (Rosa & Flores, 2017) for education in the Bahamas. Even when public schools allowed students such as Asha to use their Bahamian Creole Englishes, her responses suggested that the written expectation still remained aligned with expectations based on the white gaze and white audit.

Overt Legitimization of Bahamian Creolized English in the Bahamas

Amid this paradoxical acceptance reflected by Asha, which raised questions about how she wished to leverage her individual linguistic repertoire as a child and teenager, she used her metacultural understanding (Smith, 2019a) to speak with pride about a book that legitimized Bahamian Creolized English during her schooling and recognized the role of the school and nation in sanctioning it. She shared:

[In middle school] you probably just speak strict dialect with your friends, like jokes, it's not a big deal. Even like in eighth, ninth grade, we read a book, just in Bahamian dialect, and it's mandatory to read a book like that because we had to do an exam on it because there's a national exam that all Bahamians have to sit in like twelfth grade, or ninth grade.

In describing this book, the sound of pride in Asha's voice seemed to suggest that she was pleased with the school's decision to make the reading *as well as* assessment of the book mandatory in schools. Asha reflected then that her individual linguistic repertoire, in middle school, included the E-language – Bahamian Creolized English – that is often discounted in schools and expressed its significance in being required as part of a literacy assessment in her middle school. However, when she did acknowledge this, she used the pronoun "you" to characterize her speaking of "dialect," a practice that she repeatedly leverages elsewhere, suggesting a distancing of her personhood from the dialect even as she seems to want to support it. Asha's indications reflect that she notices how institutionally literate norms leveraged for reading in an E-language which has been inferiorly positioned her entire life (i.e., Bahamian Creolized English) as part of a book in middle school become established in the expectation for engaging with literacies that were typically not accepted in her private high school. Her recognition reveals an awareness of the translanguaging that she manifested across oral and written literacies in her individual linguistic repertoire (García & Wei, 2014). In this instance, raciolinguistic ideologies appear to have been transcended at least in part in the mandatory expectation that a book of 'Bahamian dialect' be read and become not only the basis for literacy/ELA reading in classrooms but also for a national assessment of literacy and ELA in the Bahamas. This decision-making on the part of the institution of schooling in the Bahamas, as reflected by Asha, was positioned by her in ways that reflected the possibilities of transcendence, at least in part, of raciolinguistic ideologies for education by institutions in the Bahamas while she attended middle school. This instantiation beckons the imagination to consider what institutions, such as schools, can expect of students through such a requirement to read books written in standardized Englishes ideologically relegated as inferior (often referred to as 'dialects'). It also prompts the need to consider how assessments leveraged by schools expose students to and engage students with E-languages often associated with inferiority based on the white gaze.

Overt Delegitimization of Bahamian Creolized English in the Bahamas and Jamaican Creolized English in Jamaica

In contrast to the paradoxical acceptance reflected by Asha, both Fanus and Melody alluded to the overt delegitimization of their inferiorly positioned E-languages in both the home and school. For instance, Fanus described his time as an elementary student in the Bahamas, stating:

So, in private school my mother definitely wants me to speak better than most people. [She would have me] read a lot of books. She makes read a lot. I had a book, I had some books that I didn't read ... I still won't read them. I don't know why.

And speaking of middle school and high school, he shared:

> So in middle school, my writing got worse, actually. My writing goes worse and then I spoke the same way. I spoke with the same slang, the same everything. It wasn't until after going into middle school until high school that I met a teacher. She's from England and she told me specifically that my Greek and English, they're going down and down. She pulled me to the aside and she told me "I've been looking at your essays and you write the way you talk." And if it wasn't for her, my English wouldn't elevate the way I did. In that conversation, basically it was about my grades, my progress ... because I was doing good in everything else except English and during inside the conversation, she had all my essays and then she looked at me and "I find myself writing you: y-u." She showed me, "You speaking like you write," and then it opened my eyes and she said, "You're [going to] go to college soon. You're about to be in America. You can't do that." So, I then found myself when I write my essays, I would go over them a ton of times and I would push back in my brain the way I speak and I would try to bring back proper, the way I should ... The way I should be writing in proper English. And then sooner or later, I became more efficient. [But] I just kept it in my writing. I continued [speaking the way I spoke], but in my writing I would write proper English and my speaking I just kept it the same way [with my friends]. [And my mom] would keep correcting me. She would. When I said "Bey," she would tell me "Stop speaking like that." When I said why, she would say, "Speak correctly" because she would correlate me talking like that like to like me talking like I'm ghetto ... And so, she would be like, "We're sending you to private school, we're sending you to this school, you need to speak correctly." And she would always say, "I bet that is not what you learn inside your books to talk like that."

The teacher in his middle school classroom viewed Fanus as incapable of language use based on the E-language privileged in her classroom. Describing his experience as a teenager back then in the Bahamas, Fanus alluded also to his feelings of being unable to measure up to the expectations for language use, using the words "down" and "elevate" in ways that suggested a supposed linguistic distance between the E-language of Bahamian Creolized English and the E-language of standardized language. For him, to go "up" was to seem more closely aligned to the supposedly acceptable approximation based on the white gaze and to go "down" was to somehow deviate from that approximation, signaling a descent into inferiority. In this dynamic, Fanus appeared troubled by a leveraging of his Bahamian Creolized English given its inferior status, governed by the monoglossic norm. He therefore chose Bahamian Standard English as part of his linguistic repertoire based on the white gaze with a Black teacher in what was the majority Black context of the Bahamas. Fanus also seemed to reflect that there were psycholinguistic processes in motion (see Ritchie & Bhatia, 2010), which potentially suggested that he was aware of how his brain struggled to overcome what he portrayed as the 'natural' inclination to rely on what seemed like, in his description, a neurobiologically instantiated (see Sabourin & Stowe, 2010) E-language based on the socially constructed language system of the Bahamas for this abstract cognitivist writing process aligned with Eurocentric norms (see Smith & Warrican, 2021; see also Berthele, 2020).

Through his metalinguistic understanding, Fanus reflected an evaluation of the context in which his languaging was leveraged, pondering his duty to use language 'properly' based on what seemed like an internalized white gaze operating in part due to raciolinguistic ideologies. These ideologies, operating in a context where white supremacy was supposedly instantiated, albeit covertly, but nonetheless present in the norms leveraged by racialized subjects (i.e., teacher) who superimposed this on the racialized objects (e.g., Fanus) over whom they had oversight, were visible in Fanus's depiction. In turn, Fanus seemed to reposition himself as capable of language use based on what seemed like acceptability according to the white gaze, a decision which, as Rosa and Flores (2017) observe in a raciolinguistic perspective, will not ultimately provide the acceptance that Fanus seeks. It is no wonder then that Fanus ultimately moved back and forth within a binary throughout his reflexive experiences as there is an iterative process of receiving acceptance and re-seeking the latter in literacies largely defined by his languaging.

Despite the raciolinguistic ideologies at play, Fanus appeared not to completely surrender to external demands, choosing instead to reflect a duality through his metalinguistic understanding (Smith, 2019a) that allowed him to seemingly expand his individual linguistic repertoire. Demonstrating this process, Fanus explained without hesitation and reservation, "I just kept [standardized English dialect] in my writing ... and my speaking, I just kept it the same way [with my friends]," a process that I refer to as using *translanguaging with Englishes* based on an integrated model of multilingualism (Smith, 2020c; see also Smith & Warrican, 2021). In such a case, the Black Caribbean student, Fanus, engages with raciolinguistic ideologies and understands what is expected of him institutionally and societally via the use of a certain E-language, but at the same time, he makes an executive decision to leverage his Bahamian Creolized English with his friends, emphasizing his comfort with duality of his linguistic repertoire. By doing so, Fanus chooses to exercise personhood as a function of his entanglement with two E-languages, one of which offers him a pathway to the '*success*' emphasized by his mother at home and his teacher at school while also seizing the opportunity for a pathway to joy based on the social acceptance of his friends.

Summary

The raciolinguistic injustice reflected in youth's reliance on what they referred to as 'broken English' in the Bahamas characterized simultaneously by a paradoxical acceptance of languages both at home and at school for youth such as Asha, which presented itself in the overt legitimization and also delegitimization of Bahamian Creolized English, was accompanied by a flexibility adopted while using languaging and a duality developed while retaining personhood in the context of the Caribbean. Through this act, what I refer to and discuss later as the *performance of inonsans jan nwè*, Fanus, a Black Caribbean teenager at the time, refused to be completely defined by raciolinguistic ideologies undergirding the inhibitions of white gaze. The scholarship pointing to *bilingualism* – often viewed as the use of two acceptable named languages – typically thought to be advantageous (Antoniou, 2019), has, for a long time, operated alongside contrasting views towards *bidialectalism*, which typically reflects an inferiorly positioned standardized and non-standardized variety with a "lower" societal status. Juxtaposed against the agentive renderings of translanguaging, for instance, by Fanus who chose to insist on joy through use of Bahamian Creolized English with his friends, the depictions of his self-determination join broad corpuses of research about the linguistic richness of Black students in the Caribbean, countries of Africa, and in the US, which continue to remain on the peripheries of schools. Though often relegated to inferior status despite the proven capacities of *multilingual* and *bidialectal* children being described as "advantageous" when compared to monolingual children on tests of memory, attention, and cognitive flexibility (Antoniou, 2019), Fanus's indications made it clear that his capacity to reinscribe his innocence would be retained.

Overall, the translanguaging processes used by Black youth in the Caribbean, as presented above, appear to mirror a wrestling with differential positioning of E-languages. This wrestling signals how the integrated model of multilingualism functions as a mechanism for students to both reflect their individual linguistic repertoires even while having to navigate their societally and institutionally determined realities undergirding literate and language practice in and beyond schools. It raises questions about how institutions of schooling create spaces in Caribbean schools and classrooms for students to reinscribe their linguistic innocence through interactions with peers in ways that allow them to preserve their personhoods (Rosa & Flores, 2017). Reflecting how Black Caribbean students simultaneously wrestled with raciolinguistic and raciosemiotic injustice in their home countries of Jamaica and the Bahamas while at the same time agentively used translanguaging practices to (re)read and (re)write their worlds as well as their personhoods within it, the holistic literacies of students in this context point to the ways in which institutions have positioned Black Caribbean students to exercise their self-determination or not, as a function of their individual linguistic repertoires. Emerging through this use of their individual linguistic repertoires to iteratively engage in a reshaping of their Caribbean worlds, the youth demonstrate how they leveraged holistic literacies (Smith, 2020b).

Holistic Literacies of Black Caribbean Immigrant Youth in the US

Evolving as Black Caribbean youth in the US, the primary participants in the study undergirding this book reflected (a) the body as a transraciosemiotic marker; (b) exceptionalistic discarding of Bahamian English in the US; (c) switch among E-languages; (d) raciolinguistic rejection from the inside and a burden of sounding American; (e) heterogeneous representations of Blackness as necessary but exclusive; (f) doing to escape feeling; and (g) the (un)seizing of varied liberties as expressions of safety.

The Body as a Transraciosemiotic Marker

First assuming a role as a transnational child before finally migrating to the US to live as a teenager, Asha's initial experience growing up in the US revealed, through a stranger's response to her mother, that she was viewed with more admiration than some of her peers. Asha explained:

I remember being in Macy's with my mom I was like eight maybe, I think, and this lady saw the sticker on my mom's car so she knew she was from the islands and this lady was like, "Oh, your kids are so well behaved you can tell they're from the islands" and she's like, "Some American kids are just swinging on everything ..."

In this excerpt, as provided by Asha, raciosemiotic ideologies were used to construct Black people perceived as 'Caribbean islanders' as better than some of their peers in the US by a stranger in that context. As reflected by the excerpt, at the time, Asha, though perhaps largely oblivious, was using her body semiotically, through the gestural mode, to write herself as a child in a public place and be still in ways that were associated with expectations for being a Black child in the Caribbean and in the Caribbean classroom. Societally, for a stranger in the US to leverage such ideologies based on the writing of the body of a child who has not also engaged in languaging suggests that there is a broader institutional ideology at play – one that is steeped in expectations for how the body of a Black young child should be literately written onto the spaces within which it interacts with the public. Regardless of the stranger's race, they "invoke behavioral stereotypes that are commonly associated with distinctions between Whiteness and Blackness *and* that can be used to remap these distinction among Black populations in ways that are still ultimately reproductive of anti-Blackness" (Dr. Jonathan Rosa, personal communication; see also Dr. Krystal Smalls on the anti-Black epistemes emerging between African transnational (Smalls, 2018) and African American youth; and Dr. Jemima Pierre on the myth of Black American cultural inferiority: Pierre, 2004). This dynamic mirrors the notion of "twining" put forward by Rosa and Flores (2017), which highlights how relationships are developed between linguistic and racial forms such that together they hold certain cultural values that make them intertwined (p. 11). In Asha's case, this twining occurs as semiotic and racial forms are intertwined and together hold cultural values which are in turn linked to Asha's personhood and the raciosemiotizing of her body.

It is no wonder that Asha is positioned as better than, what can only be assumed as, her Black American and other peers as a child even while she remained oblivious to the raciosemiotic impositions on her personhood. We know this because Asha's reference to the word "swinging" as she remembers its use by the woman has stuck with her. It can be said here also that "swinging" is often associated with monkeys and that the tendency to surmise a reference to Asha's peers as typically functioning like animals based on raciosemiotic ideologies could be made. However, given the absence of further context and the reliance on a memory offered by Asha, this inference is only conjecture.

Notwithstanding the above, Asha's semiotic practice of writing her body in public spaces in acceptable ways at least, in the eyes of stranger, were partly steeped in notions also made visible through E-semiotics imposed by her family, her schools, and the broader society. Her process of self-determination, having been influenced by the semiotic expectations for her writing of self as a child, were now represented in an inadvertent transgeographic presentation of herself transsemiotically in the US and its corresponding sanctioning of expectations for behavior across Bahamian and US borders. Asha's transracialization in the US, much like the norms for her languaging in and beyond schools in the Caribbean, as will be shown later, appeared to have been produced in partial alignment with the white listening subject for most of her life as a child. These institutional facets implied that her silencing of the body to align with conformity in public spaces was useful for *"raciolinguistic rewards"* in the societal system of the US, functioning as what has been referred to as a *"transraciosemiotic marker"* (Warrican & Smith, in press), operating first at home in the Caribbean to define how Asha will advance towards *"success"* even as she is now recognized as 'better' by a stranger after she has transgeographically occupied space in a new land.

Institutionally, the external construction of Asha, a Caribbean islander as 'better behaved' than Black American and other peers based on her transsemiotic repertoire, mirrors the indications of the portrayal of Black Caribbean youth as a "model minority" (Smith, 2020b) based largely on linguistic and socioeconomic modalities as a basis for rewarding approximations to whiteness. This dynamic, challenged in the framework for Black immigrant literacies (Smith, 2020b, 2023a), in turn, is steeped in broader societal notions of comportment associated with Caribbean Blacks and into which Asha's mother inadvertently is complicated, when she accepts the compliment about her daughter. It also raises questions about how Asha's body may have been read raciosemiotically as a Black immigrant child in the US classroom as potentially 'better' than that of her peers.

Greeting For Jermaine and Fanus, the writing of the body transsemiotically across the Bahamas and the US was premised on the significant change in *greetings* reflected by the society in the US as opposed to what they were used to with their social interactions in the Caribbean. Through their metacultural understanding (Smith, 2019a), the two Black Bahamian Caribbean youth immediately surmised that there was a difference in societal expectations of them for writing themselves into the interactional fabric of informality in the new world. Both youth seemed appalled that they could no longer write their bodies through greetings with people as a daily part of their interactions in the world in much the same way that they had been accustomed to doing this in the Caribbean. Jermaine explained:

I guess, greetings, back home, I mean you see someone, even if you don't know them you say good morning. You doh really get that here. They just give you a smile, if that, or they don't even look in your direction so that was different. I had to understand that people don't understand me when I talk sometimes. If they understand me, is certain parts here and there, they would or would not understand so it's just the cultural barrier that I faced.

For Fanus, he described the difference as an overall lack of friendliness in how the US society expected him to function. He shared:

Moving to the United States, I guess the adjustment was to the culture. It's so different. Like everyone, I would say they're not friendly as we [Caribbean people] are. So, when I first came back home [here in the US] and said, "Good morning" ... I find myself I stop saying good morning as often as I would because no one says that back to me. And I'm a friendly person. So, I try to conversation with anyone. So, I would say [to myself], "Good. Let it go," and ... I would say [to people], "Your hair is nice" and "How's your day going?" and [this girl] she was like ... [looking back like], Because she asked, "Why is he talking to me?" Yes. "Why is he talking to me?" I found it's weird [because] back home, I'm in a library and I sit next to a stranger, and I made a comment like that in the conversation ... I'm not trying to get with or to be interested. I'm just trying to have conversation. And we will feel more comfortable if we know each other a little bit more than [if] we just sit in front of each other [when] we don't know each other ... So, that was the biggest thing I had to deal with. The friendliness. I think Caribbean people in general are one hundred percent more friendly. So, I think that was the biggest thing for me.

Unlike Asha, who was much younger at the time of her transsemiotic writing and who may have not been as aware of it, Jermaine and Fanus both appeared, as youth, to be disturbed by the erasure of their personhood when engaging with people informally through a greeting where they smiled and appeared to be friendly. This transsemiotic rewriting of the body accompanied by explicit translingual erasure from their individual linguistic and semiotic repertoires imposed societally as a normative practice of institutions such as schools and in homes in the Caribbean meant that Jermaine and Fanus appeared to seem transsemiotically handicapped, judging from the emphatic tone in their voices as they lamented this absence of a semiolingual crutch that had been part of their entire lives as Black youth in the Caribbean. Though largely invisible, the collective interdependence of Indigeneity undergirding the expectations for informally greeting others with whom one interacts daily, via semiolinguality, was juxtaposed against a culture of individuality in the US steeped in the competitiveness fueled by white supremacy, a dynamic which Jermaine and Fanus seemed to decry. They missed greeting people and smiling at them or just making sure that strangers felt comfortable around them. They missed people just looking at them. But Fanus acknowledged that even worse than this, they had to also contend with a lack of acknowledgment of elements of their transsemiotic repertoire which were made invisible through the American society's reading of their bodies as only and just Black. Drawing on his raciosemiotic architecture as the basis for attempting to clarify his personhood in the US, as he spoke of his friendliness and its lack thereof in the university where he functioned versus the broader US society, Fanus shared:

[I found it different in the university.] It's different. I was with the ethnicity ... [for instance] in the United States ... the girl I was talking about, that was a Caucasian young lady, I guess she felt distant because I would be classified as Black, African American when I'm not African American. I'm a Caribbean person. And I guess, she felt as if, you know, so, I can't do stuff like this. [It's basically like I'm you're being framed based on the previous history that has nothing to do with it.]

Fanus's identification of being viewed as Black as a factor impacting his perceived friendliness offered a window beyond the process of adjustment for explaining why he believed people were not more friendly. Reflecting Ibrahim's (1999) notion of "becoming Black," Fanus was forced to wrestle with the fact that the first categorizing factor by which he was judged in the US was not his Caribbeanness, but rather, his Blackness. His indications, though operating on the individual level in this one instance based on one interaction, were mirrored in the long-standing positioning of Black males in the US as a threat, and their masculinities as something to reject based on literate discourses mirrored repeatedly and across time in the media and within institutions as well as the broader society (Rodriguez, 2015). His distinctiveness as a Black Caribbean male, sought after to uniquely present himself, not as an African American, but as a Caribbean, has been addressed by the framework for Black immigrant literacies which invites Black immigrants to identify, understand, and engage with the struggle for justice upon their migration to the US (Smith, 2020b).

Unlike Asha, who transsemiotically invoked notions of being 'well-behaved' because she was a Caribbean girl whose mother had the sticker of a Caribbean island on her car, Fanus was immediately read with rejection and though he rewrote himself as Caribbean, the imposed racial ideology of being inferior because of his proximity to African Americans seemed to make his

Blackness appear too potent to supersede his transsemiotic rewriting of the self as friendly, willing to say hello to a stranger, based on intentional translingual interactions linked to his Caribbean speech.

Accentuating Intriguingly, Fanus appeared to, at times, transcend the connotation that his Blackness and languaging were intimately bound to relegate his personhood to inferiority, deciding to leverage his Bahamian Creolized English E-language as a basis for attractiveness in certain social settings. He shared:

In terms of how others treat me in classes as a Black male, [if I was not Bahamian,] I would be just a Black male. I feel as if me speaking the way I speak means I have more recognition. Or I'm able to strike up more conversations and people are more interested in asking me, "Oh, where are you from?" or "Why do you speak like that?" instead of me talking like a[n] African American. Sometimes, intentionally, I put on my [Bahamian] accent, to like, if I'm trying to "soot" [call out to] a lady or something like that because I guess it gives me a certain pizzazz when I speak my Caribbean accent so sometimes I intentionally just talk like a Bahamian. I think it's more attractive. More attractive, I think, and I guess the majority of the Bahamian guys, they would say the same thing. [When I do that] I'm like a little special apple with a Bahamian flag on it. When people interact with me, or they walk past me, interested of seeing a regular apple, [they] see little blue, black, and gold – something on the apple and [they] would like to know, "Oh, how come de apple look like that?"

The transsemiotic transgressiveness engaged by Fanus that seemed to both disrupt how raciosemiotic ideologies had positioned him while, at the same time, reframe his response to them positively is linked to his metalingual (Smith, 2019a) and "metasemiolingual understanding" which allowed him to recognize how being a Black male in the US was based on the co-naturalization of race and semiotics, a dynamic that can be linked to "twining" in a raciolinguistic perspective (Rosa & Flores, 2017). Societally, the attention Fanus received from individuals who did acknowledge his E-language as an element that caused him to be unique and to stand out to them suggested that there was an emotive element steeped in transsemiotics undergirding the notion of painting the Black immigrant as superior and as a "model minority" that perhaps extended beyond the academic and socioeconomic factors often used as a basis for this discourse (Smith, 2020b; see also Chapter 2). As outlined in the framework for Black immigrant literacies, subscribing to the myth of the model minority by Black immigrants can create a dynamic where they position themselves as superior to Black American peers in ways that reinforce divisive rhetoric designed to thwart the connection through solidarity so necessary across Black diasporic populations (Smith, 2020b). While it is not entirely clear whether the response to Fanus was linked to his model minority status, this dynamic is worth further examination.

Fanus positioned himself as advantageous based on the recognition of raciosemiotic rewards linked to social currency where to be Black Caribbean was elevated over being Black American, at least by some of his peers in the US society. In that moment, he detached the use of his E-language – Bahamian Creolized English – from notions of proficiency, cognition, and white gaze (Smith & Warrican, 2021), focused only on his leveraging of the E-language in his linguistic repertoire as advantageous based on social currency. To him, in doing so, he manifested an exotic appeal and conversational advantage, in which he relished, that afforded him a social affinity to which his Black American peers could not lay claim. In positioning himself as socially advantageous based on his metalinguistic, metaracial, and metacultural understanding (Smith, 2019a), absolutely *sans* attention to white gaze, Fanus exercised self-determination and reframed societal norms that had often, as shown earlier, relegated his Blackness to the periphery of the social enterprise, much like he described the exclusion he felt in the absence of American greeting.

Home-Cooked Food For Jermaine, though seemingly unrecognizable as a literate practice, the disruption of cooking food and eating it at home – *home-cooked food* – in his semiolingual repertoire, functioned as a basis for transraciosemiotic dissonance. He shared:

I was far away from home and to be independent, it was, I wasn't nervous. I wasn't, it wasn't a hard transition. The food, couldn't get no more home cooked food. You know, everything was fast food I had to eat. I didn't have the time to cook or anything.

Jermaine reminisced about home-cooked food and the absence of it as well as the presence of and his reliance on fast food in the US, which were intertwined with the multimodality undergirding literacies surrounding the process of feeding one's self and others. Jermaine's expressions about his food as a cultural dissonance suggested a difference in literacies of feeding, requiring a reliance on the phenomenon of 'fast food' in the US with which he was largely unfamiliar. Similar in some regards to the disruption of his literacies undergirding a regular use of greetings, Jermaine appeared to be thrust into a context where he semiotically became disconnected from a practice that undergirds a basic need – sustenance through home-cooked meals. Though he did not explain exactly why this created such as major dissonance but suggested that he would cook if he had the time, his association of eating home-cooked food with a sense of well-being is one that invokes remembrances of the literacies of cooking one's own food as a practice steeped in Indigeneity and reliance on the land, a common practice in the English-speaking Caribbean.

Beyond this, Jermain's literate practice surrounding feeding as a human was also reflective of the practice of caring for the self through the time allocated in the Caribbean context to cook one's own food so that the body can be nourished. Through this signaling of investing time to sustain the body, Jermaine's transsemiotic disruption pointed to the absence of home-cooked food and a reliance on American fast food as a shift in his semiotic repertoire. In other words, Jermaine's expressions about home-cooked food symbolically represented how his linguistic repertoire had expanded such that, transsemiotically, the E-semiotic of purchasing and relying on fast food now joined the E-semiotic of preparing home-cooked meals in his evolving transgeographically informed transsemiotic repertoire. Through his metacultural understanding (Smith, 2019a), Jermaine's recognition seemed to point to the pre-established broader institutional and societal structures of US individualism (Chilisa & Ntseane, 2010) steeped in a context governed by white supremacy where instantiated sustenance of the self with food as a practice is one that is often largely entrusted to strangers (see Conrad, 2020). In turn, it appeared to disrupt the notions of collectivism and community (Chilisa & Ntseane, 2010) steeped in traditional African culture and represented by the cooking of food in the home for a family, no matter what this might look like, an existence-in-relation practice with which Jermaine had been familiar in the Majority World nation of the Bahamas for his entire life (see Conrad, 2020, for a discussion of the white supremacy culture in food systems).

Taken together with the other transraciosemiotic instantiations, Jermaine's experiences offered insight into the notion of how youth's literacies of greeting, feeding, and being, functioned as legitimate sites of dissonance, but often remained obscure in the US context because of their position on the periphery of traditional notions of literate practice often explored in schools. In turn, these observations from the lives of Jermaine and Fanus highlight how such literacies that undergird flourishing can often be overlooked by institutions and society despite being so central to the holistic literacies of immigrant youth. They also highlight the ways in which youth may use transsemiotic practices such as greetings and food in a new land to flourish as they learn to know, do, be, and live together with others (Smith, 2018).

Exceptionalistic Discarding of Bahamian English in the US

In the experience of Asha after her migration to the US, there was a seeming discarding of the influence of her accent and 'dialect' until she was thrust into her comfort zone and disrupted by the corresponding imposition of her emotions on her languaging. Asha reflected what can best be described as synesthesia (Cope & Kalantzis, 2013; Kalantzis & Cope, 2020), where the feeling of being thrust into a comfort zone with someone during interactions in the US somehow instantiated a shift in her linguistic modality. In other words, when Asha was placed in a situation where she became so comfortable with someone, she would forget that she needed to use the E-language preferred and automatically speak the E-language deemed inferior. This occurred in ways that reflected the inferiorly positioned E-language in her literate repertoire as Asha's languaging, elicited unbidden by her – at least subconsciously – reflected a sudden emergence and production of her Bahamian Creolized English – instantiated by what appeared to be the integrated modalities of hearing, seeing, and feeling operating simultaneously in her literate repertoire, functioning as a sudden replacement of the E-language of Standard American English during an interaction. Initially describing herself as almost accentless, and yet, acknowledging how comfort caused a shift in her E-language, Asha stated:

I don't have an accent as much so being in a new place with people like migrating here [to the US] doesn't affect me at all. I know last semester I got comfortable with this girl so like, I kinda switched and I started sounding more Bahamian, and she's like "Oh wow, are you from Jamaica?" and I'm like, "No." I don't switch unless I get really comfortable.

Like Melody who described being "totally" comfortable speaking the Jamaican Creolized English at home with her mom and being able to "switch it on and off," and like Jermaine and Fanus who used similar explanations to describe switching the E-languages in their linguistic repertoires "on and off," Asha used her Bahamian Creolized English to switch from Standard American English only when she became comfortable with a girl she met and with her roommate. Her inferiorly positioned E-language *suddenly* came into play as she talked about switching her language even though she had just mentioned that she almost never uses the Bahamian Creole. At the same time, her I-language was also visible because it showed that her individual linguistic repertoire was largely influenced by the emotive – her being comfortable with a person or not.

Asha's metalinguistic understanding intersecting with the metacultural (Smith, 2019a) to reflect how comfort invoked her reliance on Bahamian Creolized English allowed her to also offer an explanation about how this occurred when she goes to a football game. Presenting an even more intriguing dynamic, she stated:

Sometimes in the football games [here at the university in the US], when I get really angry about what's happening, I kind of switch. The games are not pretty a lot of the times they get really bad, like the West Virginia game, we lost really badly, 48-17, and it was just disappointing, and last game against University of Oklahoma, the refs were just not calling in favor of [name of university] at all so it appeared that they were targeting us at a point and [name of city fans where I lived] get really aggressive so they were screaming like profanity the whole game, like the whole crowd was chanting it. It gets bad sometimes. I think it's the excitement and the passion that brings it out.

The extension of Asha's metalinguistic understanding (Smith, 2019a) was visible also, when she pointed to being with Bahamians in person in the US and talking with her mother over the phone as both mechanisms that also caused her to launch unrestrictedly into her Bahamian Creolized English. Asha demonstrated how her comfort invoked this E-language in her linguistic repertoire, explaining:

I find that my accent gets a lot stronger [too] when I hang out with Bahamians so I've been hanging with the Bahamians here at [name of university] a lot more so my roommate can hear my dialect a bit stronger. When I call home, it's pretty strong for my mom, so I think that's influencing how I talk a lot more here.

In the dynamic reflected by Asha, raciolinguistic ideologies are initially used by the self to construct the personhood as similar to and not different from everyone else who is mostly white when she states, "I don't have an accent as much so being in a new place with people, like migrating here to the US, doesn't affect me at all." Through this construction, Asha positions herself in close proximity to the whiteness of the Standard American English of the US, so that, though racialized as Black, she approximates this English in a way that prevents her from having to make too many adjustments or stand out as 'foreign.' Yet, even while acknowledging this, Asha is forced, through an intersection of her metalinguistic and metacultural understanding (Smith, 2019a), to acknowledge the synesthesially motivated emotive factors that appear, produced unbidden (Canagarajah, 2011), to disrupt this semiolingual construction of her personhood. The thrusting of the E-language – her Bahamian Creolized English – as it were, upon her personhood by social engagements where her emotions associated with the personhood entangled with this English (Smith, 2022e) appear to be stronger than her capacity for maintaining a Standard American English layer of herself, seem to mean that her grip on approximating various elements of her linguistic repertoire based on raciolinguistic ideologies becomes an edict of her subconscious.

In Asha's experience, though ungeneralizable but largely transferable to other similar people and contexts, the influence of the societal and potentially the institution are at play. In the comfort of a peer who 'gets her,' a football game that moves her, a Bahamian posse that hang out with her, a phone conversation with her mother, there appears to be an instantiation of the inferiorly positioned E-language intertwined with Asha's personhood in a way that she seems helpless to stop. Her experience raises questions about how institutions, through the connection of immigrants with peers and otherwise, can create opportunities for students to engage with such situations of comfort, much like Asha, where their consciousness of the expectations triggered by raciolinguistic ideologies become subverted to such an extent that their subconscious kicks in, thrusting them into a comfort zone where their languaging comes forth uninhibited and unrestricted, in the full burst of its light. This automated instantiation of Asha's inferiorly positioned E-language in her linguistic repertoire – produced unbidden – represents her capacity for languaging and semiotizing absolutely *sans* attention to white gaze.

Switch among E-Languages

The Black Caribbean immigrant youth constantly switched among their E-languages as part of their linguistic repertoire, as reflected across the many facets of their holistic literacies. Two instances in which this occurred, singled out for independent discussion based on analysis, are the obscuring of meaning via translation and the incapacity of teaching support to change linguistic repertoire in speaking as opposed to writing.

Obscuring Meaning via Translation In Asha's trajectory, she reflected an attempt to switch from E-language Bahamian Creolized English to the E-language Standard American English in her linguistic repertoire while interacting in the US. This made visible the incapacity to fully capture ideas from the inferiorly positioned E-language to the superiorly positioned one. Asha recognized that her intent to translate Bahamian Creolized English to Standard American English did not allow her to fully express ideas from one E-language to the other. She said, "I do switch with my roommate (laughter) and most of the times she's like, 'What, did you say?'" Asha made use of the linguistic mode to attempt to convey ideas from one language in another language as part of her linguistic repertoire based on societal expectations as expressed by her roommate but her roommate failed to adequately capture the meaning-making in Standard American English that she wished to translate from her Bahamian Creolized English. Through her metalinguistic awareness (Smith, 2019a), Asha recognized that she was unsuccessful in her attempts to translate her non-standardized Bahamian English to the standardized American English, reflecting that these E-languages didn't allow her to express meaning in the same way. Asha seemed surprised and frustrated that the Standard American English could not accommodate the ideas from her Bahamian English.

Raciolinguistic ideologies that constructed Standard American English as better than Bahamian Creole English appeared to be disrupted in Asha's linguistic repertoire based on the notion of comprehension as observed through her multilingual understanding (Smith, 2019a) – she was now aware that, for some reason, meaning conveyed with what had previously seemed like an inferiorly positioned E-language did not appear to be capable of being conveyed in what seems like a superior language. This appeared to confound Asha. In an attempt to exercise self-determination, she stated:

And I repeat it for her and she still doesn't get it sometimes so I have to try to translate what I'm saying, and I think that's a big issue too at times because, I'm like, I dunno how to say that in Standard English. [It's like a lot of the things we say doesn't really have an equal translation from one English to another.]

In this dynamic, Asha is made aware that the institutional and societal realities which have positioned Standard American English as superior reflect a fallacy given that she is unable to capture meaning from such a 'low-status' language to one that is privileged based on linguistic ideologies in the US. Her indications raise questions about what may be missing in the reading of text and the designing of meanings and comprehension in literacy as it exists in schools based on ideas that can only or may not be captured by Standard American English. While this is one student whose experience is transferable and by no means generalizable, Asha's observations, instantiated by her metalinguistic and metacultural understanding (Smith, 2019a), raise questions about what is missed by institutions and societies in the absence of exploring such possibilities. For instance, *What knowledges appear to be lost and their requisite meanings eroded through the potential incapacity of such large numbers of immigrant populations to tap into the meanings undergirding E-languages that contain meanings untranslatable to Standard American English in schools?* Asha's experience points to possibilities and potential for institutions, through the connection of immigrants with peers and otherwise, to create synergistic exchanges that bring to light 'lost' literate meanings instantiated by E-languages often positioned inferiorly, to express knowledges, and epistemologies, which, though present in the linguistic and semiotic repertoires of youth, may not be visible or captured in Standard Englishes of classrooms.

Speaking versus Writing Melody described how her placement in an English as a second language (ESL) class as a Black immigrant child from Jamaica in elementary school meant being pulled out of the classroom so that she could better manage what was deemed to be her inability to use her E-languages as she should in speaking and writing. She shared:

I went to an elementary school in east Dallas which had a lot of Black kids and Hispanic kids. There're very different types. Very diverse. So my teacher, she's white but she understands. She always worked with me on reading. It's called like reading rainbow.

Oh. But they also pulled me out of the class in the middle of the day and said oh time for [an] hour of English. Ok, it was boring. I still remember how I did the keypad to spell out words and she said, "No. That's not right." I fixed it and I still get it wrong and I'm going to do it in a test and still get it wrong. So, speaking was changing, but the writing was not. [We would do] words lesson, she would always help me with the words because I would always spell it in [British] English, like "color" for "colour." Yeah, like everything was British. So yes, the elementary teachers helped a lot with that and then I got to middle school.

While it was unclear why Melody's speaking changed but her writing did not, the dynamic raises questions about the institutional efforts of schools to attempt to change how the E-languages of students are leveraged in writing to align with raciolinguistic ideologies for what writing must 'look like.'

Raciolinguistic Rejection from the Inside and the Burden of Sounding American

An analysis of Asha's transgeographic experience revealed that she recognized and understood why Bahamian people whom she interacted with, both in the US and when she visited her home country, sometimes discounted her as illegitimate based on her 'sounding American' as she used the E-language Bahamian Standard English with them. She shared:

When the Bahamians hear that you don't speak or don't sound Bahamian, they actually make fun of you or they'll be like, 'Oh, why you putting on that fake accent, like why you want to sound American?!" If they hear me sound how I'm speaking to you now, they will laugh at me. Because some people think like you're putting on airs, like you're being fake about it but this is how I sound all the time. But some people think like I'm being extra with it. 'Cuz sometimes when Bahamians come to like, Florida, or like, they put on, or they can gain an American accent really quick.

In turn, she seemed to agree with the corresponding delegitimization of other Bahamians who had traveled to the US and who had adopted Standard American English too quickly. Fanus reflected, in part, a similar approach to Asha when he stated:

To be honest, I'm only going to sound American when I'm speaking with [Americans] because I have an issue with the Bahamians who come to America and they come back home speaking like Americans. I think you are not staying true to who you are. You're going to another country and I guess personally me I identify that with weakness in a way. Because you spoke a certain way your whole life and then you come to America. Me, I switch my accent on and off, but when I go back home, I know I'm from the Bahamas. I'm a Bahamian and I speak like a Bahamian 'til the day I die, but when you're in America, I understand that you have standards, you need to speak properly. Yes. When you're in the Bahamas, you need to go back to your root.

Yet, Fanus seemed to also demonstrate a nuanced understanding of how his Bahamian peers might eventually evolve using a linguistic repertoire that was more representative of attempts to approximate the Standard American English E-language structures from the US. He shared:

[But then again] now that I am processing the thought inside my mind, I'm thinking, it will be difficult for Caribbean persons who are inside Bahamas with only Americans around them [to keep speaking Bahamian] whereas if you are a Caribbean student and you have only Caribbeans around you [that reinforces you're Caribbean].

[If people are] inside the culture and I'm thinking that Caribbean people who are just around Americans all day, they are forced to [speak American]. And then like exercise, anything, once you constantly do and then it becomes a part of you. And I'm thinking when those Bahamian or Caribbean students come back to the Bahamas, being sensitive in the environment they have been for so long, they can't help but speak the way they've been speaking [American] because they become blind to the factor.

Like Fanus, Asha was aware of how her literacies were discounted by Bahamians because of their affinity with the notion of sounding American. In the same way that certain Bahamians and the Bahamian society had insisted that she use Bahamian Standardized English so that she could 'become someone' who went to the US to study so she could come back home and show that she had been '*successful*,' the expectation from her Bahamian community was that when she did return she would not mirror what they rejected as her approximation of the E-language of the foreigner – Standard American English. Asha understood that her capacity for translanguaging was not regarded favorably by the people whom she felt the most affinity to – Bahamians – because the E-languages primarily reflected in her individual linguistic repertoire didn't seem to sound 'Bahamian enough' when she was speaking regularly based of her tendency to reflect Bahamian Standard and Standard American E-languages. Reflecting on this dynamic, she shared:

I'm not sure how people who don't switch [to Standard English] get by. Have you met [name of university peer]? She sounds really Bahamian. And [name of other peer too], when they speak, I can hear their dialect (laughter). But I understand what they are saying. But when they talk like that loud in the room, you can tell the Americans turn around to look at them and they're like, "What are you saying?" Other people don't understand but I can pick up both but ... I think they're aware of it, they're like, "Oh, I'm speaking English so you should understand me" but at the same time we went to different schools in the Bahamas too so my upbringing and how I speak is completely different from theirs.

Using her metalinguistic understanding (Smith, 2019a), Asha relayed the information about her Bahamian peers whose individual linguistic repertoires were such that their translanguaging reflected their Bahamian Creolized English in a US space boldly and unapologetically despite the presence of individuals who may have "turned around to look at them." And deploying her metacultural and metalinguistic understanding (Smith, 2019a) simultaneously, Asha attributed the use of the Bahamian Creolized English by her friends in the way they did to the fact that she has been culturally and linguistically raised differently from these peers given that she did not attend the same schools with them in the Bahamas.

Here, in recognizing this distinction, Asha seems to lay the burden for the marked difference in her linguistic repertoire as compared to her friends squarely on the institution of schooling. Her tendency to use the repertoire that she does seems, however, not to prevent her from appreciating the semiolingual transgressiveness of her friends. She speaks fondly about her peers talking "that loud in the room" and says she can hear their "dialect" while laughing and seemingly dumbfounded about their boldness but also in awe. She is smiling in amazement too when she says this, fascinated that they choose to express their self-determination in this way. Fanus shares a similar perspective and reflects a feeling of awe in terms of the unapologetic use of a linguistic repertoire that centers Bahamian Creolized English when speaking of one of his Bahamian peers. He explained:

[I'm thinking of friends I have.] Let me see. I only know [name of friend] who never really changes his accent and Bahamian speech because he mumbles like he's really quiet when he's talking. Yes. And a lot of people can't understand him. I don't know, he might be treated differently. To be honest, I think he gets more attention. I think he gets more attention.

Using his metalinguistic understanding (Smith, 2019a), for a moment, Fanus seems perturbed by the fact that his friend gets more attention than him despite the fact that Fanus believes it is difficult for people in the US to understand this friend. He recalls that he too does also sometimes leverage his inferiorly positioned E-language from the Bahamas in ways that are unapologetic but that this occurs only with some and not other peers. He shared:

When it comes to relating to African American males and African males in the US [for instance] I use my accent with them because the guys who are from Nigeria, they speak with their African accent a hundred percent of the time. So when they on the court, when we are on the court, they say, "Hey . . . [using Nigerian slang]" and all of that stuff and all African stuff that I don't understand and I feel more comfortable with my accent interacting with them. But the African American guys, for African Americans, I speak more American with them than I would speak with the Africans. I think the African Americans, I think it's because they are not exposed [to the language differences]. Some of them have only been in America and that goes for the guy whose parents are African American as well. The Africans [on the other hand], they may be African American, but [many of them] live in a family where their parents speak African slang [so they can still understand my accent well]. Those other guys on this side [though], they're just around [the] African American sound [so they wouldn't understand me].

Fanus's decision to use his Bahamian Creole English E-language with Black immigrant males – African – but not with Black Americans, both populations with distinctly different linguistic backgrounds from him, seems fueled by his admiration of the Africans, who, though immigrants, appear to Fanus as unafraid to leverage their full linguistic repertoires – *sans white gaze*. While his African American peers also do the same, he seems to believe that they have not been exposed to language differences beyond America or are not like second-generation African immigrants, whose parents may have exposed them to language differences beyond the American context. Intriguingly, Fanus appears to signal a comfort with Africans that allows him to use his Bahamian Creolized English while, instead, emphasizing communication and comprehension with African Americans with a preference for ensuring that they understand him.

Mirroring Fanus's excitement about being able to use a Bahamian E-language that was often inferiorly positioned in America, Asha explained about people who used the Bahamian Creolized English E-language in the US, providing further clarity. She stated:

It doesn't matter for me [when people speak Bahamian Creolized English] even when I think people speak dialect even in a professional setting. Like it adds just a bit more of diversity to their area. Sometimes, I would if I could switch that easily, but I can't because I'm thinking about it a lot. Sometimes it can be a little bit like embarrassing because like, sometimes on the news in the Bahamas, this guy was talking about the hurricane, that it hit, so they don't say "hurricane" [like I would, they say it differently]. For some reason, and he was like the water was so tall, it looked like a salami, and everyone was like "Ooh, tsunami," so like everyone was kind of like embarrassed about it but it's like a really big joke now in the country, but it was kind of like embarrassing at first. I think it was an error on his part, but they sound alike so ... all Bahamians wouldn't probably make that mistake [but] especially like a word like that that isn't used a lot, they might make a mistake with it.

Asha justified the decision-making of individuals whose individual linguistic repertoires were similar to hers and reflected E-languages that were frowned upon by her Bahamian peers, saying:

But it's more like they do it because they know if they speak standard dialect, they wouldn't be understood so they switch, so they talk to be understood and people think it's being fake but it's more like, "No, I have to be like this so I can be understood when I go out so people don't give me the wrong food, so people don't misinterpret what I'm saying, so you have to do it, like switch."

Fanus concurred, sharing:

My switch is more, switch so you understand me, not to switch to sound American. I just want to. My switch is I slow down, I pronounce my words more and that's it. I say, I don't like American say like "What's up, bro?" "Hey, man." I don't speak like that. I would say which in Bahamas I say when we ask someone "Ha it go?" instead of saying "How does it go?" or "How's it going?" I would say "How are you doing?" I translate it from what it is in Bahamas instead of taking its American slang. Yes, and it's be like "What's going on bro?" I would say I would think it might be American, I say "What's up?"... I say "What's up? How are you doing?" but I always follow it with "How are you doing?" after. I think it's now second nature. I don't even think about it as much as I used to.

Like Fanus, Asha's justification in the instance above was steeped in communicative needs of Bahamians. Both Asha and Fanus reflected translanguaging practices fueled by a desire to be comprehended by others. They believed this was a reasonable explanation for their abandonment of an E-language – Bahamian Creolized English – that would, with Americans, serve very little purpose. Even so, Asha lamented that her roommate from Ecuador possessed a linguistic repertoire that tended to reflect an E-language with which many Americans were unfamiliar. Asha also believed it was unfair that she could not use her Bahamian Creolized English all the time. For Asha and Fanus, communicative competence, "norms of usage and appropriacy in a given social context" in English, appeared to be a key goal (Savignon, 2018, p. 2; see also Berns, 2019; Hymes, 1972), alluding to their considerations for audience as a key basis for translanguaging in institutions and the society at large. In such an instance, the goal for being understood superseded the impositions of raciolinguistic or raciosemiotic ideologies on their part but as Asha noted, her roommate from Ecuador was not as fortunate as she was deemed incapable by the white listening subject of leveraging the E-language that would allow her to be understood and avoid ridicule in a predominantly white context. In these instances, Asha and Fanus inadvertently appeared to believe they were expected to accept the seeming raciolinguistic rewards associated with approximations of Standard English.

It is no wonder that Asha insisted, based on her metacultural and metalinguistic understanding, that the expectations of approximation of Standard American English by those in the US society which are connected to requirements such as getting a job meant that it was her duty to attempt conformity. This requirement, which she associated with linguistic conformity, appeared to itself be steeped in raciolinguistic notions that show how twining occurs, linking her linguistic and racial forms in ways that cause the US society to intricately connect her personhood to these forms. She shared:

[I feel it's unfair to not be able to use my Bahamian Creole English] but at the same time Americans, how do I put this, they're very exclusive at some times, to be honest, if you are Mexican, for instance, they're like, "Oh, you can't speak like that. You have to speak only English here in America." It's not about Spanish and those other languages. They try to make English the main language and they don't really accept ... like I've seen it happen to ... my roommate's mom is from Ecuador so she doesn't speak proper English all the time. She kinda infuses Spanish with it so she sounds a bit differently and people make fun of her because of that. Mostly when my roommate's like in [name of city] when we were high school friends [before we moved to college], it happened. Sometimes it's like pressure like you have to be this way especially like in a job market if you wanna compete, if you're probably using a dialect like in a meeting in the US, they'll be like maybe we should hire just an American 'cuz despite your qualifications, because you don't understand my accent, there will be a cultural barrier there with connecting to you.

Asha insisted, nonetheless, that institutionally, education needed to be centered on both individuals who are from and who are not from the US:

I think they need to educate the ones are from the US. Like educate them a little bit more about different cultures, how to embrace different cultures. What are the do's and don'ts of speaking, I guess, to someone else from another country?

And despite reinforcing the need for using Standard American English elsewhere to facilitate comprehension and communication, she asserted that the American society has a responsibility for engaging with Bahamian Creolized English given the overall dismissiveness of accents deemed foreign by American people in general. She shared:

[I do think Americans have a cultural responsibility to understand people like me too] sometimes especially with dialect, it's not like, some words are like made up words, I guess, but most words are the same, it's just said a bit differently, so if they just listen or like read lips, they'd be able to understand but they just like, [from the time] they hear an accent they kinda just dismiss it as maybe not just being English even if it is. They just kinda dismiss the language.

Explaining how she had seen Americans as well as immigrants educated in the US, she shared:

So they might incorporate a diversity week on each floor of the dorms and just like we'll focus on the Spanish culture this week, get to know Spanish food, culture, tradition, and then do a difference like Indonesian culture. Some people don't know how to talk to [the people from outside the US], how to fit in because some come straight here from a different country and lots of them stay in [name of hall].

Heterogeneous Representations of Blackness as Necessary but Exclusive

Asha's experiences reflected that she perceived the semiotic representations of Blackness used by African organizations on her university campus in the US to be exclusive in much the same way that the Caribbean organization of which she was then a part had also been previously exclusive. Using her metacultural understanding (Smith, 2019a), Asha perceived exclusivity in the ways that African organizations on her campus leveraged their literacies as ways of knowing, being, and doing – ways that were significantly different from how she wanted to write herself into the world. She shared:

There's a high number of African vs. African American kids here, I think. With Africans we have similar culture I guess because Caribbean is influenced by the slaves that were brought there from Africa but other than that I dunno, I do have an African friend but she's more Americanized too, in a sense since she's been here, so it's not really a barrier between us, [but] you can tell like there's differences. She sounds American. So like how we were talking about the Caribbean kids being maybe were exclusive to people from the Caribbean – I think like the African student organizations are in a sense exclusive, they might invite other people but when you see what they are doing, you are like, "Oh wow, that doesn't really cater to what I like to do." So I don't wanna be there because it's like exclusive to what they like to do. If you learn about a different culture you're not only attuned to learning about your way of things.

On the flip side, speaking of how white populations operated, Asha appeared to rely simultaneously on her metacultural and metaracial understanding to articulate the complexity of semiotic challenges that fueled a lack of heterogeneity. She stated:

I would probably get treated better if I wasn't different. You know, familiarity breeds fondness. People who are alike get together. That's a big barrier. There's a shortage of African American kids here at university anyway so we're forced to hang out with everyone but at the same time you probably don't feel the need to engage in groups of people who aren't like you. Like even the sororities on campus, if you look at them, they are completely, like whitewashed, there's only like a few that let in people of Color, and I dunno, maybe if it's because people of Color just rush the 'magnificent nine' or 'magic nine,' whatever – it's like nine fraternities or sororities, typically for like Black people because they might cater to needs that a Black person might have and they're historically Black so as a Black person you probably just want to 'rush them' [try to get in].

Like Melody and Fanus, who both also discussed the dynamics of interacting with African American, African, and white populations across school and university contexts with regards to how exclusivity functioned, Asha's description of the ways in which the semiotics of Blackness operated as a function of sororities to exclude people like her as a Black person seemed tied to broader notions of being Black in America that extended beyond being Caribbean. In this recognition, she appeared to reflect an element of the Black immigrant literacies framework – an understanding of the *shared struggle for justice* into which she was subsumed as a Black Caribbean whose ancestors had been enslaved in the Caribbean and whose African American peers had long since borne the brunt of racial injustice in the US (Smith, 2020b). In this instance, it is not her languaging that binds her to her Black American peers but rather, the ways in which she is raciosemiotized based on the "twining" of semiotics and race.

Escaping to Do and Escape as Impetus

The Black Caribbean students reflected a range of feelings in their experiences, some of which functioned in response to their desire to escape feeling. Other emotive experiences were the result of their engagement in the US, and still others represented strategic transsemiotic leveraging of feeling for desired goals.

Doing to Escape Feeling Asha acknowledged suppressing certain literacies of feeling in favor of those representing doing given the economic and other stakes involved in her education as an immigrant in the US. Asha's privileging of the linguistic mode as part of her literate repertoire, given its association with what it meant for her to "*succeed*," seemed to translate into using this and other modalities, typically, in ways that did not honor and legitimize her feelings about how it often felt to navigate the challenges in the US. In other words, Asha did not often give herself the liberty of feeling the emotions that beckoned her, nor did she allow them first priority in her life. She shared:

I feel like sometimes as Caribbean kids or as just international kids in general, we know that we don't have time to sit there and think, "Oh well, I don't fit in 'cuz my parents gonna be upset that they're spending this money to send me to school so I just need to get this, this education and spend my parents' money well, get good grades, like so I can go back home." [I don't have the chance to feel. I just have the chance to do.]

Using her metacultural understanding, Asha performed the part she was expected to play as an immigrant student in the US through an understanding of how she needed to leverage her Bahamian Standard English in the US for "*success*" despite the temptation to wallow in the pitiful lake of feeling unwelcomed. Through the transsemiotic and translanguaging elements leveraged in her individual semiolingual repertoire, she dared to feel when receiving comfort, as she has stated elsewhere, during moments where she socialized with like peers from the Bahamas. Yet, at the same time, Asha seemed adamant that it was counterproductive to do so fully, and to exercise this liberty elsewhere.

Asha's experience indicated that she wrestled with the raciolinguistic and raciosemiotic ideologies undergirding the imposition of "doing" over "feeling," inscribed by her parents' insistence that she "do well" in order to "return home" so she could occupy a rightful place in Caribbean society. This doing seemed steeped in Eurocentric norms for succeeding based on institutional rewards of "good grades" that were simultaneously intertwined with a partial negation of her "well-being" emotionally as observed through her suppression of her emotive literacies. Asha acknowledged her insistence on negating her right to feel badly about fitting in, but she also seemed to find spaces of comfort with her Bahamian peers when she did interact with them and was adamant that other students like her who were away from home "talk" about their feelings with peers who may have been experiencing similar challenges. She shared:

In the meantime, whatever it takes to fix the problem, [you do it]. For students who struggle, I tell them, "Talk about it, if you can find a group of kids like I have with the Bahamian students here who are like from similar backgrounds as you, that understand, they may be going through the same things so talk to them about it."

Her advice to leverage the linguistic modality orally by talking to someone who is similar suggests that this was what had worked for her during her experience with Bahamian students at the university.

Feeling as a Result of Interaction vs. Feeling Leveraged Strategically
Like most of the Black Caribbean immigrant youth, Melody reflected the emotions she felt as a Black Caribbean immigrant in the US having to interact in social settings. She explained:

Bullying was tough in middle school. I would speak and they were like "say that word again ... say that word again." I hated it! I hated it! That was how it was in middle school. That was really the worst time of my life. My mom realized this because my grades started to drop and I didn't want to go out of my room. I stayed in my room all the time because I don't want to talk to people, because I felt like they looked at me weird every time I say something. So then I started to just try to talk like them, so like [pronounce] my words like now I'm talking now (using standardized American English). So, that's how I usually talk (laugh), I started to say things my way. But that didn't work. And that's how I went to so many middle schools. It was because of a lot of bullying. I went to two, three middle schools and then one high school. I am still considered problem child. And the school teachers [in middle school] weren't very helpful. They never said anything to me. Middle school, nothing. Nothing. They never suggested anything but in high school they suggested counseling. High school had counseling for lots of stuff.

Melody's experience reflected how the school setting caused her to feel as a Black Caribbean immigrant teenager navigating a social terrain where the Jamaican Creolized English was deemed unacceptable by peers.

Like Melody, Fanus appeared to experience a range of feelings as he straddled interaction based on his semiolingual repertoire in the US. He described these feelings as ranging from "nerve-racking" and "timidness" to "hesitation" and "comfort." He shared:

So I am taking communication classes [in my first semester] and it's like a rolling ball. The more the ball rolls, the more confidence I get because my first speech inside the class, I was very, very timid. I have to speak in front of the class of about twenty-two, twenty-three people. [The class is not too large] but still it's like a nerve-racking experience. I could talk in front of the crowd with no hesitation, with no issues, but the minute many doors closed and I have people who one hundred percent focus on me, I then have that issue because once I don't want to say words incorrectly, and I constantly try to make sure that my second switch, my second language [is activated]. After a while I get more comfortable, more relaxed. I've done three speeches so far. Actually, I did one on Monday this week [and] it went well. Everyone reacted the way I wanted them to react. They applaud[ed]. Everyone could understand me. But for my first speech, people commented on my accent. They said, "You say words differently where you're from." And they said, "Oh, I can hear your accent," or "Are you from Africa? Are you from Jamaica?" Anywhere but the Bahamas. I told them I'm from the Bahamas. I was actually, speaking clear, I guess. And my teacher, he actually took some audios ... and sent them to our Dropbox in [Microsoft] Outlook [so] we could look at them or critique ourselves. He hasn't made any comments [but the course is basically I] guess to be more skilled, to be more well-versed, communicate on the job or inside the office or you have to make a presentation. So like [when] I'm at work on the phone and someone calls, I speak like an American in a sense and I put on my proper voice and I say all my words correctly. So, I [might] say "Hello" if I am answering the phone and say "Thanks for calling Kellogg's. How can I help?" and I speak correctly and instead of like me when I'm on the phone with my friend and I said "Yes, bey, I work for Kellogg's company" and ... "they ain't doing much."

Fanus provided further context as a basis for clarifying the dynamic that he describes above – the taking of a test that he believed was administered even when he did not think he deserved to have been asked to do it as an "English" speaker. In doing so, he reflected feelings such as "intimidation" and "anger." He explained:

When I came to the US, I had to do a test. I had to do TSI [Texas Success Initiative Assessment], I think because I am from the Caribbean country. And the TSI test was more like the SAT and the first time I took it I rush through it because [I felt like] always like I'm good at English, [I thought] it is too easy. I missed the [passing] score by ten points, I think, and then I took it again and then I took it again a second time and I did way it way better than I did the first time. There was, like, comprehension, vocabulary, something like that. It was just multiple-choice questions, reading passages. I was kind of, I don't know, I was kind of intimidated or I was kinda angry because I took SAT and everything and my SAT is what got me into the [university], so it's almost as if I was being asked to show it again [that I can enter into college]. I am thinking my English component is the reason why I have to take it because my [passing score on] English components were lower than math, but I didn't have to take math. I had to take English.

Fanus's indications in the excerpts above are understandable in light of Nero's (2000) assertion that it is often the case that Black speakers experience little to no dissonance in their Englishes until they arrive in the US and their standardized Englishes privileged in the Caribbean are deemed unacceptable for functioning in the latter context, this despite their supposed alignment with approximations sanctioned by the white listening subject (Rosa & Flores, 2017). In the class where he is learning to communicate, amid a range of feelings, he makes an effort to approximate these norms as he hopes to receive the raciolinguistic reward of a large group of peers whose expectations for his speech are steeped in notions determined by the white listening subject. Prior to this, when he is asked to take the TSI assessment, part of the Texas Success Initiative program designed to help one's college or university determine if one is ready for college-level course work in the areas of reading, writing, and mathematics, he is perturbed by this requirement because "students with a TSI assessment exemption can enroll in any entry-level college course without restrictions" and "students may ... Student may be exempt if they have met the minimum college readiness standard on SAT, ACT, or a statewide high school test," which he acknowledges may not have been present for English though it was for math.

Fanus's intimidation seems to arise from the view of his personhood as a legitimate speaker of the E-language that the US values – 'Standard English' – an assertion aligned with indications by Nero (2000) which show that this is often the case when Black Caribbean immigrants move to the US. Despite the fact that he is angry, particularly because he feels like he is being asked to show that he can enter college again, he attempts to demonstrate that he can approximate the norms of the white listening subject by taking the TSI once more as his goal is to reinscribe his supposed legitimacy based on a reward of college acceptance steeped in the white gaze (Morrison, 2020). He indicates this by describing his performance as "good" or as "better" when he "does" align with these norms. In doing so, he remains oblivious to the ways in which the institution positions him as incapable of language proficiency on the SAT and the TSI based on cognitivist norms regarding the use of a certain writing of English as literate competence. Inferiority and incapability of language are ascribed by the institution that administers the TSI based on successful approximation of norms as explained by raciolinguistic ideology (Rosa & Flores, 2017).

Jermaine too mirrors the dynamic of believing that his E-language as a Bahamian Standard English speaker should be good enough but finds that it does not seem to be. He shared, "Even when I think I'm speaking proper, professors would always say, 'Where are you from?' even though in my mind I think that I'm speaking proper, my accent, I think it naturally comes out." Rosa and Flores (2017) have observed that even when speakers such as Jermaine, Fanus, Asha, and Melody are asked to approximate norms for speaking English in the US that should allow them to be accepted, they often are not accepted in the society or by the institutions even when they use these supposed norms. Colleagues and I have described how this dynamic manifests itself with Black Caribbean immigrant educators who were former teachers in the Caribbean and who use Englishes in the US, showing how they too faced dissonance with the expectations for approximating a standard English that should be similar to theirs – Standard American English – but that is designated as superior to the E-languages of 'Standard English' that they possess (Smith, 2018, 2020b; Smith et al., 2023).

Leveraging her metaracial understanding, Asha indicated how the ways in which people responded to her and to other people like her racialized as Black in the US angered her. She stated:

Right now like America's having this issue with race where people and some of the kids, they are like, "Oh, they're just being stupid about it, they think they're being targeted but they're not being targeted," and I think sometimes that makes me a bit angry. Like we're not playing victims all the time. People are speaking based on experience or what has happened because they are a minority and I'm not only a minority, I'm a minority from a different country.

Here, Asha indicates how the reading of her, transsemiotically, is required to demonstrate the necessity for addressing responses to her Blackness that she deems inappropriate even while she reflects affinity to her Black American peers as part of the struggle for justice as outlined in the framework for Black immigrant literacies (Smith, 2020b).

In contrast to the feelings above invoked transgeographically as a result of his experience with languaging, Fanus appeared to also leverage his Bahamian Creolized English transsemiotically in strategic ways so that he could regulate his emotions. He explained:

When it comes to girls, I change my conversations so that people can understand what I'm saying most of the time. But like in my parties or social events, my accent is there because I'm excited, I doing emotion and then so, I guess girls, they then react in a way, they look back and when we [as Bahamian guys] open our mouth, they look back and they said, "Who's that?" Because it sounds different to what they normally hear. When I'm in constant conversation with them, I switch it on and off.

This leveraging of emotion strategically by Fanus mirrors, in part, his transsemiotizing of the body alluded to earlier where he summons what he believes is the exotic through his Bahamian Creolized English E-language to leverage oral literacy in a way that attracts attention.

Like Fanus, Melody also appeared to strategically leverage her translanguaging within her linguistic repertoire. She did so in high school in ways that would allow her to belong because she wanted to make friends as a Black person in a predominantly white space. Speaking of her strategic efforts to feel a sense of belonging, she shared:

So yeah, in high school I started speaking differently because I was at an all-white high school. So, it was like ok, it's immediately I'm the one [Black] person that has to live with [being in an all-white school] all the time. Ok, [so I thought] "let me change my voice in order to fit in, to make friends." I had one best friend and we're still friends till this day. But when I came here [to the university], I was looking for other caring people, I didn't know anybody here. Just like a brand-new life for me. I can just be myself here and stop worrying about all the bad stuff. I didn't know about it and my roommate was African at the time and my mom said "beware of her." So, next thing I know, I was excluded from things [in the dorm] and [I was like] "this [bad treatment] can't be happening again." So then, I ended up moving out at the end of December to a different room. I am no longer a friend to any of them. Some were white, some were African, and some were African American.

Melody also attempted to leverage her individual linguistic repertoire in ways that would allow her to belong when she arrived in college, navigating a range of responses intraracially among Black groups. She explained:

White people, they are really cool all the time. Again I am not the type of a typical Black person. Most people tell me "you're not Black." I am still struggling to find what am I because my dad is white. But I didn't know him. I didn't know him whatsoever. I've always identified with being just Jamaican. But my best friend who is white, she is very understanding. So, I've always felt comfortable around white people; I've never really had a problem too much, but African American people, that is my biggest problem. I also feel like the African Student Association, they stay with their own culture; white people, they're more curious, I should say some, about other different countries and cultures. But yea, I got there in the ASA with too many African people. I don't why I can't do this. They were like "You're very different." They look at you funny. So I was like I am not connected with this. I took myself out of that association. And then the Black Student Association group, well they're very Black power so I was like no. I don't fit in there. So now I know how to say something and I guess if I say something different, people won't look at me. I'll correct myself immediately [if I say something wrong]. Like if I say like rucksack, that means backpack. I'll hurry up to correct myself. People look at me for a second but if people don't know, I don't call it out.

The (Un)seizing of Varied Liberties as Expressions of Safety

Asha insisted on the right to feel safe and to inscribe herself as a legitimate part of the Black group in America that does so – African Americans – but at the same time, she also seemed to shirk the responsibility for feeling safe when it required making space, engaging the daily feelings associated with her individual challenges of how she was read as a Black Bahamian, as shared earlier. Her recognition of the challenges faced by people with race in the US where she believed Black peoples' stories were dismissed as "playing victim" caused her to feel angry. Asha's expressions about certain literacies of feeling that allowed her to write her Black body as safe in solidarity with other Black people in the US were juxtaposed against her negation of literacies of feeling that required her to acknowledge the ways in which her individual personhood was erased by not fitting in individually as a Black Bahamian person in the US.

As is suggested in the framework for Black immigrant literacies (Smith, 2020b), Asha's writing of herself as a part of the Black group in America occurs transsemiotically as she links her diasporic Caribbean Blackness to the global struggle for justice faced by Black peoples everywhere. The reading of the literacies of people in America who are Black in ways that relegate their translanguaging experiences about race as contrived angers her. To her, she feels like she is a part of them, and they are a part of her, even though she is "a minority from a different country." She shared:

The Bahamas issued a travel advisory to Bahamian students and people living in the United States and it was the second shooting that had happened, and some Americans were commenting on it, and it was really disgusting to hear. Like it was bad, it was like, we are in a state with majority white people, we want to stay protected, even if you feel like we're not being targeted, we feel like we're being targeted. [Name of university] is trying but it's just not there yet.

Much like Melody, who insisted that "schools and universities need more spaces like" the hall in her university for diverse students, which she liked because the "environment [was] really culturally diverse and [she felt] like if there're more places like that, they [would] help people more comfortable," Asha longed for spaces where Black people could feel safe. Unlike Asha and Melody, for Jermaine and Fanus, those spaces seemed to be reflected in their athletic pursuits where they tended to feel comfortable.

Summary

Overall, the translanguaging processes based on the integrated model of multilingualism used by Black Caribbean immigrant youth with their E-languages and E-semiotics in the US appear to reflect the functioning of the body as a transraciosemiotic marker. Black Caribbean youth were capable of leveraging their individual linguistic repertoires to exceptionalistically discard certain Englishes in the US while recognizing the limitations of this practice for fully capturing ideas across E-languages during translation. From raciolinguistic rejection experienced as a Black insider to the burden of 'sounding American,' the Black Caribbean immigrant youth reflected literacies that demonstrated an affinity for heterogeneous representations of Blackness even while highlighting the possibility of this practice as a basis for exclusivity. Illustrating how feeling functioned as an outlet for interaction and also the tendency to do as a means of escaping feeling, the Black Caribbean immigrant youth showed how they differentially (un)seized varied literate liberties as expressions of safety on the individual and societal level. The Black Caribbean immigrant students simultaneously wrestled with transraciolinguistic and transraciosemiotic injustice steeped in ideologies within the destination country of the US where they lived while at the same time agentively using translanguaging and transsemiotic practices based on language and raciosemiotic architecture in their communities to (re)structure the reading and writing of their "transworlds" (see Flores et al., 2014, on transworld pedagogy). They did this even as they "became Black" (Ibrahim, 1999), "became immigrant," and "became 'non-native English'" (Smith, 2020c). The holistic literacies of students in this context highlighted, at the same time, the ways in which institutions have positioned Black Caribbean immigrant students in the US to exercise their self-determination as a function of their individual linguistic and semiotic repertoires, or not. Amid the tensions persisting between agentive self-determination through translanguaging and transsemiotizing and a cognizance of the imposed transraciolinguistic and transraciosemiotic injustice, the remixing of semiolingual performativity in the lives of the Black Caribbean immigrants signaled what I have alluded to earlier as a stark portrayal of *"semiolingual innocence"* (discussed in detail later). Moreover, the attention to spaces for collective safety via agency even with individual negation of the same occurs emotively. This paradoxical dynamic points to the

192   Translanguaging Imaginaries of Innocence

dissonance created by institutions in the lives of Black Caribbean immigrant youth regarding how they can be agentive about their basic needs for flourishing, or not, as individuals as well as in relation to the collective within a society structured by a Black-White binary.

Holistic Literacies of Black Caribbean Youth across the Caribbean and the US

Emerging as Black Caribbean youth across the Caribbean and the US, the participants in the study undergirding this book reflected isolatory effects of (inadvertently) imposed homogeneity.

Isolatory Effects of Imposed Homogeneity

Asha felt isolated in the writing of her Bahamian self into the American world based on her experiences. She shared:

I feel isolated sometimes. I feel like sometimes Americans kind of they just kinda pull away from people that are different from them. They just don't want to be almost like friends with you, like they just want to hang out with people similar to them all the time. They won't create a bridge to connect like, "Oh well, that's cool," then they go hang out with [whoever they want to be with]. So whether you be from the Caribbean, Mexican, Asian, they just kinda pull away. I'm in a student group. It's a Christian organization on campus and I feel like sometimes in there they feel like, very exclusive, like my roommate they're like, "Oh, you should hang out with other people." But at the same time they are like they're all similar. So they're already friends and they are same backgrounds, they're all from [name of state] and stuff, so they connect much better.

Asha struggled with isolation imposed by a writing of herself into the world over which she had no control. Even if she seemed to use the linguistic modality that reflected Englishes based on what the American system deemed acceptable, the society did not seem to accept her. Asha reflected the capacity for translanguaging that allowed her to navigate this process in a way that linguistically did not cause her to stand out or be labeled as "inferior" based on her language use for community in a Christian group. However, it also did not prevent her from being treated like *she* didn't belong given that her personhood was linked to the notion of inferiority despite her approximations of language use based on the white listening subject. She shared:

So I feel like I'm excluded when I'm in there. I still go because I like the music that they play, it's really good Christian songs and stuff, and I like to experience that, and they're like awesome people there that are really like, "Oh, we love everyone." They include you, they try to go out of their way to talk to you but then there are some people in the group that are like okay, "I don't really care. We already have our friends that we are gonna talk to all the time." [So I go there] but I'm still aware that there's like that, "I'm not going to include her [in here]." You sometimes feel like, like it's just that, I feel like just the experience of like being included by one person is really nice and really, they feel that Jesus loves them is much better than that two people that's like, "Oh well, we wanna stay together, we're similar."

Asha's capacity for translanguaging that allowed her to use her E-languaging to leverage a linguistic repertoire that seemed to position her as privileged was betrayed by raciosemiotic ideologies from society that ascribed to her the perceived counter-transgressiveness of being Black and linguistically different, thereby intertwining her Caribbeanness with her Blackness and its associated language differentness, preventing her from exercising belonging in predominantly white spaces.

Leveraging her metacultural understanding, she explained:

I feel like many Americans here they just build stereotypes where they see like on the news about these places, like oh, if you're just from the Caribbean they just automatically assume you're Jamaican. If you're from Asia they just assume you're Chinese. They don't really care about what else your culture is or whatever, they kinda just pull away from it.

Yet, Asha insisted that even as she felt isolated, the spaces where she semiotically wished to find community were sometimes not those provided by institutions. For instance, speaking of how sororities did not ultimately serve her needs, given her personality as an introvert, she explained:

[I don't do the sorority thing.] It's like a good way to network but at the same time they have a lot of events, a lot of parties and stuff, and I'm not about being that social all the time. I'm more of an introvert. I like to stay small groups spend time to myself to get take myself together like think about my thoughts, I don't really like being in large groups and in social contexts like that especially, it just would be so draining on me.

Semiolingually, Asha used her metalinguistic, metacultural, as well as her metaracial understanding, reflecting a both-and perspective that allowed her to adopt multiple and opposing viewpoints, much like the individual dynamic described in "a transraciolinguistic approach," having the capacity to see both sides and to operate from this vantage point. She shared:

I think that it would be very helpful if [name of university] sets up cultures to learn from other cultures. If you learn about a different culture, you're not so in tune to only think about your way of things, you experience like, both sides of the spectrum so you can say, "Oh, I know from personal experience, this and this," but I seen the other side so I can say, "Oh, maybe this experience is great for me, but it's not great for another person" and understanding their point of view. For me I can say that 'cuz I've experienced the American culture and I know what the culture is like back at home. Different. Sometimes I don't really get the culture shock thing that some people get but I still experience it sometimes. But I haven't met a lot of kids who haven't adjusted well to the US.

Institutionally, Asha described how attempts to address the semiotic challenges with homogeneity and how they affected people like her sometimes were not enough, sharing:

> I know [name of university] is like big on diversity right now so ... but I don't think any changes have really happened. They just reported the campus numbers. There's 60 percent Caucasian kids here and they just said 40 percent different minorities. They didn't break it down, they didn't say well, "Oh, they are thirty Hispanics and ten Black kids or like kids from the Caribbean." They don't break it down. And for me, most of the time, I'm the only Black kid in some of my labs. Or in history, so when we learn about certain things. It's kinda like, they just kinda look at you as the person who's gonna respond, how do you speak about it, like, or like relations ... Overall, like, I feel like numbers wise in terms of the Black population, [name of university] has actually decreased. Hispanic numbers are going up but Black numbers are going down. I definitely feel like [name of university] has an atmosphere that's more Hispanic. A lot of Mexican foods on campus, tacos, a lot of Mexicans, I think if like they could have Caribbean foods there, that would definitely help bring more Caribbean people to [the university]. Sometimes it's just difficult to find a worker on campus like you and in classes and stuff.

Using her metacultural and metaracial understanding (Smith, 2019a), Asha insisted on the institutional responsibility to foster semiotics in the literacies designed to build community among diverse populations of students like her in ways that both disrupted efforts to maintain homogeneity while also addressing raciosemiotic injustice, stating:

> If the university can include diversity, or if you can prove that a group is specifically just targeting individuals that look like them or that are blonde, you can target that. I think groups like that should be disbanded. Because they're targeting people just like them, they're not trying to look for diversity. They're just building like an ultimate thing, that oh maybe people that look just this way, they are just better than everyone else. And that's kind of scary. I think that soon, they'll just put one little Black person in the group like if you seen posters around campus, they also throw like one Black person in there to make it look like, "Oh, we are diverse." If you go into classes at the university, you will see that it's not like that. It's more like nine white kids to every half a Black kid. The numbers aren't the same as they are represented. [I think that the numbers prevent us from addressing the problem of relations between white and Black kids.]

Insider Knowledges and Experiences

As a secondary participant insider who served as a former teacher in Jamaica and was now a teacher educator, Sahara spoke of her familiarity with the E-languages to which Melody, one of the Black Caribbean youth, alluded, confirming:

> So in Jamaica, we are part of the English-speaking Caribbean so we're expected to use Standard English which is British English, but our native language is Jamaican Creole.

Now you were looked down upon if you used Creole as a teacher, so you're supposed to use what quote unquote, "the Queen's language" but here I was with a second grade of forty-six children who speak Jamaican Creole and are learning to read and write Jamaican Standard English. Now I realized when I wanted those students, when I wanted to be funny, just to enlighten the air or make them laugh, I had to use the Creole. And it was when, it was moments like that that the students realized that I was not ... when I first, when they first heard me speak Jamaican Creole, they laughed, and they realized that I was not somebody who was far away from [who they were]. I realized that when I wanted to get their attention, I could switch from Standard English to Creole and I would have them. So again, having children who, their whole language is Jamaican Creole and to get them to use English in class, it was hard for them. To learn to read English, to write it so they had a lot of I would call language interference. Mind you, I didn't know that this [was what it was at the time], I just thought my children were struggling to read and write but now I can say it was the language difference that was interfering with their reading and writing because we weren't really teaching them to co-switch. We were just teaching them in Standard English not acknowledging that they are Creole speakers and then those issues what were present when they talked to each other. When they would talk to me, they attempted to use English and then they would have mixed Creole with Standard English which now sounds weird ... right? But once they were talking to each other, [they were] then talking in Jamaican Creole.

Similarly, as an insider teacher educator from the Bahamas, Davina, speaking of how teachers functioned in school using Bahamian Creolized English and Bahamian Standard English in the Caribbean, where Asha and Fanus had functioned, reflected a similar dynamic, sharing:

I think dialect was used more for emphasis than content. I think when I was trying to say something to students, it was just easier sometimes to speak in a Bahamian dialect which they all understand as opposed to a more standard English, which my kids called "The bigger words" – more standard English. It was just easier to use dialect, so it was not necessarily in terms of content, but it was in terms of emphasis and comprehension that I would use the dialect.

But she also exclaimed:

Oh, you know what, we were real flexible. We were really flexible. We did make it a point that when we got in front of students, when we were in our classrooms to ... to use a Standard English and not our dialect. So we made that a point because of course we are in the content of education. However, as we were communicating with ourselves, we were very comfortable using our dialect.

Indications from the insider Sookdeo, a Trinidad and Tobagonian functioning as a teacher educator in the Caribbean region, confirmed that indeed students in the Caribbean context are made to start paying attention to that difference in Englishes between themselves and others or among different people at a very young age. He shared:

I think that would have happened – well, probably it happened in primary school, but would not have been – and secondary school, but would not have been obvious until

I got to university, actually ... Because the thing is that – okay. So when you are in school, right, when you are in primary or high school, the thing is that you know that you are speaking Creole [English]. Your friends are speaking in Creole. That's natural. You come to expect that your teachers are speaking differently. And they say to you, "Well, you have to speak in a particular way. Speak correctly." ... They say to you to speak correctly. "Don't speak broken language," right? And that's accepted. You don't question it. You know that once you're in class, especially when the English teacher is there, that you speak English. You speak English, right? They didn't call it Creole, by the way.

This evidence from Sookdeo is bolstered by insights from Wilbertha and Jasmine, teacher educators from Jamaica, who reiterated the notion of "brokenness" often advanced in the English language arts curriculum used to train teachers in the Caribbean, stating:

As language teachers, though, teachers have to be able to distinguish when they're using which language, because the curriculum now is encouraging students to translate from English to Creole. So our teachers must really be able to translate. [The curriculum now] asks them to allow students to express in the language they're comfortable with. So you will have students talking Creole. So our teachers, when they leave here, they should know the difference in structure between English and Creole. They have to learn that. And when they're in the classroom teaching, they must be competent in [Standard] English. They must be comfortable enough to switch when necessary. So they should teach in English, but they should know that if they need to explain a concept, they can do so in Creole if necessary, depending on who they're with. They should be comfortable enough with English to teach the students the differences between the two languages, the Jamaican Creole and the Standard English. And for all students, before they leave here in the degree program, they have to do more personal development activities to make themselves more fluent in Standard English, and that they don't have a lot of time to do unless they are already teaching. If they are in the classroom, you'll get students who are more proficient in spoken Standard English. But if you have students who are not teaching, who are probably doing other jobs, and they get by using very informal English or Creole, it'll be difficult for them to become more fluent in Standard English. So, they have to work a little harder at it. There's another difficult – there's another aspect that they need to work on generally. It's the written version of English. We still have students who are competent in Standard English, but the written version is marred with several errors.

Cecelia, another insider and teacher educator who hailed from Barbados, affirmed this notion of brokenness, putting it in this way:

[There is a] whole notion that Bajan [Barbadian Creolized English] is just broken English, and it is bad, and you shouldn't speak it, and which is what the schools tended to want to – or at a policy level ... but trying to rescue the local language by denigrating Standard English ... I think you have to find a way of helping people to understand that there's nothing wrong with being able to communicate in both. And if you can communicate in Standard English, you can reach more people than if you just communicate in your home language. And we have to get the situation stopped, where the home language is a "language" spoken in inverted commas. Any time you write anything that's supposedly Bajan or whatever, it always comes in inverted commas. No matter what the context is, there's always a sense that it is wrong. So we're going to put it in inverted commas.

As the insider knowledge shows, the raciolinguistic ideologies undergirding Ashley and Melody, and the decision-making by Fanus to describe certain Englishes in their individual linguistic repertoires as broken, were steeped in the institutional processes of schooling and of other organizations as well as the broader Caribbean society that purported an acceptance of such Englishes for certain informal purposes even while reinforcing students' need to approximate what was viewed as the "standard" for other more well-defined pathways to "*success.*"

Speaking of her experience with the E-languages at play as a former teacher in the Bahamas, where Fanus had grown up, Davina, mentioned above, shared:

In the Bahamas, when I was teaching, I predominantly used just very standard English. It's often infused with Bahamian dialect but it's infused with Bahamian dialect in order to connect with the students. Often times, students would say to me, "Oh, you sound American," which meant you're using Standard English, not dialect. I think in an education context, it's important to be able to speak to young persons in a standard form of English as opposed to using the dialect. Not that I'm adverse to it because it certainly had its place depending on what we were doing. It certainly had its place, but I think it's important, particularly for my students in the Bahamas to, for me to use a Standard English so that they too can learn from that no matter what the subject is I'm teaching.

In slight contrast, Cordelia, an insider and teacher educator in the English-speaking nation country of Barbados, provided context about how teachers evolved in the Caribbean with their relationship to the E-languages reflected on by Fanus, sharing the following:

Well, first of all, for me – because many teachers, like all of us before, would have come not even recognizing, yes, they were [inaudible] about Standard English and [referable?] dialect. But by the time I got to the teacher's college, I found that there was a different sentiment within the whole society. In my earlier years, as I told you earlier, we aspired to speak the standard [English] because we saw it as an achievement. By the time I got to teacher's college ... [I realized that] as [far as teacher candidates] are concerned, they did not see the need. There was no dire need to try to even speak the Queen's English ... But what I'm saying is that they felt comfortable [with the] dialect. I think independence [changed things], I think. And then the whole awareness that Standard English is not the best thing since sliced bread, and that we in the Caribbean have our own [Creolized English] – so what I'm saying is that those were positive things which started in the Caribbean and those things are important. The fact that the dialect is not necessarily inferior, it's just different. So I needed to have [teacher candidates] understand the whole idea of being able to code switch. Because at first, when I would have begun, many of the students, somebody [else] would have taught initially [because] they were doing their associate degree in education. There were some who would have been exposed to the formal language class. But of course, we would have taught them there, using one of the texts that was used here too. So it was I who needed to have them change the way they thought about the language. So it was an attitudinal change first, and when you got them into understanding that, not that didn't know it, they knew it, but they knew that, in terms of society, which language would have been accepted as the language of the society in terms of what education use and governments. So they knew that, even if they might not have known it in a very formal way. But as far as they were concerned, the distinctiveness of being a Bajan was important. I remember when we passed through the sixties and so where you want to throw away your Afro and become a West Indian. All that. So it was a way of seeing life that was very different from the way we saw it in my former years, my younger years. But then again, the advantage to Teachers College would be that you're helping them to understand their society, helping them to understand how things work, and what would be their role in the classroom as a teacher. So once you got them to get that transition in their minds, then it was easier in terms of attitude.

Holistic Literacies of Black Caribbean Immigrant Youth: Articulating a Heuristic of Semiolingual Innocence

As articulated in this chapter, the painting of a portrait of the literacies of Black Caribbean immigrant youth presented above reflects six holistic literacies as follows, each of which raises questions for research, teaching, and policy-making that are correspondingly presented below:

(1) **Literacies of Perceived Success:** Literacies of perceived success were reflected via translanguaging and transsemiotizing in the form of Black Caribbean immigrants' reading and writing through the linguistic mode, orally with various representations of what students believed was 'Standard English,' reading and writing the body into the Caribbean and US as well as across these spaces transsemiotically in ways that signal efforts to be accepted based on such notions of success, whether cognizant of this or not, as well as other methods of representing (e.g., visually) in ways that would lead to "success" as determined externally by society and by others. In other words, these literacies often involved phonetic constructions, meaning-making, as well as the use of vocabulary and comprehension often associated with a view of success that aligned with what schools and parents as well as organizations in society perceived as being successful. They raise questions such as:
  (a) How can phonics and phonemic awareness be different for immigrants from the Bahamas and Jamaica and for other Black Caribbean immigrants?
  (b) What differences are presented in the phonetic pronunciations of each island and how do these differences present themselves in literacy and ELA, as well as other classrooms in the US?

(c) How do teachers avoid marking as inaccurate these broadly acceptable phonemic and phonetic structures that are part of Black Caribbean students' linguistic repertoires, as miscues on running records?
(d) What assessments can be designed to capture these as non-miscues?
(e) How can reading and writing through the broader semiotic repertoire for immigrants as well as synesthesia be positioned as equally viable paths to human flourishing as is the tendency to do so for the linguistic mode?
(f) How can parents of Black Caribbean immigrants be supported to allow children to be children with their bodies in ways that don't necessarily have to approximate whiteness to be accepted? How can Black Caribbean immigrant literacies position the teaching of literacy and ELA in classrooms more broadly, for flourishing (Keyes, 2002) and not merely "success" with the affordances of translanguaging and transsemiotizing?
(g) How can schools include specific directives for engaging with the varied ways in which the differentiated E-languages of Black Caribbean immigrants are acknowledged and addressed in literacy and ELA as well as other US classrooms?

(2) **Literacies of Human Sensitivity:** Literacies of human sensitivity were reflected via translanguaging and transsemiotizing as what Black Caribbean immigrants loved about the use of languaging, how they felt about people responding to them, how they became angry about what they perceived as raciolinguistic injustice, in the love for a father's use of his racialized Englishes, in the pervasive isolation, a refusal to feel, among other representations. These literacies raise questions such as:

(a) How can Black Caribbean immigrant students be allowed spaces that are so comfortable that they forget themselves and the impositions of society to such a large degree that they are thrust into using E-languages often deemed inferior within their repertoires in ways that equally allow for and legitimize the expression of their joy, pain, anger, frustration, happiness, etc. – disrupting the fragmentations that may persist on their lives?
(b) How can parents of Black Caribbean immigrants be supported to explore and use E-languages positioned as inferior with their children in ways that convey the love that the children feel through the use of these languages versus others?
(c) How can institutions create spaces that are more intentional about keeping Black Caribbean immigrants in community with others who have similar literacies or who wish to understand and connect with them?
(d) How can addressing the anger and impatience or the frustrations of Blackness in the immigrant life be legitimized by institutions in ways that use foster their holistic literacies for flourishing?

(e) How can schools position the teaching of literacies for subconscious elicitation of emotion as a basis for cultivating animation and imagination emerging in the evolving experiences of Black Caribbean immigrant students?

(3) **Literacies of Paradox:** Literacies of paradox were reflected as using translanguaging and transsemiotizing to seemingly represent one's self as a certain person on one context and as another person in another context, or seemingly representing one's self as a certain person with members of a defined societal group and as another person with members of another societal group via translanguaging and transsemiotizing, even when this practice doesn't make sense to the self or to others. Such literacies were seen to be intertwined with the emotive where, for instance, a Black Caribbean immigrant student would often make a certain claim about how they used language in one space but make an opposite claim about language and semiotics in another based on the instantiation of their emotions. These literacies were also seen to be present when Black Caribbean immigrant youth would say that they used semiolingual practice in one way, but their anecdotes reflected the opposite. They were also seen in the constant movement between extremes of their use of languaging and semiotics in ways that were paradoxical – "*semiolingual polarization*" – reflecting often that they couldn't get rid of instantiations of the self that were preferred by various publics but choosing to instead decide on which polar opposites functioned as the best translanguaging and transsemiotic version of the self for the right reason. Literacies of paradox raise questions such as:

(a) How can spaces for translanguaging practices be created that foster engagement with navigating extremes, albeit that are morally and ethically sound, through languaging and semiotics for developing a both-and approach to using literacies to read and write the world?

(b) How can schools position the teaching of literacies to seek and to leverage intentional as well as morally and ethically sound paradoxical confrontations towards the cultivation of a both-and ethos in literacy, ELA, and other subject areas?

(4) **Communicative Literacies:** Communicative literacies were reflected as speaking to be understood as opposed to merely translanguaging and transsemiotizing for its own sake. These literacies were visible in seeking comprehension based on lack of transferability of meaning across E-languages. They raise questions such as:

(a) How can assessments and instructional practices allow for capturing originality of meaning from Black Caribbean immigrants so that it is not lost in Standard American English? How do we do this in a way that equally presents meanings lost in tandem with those meanings captured only by SAE?

(b) How can schools create spaces for communicative literacies of social spaces such as TikTok and Instagram that others can understand but that are not dictated by the Eurocentric norm?
(c) How can assessments be designed to leverage such literacies?
(d) What about the ELA curriculum as it stands? What literacy modules can facilitate this process?

(5) **Literacies of Intraracial and Interracial Interdependence:** Literacies of intraracial and interracial interdependence were represented via translanguaging and transsemiotizing in groups that the Black Caribbean immigrants joined for community such as athletics, religion, Caribbean associations, sororities, other associations, and organizations that they *attempted to* but could not join as well as those they decided not to try to join. These literacies were also visible in the interdependence established beyond persons such as foods while also seeking community with persons in the broader society with mechanisms such as greetings. These literacies raise questions such as:
(a) How can schools position the teaching of literacies for intraracial and interracial interdependence?

(6) **Literacies of Possibility:** Literacies of possibility were represented in indications of how the Black Caribbean immigrant students' presents and futures could be better, and they could enjoy greater flourishing via their translanguaging and transsemiotizing. These literacies raise questions such as:
(a) How can schools position the teaching of literacies for harnessing the imagination to solve local and global problems imposed upon themselves and the world?

As implied, these literacies transcend dichotomies typically relegating students' literate repertoires to notions of "academic language" and "academic literacy" or "invisible literacies" and "home language" vs. "school language" given the reliance on language and raciosemiotic architecture (Flores, 2020; Smith, 2023a) used by the students as a function of their metalinguistic, metacultural, metaracial, and metasemiotic understanding, both in the Caribbean and in the US. In relying on modalities across their multiliteracies, the Black Caribbean youth also reflected the transgressiveness in the transracialization (Alim, 2016) undergirding their linguistic and semiotic repertoires which relies on broader transsemiotizing as much as it does on translanguaging to reflect how they demonstrate agency with their E-languages and E-semiotics while also engaging the (trans) raciosemiotic and (trans)raciolinguistic ideological norms across geographic, virtual, and other spaces. In doing so, the holistic literacies of the Black Caribbean immigrant youth correspond to the individual analyses of students' literate practices to occur in the context of the broader global perceptions by which they are surrounded, as called for by Rosa and Flores (2017), perceptions that systematically dictate how racial and linguistic structures function together to maintain (perceptions of) literate inequities.

Operating as presented here, based on "individual-to-global" analyses that examine how linguistic and semiotic practices are racialized in literacy both at the individual and global level, allows the holistic literacies of these youth to make visible the reification of structures of government in literacy, English language arts, language, and other curricula that continue to overlook the legitimate literacies of underrepresented youth (Rosa & Flores, 2017; Smith, 2019a). Analyses such as these, that show how students' literate practices at the micro level are connected to hegemonic perceptions about racialized language and semiotics at the macro level, present opportunities to challenge deficit notions of underrepresented youth that tend to consistently question students' linguistic competence and sense of self (Rosa, 2016; Rosa & Flores, 2017, Smith, 2019a). In these holistic literacies, we see also the significance of centralizing race as a unit of analysis beyond the US context and *as equally important as* constructs such as class, gender, ethnicity in examinations of the co-naturalization of race and language for furthering research on intersectionality, as espoused in a raciolinguistic perspective (Rosa & Flores, 2017). Moreover, through the holistic literacies of Black Caribbean youth presented, there is a reiteration of the need to shift the focus away from how racialized populations modify their linguistic practices and instead, to equally identify the ways in which dominant white perspectives are complicit in reifying colonial practices that use co-naturalization of race and language as well as race and semiotics to define academic and other institutions (Rosa & Flores, 2017; Smalls, 2020).

In thinking of these holistic literacies from the perspective of the framework for '*Black immigrant literacies*' (Smith, 2023a) alluded to previously, I have established, through the foregoing depictions of youth's literacies, that their instantiations reflect, to varying degrees, the five elements of this framework designed to facilitate researchers, practitioners, and parents who wish to better understand and support Black immigrant youth (see Figure 6.1). These five elements, alluded to earlier in this book, are:

(1) *Claim to the Struggle for Justice:* allows for emerging understanding through intentional and adept communication between Black immigrant and Black Americans about the distinctive historical experiences surrounding slavery that they have endured in what has evolved into a white supremacist context that inadvertently frames their ability to lay claim to the struggle for justice.

(2) *Myth of the Model Minority:* facilitates critical understanding of the ways in which a meritocratic model minority myth, as applied to Black immigrant youth, is steeped in divide-and-conquer racial politics that sustains interracial divisions between Black immigrant youth and their Black American peers and other minoritized immigrant populations.

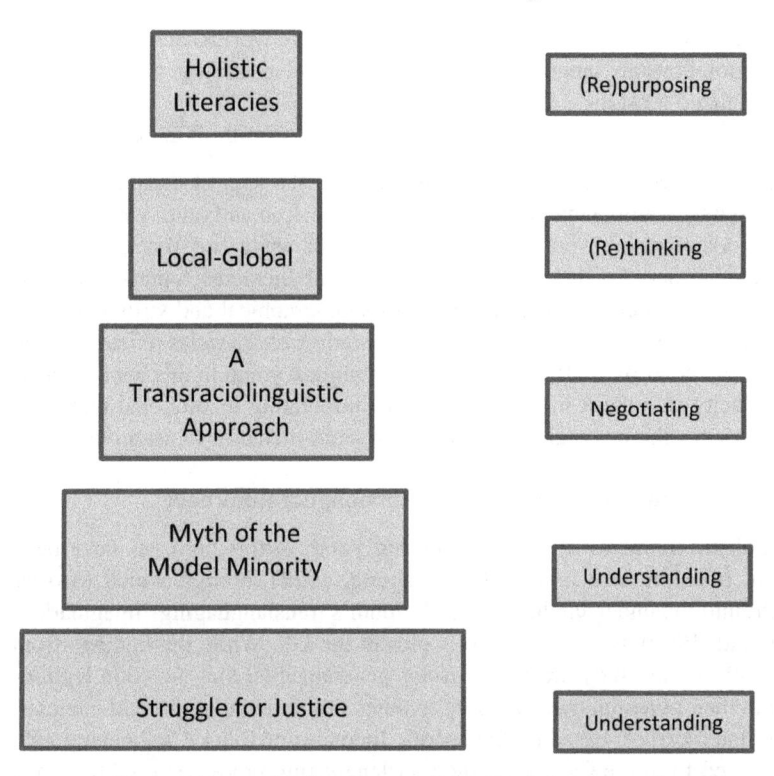

Figure 6.1 A model for conceptualizing Black immigrant literacies

(3) *A Transraciolinguistic Approach:* creates opportunities for youth, teachers, parents to discuss and to leverage a transraciolinguistic approach (Smith, 2019a, 2020a) through opportunities presented for developing metalinguistic, metacultural, and metacultural understanding as youth *keep learning and acknowledging their 'not knowing'* about race through an iterative diagnostic and feedback loop (Guinier, 2004).
(4) *Local-Global:* instantiates a rethinking of the global through lived experience with the local by recognizing duality and hybridity in how racialization is implicitly embedded in the 'postcolonial' structures of youth's home countries as they encounter its explicit enactment through hegemonic whiteness and individual racialized encounters within the US.
(5) *Holistic Literacies:* re(purposes) literacies as holistic (as opposed to fragmented based on a privileging of literacy performance on tests) where youth use language, multiliteracies, and cross-border shifts to function as language architects who reread and rewrite text (i.e., which include

Englishes and semiotic resources from their life worlds) across home and school through languaging based on an understanding of inescapable racialized tensions.

(Smith, 2020b, pp. 26–28)

Developed intersectionally by drawing from (a) the lens of diaspora literacy often used to examine the literacies of Black American and other youth; (b) the framework of racial literacy often used for both white and Black American populations; and (c) the notion of transnational literacies typically used to understand the literacies of youth who cross geographical and virtual borders, these elements of the framework for *Black immigrant literacies* reflected in the holistic literacies of the Black Caribbean immigrant youth in this book point to the capacity that these literacies have for illuminating institutional pathways that allow for the leveraging of Black immigrant literacies in agentive ways.

Articulating a Heuristic of Semiolingual Innocence

The holistic literacies of Black Caribbean youth in this book, as have been shown, function as a prism (Bryce-Laporte, 1972) through which to offer insight into the understanding of Black youth's translanguaging "imaginaries" (Mahmud, 1999) as immigrants of Color in the US. While the findings from the youth in this study are by no means generalizable, they function legitimately in their potential transferability to other similar populations and contexts.

As stated earlier, based on the holistic literacies of Black Caribbean youth, as reflected from the Caribbean, the translanguaging processes used by Black youth in the Caribbean appear to mirror a wrestling with differential positioning of E-languages and E-semiotics, signaling how the integrated model of multilingualism functions as a mechanism for students to both reflect their individual linguistic and semiotic repertoires even while having to navigate their societally and institutionally determined realities undergirding literate and language practice in and beyond schools (Smith, 2020c). This dynamic, in turn, raises questions about how institutions of schooling create spaces in Caribbean schools and classrooms for students to reinscribe their linguistic innocence through interactions with peers in ways that allow them to preserve their personhoods (Rosa & Flores, 2017). By "innocence" here, I refer to the inherently imbued capacity of institutional-individual spaces created by Black students which operate legitimately *sans* attention to white gaze, juxtaposed against and disrupting the long-standing a societally imposed "Black abstraction" that has for so long operated legally and otherwise to uphold an imagined "white innocence" (Ross, 1990). And by "linguistic innocence" – I refer to the instantiation of these spaces through languaging.

Reflecting how Black Caribbean students simultaneously wrestled with raciolinguistic and raciosemiotic injustice in their home countries of Jamaica and the Bahamas while at the same time agentively using translanguaging practices to (re)read and (re-)write their worlds as well as their selves within it, the holistic literacies of students in this context point at the same time to the ways in which institutions have positioned Black Caribbean students to exercise their self-determination or not, as a function of their individual linguistic and semiotic repertoires. Emerging through this use of their individual linguistic repertoires to iteratively engage in a reshaping of their Caribbean worlds is what I posit shortly as *"semiolingual innocence."*

Also as presented earlier, based on the holistic literacies of Black Caribbean youth as reflected by their experiences as immigrants in the US, the translanguaging processes steeped in the integrated model of multilingualism used by Black Caribbean immigrant youth with their E-languages and E-semiotics in the US appear to reflect the functioning of the body as a transraciosemiotic marker. They were capable of leveraging their individual linguistic repertoires to exceptionalistically discard English in the US while recognizing the limitations of this practice for fully capturing ideas across E-languages during translation. From raciolinguistic rejection experienced as a Black insider to the burden of 'sounding American,' the Black Caribbean immigrant youth reflected literacies that demonstrated an affinity for heterogeneous representations of Blackness even while highlighting the possibility of this practice as a basis for exclusivity. Illustrating how feeling functioned as an outlet for interaction and also the tendency to do as a means of escaping feeling, the Black Caribbean immigrant youth showed how they differentially (un)seized varied literate liberties as expressions of safety on the individual and societal level. The Black Caribbean immigrant students simultaneously wrestled with transraciolinguistic and transraciosemiotic injustice in the destination country of the US where they lived while at the same time agentively using translanguaging and transsemiotic practices based on language and raciosemiotic architecture to reread and rewrite their "transworlds" (see Flores et al., 2014, on transworld pedagogy) – remixing their semiolingual performativity and reflecting *"semiolingual innocence."*

Based on the holistic literacies of Black Caribbean youth across the Caribbean and the US, as shown in the findings of the study undergirding this book, the translanguaging processes steeped in the integrated model of multilingualism used transgeographically by Black Caribbean immigrant youth with their E-languages and E-semiotics, signaling a capacity for translanguaging that allows for the use of E-languaging to leverage a linguistic repertoire which seems to position them as privileged, is betrayed by raciosemiotic ideologies from society that ascribe a perceived countertransgressiveness of being Black and linguistically different. In doing so, the youth's Caribbeanness is intertwined with their Blackness and its associated language differences, seemingly inhibiting the exercise of belonging in white spaces. Even so, metasemiolingual, metalinguistic, metacultural, as well as metaracial understanding are leveraged, reflecting a "both-and" perspective (Smith, 2013a, 2013b, 2017, 2018) that allows for adopting multiple and opposing viewpoints to be held in consciousness at the same time, much like is fostered among the individuals presented in *"a transraciolinguistic approach"* (see Figure 4.1). Here, where there is a capacity to see both sides, albeit morally and ethically informed, and to operate from this vantage point – a position is occupied made possible through *"semiolingual innocence."*

Considering these characterizations emerging from the above-painted portrait of the holistic literacies of Black Caribbean youth, I assert that in the holistic literacies of these youth, *"semiolingual innocence"* emerges and operates as instantiated by space – functioning not within the student, but rather, emerging in the infinitely shifting space between and among individuals or between and among individuals and the ever-evolving institutional or societal (see Smith, 2023a). In the spaces between the racialized and dominant individuals presented in a transraciolinguistic approach and in the interstices instantiated by their metalinguistic, metaracial, metasemiotic, and metacultural understanding, spurred on by their relations to institutions and to the society, their semiolingual innocence emerges, not statically, but intermittently reinscribed through their holistic literacies, leveraged absolutely *sans* white gaze. Operating constantly as a function of this dialectic where the raciolinguistic and raciosemiotic challenges of the institution, community, and society incessantly meet the individual even while self-determination (Fanon, 1991/1961) simultaneously flourishes *sans* attention to white gaze, semiolingual innocence emerges beyond the interstices of third space (Bhabha, 1994; Soja, 1996) – representing just one articulation of Freire's vision of the new human. Visible when instantiated through experiences in the lives of humans such as the Black Caribbean students in this book, as the unapologetic and inhibited capacity to pursue and persist toward "flourishing" (Keyes, 2002) while unapologetically operating semiolingually *sans* white gaze, even while naming and engaging the raciolinguistic and raciosemiotic influences on the personhood, *semiolingual innocence* is acknowledged in the holistic literacies of Black Caribbean immigrant youth made visible through their translanguaging and transsemiotizing, as a long-established and entrenched *capacity* – one accessible to all humans.

Just as the Black Trinidadian and Tobagonian Soca artist Rodney LeBlanc observed in the song "Phenomenal" at the beginning of this chapter, "semiolingual innocence" in the holistic literacies of the Black Caribbean youth can be captured in the following lyrics:

> We partying sun or rain
> We doh care what the people say

Once the music hit meh veins
So much powers ah cyah explain
Until ah cool again, when the father take me away
All wey meh friends will say
I'm Phenomenal
I'm Phenomenal
I'm Phenomenal
I'm Phenomenal

(Kan Kan Riddim, 2015)

Reflected repeatedly across the Black Caribbean students' holistic literacies in this book, *semiolingual innocence* emerged in glimpses within the spaces instantiated by the transraciolinguistic, translanguaging, and overall transsemiotic practices of youth but failed to be limited by the racialization accompanying these.

Just as the sun has hung infinitely suspended in liminal perfection between what is often humanity on an earth insistent on bringing about its own destruction, and a celestial heaven that never hesitates to inspire with its majestic beauty – no matter how deviant this humanity from the quantum and moral order of the universe – never once hesitating to shine on anyone because of the evil manifested in the world, *semiolingual innocence* finds its inception in the "transcendent literacies" (Willis, 2022) of our ancient pasts before the white gaze had ever been conceived, persisting across centuries to be manifested in the Black Caribbean immigrant literacies leveraged through translanguaging and transsemiotizing today. Liberated from the incessant need to view the self as oppressed while at the same time, also capable of engaging with the raciolinguistic and raciosemiotic invoked by oppression in ways that nonetheless allow a functioning absolutely *sans* white gaze, semiolingual innocence as illustrated through the holistic literacies of Black Caribbean youth, holds potential as a much-needed heuristic for advancing holistic literacies of youth in a myriad of ways.

Here, I articulate eight mechanisms that become immediately visible in such a heuristic:

(1) **Flourishing:** Semiolingual innocence positions teaching for *"flourishing"* (Keyes, 2002; see also Toussaint et al., 2023) with translanguaging and transsemiotizing, discarding a sole reliance on archaic notions of success (*Flourishing*).
(2) **Purpose:** Semiolingual innocence positions teaching solely for *purpose* such that children and their parents together hold the right to determine the codes undergirding E-languages and E-semiotics needed to foster life pursuits with mediation by the teacher (*Flattening*).
(3) **Comfort:** Semiolingual innocence positions the teaching for subconscious elicitation of emotion through immersion in *spaces of comfort* as a basis

for cultivating "animation" (Orellana, 2015) and imagination through translanguaging and "transsemiotizing" (*Feeling*).
(4) **Expansion:** Semiolingual innocence positions teaching as an opportunity for leveraging metalinguistic, metacultural, metaracial, and metasemiotic understanding that recognizes intralinguistic capacity of 'monolingual,' 'monocultural,' and 'monoracial' repertoires while expanding these at the same time (see Smith, 2022b, on transraciolinguistics; see Smith, 2016, on monolingual students at risk) (*Fostering*).
(5) **Paradox:** Semiolingual innocence positions teaching to instantiate intentional paradoxical confrontations towards the cultivation of a "*both-and*" ethos, critical for emerging through the dialectic of 'oppressed' versus 'oppressor,' into an ever-evolving flourishing (Freire, 1970/2000; Smith, 2016) (*Finessing*).
(6) **Originality:** Semiolingual innocence positions teaching to prioritize communicative capacities through translanguaging and broader transsemiotizing approaches to comprehension that preserve *originality of meaning* steeped in cultural indigeneity, regardless of the source (*Factualizing*).
(7) **Interdependence:** Semiolingual innocence positions teaching for intraracial and interracial as well as intracultural and intercultural, intralinguistic and interlinguistic, and other forms of interdependence, recognizing the shared humanity of all peoples (*Friending*).
(8) **Imagination:** Semiolingual innocence positions teaching for harnessing the imagination via translanguaging and transsemiotizing to solve local and global problems currently assailing the currents and futures of the world (*Facilitating*).

The Promise of Semiolingual Innocence

Through "semiolingual innocence" presented as a much-needed heuristic for navigating with wisdom, the increasingly polarized nature of racial, linguistic, and cultural relations in the US and elsewhere, this book illustrates how Black Caribbean immigrant youth reinscribe this innocence, or attempt to, both in the Caribbean and transgeographically, upon their migration to the US. As a function of this heuristic, I acknowledge how these youth, no matter the Englishes they speak, reflected varying degrees of translanguaging in their literate practice on which schools are positioned to draw as a basis for cultivating novel and liberatory imaginary presents and address the pressing problems of immediate and distant futures. In doing so, I assert that contrary to broadly held notions that dichotomize translanguaging practices, seemingly portraying this construct as characteristic of certain students who use often privileged named languages (e.g., 'Standard English,' 'Standard Spanish,' codified languages, or superiority), *all youth*, no matter the color of their skin, have literacies and translanguaging practices that are either rendered less than agentive in classrooms or that are placed at risk by a disengagement with diverse linguistic repertoires when the Eurocentric method is used as a basis for determining what children and youth can and cannot do as literate beings (see Smith, 2016, on the ways in national policies on language and literacy curricula in the US reinforce standardized language approaches that place 'monolingual speakers' at risk). The Black gaze (Campt, 2023; hooks, 1992) makes this clear in the case of students racialized as white. The white gaze imposed on students racialized as Black as well as other students of Color also makes this visible. The prism (Bryce-Laporte, 1972) of Black immigrant literacies is illustrated through the rich voices of these youth, to argue that Black immigrant children and youth, every Black student, and students of Color, much like all students across the globe, deserve the right to reinscribe their *semiolingual innocence* via their holistic literacies in a (re)reading and (re)writing of the world, and themselves in it.

Based on the eight mechanisms presented above, as elements of the heuristic of *semiolingual innocence*, I call for an expansion of the conceptual and pedagogical reach of translanguaging that offers millions of children who speak Englishes in the US and across the globe an opportunity to leverage their *semiolingual innocence* through *"translanguaging with Englishes"* (TWE) (Smith, 2020c; Smith & Warrican, 2021). Through this opportunity, I facilitate an instantiation of the long-standing dream of Paulo Freire, to allow an emergence at last, from the persisting dialectic of 'oppressor' vs. 'oppressed' into scholarly and practical avenues for positioning a new literate being as agentive – a semiolingual innocence that for certain Black Caribbean youth in this book functions absolutely *sans* attention to white gaze. At the same time, I paint a portrait of the ways in which the framework of semiolingual innocence can provide institutions with opportunities to position the translanguaging and transsemiotic capacities undergirding Black Caribbean immigrant youth's literacies, much like that of *all* youth, as they functioned pre-coloniality and pre-white gaze, as sites of "imagination" and not merely representation (Gutiérrez et al., 2017; Wartofsky, 1979, p. 189).

Through the envisioning of a new being as invoked by Paulo Freire – whether Black, Native American, Native Caribbean American, Haitian Creole, Latinx, Afro-Latinx, Asian, mixed, or otherwise – that leverages *semiolingual innocence*, I ultimately assert that Black immigrant students, and all students of Color, whose Englishes inadvertently remain the basis for literacy and English language teaching across the globe, stand positioned, through *semiolingual innocence*, to bridge barriers through "transcendent literacies" (Willis, 2022) as they center their personhoods for making visible the vast range of their translanguaging and transsemiotic imaginaries. Ultimately, for those who speak other languages too, and for white students at large whose linguistic repertoires have been maimed by the seeming privilege and promise of monoglossia, utilizing the Black gaze to disrupt 'whiteness' and thus embrace semiolingual innocence can potentially function as a much-needed heuristic for cross-ancestral redemptiveness. This redemptive shift allows for a reinscribing upon children whose legacies often remain tainted by legacies of a cruel past and whose currents and futures largely long (we very much hope) for a reconciliatory peace, the opportunity to emerge *semiolingually innocent* – invoking *translanguaging imaginaries of innocence*. They hold the opportunity to do so, by engaging with the Black gaze to function fully with holistic literacies themselves, which can, in conjunction with those of students of Color, function reconciliatory and restoratively for a troubled world – a reconciliation and restoration, invoked in part by Amanda Gorman, when she states:

When day comes, we step out of the shade of flame and unafraid. The new dawn balloons as we free it. There is always light. If only we're brave enough to see it. If only we're brave enough to be it. (Gorman, 2021)

7 Reinscribing Lost Imaginaries of Semiolingual Innocence

Futurizing Translanguaging for Flourishing

> We've seen a force that would shatter our nation, rather than share it.
> Would destroy our country if it meant delaying democracy.
> And this effort very nearly succeeded.
> But while democracy can be periodically delayed, it can never be permanently defeated.
> In this truth, in this faith we trust, for while we have our eyes on the future, history has its eyes on us.
> This is the era of just redemption.
> We feared at its inception.
> We did not feel prepared to be the heirs of such a terrifying hour.
> But within it we found the power to author a new chapter, to offer hope and laughter to ourselves.
> So, while once we asked, how could we possibly prevail over catastrophe, now we assert, how could catastrophe possibly prevail over us?
> We will not march back to what was, but move to what shall be: a country that is bruised but whole, benevolent but bold, fierce and free.
>
> Gorman, 2021

In 2015, the Trinidadian and Tobagonian performer and songwriter Soca artist Olatunji Yearwood, known by his mononym "Olatunji" or just "Ola," winner of the famous Soca Groovy Monarch competition, released his hit single "Ola," the music video which was produced in South Africa. In the song, Ola provocatively alludes to a beautiful Black woman who has captured his attention, chanting evocatively:

This gyal prettier than a rainbow, Smile bright than day light, Girl I want you ah say so, Ah Follow you like ah tail light, Standing there with you halo, More dangerous than a snake bite, Whenever that ah see you, Yuh take away all meh stage fright. (Olatunji, 2015)

Having grown up in Trinidad and Tobago, "one of the world's true melting pots" and "an island nation whose citizens have pulled from their African, Asian, Latin, European and Amerindian heritage to innovate in the fields of music, art, food and having a good time" (Kes the Band, n.d.), Olatunji boasts a West African Nigerian name, "Ọlátúnjí," drawn from the Yoruba personal name "ọlá tún jí," meaning *"nobility has awoken again,"* a name that dares to reawaken the innocence of Blackness much like *Black Panther* and *Black Panther: Wakanda Forever* – the films invoked at the beginning of this book; a name in song to transcend the diasporic divide, painting a South African semiolingual imaginary on the largely Trinidadian and Tobagonian translanguaging canvas of the Caribbean (Dictionary of American Family Names, 2022). It is therefore fitting that this song, "Olatunji," sang by a Caribbean artist racialized as Black in the world and invoking "Black Diasporic possibilities" (Austin, 2022) through the inscription of Black innocence on the historically warped imaging of Black womanhood, be used to reinforce the Black semiolingual innocence of Black Caribbean immigrant youth, steeped in "transcendent literacies" (Willis, 2022) as presented in the movie *Black Panther*. Extending the symbolism of this film invoked at the beginning of this book, the name "Olatunji" functions as the necessary crescendo for acknowledging "phenomenality" (Kan Kan Riddim, 2015) emerging in the articulated translanguaging imaginaries of *inonsans jan nwè*.

In this book, I have painted a portrait of the holistic literacies of six Caribbean immigrant youth, racialized as Black. Using a nuanced (decolonizing) interpretive approach, I have shown how the youth used their self-determination to reclaim their linguistic and semiotic – *semiolingual* – innocence while working towards imagined futures even as they simultaneously engaged with the influence of institutional factors, raciolinguistically and raciosemiotically, on their literacies. Relying on the intersecting lenses of translanguaging with Englishes, multiliteracies, and a raciolinguistic perspective in concert with transracialization (Alim, 2016) to explore the insights of these youth, I demonstrated how the fields of language and literacy are positioned to disrupt what have long been considered dichotomies that characterize the *academic* and *invisible* literacies of youth, and extend beyond tensions concerning such dichotomies to focus instead on notions such as "language architecture" (Flores, 2020) and raciosemiotic architecture (Smith, 2022d) as well as their affordances for understanding the multiliteracies of Black immigrant youth. Making visible awareness of instances where the Black Language – Englishes (i.e., E-languages) – and Black semiotics – broader range of semiotic resources (i.e., E-semiotics) – of immigrant youth may be racialized by institutions and society even as they engage in architecting, I illustrated in this book how transraciolinguistics and transsemiotizing function in the semiolingual repertoires of these youth as a function of their "*transcendent literacies*" (Willis, 2022).

In the juxtaposition of youth's translanguaging with Englishes based on an integrated model of multilingualism against their superimposed negotiation of literacies through the lens of the white listening subject undergirding their contestation of raciolinguistic and raciosemiotic ideologies, I show how Black Caribbean immigrant youth, through their holistic literacies, reclaim 'lost' translanguaging imaginaries and reinscribe their *"semiolingual innocence"* as they evolve into the "new beings" envisioned by Paulo Freire. Operating based on "individual-to-global" analyses called for in a raciolinguistic perspective by Rosa and Flores (2017) and responding to the questions "By what processes are we all involved in the construction and maintenance of a 'standard' language, and further, that the 'standard' is somehow better, more intelligent, more appropriate, more important, etc. than other varieties?" and "How, when and why are we all implicated in linguistic supremacy?" (Alim, 2004, p. 194), I used a holistic a portrait of Black Caribbean immigrant youth in this book to challenge obscured discourses where institutional structures reinforce the transgeographic burden imposed on such youth to navigate inescapable tensions surrounding Black languaging and more broadly, Black semiotics.

In doing so, findings from the analyses of the experiences of the six Black Caribbean youth in the English-speaking Caribbean illustrated holistic literacies reflected as they grew up as Black children in Jamaica and the Bahamas, which meant: (a) a reliance on 'broken English'; (b) paradoxical acceptance of languages both at home and at school in the Bahamas; and (c) overt legitimization of Bahamian Creolized English. In addition, findings from these analyses of the experiences of the Black Caribbean youth migrating to the US also reflected holistic literacies evolving in their lives, illustrated as follows: (a) the body as a transraciosemiotic marker; (b) exceptionalistic discarding of Bahamian English in the US; (c) incapacity to fully capture ideas in translation; (d) raciolinguistic rejection from the inside and a burden of sounding American; (e) heterogeneous representations of Blackness as necessary but exclusive; (f) doing to escape feeling; and (g) the (un)seizing of varied liberties as expressions of safety. In these findings from analyses of the experiences of Black Caribbean youth migrating across the Caribbean and the US, their holistic literacies emerged as representations of the isolating effects of (inadvertently) imposed homogeneity. Through the use of the Black Caribbean immigrant youth literacies as a "prism" (Bryce-Laporte, 1972), I have dared to silence their invisibility (Smith, 2020b), and resurrect, through the painting of the portrait of these holistic literacies (Smith, 2020b), the long-held but largely obscured Black translanguaging and Black transsemiotic imajinè inosan of this student population, both in the Caribbean and in the US.

These findings pointed to eight mechanisms in the heuristic of semiolingual innocence – *flourishing, purpose, comfort, expansion, paradox, originality, interdependence, and imagination* – capable of advancing the holistic literacies of Black Caribbean immigrant youth, mechanisms that I assert can be cultivated by all youth, in a myriad of ways. Based on the holistic literacies of Black Caribbean immigrant youth and the corresponding elements emerging via the heuristic of semiolingual innocence, the question becomes: *How does the painted portrait of Black Caribbean literacies of migration presented function as a lens for imagining the potential of translanguaging as a scholarly and pedagogical practice of equity for Black Caribbean immigrant students in particular, and beyond this, for all?*

Translanguaging beyond Privileged Languages

To do justice to this question, I assert that first, we must use the notion of semiolingual innocence to problematize translanguaging as a practice, which though in its conception operates as a characteristic of all, has thus far in its pedagogical application appeared to be largely inhibited in its potential by its tendency to be restricted to a privileging of certain student populations, named languages, and school settings over others. This privileging, represented in scholarship that often examines the crossing of named E-languages deemed superior (e.g., Spanish–English) (see Martínez, 2010, on Spanglishes for an exception) as opposed to the centering of 'unnamed' E-languages deemed inferior (e.g., African American English, Haitian Creole), fuels a supposition that linguistic repertoires necessarily operate only for those who possess certain variations of such named languages, an intention that foundationally functions in opposition to the stated goals of translanguaging (García et al., 2021). This privileging, though perhaps inadvertent, yet articulated often in the positioning of translanguaging as a function of dual-language programs that tend to center Spanish and English in the US for certain students of Color, or not, while overlooking others (i.e., African American English, Haitian Creole), runs counterproductive to the stated pedagogical and conceptual intentions of translanguaging.

Problematizing the potential of translanguaging based on semiolingual innocence, given the racially disruptive practice that translanguaging is, or has been articulated to be (García et al., 2021), disrupts the tendency to advance it, pedagogically and scholarly, based on linguistic repertoires steeped in named standardized languages (i.e., 'Standard English,' 'Standard Spanish') privileged by schools, teachers, curricula, and classrooms in the Minority World of the US and the Majority World at large. This problematization also disrupts the tendency to present translanguaging as a mechanism for liberation even while the advancement of the construct, in large part, often overlooks the multiplicities and hybridities of languaging mixing and fluidity that occur in the personhoods of students based largely on linguistic repertoires positioned on the linguistic margins of inferiority (i.e., African American English, Black Caribbean English) (see Bauer et al., 2017, for an exception on translanguaging of African American students).

The silencing of these Black linguistic repertoires in the burgeoning scholarship of translanguaging (Smith, 2020c) – repertoires that draw in large part, from 'unnamed' languages often peripheral to legitimized languages of schooling – supports problematization of translanguaging as a necessary interruption of the corresponding tendency to privilege the largely Eurocentric practice of traditional writing in classrooms as a literate practice represented by the standardized forms of privileged named languages based on accepted norms of these legitimized languages in schools while tending to overlook the vast range of transsemiotizing and translanguaging in the oral and multimodal inscriptions characterizing the holistic literacies of populations from the Majority World. This dynamic, I assert, where translanguaging often foregrounds traditional notions of writing as a Eurocentric practice – steeped in a privileging of certain forms of codification even when it is positioned as a pedagogical tool for redeeming the futures of students of Color – deviates from its intended capacity to reinscribe the *semiolingual innocence* of youth of Color, and specifically, of Black youth.

If translanguaging as a scholarly and pedagogical practice is to avoid the paradoxical failure of centering semiolingual repertoires based largely on languages and their accompanying Eurocentrically driven writing practices privileged by schooling, a departure from how it has functioned in large part as a long-held practice of Majority and Minority World youth for centuries, and through which it has now been (re)membered as a redemptive pathway for reinscribing semiolingual innocence, it becomes necessary, at its core, to address the tendency of translanguaging to largely overlook a focus on how marginalized 'unnamed' languages (often referred to as "Creoles" and "dialects") function pervasively on the social periphery due to the raciolinguistic and raciosemiotic ideological enterprise. In turn, it also becomes necessary to engage how certain forms of translanguaging are necessarily sidelined by its very privileging of certain instantiations of students' linguistic and semiotic repertoires over others based on the theoretical and conceptual examples that tend to characterize examinations in which it is steeped. In other words, the examples used to present translanguaging as a practice must intentionally account for deviations in the rationale undergirding its conceptualized intention given that they are often so deeply distanced from its capacity to function concretely as a pedagogical tool that accommodates intralinguistic variation, as represented in the repertoires of the world's population of speakers of Englishes.

As the prism of Black immigrant literacies undergirding the translanguaging imaginaries steeped in the Englishes of Black Caribbean immigrant youth has shown, translanguaging, in theory and practice, holds the potential to function as a mechanism through which to re-envision its original intention and to reinscribe the semiolingual innocence of Black youth, vast numbers of whom in the US (e.g., African Americans) and across the world (Africans, Caribbeans) are speakers of Black Englishes (see also Rampton, 1997; Winer, 1988).

Alim (2005) has clearly articulated in the chapter "Hearing What's Not Said and Missing What Is: Black Language in the White Public Space," based on research with Black English speakers in the US, this original intention, reflected as follows:

Many well-meaning teachers and scholars who insist on the teaching of "standard English" to Black youth are under the assumption that Black Language is a monostyle, i.e., that BL can be described as one style of speaking that is identifiably Black. As these data [in the study referenced] have shown, Black youth possess a broad range of speech styles (review Bilal's [the youth's data in the referenced study] stylistic flexibility when talking to a White female non-Hip Hopper and in his peer group, for example) ... It makes more sense, that is, it is more in line with the data on Black stylistic variation, to consider BL as the whole range of styles within speakers' linguistic repertoires. Part of speaking BL is possessing the ability to styleshift in and out of in-group ways of speaking. This is not astonishing. But somehow, when it comes to Black youth, some are under the impression that they are mired in this monostylistic linguistic ghetto (this is certainly a contemporary strain of linguistic depravation thinking). But the ghetto is a beautiful thang – that is, speakers such as Bilal, who had had a full range of experiences as Black youth, naturally (and quite obviously) vary their speech styles in different situations and contexts. Any time spent in Black communities would reveal that Bilal speaks to his Minister in the Nation of Islam mosque in one way, to his White teachers in another, to his grandmother in another, to his girlfriend, father, brothas on the block in yet another. And certainly, since he's forced to look for employment outside of his community, as a sporting goods store employee he will speak to White customers and non-English speaking customers in yet another style. Any why should we expect him not to? The question is: If the Black speech community possess a range of styles that are suitable for all of its communicative needs, then why the coercion and impositions of White styles? (Alim, 2005, pp. 194–195)

Alim's observation mirrors long-standing observations of Labov (1972) – all of which reflect translanguaging – that countered the "verbal deprivation" often used to characterize Black speech – then as it still is now – acknowledging how Black speech events were reflexive of a "competitive exhibition of verbal skills" such as "sounding, singing, toasts, rifting, louding [and battlin]" functioning as "a whole range of activities in which the individual [Black] person' gain[ed] status through [their] use of language" (Alim, 2005, pp. 212–213).

Given these historical observations, I argue here that to leverage semiolingual innocence for returning translanguaging to the intralinguistic and intrasemiotic variations of Black speakers in which its remembering (Dillard, 2012a) as a practical construct in the US was originally steeped (e.g., Labov, 1972; Rickford & Rickford, 1980/2015; Smitherman, 1977) necessarily opens it up to the possibilities that it globally affords. These possibilities allow for reinscribing semiolingual innocence of Black youth and youth of Color whose Englishes often function as intralinguistic and broader intrasemiotic representations undergirding the holistic literacies of marginalized Majority and Minority World linguistic populations. Specifically, through this process, translanguaging also allows for a recentering of race, and of Black Language, which, in response to continued and pervasive anti-Blackness that has kept Black Englishes on the periphery of the literacy enterprise for so long, as scholars such as Nero (2006) and Alim (2004) observed from the inception, has been propelled by the need for engaging with intersections of how racialized language deserved treatment in scholarship and in practice, both from the vantage point of the institutional as well as an individual. In articulating this dynamic, Alim (2004) asked the poignant questions:

Why is it that, despite ample evidence of sociolinguistic studies and theory that different speech communities possess different, yet theoretically equivalent, linguistic rules and riles of language use, [Black Language] and linguistic practices continue to be denigrated and underappreciated by Whites, particularly in educational institutions? What is the root of this denigration and misinterpretation? How is it that the theology and practice of linguistic supremacy – the unsubstantiated notion that White linguistic norms are inherently superior to the linguistic norms of other communities, and the practice of mapping White norms onto "the language of school," "the language of economic mobility," and the "language of success" – persists, even within the subjugated group? What is the role of communicative misunderstanding in maintaining and perpetuating tensions between communities? How do we understand communicative differences not as the source of tensions but as a means of perpetuating and reinforcing these tensions? How do we move beyond searching for communicative mismatches to explain intercultural tensions and conflicts that already exist due to the larger and systematic social, political and economic subjugation of a group? Or worse yet ... will greater knowledge of communicative differences be used for or against justice? As overt forms of racism begin to be publicly sanctioned in most areas of the US, linguistic differences are currently being used to exclude Blacks from full participation in society in a number of ways (see Baugh, 2003 on linguistic profiling in housing discrimination based on "Black-sounding" voices, and Bertrand and Mullainathan 2003 on differential access to employment based on "Black-sounding" names). Studies of intercultural communication need to address these questions if the field is to remain relevant to dominant populations. Such studies are essential since the problem with [Black Language] has more to do with Black people than Black language. Given the emerging studies addressing the role of BL in various forms of discrimination, more scholars are beginning to see the BL "Problem" as one that is part and parcel of a sociostructural system of White racism in the US. (Alim, 2004, pp. 192–193)

Alim's (2004) observations reiterated then as they continue to do now, through a return to translanguaging from its inception, the call for "avoid[ing] explanations of Black academic failure as the result of Black 'opposition' to formal schooling and begin[ning to interrogate] the daily cultural combat (conscious or unconscious) against Black language and culture in White public space" (p. 193). Through the problematizing of translanguaging and transsemiotizing based on an integrated model of multilingualism, allowing for semiolingual innocence to be visible through the prism of Black Caribbean immigrant literacies, I assert that intentional attempts must be made to articulate how these practices function beyond the named languages that translanguaging critiques so that translanguaging operates as a mechanism for liberating racialized/immigrant and other students in school systems whose linguistic repertoires often reflect intricacies of inferiority based on uses of 'unnamed' languages that are often not accepted, centered, captured, or integrated into translanguaging writing practices in schools. Questions arise such as: *Why, for instance, has translanguaging, though originally steeped from the inception in the discourse that intersects language and race based on the holistic literacies of Black Language in "White public space" (Page & Thomas, 1994), failed to be largely taken up as a key mechanism for articulating the linguistic strengths of African American learners? Or why, for instance, have the linguistic repertoires of students whose numerous Englishes and 'unnamed' languages functioned primarily based on translanguaging seemingly escaped its gaze?*

Aligned with these questions, some of which are instantiated in the article "The Case for Translanguaging in Black Immigrant Literacies" (Smith, 2020c) and the chapter "Migrating While Multilingual and Black: Beyond the '(Bi) dialectal Burden'" (Smith & Warrican, 2021), Ofelia García has since recently described, as alluded to earlier, and appears to acknowledge, the possibility of a consolidation of Global English Language Teaching (GELT) and translanguaging. This acknowledgment holds possibility for liberating millions of students whose 'unnamed' languages nonetheless are more pronounced in their linguistic repertoires yet often function on the periphery of schools. Imagining the possibilities of *translanguaging with Englishes*, as my colleagues and I have articulated (Smith, 2020c; Smith & Warrican, 2021), García (2022) has since observed, "Without GELT translanguaging does not offer the English teaching profession a way to think beyond named languages in the ways that students make sense of language, and the ways in which they interact in language" (p. 6). Inspired by the potential of considering how translanguaging and transsemiotizing imaginaries can be broadened when viewed through the lens of Black immigrant literacies, as supported by García (2022), there remains an urgent need to illuminate understandings of what it means for linguistic and semiotic repertoires as originally identified in the stylistic choices of Black Language speakers (Alim, 2004), to function as representations of *semiolingual innocence*, completely sans attention to white gaze.

Translanguaging beyond the Nation-State

Considering how the portrait of Black Caribbean immigrant literacies presented in this book functions as a lens for imagining the potential of translanguaging as a scholarly and pedagogical practice of equity for all, through semiolingual innocence, I argue that in conjunction with the foregoing necessitations of translanguaging, we must secondly problematize the latter as largely confined to instantiation within the nation-state and resurrect its potential as a transgeographic and transborder practice to be harnessed by schools. The framework for Black immigrant literacies, which presents five elements to be considered as Black immigrants use Englishes in the US, functions as a legitimate starting point for advancing the conversation on translanguaging as a transgeographic practice (Smith, 2020c; Smith & Warrican, 2021). These five elements – *claim to the struggle for justice, myth of the model minority, a transraciolinguistic approach, local-global,* and *holistic litera*cies – allow for an understanding of how the Black immigrant engages with translanguaging practices as a function of being subsumed within the Black population in the US racially ("becoming Black": Ibrahim, 1999) though culturally reflecting differences as well as complicating discourses of superiority that tend to be attached to Black immigrants in relation to their African American peers in much the same way that such notions of superiority are attached to Asian Americans as relates to all other peers. In doing so, the elements of the Black immigrant literacies framework offer opportunities for acknowledging that the influence of transraciolinguistics on translanguaging in the local context in which students operate in the US is tied to how this practice was leveraged in the global context of their home countries. Demonstrating how *translanguaging and transsemiotizing with and beyond Englishes* allows for recognition of raciolinguistics and raciosemiotic ideologies impacting Black students' holistic literacies in their home countries while also reflecting the role of transracialization in these literacies in the US as they "become immigrant" and "become non-native English speakers" (Smith, 2020c), the discourse concerning translanguaging and transsemiotizing is extended as a function of racialized transborder realities that help to address the often-obscured impositions of colonially driven nation-state norms. Such a notion troubles the demarcations proposed by Orellana (2015) alluding to this movement *"beyond borders"* as the process of "transculturation" where there is "a transcendence or transformation of things that were being held apart, or artificially constructed as separate and distinct" and allows for a "questioning [of] the ontologies that hold things apart" (p. 91). In turn, this transformation, alluded to in "transcendent literacies," sees the evolution through "both-and" and the conception of "transracialization" which both allow for Paulo Freire's emersion of the "new being" through the dialectic. And as highlighted in the call for attention to race in "transnational literacies" more broadly, it also invokes a need for addressing how institutional and societal realities are enacted in translanguaging and transsemiotizing as a function of *immigrant of Color literacies* across borders (Smith, 2020b; Smith et al., 2023).

Translanguaging beyond the Individual

The third consideration in using the portrait of Black Caribbean immigrant literacies as a lens for imagining the potential of *translanguaging* and *transsemiotizing* as a scholarly and pedagogical practice of equity for all relates to interdependence – a mechanism of semiolingual innocence. As the holistic literacies of Black Caribbean immigrants have shown, translanguaging must function as instantiation for its own sake but also with the intention as a practice that facilitates interdependence and intradependence across racial, linguistic, cultural, and other lines. Challenging the grounding of translanguaging as a pedagogical practice steeped in individuality of the Majority World US context based on a foregrounding of standardness that foundationally, at its core, insists on positioning one child's languaging as better than another, translanguaging with Englishes as represented in the holistic literacies of the youth in this book reflects the need for recognizing the power of its potential for reclaiming connectivity through cultivating interdependence across linguistic, racial, and cultural boundaries. Dr. Belinda Flores and colleagues have used the term "transworld pedagogy" (Flores et al., 2014) to discuss how broad questions concerning the nature of 'community' emerge as students cross transgeographic boundaries, and Dr. Marjorie Elaine (formerly Faulstich Orellana), Professor of Education and Associate Vice Provost of the International Institute at the University of California, Los Angeles, has asserted, in her work with colleagues in collaboration with immigrant children, that they "try to honor the connections participants have to places far away and recognize the history in our dynamic and changing corner of the world" (Kinloch et al., 2016, p. 12). The notion of "language brokering," emerging from the interactions of immigrant children in the US, represents just one example of how translanguaging might function among Black youth and their peers as a basis for interdependence (Orellana, 2015). With a colleague, Orellana illustrated how "language and culture brokering (translating and interpreting language and culture for others) influences the acculturative experiences and self-perceptions of young adults from immigrant Arab, Asian, and Latino American backgrounds" highlighting the ways in which "mediating information for members of different cultural and linguistic groups strengthens awareness of linguistic, cultural, and social processes," an awareness that, in turn, "is leveraged for social and cultural processes as identity formation and transcultural competencies" (Guan et al., 2016, p. 150). The authors observed that "experiences both prior to immigration and in the new immigrant context also differently shape the experiences of brokers from different ethnic groups," demonstrating how various populations of immigrant students might support interdependence across multiple populations in varied ways.

Considering these insights, I argue here that the presentation of semiolingual innocence as a function of translanguaging and transsemiotizing positions the latter as a pathway for interdependence and not merely as an end in itself that functions irrelevant of context. Despite the legitimacy of translanguaging as an acknowledged and inherent right of the Black individual, and of people of Color as established, it is possible to extricate the relegation of translanguaging from the often-contrived spaces of schools to observing how it emerges "unbidden" (Canagarajah, 2011) for cultivating interdependence in the linguistic and semiotic repertoires of youth. It is possible also to use translanguaging imaginaries visible in these holistic literacies of youth, to capture and consolidate meanings often lost in isolation across disparate and divided inter- and intraracial communities in ways that hold ultimate potential for developing solutions to address pressing problems of this contemporary world. At the same time, institutions at large, too, are positioned by semiolingual innocence as a function of translanguaging to consider how such critical lenses necessitate a rethinking of transcultural flows leveraged by both the individual and society at large. They may do so by using transraciolinguistics to (a) identify the ways in which assets of metacultural, metaracial, and metalinguistic understandings from racialized populations form the basis for rethinking norms steeped in monocultural, monoracial, and monolinguistic traditions; (b) revamp practices and policies based on the assets presented and on these understandings; and (c) create opportunities for building solidarity across racialized and dominant groups. They may also think futuristically about the ways in which transraciolinguistics can be used to design just experiences in the emerging virtual realities of the metaverse (Smith, 2022b).

The promise of translanguaging imaginaries brings the holistic literacies of those long oppressed and descendants of those long serving as oppressors into redemptive recognition of the humanity that reconciliatorily binds, even as powerful structures operating as a function of white supremacy threaten to erode the interdependence of people from both sides of a divide characterized by the fragility of a shared yet distant solidarity. Through translanguaging imaginaries as those presented in this book, the necessary and urgent reinscribing of semiolingual innocence of Black students and students of Color by institutions is portrayed as intertwined with the redemptive and reconciliatory purpose of semiolingually inscribing such innocence operating *sans white gaze* also to the white student, whose current inheritance, though deemed privileged, loses an often imposed virtue when placed squarely in light of the largely complicated raciolinguistic and raciosemiotic burdens of a horrific ancestral past. This virtue, markedly stripped often from many a white child in the US due to such a past, challenges long-standing and inherent claims to "white innocence," and runs parallel to an often-limited linguistic dexterity, plurilinguality, and fluidity typically held, but which for so long has been touted as 'privileged' (Ross, 1990; Wekker, 2016). But how can a markedly limited capacity to use translanguaging and broader transsemiotizing or to adeptly leverage metalingustic, metacultural, and metaracial and other understandings ever be positioned as privileged? And how can an ancestral history often imbued with a virtueless past allow for a claim to semiolingually functioning by white peoples sans a *white gaze* with which they are often intentionally or unintentionally complicit?

Translanguaging imaginaries as presented here, in the lives of Black Caribbean youth, disrupt the long-standing perception perpetuated by institutions and societies alike that there is any semblance of privilege in having a limited view of the world merely because of a precarious power wielded for so long as a function of this limitation. In so doing, it operates based on quantum notions of multiple levels of reality, reclaiming the invisible and thus long-lost semiolingual innocence of Black peoples as legitimate pathways that blatantly shatter notions of "white privilege" and "white innocence." At the same time, translanguaging imaginaries represent an overt anti-racist (Kendi, 2019) call to flourishing via a recognition that the holistic literacies of Black students are intricately bound to that of the dominant population – a population that remains linked to an oppressive system within which the *semiolingual innocence* of Black youth must function sans white gaze even as it acknowledges the value of its shared humanity with all lives. This institutionally informed interdependence, invoking an invitation to whites to translanguage sans leveraging the white gaze, only then, makes it possible for those racialized as white, like all peoples, to lay claim to semiolingual innocence. In the end, and as symbolized in the "both-and" of a transraciolinguistic approach (see Figure 4.1), translanguaging imaginaries of semiolingual innocence, much like the transsemiotizing imaginaries presented, offer a pathway, through the holistic literacies illustrated, to instantiate a return to flourishing by acknowledging and relying on the interdependence of our shared humanity, a humanity that must be wrestled with through an intentional establishment of the quantum-informed potentiality that can only be ours through recognizing the inextricable threads of consciousness – Ubuntu: I am because we are.

The call for an urgent resurrection of long-established translanguaging and transsemiotizing imaginaries of semiolingual innocence on the part of Black children, youth, and peoples across the globe, even as it acknowledges the devastating raciolinguistic and broader raciosemiotic effects of a system operating based on the warped semiolinguality that they are often ascribed, has often made it almost impossible to see that there is humanity in the dominant population in the US, or in white people elsewhere. Emerging in the Black languaging and semiotizing of Black Caribbean youth as it does in this book, *semiolingual innocence* beckons the possibilities of translanguaging as a mechanism for its inscription, not only as leveraged by Black peoples and people of Color traumatized historically by centuries of a colonial and/or enslaved past sans "white gaze," but also capable of being reflected, as we have seen in US history, by white descendants of the 'Master.' These white descendants, many of whom translanguage daily and often intralinguistically in the US, wrestle with a perception of the self constantly reminded of the truthfulness of a tainted ancestral history emerging often from "Black gaze" (Campt, 2023; hooks, 1992). This occurs given the intricately interwoven legacies intertwined with their white ancestors' oppressive histories. Reaching across the long-standing intergenerational racial abyss through a "both-and" approach, *semiolingual innocence* is instantiated by institutions as the right of a Black person and person of Color to use translanguaging and transsemiotizing, completely oblivious to white gaze even as it invites the persons racialized as white to enjoy such innocence by discarding the white gaze with which they tend to be coupled, at last. This act, allowing for the seeing and rewriting of white personhoods as a peoples anew, would see institutions and the broader society acknowledge how Black gaze, through the lens of Black people, exposes the 'unmarked narrative' of whiteness (Solomona et al., 2005). As suggested by bell hooks:

Although there has never been any official body of black people in the United States who have gathered as anthropologists and/or ethnographers to study whiteness, black folks have, from slavery on, shared in conversation with one another a 'special' knowledge of whiteness gleaned from close scrutiny of white people. (hooks, 1992, p. 165)

We have seen the capacity and potential for a shared semiolingual innocence emerging societally and individually in the interdependence of knowledges across the Black-white spectrum made starkly visible recently in the women's march of 2017 that drew 3–5 million people in the US (Chenoweth & Pressman, 2017). We have seen it in the Black Lives Matter protests in 2020 following the death of George Floyd which drew 15–26 million people (Buchanan et al., 2020) where the shared humanity of millions of Blacks, whites, and others erupted together in protest in the US, bolstered by protests across the world in vehement opposition to the deliberate taking of one Black life. We have seen it in the professor at the University of South Florida, who, working with her student, and an organization, filed a lawsuit against the "Stop WOKE Act" as an infringement on First Amendment rights (Saunders, 2022) to give pause to the blatant fueling of flames of hatred of Blacks and peoples of Color, functioning as a backlash to the recent re-inscriptions of *inonsans jan nwè*. We see it daily in evidence which reiterates a concomitant intention by the certain facets of the dominant population to undo much of the erasure of Black life that has existed concurrently with a privileging of white life and which has persisted for centuries even while an opposing intention remains visible in blatant displays such as the bold attack on the US Capitol and the banning of "Critical Race Theory" in schools. The truth is that even with an imaginative reinscribing of the semiolingual innocence of Blacks, hopes for the flourishing of humanity remain incomplete without an acknowledgment of the intertwined redemptiveness with whites, whose wrestling with ancestral histories of a faux claim to white innocence requires a reckoning with Black gaze if there must be an inscription of their semiolingual innocence.

The insights from the authentic narratives of Black Caribbean immigrants in this book beg the questions *What would it look like for translanguaging imaginaries of innocence to be explored and cultivated by universities as a key tenet of teacher preparation programs? What would it look like for schools to use semiolingual innocence to foster the holistic literacies of the dominant student population in the US? To what end would the examination and use of their metalinguistic, metacultural, and metaracial understanding by schools foster clarity in how they respond, via translanguaging, to the self, Black Caribbean immigrants, and other students? What institutional opportunities exist to explore the raciolinguistic and raciosemiotic ideological positions occupied by white students, and white peoples, as a function of their roles as the dominant population within institutions, and in relation to Black students and Black peoples at large? What would a project of exploring interdependence as a function of institutions through translanguaging imaginaries look like if the shared humanity of Blacks and whites are placed at the center of this enterprise? To what end can institutions foster clarity about how the linguistic repertoires of Black children in relation to their white peers, and vice versa, intersect to either reinforce or dismantle hegemonies that threaten our collective futures? How can societies make visible transraciosemiotic, transgeographic, and transraciolinguistic ideologies, explored as a function of interdependence between whites and immigrant Black peoples/people of Color, and reveal how we might redeem ourselves from what seems to be the incessant rendering of Black illegality and foreignness? What would it look like for the situating of semiolingual innocence as an articulation of translanguaging imaginaries across racial, linguistic, gendered, religious, and other populations to be done with a goal of revealing our shared interdependence to shift the locus from a competitiveness centered in individuality to a flourishing inspired by the wish for collective healing?*

From these questions, we are forced to reckon also with the following: *How can our schools, churches, universities reinscribe the semiolingual innocence of Black Caribbean immigrants and people of Color through translanguaging via holistic literacies, disrupting the silenced and stained impositions of a lineage of ancestors whose enslavement condemned both Black and white descendants of the current day at large? And how can they do the same for all children and youth, youth whose whiteness has long been a visible burden due to their inadvertent heritage as the progeny of slave owners, lynchers? What does it look like, specifically, to leverage this for teachers who work with students in literacy English language arts and literacy classrooms? And what would it look like for teachers to do so through the E-languages – Englishes – with which populations both in the Majority and Minority World remain involuntarily entangled, but which at the same time offer a pathway for painting global translanguaging imaginaries?*

The truth is that amid decades of debate about the colonized Englishes that people of Color, and specifically Black peoples, have inherited from the Master's Language, we cannot, given our double consciousness (Du Bois, 1903/1999), seem to extricate ourselves from Englishes and unentangle them from us. But we can *disentangle* (Smith, 2022a). As I observed in "Black Immigrants in the United States: Transraciolinguistic Justice for Imagined Futures in a Global Metaverse," the Englishes that we wish to sequester have long since functioned as the primary mechanism through which it appears we have been destined to restore our individual and collective "phenomenality" via semiolingual innocence through the translanguaging imaginaries that we now exhibit. There is no extricating the personhood from the twining of language and race, Rosa and Flores (2017) have observed, and the interrelations of race and language from the personhood. These racialized entanglements, as I have explained, reflect a dynamic where the racialized body impacts Englishes as much as the Englishes impact the racialized body – Englishes and the racialized body are one (Smith, 2022a). And as such, as illustrated in the lives of Black Caribbean and Black Caribbean immigrants, entanglements emerge in unique ways between Englishes and racialized migrants in the US ("white world"); entanglements occur in unique but similar ways between Englishes and racialized English-speaking Caribbean nationals ("Black world"); and entanglements are constantly being redefined in dynamic spaces between Englishes and the racialized bodies based on institutional and local norms within and across global contexts ("Black and white worlds") (Smith, 2022a). What this means, then, is that any program of literacy and English language arts that seeks to reinscribe semiolingual innocence for Black peoples and for Black immigrants in particular is compelled to recognize interrelationships such as these that undergird the holistic literacies and translanguaging imaginaries of youth and legitimize youth as entangled with languaging that have become part of the self. It is only in doing so that we can fully re-envision Englishes, despite their colonial legacies, as implicated pathways for reinscribing semiolingual innocence. The questions remain, *What specific affordances does this pathway of Englishes provide through institutions for Black immigrant and Black students and peoples as a basis for reinscribing semiolingual innocence through holistic literacies via translanguaging imaginaries? And what specific affordances does it also provide for other students and peoples of Color as well as for all students and peoples? How can the institutional invocation of "unbroken Englishes" (Smith, 2023b) inspire a promise of identifying, excavating, and leveraging translanguaging imaginaries that signal raciolinguistic redemption?*

Through a deliberate nuancing of the intricacies of raciolinguistics and raciosemiotics in the lives of Black Caribbean immigrant youth, I have introduced eight mechanisms in the heuristic of semiolingual innocence – *flourishing*, *purpose*, *comfort*, *expansion*, *paradox*, *originality*, *interdependence*, and *imagination* – functioning as a basis for advancing holistic literacies of Black Caribbean immigrant, as well as all youth. I assert that it is possible in scholarship, policy, and in teaching to instantiate these practices in ways that extend the capacity of translanguaging and transsemiotizing to function as a pathway to redemptiveness and reconciliation across groups even as these mechanisms address inequitable institutional and societal norms via Englishes in and beyond schools. And for the many Protestant Christians, like me, who often wonder about circumventing individual and institutional pathways of forgiveness (Smith, 2024) to reconciliation, forgiveness, and to love, make no mistake. There can be only a feigned peace, tainted with hopes of flourishing in the absence of *linguistic and broader semiotic reparations* bolstered by a corresponding languaging of forgiveness steeped in the great commandment and golden rule: "Love thy neighbor as thyself" (Matthew 22:39).

Reinscribing Lost Imaginaries of Semiolingual Innocence

Martin Luther King Jr., a radical of his time, and only later touted as a beacon of peace, is well known for his "I Have a Dream" speech. He shared:

> I have a dream that one day out in the red hills of Georgia the sons of former slaves and the sons of former slaveowners will be able to sit down together at the table of brotherhood. He say by faith With this faith we will be able to transform the jangling discords of our nation into a beautiful symphony of *brotherhood* [emphasis added].

In the words of Martin Luther King Jr., we see a nudge towards semiolingual innocence and towards a translanguaging imaginary such as that presented through the holistic literacies of the Black Caribbean immigrant youth in this book. Martin Luther King Jr. believed that those whom we describe today as descendants of slaves – "the sons [daughters, and others] of former slaves" – would sit together with those whom we refer today as descendants of white oppressors – the "sons [daughters, and others] of former slaveowners" – would "sit down together at the table of brotherhood." In Martin Luther King Jr.'s dream, we see a subtle yearning for engaging silenced nuances such as those undergirding the often overlooked and obscured translanguaging of white Appalachian youth, whose *"white Englishes,"* positioned as superior given their race are also often deemed inferior because of their class.

Invoking this martyr, assassinated in his time for his daring to inscribe semiolingual innocence for all while reminded of the vision of Du Bois (1903/1999) for humanity's cultivation of moral and aesthetic insights in their cultures that become valuable to all, I ask, *How can the descendants of slaves and slaveowners, many of whom shae ancestral histories, join each other at the table of brotherhood without the corresponding holistic literacies emerging from their representative translanguaging and transsemiotizing practices? And how can the translanguaging practices of Black immigrants as presented and of people of Color be advanced to achieve such brotherhood as envisioned by Dr. King if by its conceptual and pedagogical nature, it results in an alienation of "whites"?* For Martin Luther King Jr., the deferred dream that has prevented us still from engaging fully "into a beautiful symphony of brotherhood [sisterhood, otherhood]" stirs the conscience to grapple, though hesitantly, with what remains indelibly the often silenced and discomfiting question for many, namely, *What will it look like to simultaneously engage with a study of the translanguaging and transsemiotizing practices undergirding the Black Englishes of youth in direct relation to an equal consideration of the translanguaging and transsemiotizing white Englishes of their counterparts, whose class positions their translanguaging and transsemiotizing on the peripheries of society even while their race deems them an insider to it?* Simultaneously, it becomes also critical to ask often obscured questions such as *What would it look like to address Spanglishes in the translanguaging and transsemiotizing of children whose E-languages and E-semiotics often transcend norms for codification in classrooms and therefore are not often visible in the written translanguaging scholarship?* (See Martínez, 2010, for a noted exception.) *What would it look like to center Black Englishes and Frenches of Haitian Creole speakers whose translanguaging and transsemiotizing places them within the English learner population but often not the dual-language classroom? By the same token, how is the notion of "dual-language" classroom, in turn, designed to accommodate 'unnamed' languages of some, by default, obscuring the translanguaging imaginaries of others? What will it look like to finally address African American students' rich linguistic histories, curated for so long on the peripheries of mainstream literacy instruction, as translanguaging and broader transsemiotizing, which, though largely established based on scholarship, remain oblivious in their explicit naming as such, and thus whose imaginaries of languaging and broader semiotizing remain obscured as a key facet of developing a long-awaited interdependence with white peers? What will it look like for translanguaging and transsemiotizing across racial linguistic, ethnic, cultural groups – for interdependence – to become a key study of every teacher who prepares to teach holistic literacies for flourishing and purpose – two key elements of semiolingual innocence?*

Aware of what remained at stake for children of Color during his time, Martin Luther King Jr. lamented the impasse then as the Black Caribbean immigrants in this book invoke now, stating:

It is obvious today that America has defaulted on this promissory note insofar as her citizens of color are concerned. Instead of honoring this sacred obligation, America has given its colored people a bad check, a check that has come back marked "insufficient funds." But we refuse to believe that the bank of justice is bankrupt. We refuse to believe that there are insufficient funds in the great vaults of opportunity of this nation. So we have come to cash this check, a check that will give us upon demand the riches of freedom and security of justice.

The cashing of this symbolic check, to which Martin Luther King Jr. alluded generally, I assert, in my presentation of the translanguaging imaginaries of Black immigrant youth, must also now be cashed in the education of our children, and specifically via the "riches of freedom" and the "security of justice," through the opportunity to reinscribe semiolingual innocence via these translanguaging imaginaries. Like Martin Luther King Jr., I concur in the present as it was in the past that, "Now is the time to lift our nation from the quicksand of racial injustice to the solid rock of brotherhood" via the translanguaging imaginaries emerging through an understanding of Black immigrants' holistic literacies.

And for those who insist on demarcating African Americans as the *primary* "descendants of slaves" (DOS), furthering what has been viewed as the rhetoric of white supremacist divide-and-conquer politics, let us not for a moment forget that even as slavery was running rampant in the Caribbean, the colonizing of Africa was wreaking havoc across its countries, all while white supremacy became overtly constructed as the most blatant representation of injustice in the US. For Black Caribbean, Black American, Black African, and Black peoples worldwide, there can be no insistence, as is often the case, on a tendency to weigh comparative trauma as a basis for determining moral, economic, and other worth. The powers exercised and associated with colonization operating in Africa where Black people were restricted from accessing and owning their own land, inspiring Nelson Mandela to tear down an oppressive government and install democracy, should be no less horrific to our consciousness than the brutality and devastating effects of slavery against Black peoples in the Caribbean and the US. In the end, trauma is trauma, and generationally, through this trauma, Black peoples both in Africa and across the diaspora have since been made to forget the collective and quantum power of our *semiolingual innocence*, looking instead, as Willis (2022) asserts, to the white gaze as a basis for defining the potential of the self. But though the white gaze remains absolutely necessary for naming and deconstructing the Black rac(e)ing of place, it is only *also* transcending beyond coloniality to the pre-white gaze that allows the Black person to truly see the capacity of the collective imaginary for *flourishing* through translanguaging. This seeing, sans white gaze, but also with it, as Alim (2016) has described in transracialization, makes visible the capacity of the human who has only eventually come to be defined by the color of their skin. Even as the killing of George Floyd by a white officer and the horrific beating in broad daylight to death of a Black man by five Black officers over what seemed like a speeding ticket, has placed in clear sight how a failure to believe in Black innocence by both white and Black people manifests itself as erasure propelled by the system, the potential for reinscribing semiolingual innocence beckons – longing for a tsunami of the soul.

Alas, as descendants of slaves indelibly impacted by and often sharing ancestral histories with descendants of the Master, our collective destinies as Black descendants of slaves – or not – remain intertwined largely with the destinies of the former, involuntarily bound by the persistence of languaging and broader semiotizing across our worlds. We see now from the complex nuancing and historicizing across the Black diaspora coupled with the vivid elucidating of the holistic literacies of the Black Caribbean immigrant youth presented in this book, that intergenerational brutality, economic depravity, and an unwillingness, or inability, to semiolingually reach across the abyss reparatively in reconciliation now places us *all* in the US at an impasse, yes, at perpetual risk, even as the world looks on wondering what will become of our children. The urgency of a call for semiolingual innocence is by no means limited to the field of literacy. In fact, it emerges pivotally as a call that extends beyond – inviting if not cajoling the unsilencing of our collective consciousness and imaginations – signaling a yearning to see the futures of *all* our children and youth redeemed through a reinscribing of their *semiolingual innocence*, sans white gaze and with Black gaze alike.

To what end would scholarship and practice across the educational spectrum steeped in a view towards semiolingual innocence lend itself to the use of translanguaging and transsemiotizing as a basis for identifying how raciolinguistics and raciosemiotics emerge as a function of efforts to leverage interdependence or to avoid its grip across racial, linguistic, gendered, and other institutions and communities? And how can institutional and societal structures that rely on the divisiveness created through a silencing of these translanguaging and transsemiotizing imaginaries be disrupted through a transition to reinscribing semiolingual innocence that allows for a leveraging of metalinguistic, metacultural, metaracial, and metasemiotic understanding that expands 'monolingual,' 'monocultural,' and 'monoracial' repertoires even while enhancing those that are "multilingual," "multicultural," and "multiracial" (see Smith, 2022b, on transraciolinguistics)? How also can a semiolingual innocence for youth based on the "both-and" (not "both-sides") "paradox" steeped in multiple levels of reality, as informed by a sound moral and ethical compass, position teaching for intraracial and interracial interdependence, recognizing the shared humanity of all peoples – *interdependence*? And in doing so, how can semiolingual innocence position teaching to instantiate intentional paradoxical confrontations towards the cultivation of a *"both-and"* ethos, critical for emerging through the dialectic of 'oppressed' versus 'oppressor,' through flourishing (Freire, 1970/2000; Smith, 2016) – *paradox*?

From the invocation to brotherhood put forward by Martin Luther King Jr. in the urge to work against the divisiveness of a haunting past, we see, based on the Black Caribbean immigrant youth's holistic literacies, that it is the literacies that indelibly tore us apart and which we all use now, according to our racialized entanglements with Englishes, both as descendants of the slave and descendants of the oppressor, with our translanguaging and transsemiotic capacities, which remain inherently positioned to doom or redeem us. And so the question, though ultimately and long-since acknowledging, also extends beyond whether Englishes undergirding the literacies of one of us is better or worse, superior or inferior, articulate or inarticulate. We are tasked now, in a world assailed by a horrific present as has been made visible in the continuing and innocent deaths of thousands of Palestinians and hundreds of Israelis, and heading towards a terrifying future, to collectively paint a vision of how translanguaging and transsemiotizing can be used interdependently as a function of semiolingual innocence to emerge through the contestations of raciolinguistics and raciosemiotics in ways that create new imaginary presents for all children. In the portrait of interdependence as an imaginary by Martin Luther King Jr., we see the promise of semiolingual innocence, not as a return to "either-or," but only as a call to "both-and" (Smith, 2016, 2018). This both-and, which asserts that power is possible and present, though yet not fully accessible, through evolving understandings and applications of quantum physics, quite markedly extends beyond Du Boisian notions that maximize the power of the Master and limit the possibilities of the Slave, allowing the 'second sight' of double consciousness to transcend its burden as it works in concert with multiple levels of reality to restore balance between the universe and humanity (Du Bois, 1903/1999).

For Black Peoples in the Caribbean

As I have previously discussed in part, for Black peoples in the English-speaking Caribbean, the call to *semiolingual innocence* can be largely made possible through *"liberatory Caribbean imaginaries"* (Smith, in press; Waldron et al., 2023). The legacy of colonialization in the English-speaking Caribbean, though once vehemently opposed, has increasingly come to function during the past few decades as a key foundation for the ways in which literacies and languaging are taught, researched, and leveraged in schools. As I have shown to some degree in this book, a global project of white supremacy, designed intricately for curricular development, design, and implementation, has functioned subtly yet powerfully as the mechanism through which we, as a Caribbean people, have maintained our long-held inheritance of "the Master's Language." Through uncontested entanglements of the self and languaging premised on the careful maintenance of literacies that safeguard the foundation of this language, we have become dependent on the Master's Languaging as a mechanism for supposed advancement even while key tenets inherited from our African ancestors are eroded, excised, expunged. These tenets of Afrocentric practice (King, 2020), brought by our enslaved ancestors to the Caribbean not too long ago, functioned as languaging and literacies of care, humanity, unity, and character development, yet continue to be usurped in favor of those that foster prescriptiveness, standardness, individuality, competition, all under the guise of a commitment to excellence, on the one hand, and a celebration of our culture, on the other. It is not surprising, then, that the effects of an inheritance of racialized entanglements (Smith, 2022e) advanced rigorously in our educational system since the supposed independence of many of our island nations now shows up in the reckless abandon that we see across our schools, communities, societies, and nations. The Master's Language that we have so resoundingly and rigorously reinforced now reiterates its resounding inability to liberate the mind and to give students hope. We face, at this moment, in our 'post-pandemic' Caribbean history, much as is the case in the US, an impasse that requires a reckoning with the psyche of a people to determine the path that we will take as a region.

I offer, based on the call for semiolingual innocence in this book, that to contest the inheritances of entanglements that have continued to remain a pervasive part of our literacy and language education in the English-speaking Caribbean, we must free the self to cultivate what I am calling *"liberatory Caribbean imaginaries"* (Smith, in press). By liberatory Caribbean imaginaries, I am referring to imaginaries steeped in translanguaging that invoke semiolingual innocence, and which allow us to acknowledge our entanglements with the Master's Language as a legacy of our inheritance of His House, His Tools – all of which are entangled with us – *even while we also* transcend the limitations imposed by the Master in our current(s) and past(s) to engage and engineer a present and a future that emerge from our literate potentiality (Edwards & Smith, 2023; Waldron et al., 2023). We have long since claimed that the Master's Tools cannot dismantle the Master's House (Lorde, 2003) but it is these very tools that are entangled with our psyche of the self through languaging and it is these very tools that are the basis of all the literacies that we have relied on for decades as a basis to facilitate a dismantling (Waldron et al., 2023). You see, if the Master's Language lives within and we are entangled with it, any mechanism that touts eradication of this language, by its very definition and intent, is bound at the same time to destroy the personhood. And the privileged proximity to whiteness that we have amassed with it.

The holistic literacies of Black Caribbean immigrant youth presented in this book demonstrate the impossibility of extricating the Master's Language from the self (see Du Bois, 1903/1999, on double consciousness). Through the preceding illustrations in the lives of Black Caribbean immigrant youth, I have provided a basis for understanding why cultivating liberatory Caribbean imaginaries must first require an acceptance of the racially entangled self even as it perseveres through literate potentiality to semiolingually innocent pathways that engineer a gradual return to languaging and literacies that reclaim and sustain our humanity. To consider these possibilities necessitates, via quantum reality, holding two opposing viewpoints in the mind at the same time (Nicolescu, 1999; Smith, 2013a, 2018). Specifically, alluding to the Du Boisian notion of double consciousness (1903/1999) but also extending beyond it, it requires (a) acknowledging and accepting the racially entangled self-emerging out of a legacy of horrific white supremacy as legitimate; *and also* (b) acknowledging and accepting the "transcendence" of the racially entangled self beyond white supremacy as a possibility through literate potentiality (see Willis, 2022, on "transcendent literacies").

By offering liberatory Caribbean imaginaries steeped in semiolingual innocence as a pathway, I seek to help us – my brothers, sisters, others in the Caribbean, America, and elsewhere – bridge the gaps between the parts of our broken psyche as a people that reject the trauma imposed on our enslaved yet leveraged by our captor ancestors ancestors *and* those elements of our personhoods that long to create new worlds where our psyche heals, through an extending beyond. Liberatory Caribbean imaginaries reposition the discourse of 'both-and,' 'either-or,' 'neither-nor,' 'us-them,' 'standard-non-standard,' 'native-non-native,' 'academic-invisible,' 'home-school' that has plagued our language and literacy and ELA systems for so many decades. It asks us not whether a child should choose a home language over the Master's Language, or whether schools should tout the Master's Language and not home language for student success. Rather, liberatory Caribbean imaginaries allow the child to legitimately draw from what Alim (2005) has referred to as their full linguistic repertoire, and what later García and Wei (2014) described as "translanguaging" – originally coined by Cen Williams as 'trawsieithu' in Welsh – to self-determine who they wish to be in the world. Liberatory Caribbean imaginaries invite us to allow each child the privilege of working as a "language architect" (Flores, 2020) and also, whether racialized as Black, a person of Color, or as white, as a raciosemiotic architect (Smith, 2022a, 2023c) in their own right, to interdependently engineer their destinies.

Through liberatory Caribbean imaginaries that make visible students' semiolingual innocence, the literacy/ELA curriculum is focused on cultivating the child's purpose by exposing them to various literacies and languaging designed to enhance what they wish to do in the world. An English language arts curriculum built around such a vision of liberatory translanguaging imaginaries would draw upon what Dr. Gholnescar (Gholdy) Muhammad describes as "pursuits" and not on standards (Muhammad, 2020). It would center discourse in the curriculum that is not dedicated entirely to pursuing a standard designated by the colonial enterprise and that allows the child to identify how the Master's Language functions in ways that impede the child's humanity. But it would not stop there. At the same time, it would support the child with transcending the limitations that the Master's Language may have imposed, allowing the child to see, create, and build an imagined future steeped in their pursuits as legitimate people in the world. Recreating a system of languaging and literacies that allows for a restoration of hope would require a novel focus on pursuits by reimagining the educational system in the

Caribbean and around which the learning of literacies revolve. For instance, a child in the first grade who comes to the classroom with an incessant love of bicycles would be nurtured to develop the code as they work on researching how bicycles function, their creation, connect with bicyclists around the globe, develop a library of books on bicycles, participate in bicycle races around the country, and the list goes on. As they progress through to second grade, their pursuits might change, as is expected in children and when this happens, the process would begin again. When they get older, they might be supported with inventing a new type of bicycle as they are connected to experts in an innovative lab much like the lab invoked in *Black Panther: Wakanda Forever*. This invention that they create might be focused on their goal to help, for instance, reduce the carbon footprint on the earth or it might be a cost-saving mechanism for parents who have limited financial means. Children already do these things, but schools are not currently designed to intentionally cultivate pathways for this to happen as a function of their semiolingual innocence, which is often obscured due to a silencing of their translanguaging imaginaries. Creating hubs across the schooling progression into which each child can tap, via their translanguaging and broader transsemiotic practices, as they focus on varied pursuits throughout the developmental process, is critical as this is by necessity a departure from the normative schooling enterprise that continues to fail millions of children and youth across the Caribbean. In a world where purpose is daily denied and a mental health pandemic threatens the futures of so many children, cultivating purpose through pursuits via liberatory Caribbean imaginaries is critical (Muhammad, 2020).

In effect, through liberatory Caribbean imaginaries, schools as we know them in the region would be deconstructed, revamped, redesigned, transformed, recreated, into pathways for cultivating what I have referred to in the Black immigrant literacies framework, as the "holistic literacies" of every child (Smith, 2020b). In every school the central unifying elements would revolve around pursuits (Muhammad, 2020), not standards, and also around interconnections across these pursuits. Unlike the current system where a teacher possesses expertise in one area or focuses only on elementary subjects, a teacher would have multiple specialties and not just one as well as a range of developmental pathways through which they support students, much like Nicolescu (1999) envisioned in a 'new kind of education' premised on reconnecting the intellect and the human sensitivity through a focus on learning to know, learning to be, learning to do, and learning to live together (see also Smith, 2013a, 2018). This would allow for the unity, collaboration, and building together via interdependence that our ancestors brought from the Mother Land and used as a key mechanism to escape physical slavery to again become achievable as a mental emancipation given our continued and fettered enchantments with the racialized residues of the colonial entanglements of the

Master. Through a system where new models of teacher preparation are themselves imagined to address a novel type of learning focused equally on both intellectual capacity and human sensitivity designed to address existence rapidly descending into a moral, social, and mental abyss, through translanguaging and transsemiotizing, across schools and the broader Caribbean and global society, a teacher would be able to tap into the multiple knowledge bases required to encourage, sustain, support, and advocate for multiple pursuits in one child or many children. In doing so, the teacher would reduce the focus on the intellect as a main part of schooling and literacy instruction, as we have so markedly done in honor of the Master and would instead equally center attention on the body and the child's sensitivity as they do the mind (Nicolescu, 1999; Smith, 2013a, 2018). The teacher would also be very connected to the real-world problems in the local community, nation, society, and Caribbean region, allowing the pursuits being explored by each child to be mapped on directly to solutions requiring sustenance of the Caribbean region, and thus the planet at large. And yes, to emerge through racialized entanglements into a promise of imaginaries is to intentionally return to the Afrocentric legacy that our ancestors possessed and brought to the Caribbean in ways that represent a marked departure from merely and simply revising curricula as we have done for so many decades.

Overall, a vision of liberatory Caribbean imaginaries would leverage, semiotics at large, and not just languaging, for holistic literacies with a focus on cultivating the inherent *purpose* of children for *flourishing* while connecting them *interdependently* to community and to creating comfort zones that function as *"sites of animation"* – a direct pathway for solving problems faced in the real world. After all, they have shown us now, through the descent into chaos that plagues our societies, that our methods, long held dear, have not worked. Are we so dedicated to these methods that we will choose not to abandon them for the sake of redeeming the collective presents and futures of our children? Through semiolingual innocence, the vision of liberatory Caribbean imaginaries that acknowledges racialized entanglements *even while* allowing for literate potentiality that transcends them would significantly reduce the emphasis on dichotomous relationships that continue to result in a distancing of humanity and would instead be premised on reconciliatory literacies (Smith, in press) that allow for an advancing of our shared humanity – channeling Ubuntu – "I am because we are" (Waldron et al., 2023).

For People of Color

In "Literacy, Equity, and Imagination: Researching with/in Communities," Kinloch and colleagues speak of the ways in which research is conducted to foreground community via what is presented as a "New Childhoods" framework. This framework is presented as one "that takes seriously children's actions, perceptions, experiences, and viewpoints" (Kinloch et al., 2016, p. 105). In this "community of learners' pedagogical model" informed by Rogoff (2003), which Kinloch and colleagues describe as being framed by sociocultural perspectives on literacy as informed by the New London Group (1996), the authors explain that they use "'acuerdos,' not 'warnings,' which are agreements to be nice, respectful, safe, say hi!, give advice, and have fun" (Kinloch et al., 2016, p. 105). Kinloch and colleagues state this environment allows their research team to "create spaces for kids to spell, utter, write, draw, speak, dance, and invent language in their own ways" and to then "study what happens" (Kinloch et al., 2016, p. 105). Through practices such as interactive dialogue journals (Díaz & Flores, 2001), "writing on the wall," explorations of digital literacies, and story club (Enciso, 2011), the scholars demonstrate how students' "authentic literacies" offer an avenue for "participants to create, swap, and build on each other's spoken and written stories in different ways" and for kids to write "letters of friendship to each other" and to others as well as share them via a "club mail system" (Kinloch et al., 2016, p. 106). Even so, the scholars note, though the research team believed themselves to be exhibiting freedom with their approach to engaging students with literacy as they encouraged experimentation, imagination, and play, "and not trying to keep words or ideas within boxes or boundaries," they eventually "came to see that in certain ways, [they] were keeping things in their place" (Kinloch et al., 2016, p. 106). Kinloch and colleagues urged a rethinking of "try[ing] to engage students and communities into our visions" to instead, foster "animation" as "a quality of participation that emerges from within" (Kinloch et al., 2016, p. 107).

In offering this concept of *animation*, which "refers to the soul or spirit level of the human experience, our very life force, which comes from within" (Orellana, 2015, p. 56), Orellana highlighted in *Immigrant Children in Transcultural Spaces: Language, Learning, and Love* how children in "B-Club lit up or became animated when they had the opportunity to remember, talk, and share their families' or their own transnational experiences" (p. 14). Acknowledging how "engagement" is typically used in education, Orellana (2015) questions the constant seeking to "engage" students based on extrinsic factors, and asks: "What would it mean to spark animation – or just notice when it is sparked – and then help kindle it, fanning fires of excitement about learning and social transformation wherever we go?" (p. 14).

In these offerings of Dr. Marjorie Elaine (formerly Faulstich Orellana) to the field that invite a call to foster animation, we see glimpses of the notion of imagination highlighted in the heuristic of semiolingual innocence. As described earlier, semiolingual innocence positions teaching for harnessing the imagination, via translanguaging and transsemiotizing, to solve local and global problems currently assailing the currents and futures of the world much like Asha symbolizes for the youth who each presented solutions to polarization, isolation, and delegitimization. As Maldonado-Torres reminds us:

> Standards of rational acceptability completely change when a rational exchange with a black person is supposed to take place. The reason for this is simple: since the very existence of the Black rational body threatens the logic of the system, the paradox must be negated. For the black person who believes and trusts in the force of rational argument, the encounter with epistemic racism is traumatic. She or he is led either to choose irrationality as a means to claim her or his humanity, to abandon herself or himself purely in politics or material change, or to examine the contradictions and unsurpassable limits in the hegemonic concept of reason and propose new formulas. (Maldonado-Torres, 2005, p. 152)

By facilitating a harnessing of the imagination through translanguaging and transsemiotizing, semiolingual innocence offers literate potentiality (Edwards & Smith, 2023) as a pathway to animation, a new formula is instantiated, allowing for animation's spark to emerge amid the evocation of students' holistic literacies based on their linguistic and semiotic repertoires.

For All Peoples

In "Black Immigrants in the United States: Transraciolinguistic Justice for Imagined Futures in a Global Metaverse," I drew upon the prism of Black immigrant literacies in conjunction with Alim's (2016) notion of the "transracial subject" and Kates's (2010) conception of the "soul" to respond to the recent wave of racial reckoning and its associated backlash, asserting the urgency of drawing from the Black immigrant experience in the US to

> demonstrate why the future of applied linguistics in a global metaverse must be concerned with what I refer to as "transraciolinguistic justice" that: (a) creates opportunities beyond racialized [language] as a function of the imminent global metaverse; (b) disrupts the racialization of [language] for relegating citizenship based on national norms as a function of civic engagement; and (c) dismantles racialized [language] and borders that hold up the exclusion of "foreignness" to transform the relational experience of the soul. (Smith, 2022a, p. 112)

Acknowledging the impending verge of an imminent global metaverse in which the world will soon exist, I provoked the field to consider the degree to which (racialized) language and semiotics can, in fact, continue to function "as the primary mechanism for operating in a future world order" (Smith, 2022a, p. 111). By the "global metaverse," I referred to a "highly immersive and global virtual world in which people engage socially, play, and work" (Merriam Webster, 2021), and a space where

- the real world merges into a virtual reality;
- virtual worlds converge;

- social/professional/learning spaces transcend physical borders;
- avatars exist making use of multiple languages;
- language translation tools are utilized;
- characteristics such as race, ethnicity, nationality, cultural and linguistic background potentially lose or gain power as they are eliminated, blended, forged, or masked;
- communication is further unrestricted to varying languages, and is even more possible through universal signs, symbols, and pictures for meaning-making, across and within language groups.

(Smith, 2022a, p. 111)

Using Black immigrant literacies as a lens to describe the potential for "creating opportunities beyond racialized language and semiotics in a global metaverse," for "disrupting the racialization of language and semiotics in legal and civic engagement," and for "dismantling racialized language, semiotics, and borders that exclude 'foreignness' to transform the relational experience," I urged the field of applied linguistics to

consider how we might potentially utilize transracio[linguistic] justice to disrupt and dismantle racialized language in relation to "foreignness" while imagining and co-designing just futures for people of color through transformed interactions for all peoples in a global metaverse. (Smith, 2022a, p. 116)

I also asked the question *"What is the role of applied linguistics in undoing transracio[linguistic] harm as we co-create, co-imagine, and co-invent a global metaverse?"* (Smith, 2022a, p. 116).

The question I posed then lingers now, in the call for a reinscribing of semiolingual innocence by institutional and organizational mechanisms, all of whom will soon operate in an impending global metaverse where languaging and semiotizing that lacks a moral basis can just as easily "signal further calamity" in our collective futures if failed to be harnessed for opportunity (Buni, 2021). As the world has recently seen with translation mechanisms, virtual reality, augmented reality, and AI ChatGPT, to name a few, the capacity for translanguaging and transsemiotizing increasingly functions now largely *beyond the human*, reiterating the need for attention to flourishing based on purpose as instantiated by comfort to expand the capacity for reconciling now more than ever seemingly opposing and paradoxical viewpoints in ways that cultivate an originality steeped in interdependence critical to the imaginative potential for solving the pervasive problems of a perplexed world. The burgeoning climate crisis remains intertwined with political instability that renders physical interaction daily more dangerous than before and continues to threaten the balance and harmony long overlooked but necessary for the survival of humanity with the universe; a restoration of semiolingual innocence positions a return to unity needed for redemptive presents and futures. Amid this crisis, we are reminded:

The question is whether black solidarity can be pursued toward an end in complete juxtaposition to that which white solidarity has tried to fulfill. Can it be to the end that no more must men have to dream and die as West Indian Malcolm, black American Martin, West Indian Garvey, and black American DuBois, African-West Indian Vessey, black North American Nat Turner, and white American John Brown did? Will it serve to deter unjust and unequal practices by powerful or privileged black peoples or nations against less-powerful or less-privileged black peoples or nations? Will it affect the policies of powerful white governments in their relations with less-powerful black groups or governments? Hopefully, it will serve to give new humanitarian meaning and use to the notion of collective strength and thus assure positive answers to all these inquiries. The effective and just execution of equality is a universal challenge that blacks in superordinate positions will not be allowed to ignore or avoid, any more than their white counterparts. Power is power, color notwithstanding – and most black immigrants have come to learn this by their experiences "back home." (Bryce-Laporte, 1972, pp. 53–54)

Reinscribing semiolingual innocence therefore, through the cultivation of translanguaging imaginaries, in or beyond the metaverse, positions each child, human, and peoples, much like it does the Black Caribbean immigrant and Black people in general, and much like it does the person racialized as white, in a position to work together sans white gaze, emerging through the dialectic as new beings each imbued with quantum power – a quantum power that harnesses the potential of multiple levels of reality to instantiate institutional interconnectivities across the abyss of racially motivated abandonment, beckoning humanity to embark with spirit and soul on preparing pathways for flourishing (Smith, 2023a). To echo Fanon:

The living expression of the nation is the moving consciousness of the whole of the people; it is the coherent, enlightened action of men and women. (Fanon, 1991, p. 204)

And Amanda Gorman reminds us of this potential with the words

> But while democracy can be periodically delayed, it can never be
> permanently defeated. In this truth, in this faith we trust, for while we
> have our eyes on the future, history has its eyes on us. This is the era of
> just redemption. We feared at its inception. We did not feel prepared to
> be the heirs of such a terrifying hour. But within it we found the power
> to author a new chapter, to offer hope and laughter to ourselves.
> (Gorman, 2021)

In these words, we see the potential summoned for an instantiated power emanating from Gorman's languaging and from the beckoned semiotics of hope and laughter, invoking the present as an opportune moment for reclaiming our quantum power – all of us – through a compendium of lost imaginaries of semiolingual innocence that beckon – with bated breath, as it has for centuries – and our current generations and their futures with it.

Afterword: Imagining Pedagogical Possibilities beyond Normative Educational Perspectives

What might it mean to reject the white gaze when seeking to understand the language and literacy practices of Black immigrant youth from the English-speaking Caribbean? What does it mean for these youth to refuse to be defined by the raciolinguistic ideologies that have historically and systematically misapprehended and distorted their multiple literacies and rich everyday forms of translanguaging? How can focusing our attention on these youth's perspectives on their own language and literacy practices help to redirect and expand our understanding of language, literacy, and race more broadly?

In the pages you have just finished reading, Dr. Patriann Smith offers some very fresh and compelling answers to these timely and important questions. For the past six years, it has been my distinct privilege to know and learn from Smith, to engage with her groundbreaking scholarship, and to see her ideas develop into the book you have in your hands now. In my view, Smith has accomplished something supremely beautiful and powerful with this book. Her crucial intervention seeks to draw scholarly attention to Black immigrant youth from the English-speaking Caribbean – a growing population of students that has been overlooked and invisibilized in the literature, and that has been misapprehended and misrepresented in everyday educational contexts across national borders. Not content to highlight the novelty or uniqueness of this student population, however, Smith shows us that Black immigrant youth are discursively recruited to serve as a kind of *new model minority*, and she situates this contemporary phenomenon within longer colonial histories of racism, racial thinking, and racial violence.

What I find perhaps most inspiring about Smith's scholarly intervention is that she refuses to subordinate her understanding of Black immigrant youth's language and literacy practices to contemporary theoretical frameworks that have gained traction in the academy. While she engages directly and deftly with such frameworks, she deliberately refuses to let them do the proverbial heavy lifting. Instead, as Smith explains beautifully in the preceding pages, she draws directly on Black immigrant youth's perspectives, as well as on her own experiences and identities (e.g., as a "Black-immigrant-single-parent-mother-scholar-educator," a former "well-meaning" teacher in the Eastern Caribbean, and "a 'foreign-born,' 'international,' and 'immigrant' student") to frame contemporary language and literacy in relation to centuries-long histories of colonization, colonialism, and coloniality. Smith reminds us that, geographically, the Caribbean has been central to European colonial histories in the Americas, and that, conceptually, it should be central to our scholarly efforts to understand the ongoing colonial legacy of racial thinking. Crucially, she also reminds us that the everyday practice of translanguaging was a communicative norm in the Caribbean long before it gained recognition in Western scholarship. In her own words, translanguaging is "deeply entrenched in our ancestral histories" (p. 108). It strikes me that, by deliberately subordinating contemporary theoretical constructs to her own lived experiences and ancestral histories, Smith mirrors some of the moves that her youth research participants make as they reinscribe what she calls *semiolingual innocence*. To quote Smith herself, "this is what it looks like when Black languaging dares to function with zero attention to white gaze" (p. 139).

With this beautifully written and powerfully framed scholarly intervention, Smith points us towards important conceptual, political, and pedagogical ground. First, she points us to peripheralized populations. Despite the geographic and political centrality of the Caribbean, diasporic African populations in that region have been peripheralized – or made to seem peripheral – with respect to contemporary conversations about race in the US. As Smith reminds us, there is a direct connection here to the ways in which Caribbean youth's multiliterate practice has been made "peripheral to the educational enterprise" (p. 132). By pointing to these related processes of peripheralization, Smith re-centers the Caribbean and its histories of translingual and multiliterate practice.

Smith also points us beyond the white gaze and beyond white supremacy. By centering the notion of *semiolingual innocence*, she points us beyond the colonial logic of race and racial thinking and towards a framing of Black Caribbean language and literacy practices by Black Caribbean immigrant youth themselves. These youth can and do practice – and conceptualize – their languaging and literacies on their own terms. This quotidian reality, Smith shows us, is reflective of and replete with radical political possibilities.

And this is, ultimately, where Smith points us – towards *possibility*. Smith shows us a possible path forward – a path towards imagining pedagogical possibilities beyond normative educational perspectives, policies, and practices, and beyond the colonial logic of race itself. In doing so, she also necessarily points us towards solidarity, which she highlights as a key impetus for this work in the first place. Indeed, Smith imagines possible futures in which Black Caribbean youth build solidarity with other racialized and marginalized populations of students. As she so thoughtfully and compellingly illustrates in this book, rejecting the white gaze and reinscribing semiolingual innocence can help us all better discern and understand the "long-established and entrenched capacity – one accessible to all humans" (p. 206) to engage in multiliterate and translingual communicative practice. In my view, Dr. Patriann Smith is inviting us to join her in imagining and pursuing radical conceptual, political, and pedagogical possibilities.

Ramón Antonio Martínez
Stanford University

Notes

1 **Immigrant:** The term "immigrant," as per the Internal Revenue Service's description in 2020, referred to: "An alien who has been granted the right by the USCIS to reside permanently in the United States and to work without restrictions in the United States. Such an individual is also known known as a Lawful Permanent Resident (LPR). All immigrants are eventually issued a 'green card' (USCIS Form I-551), which is the evidence of the alien's LPR status. LPR's who are awaiting the issuance of their green cards may bear an I-551 stamp in their foreign passports. Immigrant visas are available for aliens (and their spouses and children) who seek to immigrate based on their job skills. An alien who has the right combination of skills, education, and/or work experience, and is otherwise eligible, may be able to live permanently in the United States. Per USCIS, there are five employment-based immigrant visa preferences (categories): EB-1, EB-2, EB-3, EB-4 and EB-5" (Mattix, 2018). Unlike an "immigrant," a nonimmigrant is considered to be "an alien who has been granted the right to reside temporarily in the United States. Each nonimmigrant is admitted into the U.S. in the nonimmigrant status which corresponds to the type of visa issued. Aliens in some nonimmigrant statuses are permitted to be employed in the United States, and others are not. Some nonimmigrant statuses have strict time limits for the alien's stay in the U.S., while others do not. Each nonimmigrant status has rules and guidelines. A nonimmigrant who violates one of these rules or guidelines will fall 'out of status.' A nonimmigrant who remains 'out of status' for at least 180 days is deportable and if deported will be unable to re-enter the United States for 3 years. A nonimmigrant who remains 'out of status' for at least 365 days is deportable and if deported will be unable to re-enter the United States for 10 years. Each nonimmigrant status has rules and guidelines, which must be followed in order for the nonimmigrant to remain 'in status.' A nonimmigrant who violates one of these rules or guidelines will fall 'out of status.' A nonimmigrant who remains 'out of status' for at least 180 days is deportable and will be unable to re-enter the United States for 3 years. A nonimmigrant who remains 'out of status' for at least 365 days is deportable and will be unable to re-enter the United States for 10 years" (Mattix, 2018).

2 **Standardized Englishes:** The term "Englishes" refers to the many different varieties of English that represent a plurality, variation, and change within the English language as a norm (Kachru, 1992). Englishes represent the interweaving of both standardized (e.g., Standard American English) and non-standardized (e.g., African American English) forms. I use non-standardized Englishes in this book to refer to Englishes that do not adhere to what has been determined to be a Standard English within a given context. Linguists refer to these variations as dialects, or New Englishes (Kirkpatrick & Deterding, 2011) and to their counterparts, standardized Englishes, as those that have been typically adopted for use in literacy classrooms (e.g., Standard American English).

References

ABC News. (2020, February 10). *Backlash emerges behind Cynthia Erivo's role in 'Harriet'* [Video]. YouTube. www.youtube.com/watch?v=zr3fiKJitmo

Agyepong, M. (2013). Seeking to be heard: An African-born, American-raised child's tale of struggle, invisibility, and invincibility. In I. Harushimana, C. Ikpeze, & S. Mthethwa-Sommers (Eds.), *Reprocessing race, language and ability: African-born educators and students in transnational America* (pp. 155–168). Peter Lang.

(2019). *Blackness and Africanness: Black West African immigrant students' experiences in two New York City high schools* [Doctoral dissertation, University of Wisconsin–Madison]. ProQuest Dissertations & Theses Global.

Alegría, M., Álvarez, K., & DiMarzio, K. (2017). Immigration and mental health. *Current Epidemiology Reports*, *4*(2), 145–155. https://doi.org/10.1007/s40471-017-0111-2

Alim, H. S. (2004). *You know my steez: An ethnographic and sociolinguistic study of styleshifting in a Black American Speech community*. Duke University Press.

(2005). Hearing what's not said and missing what is: Black language in white public space. In S. F. Kiesling & C .B. Paulston (Eds.), *Intercultural discourse and communication* (pp. 180–197). Blackwell Publishing Ltd.

(2016). Who's afraid of the transracial subject? Raciolinguistics and the political project of transracialization. In S. Alim, J. R. Rickford, & A. F. Ball (Eds.), *Raciolinguistics: How language shapes our ideas about race* (pp. 34–50). Oxford University Press.

Alim, H. S., Rickford, J. R., & Ball, A. F. (Eds.). (2016). *Raciolinguistics: How language shapes our ideas about race*. Oxford University Press.

Alim, H. S., & Smitherman, G. (2012). *Articulate while Black: Barack Obama, language, and race in the US*. Oxford University Press.

(2020). Raciolinguistic exceptionalism: How racialized "compliments" reproduce white supremacy. In Alim, H. S., Reyes, A., & Kroskrity, P. V. (Eds.), *The Oxford handbook of language and race* (pp. 472–498). Oxford University Press.

Allen, K. M., Jackson, I., & Knight, M. G. (2012). Complicating culturally relevant pedagogy: Unpacking African immigrants' cultural identities. *International Journal of Multicultural Education*, *14*(2). https://doi.org/10.18251/ijme.v14i2.506

Alleyne, M. C. (1961). Language and society in St. Lucia. *Caribbean Studies*, *1*(1), 1–10.

American Psychological Association. (2021, October 29). *APA apologizes for longstanding contributions to systemic racism* [Press release]. www.apa.org/news/press/releases/2021/10/apology-systemic-racism

Anekwe, P. N. (2008). *Characteristics and challenges of high achieving second-generation Nigerian youths in the United States males* [Unpublished doctoral dissertation]. Western Connecticut State University.

Antoniou, M. (2019). The advantages of bilingualism debate. *Annual Review of Linguistics, 5*, 395–415.

Anya, U. (2016). *Racialized identities in second language learning: Speaking Blackness in Brazil*. Taylor & Francis.

Aponte, G. Y. (2018). Centering the marginalized identities of immigrant students of color in the literacy classroom. *Texas Education Review*.

Armstrong, L. A., & Campos, J. (2002). *Assessment of teacher training and reading instruction needs and capacities in the Caribbean*. USAID: Centers of Excellence for Teacher Training (CETT). http://pdf.usaid.gov/pdf_docs/PNACX198.pdf

August, D., Shanahan, T., & Escamilla, K. (2009). English language learners: Developing literacy in second-language learners – Report of the National Literacy Panel on language-minority children and youth. *Journal of Literacy Research, 41*(4), 432–452. https://doi.org/10.1080/10862960903340165

Austin, T. (2022). Linguistic imperialism: Countering anti Black racism in world language teacher preparation. *Journal for Multicultural Education, 16*(3), 246–258. https://doi.org/10.1108/JME-12-2021-0234

Austin, T., & Hsieh, B. (2021). # SayHerName: Addressing anti-Blackness and patriarchy in language and literacy curricula. *Journal of Adolescent & Adult Literacy, 65*(3), 237–244.

Awokoya, J. T. (2009).*"I'm not enough of anything!": The racial and ethnic identity constructions and negotiations of one-point-five and second generation Nigerians* [Doctoral dissertation, University of Maryland]. ProQuest Dissertations & Theses Global.

BabyNames.com. (n.d.). *Wakanda*. Retrieved January 24, 2023, from https://babynames.com/name/wakanda

Bachoo, R. (Producer). (2023, January 2). *Concordat: A battle of power, race and religion* [Video]. Facebook. www.facebook.com/watch/live/?ref=watch_permalink&v=1451915352004028

Bailey, E. K. (2019). Resetting the instructional culture: Constructivist pedagogy for learner empowerment in the postcolonial context of the Caribbean. In S. Blackman, D. Conrad, & L. Brown (Eds.), *Achieving inclusive education in the Caribbean and beyond* (pp. 173–191). Springer.

Bailey, G. (2001). The relationship between African American Vernacular English and white vernaculars in the American South: A sociocultural history and some phonological evidence. In S. L. Laneheart (Ed.), *Sociocultural and historical contexts of African American English* (pp. 53–89). John Benjamins.

Bajaj, M., & Bartlett, L. (2017). Critical transnational curriculum for immigrant and refugee students. *Curriculum Inquiry, 47*(1), 25–35.

Baker, M. M., & King, J. E. (2022). Africana intellectual/pedagogical work: Teaching to answer the call to the African Renaissance in the African Diaspora context. *Journal of Black Studies, 53*(6), 511–533. https://doi.org/10.1177/00219347221087397

Baquedano-López, P., & Gong, N. (2022). Indigenous mobilities in diaspora: Literacies of spatial tense. In A. N. Shaswar & J. Rosén (Eds.), *Literacies in the age of mobility: Literacy practices of adult and adolescent migrants* (pp. 25–49). Springer.

Barth, E. A. T. (1961). The language behavior of Negroes and Whites. *Pacific Sociological Review, 4*(2), 69–72. https://doi.org/10.2307/1388674

Bartlett, L. (2012). South-South migration and education: The case of people of Haitian descent born in the Dominican Republic. *Compare: A Journal of Comparative and International Education, 42*(3), 393–414.

Bartlett, L., Oliveira, G., & Ungemah, L. (2018). Cruel optimism: Migration and schooling for Dominican newcomer immigrant youth. *Anthropology & Education Quarterly, 49*(4), 444–461.

Bauer, E. B., Presiado, V., & Colomer, S. (2017). Writing through partnership: Fostering translanguaging in children who are emergent bilinguals. *Journal of Literacy Research, 49*(1), 10–37. https://doi.org/10.1177/1086296X16683417

Baugh, J. (1983). *Black street speech: Its history, structure, and survival.* University of Texas Press.

(2003). Linguistic profiling. In A. Ball, S. Makoni, G. Smitherman, & A. K. Spears (Eds.), *Black linguistics: Language, society and politics in Africa and the Americas* (pp. 155–168). Routledge.

Becker, H., & Geer, B. (1957). Participant observation and interviewing: A comparison. *Human Organization, 16*(3), 28–32.

Bell, D. (1995). Racial realism. In K. Crenshaw, N. Gotanda, G. Peller, & K. Thomas (Eds.), *Critical race theory: The key writings that formed the movement* (pp. 302–312). New Press.

Berns, M. (2019). World Englishes and communicative competence. In C. L. Nelson, Z. G. Proshina, & D. R. Davis (Eds.), *The handbook of world Englishes* (pp. 674–685). John Wiley & Sons.

(2020). *Black Athena: The Afroasiatic roots of classical civilization: Vol. 3. The linguistic evidence.* Rutgers University Press.

Berthele, R. (2020). The extraordinary ordinary: Re-engineering multilingualism as a natural category. *Language Learning, 71*(S1), 80–120. https://doi.org/10.1111/lang.12407

Bhabha, H. K. (1994). *The location of culture.* Routledge.

Birmingham, J. C. (2015). Black English near its roots: The transplanted West African Creoles. In J. L. Dillard (Ed.), *Perspectives on American English* [Originally published 1980], Vol. *29* (pp. 335–346). De Gruyter.

Blackman, S. & Conrad, D. (2017). *Caribbean discourse in inclusive education: Historical and contemporary Issues.* Information Age Publishing.

Blackman, S., Conrad, D., & Brown, L. (Eds.). (2019). *Achieving inclusive education in the Caribbean and beyond.* Springer.

Blair, E. J., & Williams, K. A. (Eds.). (2021). *The handbook on Caribbean education.* Information Age Publishing.

Blake, R., & Shousterman, C. (2010). Second generation West Indian Americans and English in New York City. *English Today, 26*(3), 35–43. https://doi.org/10.1017/S0266078410000234

Blommaert, J. (2007). Sociolinguistics and discourse analysis: Orders of indexicality and polycentricity. *Journal of multicultural discourses, 2*(2), 115–130.

Bogle, M. (1997). Constructing literacy: Cultural practices in classroom encounters. *Caribbean Journal of Education, 19*(2), 179–190.

Boutte, G., Johnson, G. L., Wynter-Hoyte, K., & Uyoata, U. E. (2017). Using African diaspora literacy to heal and restore the souls of young black children. *International Critical Childhood Policy Studies Kournal, 6*(1), 66–79.

Braden, E. (2020). Navigating Black racial identities: Literacy insights from an immigrant family. *Teachers College Record, 122*(13), 1–26. https://doi.org/10.1177/016146812012201310

Braden, E., Bryan, K., Chang, B., Hotchkins, B., Kiramba, L., Knight-Manuel, M., Smith, P., & Watson, V. (2020, April). *Clarifying the role of race in the literacies and Englishes of Black immigrant youth* [Symposia]. American Educational Research Association Annual Meeting, San Francisco, CA, United States.

Brereton, B. (2004). *General history of the Caribbean: The Caribbean in the twentieth century.* UNESCO.

Bristol, L. (2012). *Plantation pedagogy: A postcolonial and global perspective.* Peter Lang.

Bronfenbrenner, U., & Morris, P. A. (2006). The bioecological model of human development. In W. Damon (Series Ed.) & R. M. Lerner (Vol. Ed.), *Handbook of child psychology: Theoretical model of human development* (pp. 793–828). John Wiley & Sons.

Brooks, M. D. (2015). "It's like a script": Long-term English learners' experiences with and ideas about academic reading. *Research in the Teaching of English, 49*(4), 383–406.

Brown, D. S. (2000). Democracy, colonization, and human capital in sub-Saharan Africa. *Studies in Comparative International Development, 35*(1), 20-40.

Bryan, B. (1997). Investigating language in a Jamaican primary school: Perceptions and findings of a group of primary school teachers. *Changing English, 4*(2), 251–258. https://doi.org/10.1080/1358684970040207

Bryce-Laporte, R. S. (1972). Black immigrants: The experience of invisibility and inequality. *Journal of Black Studies, 3*(1), 29–56. https://doi.org/10.1177/002193477200300103

Buchanan, L., Bui, Q., & Patel, J. K. (2020, July 3). Black Lives Matter may be the largest movement in U.S. history. *The New York Times.* www.nytimes.com/interactive/2020/07/03/us/george-floyd-protests-crowd-size.html

Buni, C. (2021, October 11). If social media can be unsafe for kids, what happens in VR? *Slate.* https://slate.com/technology/2021/10/facebook-virtual-reality-metaverse-safety-children-jakki-bailey.html

Burkhard, T. (2021). "They prefer you to have a conversation like a real American": Contextualizing the experiences of one Somali (former) refugee student in adult ESL. In D. Warriner (Ed.), *Refugee education across the lifespan* (pp. 179–195). Springer.

Butcher, K. (1994). Black immigrants in the United States: A comparison with native Blacks and other immigrants. *Industrial and Labor Relations Review, 47,* 265–284.

Cabrera, N. L. (2018). Where is the racial theory in critical race theory? A constructive criticism of the Crits. *Review of Higher Education, 42*(1), 209–233. https://doi.org/10.1353/rhe.2018.0038

Calhoun-Brown, A. (1999). The image of God: Black theology and racial empowerment in the African American community. *Review of Religious Research, 40*(3), 197–212.

Calvet, L.-J. (1974). *Linguistique et colonialisme: petit traité de glottophagie*. Payot.
Calzada, E., Barajas-Gonzalez, R. G., Dawson-McClure, S., Huang, K.-Y., Palamar, J., Kamboukos, D., & Brotman, L. M. (2015). Early academic achievement among American low-income Black students from immigrant and non-immigrant families. *Prevention Science, 16*(8), 1159–1168. https://doi.org/10.1007/s11121-015-0570-y
Cameron, D. (2018). 'Respect, please!': Investigating race, power and language. In D. Cameron, E. Frazer, P. Harvey, M. B. H. Rampton, & K. Richardson, *Researching language: Issues of power and method* (pp. 113–130). Routledge.
Campano, G. (2007). *Immigrant students and literacy: Reading, writing, and remembering*. Teachers College Press.
Campano, G., & Ghiso, M. P. (2011). Immigrant students as cosmopolitan intellectuals. In S. Wolf, K. Coats, P. Encisco, & C. Jenkins (Eds.), *Handbook of research on children's and young adult literature*. Taylor & Francis.
Campt, T. M. (2023). *A Black gaze: Artists changing how we see*. MIT Press.
Canagarajah, S. (2006). Changing communicative needs, revised assessment objectives: Testing English as an international language. *Language Assessment Quarterly, 3*(3), 229–242. https://doi.org/10.1207/s15434311laq0303_1
  (2011). Codemeshing in academic writing: Identifying teachable strategies of translanguaging. *The Modern Language Journal, 95*(3), 401–417.
  (2013). *Translingual practice: Global Englishes and cosmopolitan relations*. Routledge.
Canagarajah, S., & Ben Said, S. (2011). Linguistic imperialism. In J. Simpson (Ed.), *The Routledge handbook of applied linguistics* (pp. 388–400). Routledge.
Capstick, T. (2016). *Multilingual literacies, identities and ideologies: Exploring chain migration from Pakistan to the UK*. Palgrave Macmillan.
Carrington, L. (1992). Caribbean English. In T. McArthur (Ed.), *The Oxford companion to the English language* (pp. 191–193). Oxford University Press.
Centers for Disease Control and Prevention. (2022, March 31). *New CDC data illuminate youth mental health threats during the COVID-19 pandemic* [Press release]. www.cdc.gov/media/releases/2022/p0331-youth-mental-health-covid-19.html
Chandran, N. (2023, January 9). An 'unapologetically Indian' universe. www.bbc.com/culture/article/20230106-the-ancient-indian-myths-resonating-now
Charmaz, K. (2006). *Constructing grounded theory: A practical guide through qualitative analysis*. Sage.
Chenoweth, E., & Pressman, J. (2017, February 7). This is what we learned by counting the women's marches. *The Washington Post*. www.washingtonpost.com/news/monkey-cage/wp/2017/02/07/this-is-what-we-learned-by-counting-the-womens-marches/
Chilisa, B., & Ntseane, G. (2010). Resisting dominant discourses: Implications of indigenous, African feminist theory and methods for gender and education research. *Gender and Education, 22*(6), 617–632. https://doi.org/10.1080/09540253.2010.519578
Chiswick, B. R. (1979). The economic progress of immigrants: Some apparently universal patterns. In W. Fellner (Ed.), *Contemporary economic problems* (pp. 357–399). American Enterprise Institute for Public Policy Research.

Chow, R. (2014). *Not like a native speaker: On languaging as a postcolonial experience*. Columbia University Press.
Christie, P., & McKinney, C. (2017). Decoloniality and "Model C" schools: Ethos, language and the protests of 2016. *Education as Change, 21*(3), 1–21.
Clachar, A. (2003). Paratactic conjunctions in creole speakers' and ESL learners' academic writing. *World Englishes, 22*(3), 271–289. https://doi.org/10.1111/1467-971X.00296
(2004). Creole discourse effects on the speech conjunctive system in expository texts. *Journal of Pragmatics, 36*(10), 1827–1850. https://doi.org/10.1016/j.pragma.2004.05.002
Clark, V. V. A. (2009). Developing diaspora literacy and *marasa* consciousness. *Theatre Survey, 50*(1), 9–18. https://doi.org/10.1017/s0040557409000039
Clayton, K. E., & Zusho, A. (2016). A cultural heuristic approach to the study of Jamaican undergraduate students' achievement motivation. *British Journal of Educational Psychology, 86*(1), 8–36. https://doi.org/10.1111/bjep.12081
Coard, B. (1971). *How the West Indian child is made educationally subnormal in the British school system: The scandal of the Black child in schools in Britain*. New Beacon Books.
Cohen, L., Manion, L., & Morrison, K. (2011). *Research methods in education* (7th ed.). Routledge.
Collins, P. H. (2000). *Black feminist thought: Knowledge, consciousness, and the politics of engagement* (2nd ed.). Routledge.
Collins English Dictionary. (n.d.). Wakanda. In *Collins English Dictionary*. Retrieved January 24, 2023, from www.collinsdictionary.com/us/dictionary/english/wakanda
Compton-Lilly, C., Papoi, K., Venegas, P., Hamman, L., & Schwabenbauer, B. (2017). Intersectional identity negotiation: The case of young immigrant children. *Journal of Literacy Research, 49*(1), 115–140. https://doi.org/10.1177/1086296x16683421
Conference on College Composition and Communication. (1974). Students' right to their own language. *College Composition and Communication, 25*(3), 1–18.
Conrad, A. (2020). *Research brief: Identifying and countering white supremacy culture in food systems*. Duke World Food Policy Center. https://wfpc.sanford.duke.edu/wp-content/uploads/sites/15/2022/05/Whiteness-Food-Movements-Research-Brief-WFPC-October-2020.pdf
Conrad, A., & Zuckerman, J. (2020). Identifying and countering white supremacy culture in food systems. *World Food Policy Center, 1*, 1–10.
Cook, A. L. (2015). Building connections to literacy learning among English language learners: Exploring the role of school counselors. *Journal of School Counseling, 13*(9), 3–43.
Cooper, A. (2020). Justice for all: Realities and possibilities of Black English learners in K–12 schools. *Teachers College Record, 122*(13). https://doi.org/10.1177/016146812012201311
Cope, B., & Kalantzis, M. (2013). "Multiliteracies": New literacies, new learning. In M. Hawkins (Ed.), *Framing languages and literacies* (pp. 105–135). Routledge.
Council of Europe. (2020). *Common European Framework of Reference for Languages: Learning, teaching, assessment – Companion volume*. https://rm.coe.int/common-european-framework-of-reference-for-languages-learning-teaching/16809ea0d4

Cowley, S. J. (2017). Changing the idea of language: Nigel Love's perspective. *Language Sciences*, *61*, 43–55.

Craig, D. (1974). Education and Creole English in the West Indies: Some sociolinguistic factors. In D. H. Hymes (Ed.), *Pidginization and Creolization of languages* (pp. 371–392). Cambridge University Press.

Crenshaw, K. (1991). Mapping the margins: Intersectionality, identity politics, and violence against women of Color. *Stanford Law Review*, *43*(6), 1241–1299.

(2021). *A primer on intersectionality*. American Policy Forum. www.aapf.org/_files/ugd/62e126_19f84b6cbf6f4660bac198ace49b9287.pdf

Crenshaw, K., Gotanda, N., Peller, G., & Thomas, K. (1995). Introduction. In K. Crenshaw, N. Gotanda, G. Peller, & K. Thomas (Eds.), *Critical race theory: The key writings that formed the movement* (pp. xiii–xxxii). New Press.

Crotty, M. (1998). *The foundations of social research: Meaning and perspective in the research process*. Sage.

Cukor-Avila, P. (2001). Co-existing grammars: The relationship between the evolution of African American English and White Vernacular English in the South. In S. L. Lanehart (Ed.), *Sociocultural and historical contexts of African American English* (pp. 93–127). John Benjamins.

Curry, M. J. (2004). UCLA community college review: Academic literacy for English language learners. *Community College Review*, *32*(2), 51–68. https://doi.org/10.1177/009155210403200204

Cushing, I. (2022). *Standards, stigma, surveillance: Raciolinguistic ideologies and England's schools*. Springer.

Cushing, I., & Carter, A. (2022). Using young adult fiction to interrogate raciolinguistic ideologies in schools. *Literacy*, *56*(2), 106–119.

Cushing, I., & Snell, J. (2022). The (white) ears of Ofsted: A raciolinguistic perspective on the listening practices of the schools inspectorate. *Language in Society*, *52*(3), 363–386.

Dancy, T. E., Edwards, K. T., & Earl Davis, J. (2018). Historically white universities and plantation politics: Anti-Blackness and higher education in the Black Lives Matter era. *Urban Education*, *53*(2), 176–195.

Daniel, S. M., & Pacheco, M. B. (2016). Translanguaging practices and perspectives of four multilingual teens. *Journal of Adolescent & Adult Literacy*, *59*(6), 653–663.

Daoud, N., English, S., Griffin, K. A., & George Mwangi, C. A. (2018). Beyond stereotypes: Examining the role of social identities in the motivation patterns of Black immigrant and Black native students. *American Journal of Education*, *124*(3), 285–312. https://doi.org/10.1086/697211

Darder, A. (2015). Decolonizing interpretive research: A critical bicultural methodology for social change. *International Education Journal*, *14*(2), 63–77.

Darvin, R., & Norton B. (2014). Transnational identity and migrant language learners: The promise of digital storytelling. *Education Matters: The Journal of Teaching and Learning*, *2*(1), 55–66. https://journalhosting.ucalgary.ca/index.php/em/article/view/62890

Davies, C. B. (1995). Hearing Black women's voices: Transgressing imposed boundaries. In C. B. Davies & 'M. Ogundipe-Leslie (Eds.), *Moving beyond boundaries: Vol. 1. International dimensions of Black women's writing* (pp. 3–14). New York University Press.

(2013). *Caribbean spaces: Escapes from twilight zones*. University of Illinois Press.

Dávila, L. T. (2015). Diaspora literacies: An exploration of what reading means to young African immigrant women. *Journal of Adolescent & Adult Literacy, 58*(8), 641–649.

(2019). Multilingualism and identity: articulating 'African-ness' in an American high school. *Race Ethnicity and Education, 22*(5), 634–646, https://doi.org/10.1080/13613324.2018.1424709

De Costa, P. I. (2010). From refugee to transformer: A Bourdieusian take on a Hmong learner's trajectory. *TESOL Quarterly, 44*(3), 517–541. https://doi.org/10.5054/tq.2010.226856

(2014). Reconceptualizing cosmopolitanism in language and literacy education: Insights from a Singapore school. *Research in the Teaching of English, 49*(1), 9–30.

Dei, G. J. S. (2000). Rethinking the role of Indigenous knowledges in the academy. *International Journal of Inclusive Education, 4*(2), 111–132. https://doi.org/10.1080/136031100284849

de Kleine, C. (2006). West African World English speakers in U.S. classrooms: The role of West African pidgin English. In S. J. Nero (Ed.), *Dialects, Englishes, Creoles, and education* (pp. 205–232). Routledge.

Delgado, R., & Stefancic, J. (Eds.). (2001). *Critical race theory: The cutting edge* (2nd ed.). Temple University Press.

De Lisle, J. (2019). Insights on the marginalization of poor children in the education system of Trinidad and Tobago. In S. Blackman, D. Conrad, & L. Brown (Eds.), *Achieving inclusive education in the Caribbean and beyond* (pp. 89–119). Springer.

De Lisle, J., Seunarinesingh, K., Mohammed, R., & Lee-Piggott, R. (2017). Using an iterative mixed-methods research design to investigate schools facing exceptionally challenging circumstances within Trinidad and Tobago. *School Effectiveness and School Improvement, 28*(3), 406–442. https://doi.org/10.1080/09243453.2017.1306570

de los Ríos, C. V., & Seltzer, K. (2017). Translanguaging, coloniality, and English classrooms: An exploration of two bicoastal urban classrooms. *Research in the Teaching of English, 52*(1), 55–76.

Delva, R.-J. (2019). "Kreyòl Pale, Kreyòl Konprann": Haitian identity and Creole mother-tongue learning in Matènwa, Haiti. *Journal of Haitian Studies, 25*(1), 92–126. https://doi.org/10.1353/jhs.2019.0003

Devonish, H. (1986). *Language and liberation: Creole language politics in the Caribbean*. Karia Press.

Devonish, H., & Carpenter, K. (2007). Towards full bilingualism in education: The Jamaican bilingual primary project. *Social and Economic Studies, 56*(1/2), 277–303.

(2020). *Language, race and the global Jamaican*. Springer.

Díaz, S., & Flores, E. (2001). Teacher as sociocultural, sociohistorical mediator. In M. de la Luz Reyes & J. J. Halcón (Eds.), *The best for our children: Critical perspectives on literacy for Latino students* (pp. 29–47). Teachers College Press.

Dick, H. P. (2020). Mexican and Central American migration in the time of Trump. In H. S. Alim, A. Reyes, & P. V. Kroskrity (Eds.), *The Oxford handbook of language and race* (pp. 447–471). Oxford University Press.

References

Dictionary.com. (n.d.). Wakanda. In *Dictionary.com*. Retrieved January 24, 2023, from www.dictionary.com/e/pop-culture/wakanda/

Dictionary of American Family Names. (2022). Olatunji. In *Dictionary of American Family Names*. Retrieved January 24, 2023, from www.oxfordreference.com/display/10.1093/acref/9780190245115.001.0001/acref-9780190245115-e-54938?rskey=jwhQf6&result=54961

Dillard, C. B. (2012a). *Learning to (Re)member the things we've learned to forget: Endarkened feminisms, spirituality, & the sacred nature of research & teaching*. Peter Lang.

— (2012b). *On spiritual strivings: Transforming an African American woman's academic life*. State University of New York Press.

Dillard, J. L. (Ed.). (1980). *Perspectives on American English*. Mouton.

Dodoo, F. (1991). Earnings differences among Blacks in America. *Social Science Research*, 20, 93–108.

— (1997). Assimilation differences among Africans in America. *Social Forces*, 76(2), 527–546. https://doi.org/10.1093/sf/76.2.527

Dornan, I. (2019). 'Book don't feed our children': Nonconformist missionaries and the British and Foreign School Society in the development of elementary education in the British West Indies before and after emancipation. *Slavery & Abolition*, 40(1), 109–129. https://doi.org/10.1080/0144039X.2018.1505144

Dovchin, S. (2019a). Language crossing and linguistic racism: Mongolian immigrant women in Australia. *Journal of Multicultural Discourses*, 14(4), 334–351.

— (2019b). *Language, social media and ideologies: Translingual Englishes, Facebook and authenticities*. Springer.

— (2020). Introduction to special issue: Linguistic racism. *International Journal of Bilingual Education and Bilingualism*, 23(7), 773–777.

Du Bois, W. E. B. (1999). *The souls of Black folk: A Norton critical edition*. Edited by H. L. Gates Jr. & T. H. Oliver. Norton [Originally published 1903].

Duong, M. T., Badaly, D., Liu, F. F., Schwartz, D., & McCarty, C. A. (2016). Generational differences in academic achievement among immigrant youths: A meta-analytic review. *Review of Educational Research*, 86(1), 3–41.

Dyson, A. H. (2003). *The brothers and sisters learn to write: Popular literacies in childhood and school cultures*. Teachers College Press.

Edwards, P. A., & Smith, P. (2023). From illiterate assumption to literate potentiality: Harnessing the possibility of parent-of-Color stories. *Contemporary Issues in Early Childhood*. https://doi.org/10.1177/14639491231209586

Edwards, P. A., & Smith, P., & McNair, J. C. (2023). Toward culturally relevant literacies with children and families of Color. In R. J. Tierney, F. Rizvi, & K. Ercikan (Eds.), *International Encyclopedia of Education* (4th ed.) (pp. 180–197). Elsevier.

Enciso, P. (2011). Storytelling in critical literacy: Removing walls between immigrant and nonimmigrant youth. *English Teaching*, 10, 21–40.

Engerman, S. L. (1982). Economic adjustments to emancipation in the United States and British West Indies. *Journal of Interdisciplinary History*, 13(2), 191–220.

Fanon, F. (1988). *Toward the African revolution: Political essays*. Translated by H. Chevalier. Grove Press.

— (1991). *The wretched of the earth*. Translated by C. Farrington [Originally published 1961]. Grove Press.

Farah, L. A. (2015). *Somali parental involvement in education: Case studies of two urban public schools in the United States of America* [Unpublished doctoral dissertation]. University of Minnesota.

Fine, M., & Jaffe-Walter, R. (2007). Swimming: On oxygen, resistance, and possibility for immigrant youth under siege. *Anthropology & Education Quarterly, 38*(1), 76–96. https://doi.org/10.1525/aeq.2007.38.1.76

Fisher, M. T. (2003a). Open mics and open minds: Spoken word poetry in African diaspora participatory literacy communities. *Harvard Educational Review, 73*(3), 362–389. https://doi.org/10.17763/haer.73.3.642q2564m1k90670

(2003b). *Choosing literacy: African diaspora participatory literacy communities* (Publication No. 305337929) [Doctoral dissertation, University of California, Berkeley]. ProQuest Dissertations & Theses Global.

(2005). Literocracy: Liberating language and creating possibilities. *English Education, 37*(2), 92–95.

(2006). Building a literocracy: Diaspora literacy and heritage knowledge in participatory literacy communities. *The Yearbook of the National Society for the Study of Education, 105*(2), 361–381. https://doi.org/10.1111/j.1744-7984.2006.00090.x

FitzGerald, S., & Cook-Martín, D. (2015). *The geopolitical origins of the U.S. Immigration Act of 1965*. Migration Policy Institute.

Flores, B. B., Vasquez, O. A., & Clark, E. R. (2014). *Generating transworld pedagogy: Reimagining La Clase Mágica*. Lexington Books.

Flores, N. (2013). Silencing the subaltern: Nation-state/colonial governmentality and bilingual education in the United States. *Critical Inquiry in Language Studies, 10*(4), 263–287.

(2020). From academic language to language architecture: Challenging raciolinguistic ideologies in research and practice. *Theory Into Practice, 59*(1), 22–31. https://doi.org/10.1080/00405841.2019.1665411

Flores, N., & Rosa, J. (2015). Undoing appropriateness: Raciolinguistic ideologies and language diversity in education. *Harvard Educational Review, 85*(2), 149–171.

(2019). Bringing race into second language acquisition. *The Modern Language Journal, 103*, 145–151.

Foner, N. (1985). Race and color: Jamaican migrants in London and New York City. *International Migration Review, 19*(4), 708–727.

Fordham, S., & Ogbu, J. U. (1986). Black students' school success: Coping with the "burden of 'acting white.'" *The Urban Review, 18*(3), 176–206.

Franco, K., Patler, C., & Reiter, K. (2020). Punishing status and the punishment status quo: Solitary confinement in U.S. immigration prisons, 2013–2017. *Punishment & Society*. https://doi.org/10.31235/osf.io/zdy7f

François, R. (2015). *An investigation of Catholic education and the predicament of democracy in Haiti* (Publication No. 2512770152) [Doctoral dissertation, McGill University]. ProQuest Dissertations & Theses Global.

Franklin-Brown, G. R. E. T. A. (2013). *Two generations of Black Caribbean women's experiences of the education system* [Unpublished doctoral dissertation]. London South Bank University.

Freeman, S. V. (2016). *Counter-narratives of African American academic persistence: Identity maps and funds of knowledge* [Unpublished doctoral dissertation]. Arizona State University.

Freire, P. (2000). *Pedagogy of the oppressed (30th anniversary ed.)*. Translated by M. B. Ramos [Originally published 1970]. Continuum.
Freire, P., & Macedo, D. (1987). *Literacy: Reading the word and the world*. Bergin & Garvey.
Galloway, N., & Rose, H. (2015). *Introducing global Englishes*. Routledge.
García, O. (2009). *Bilingual education in the 21st century: A global perspective*. John Wiley & Sons.
(2022). Designing new ownership of English: A commentary. *Teaching English as a Second Language Electronic Journal (TESL-EJ)*, *26*(3). https://doi.org/10.55593/ej.26103a10
García, O., Flores, N., Seltzer, K., Wei, L., Otheguy, R., & Rosa, J. (2021). Rejecting abyssal thinking in the language and education of racialized bilinguals: A manifesto. *Critical Inquiry in Language Studies*, *18*(3), 1–26. https://doi.org/10.1080/15427587.2021.1935957
García, O., Flores, N., & Woodley, H. H. (2015). Constructing in-between spaces to "do" bilingualism: A tale of two high schools in one city. In J. Cenoz & D. Gorter (Eds.), *Multilingual education: Between language learning and translanguaging* (pp. 199–224). Cambridge University Press.
García, O., & Kleyn, T. (Eds.). (2016). *Translanguaging with multilingual students: Learning from classroom moments*. Routledge.
García, O., & Torres-Guevara, R. (2022). Monoglossic language education policies and Latinx students' language. In E. G. Murillo, D. Delgado Bernal, S. Morales, L. Urrieta, E. Ruiz Bybee, J. Sanchez Muñoz, V. B. Saenz, D. Villanueva, M. Machado-Casas, & K. Espinoza (Eds.), *Handbook of Latinos and education: Theory, research, and practice* (pp. 93–102). Routledge.
García, O., & Wei, L. (2014). *Translanguaging: Language, bilingualism and education*. Palgrave Macmillan.
Getty, G. A. (2010). The journey between Western and Indigenous research paradigms. *Journal of Transcultural Nursing*, *21*(1), 5–14. https://doi.org/10.1177/1043659609349062
Ghabra, R. (2022, February 17). Black immigrants face unique challenges. *Human Rights First*. https://humanrightsfirst.org/library/black-immigrants-face-unique-challenges/
Ghong, M., Saah, L., Larke, P. J., & Webb-Johnson, G. (2010). Teach my child, too: African immigrant parents and multicultural educators sharing culturally responsive teaching tips. *Journal of Praxis in Multicultural Education*, *2*(1). https://doi.org/10.9741/2161-2978.1023
Gilbert, S. (2008). *The relationship of immigrant status to perceptions of reading and reading literacy among young Black students: A test of the Cultural-Ecological Theory of School Performance* [Doctoral dissertation, Florida International University]. ProQuest Dissertations & Theses Global.
Givens, J. R. (2016). A grammar for black education beyond borders: Exploring technologies of schooling in the African Diaspora. *Race Ethnicity and Education*, *19*(6), 1288–1302. https://doi.org/10.1080/13613324.2015.1103724
Goodwin, A. L. (2002). Teacher preparation and the education of immigrant children. *Education and Urban Society*, *34*(2), 156–172.
Gorman, A. (2021). *The hill we climb: An inaugural poem for the country*. Viking.

Gort, M. (2012). Code-switching patterns in the writing-related talk of young emergent bilinguals. *Journal of Literacy Research, 20*(10), 1–31.

Guan, S. S. A., Nash, A., & Orellana, M. F. (2016). Cultural and social processes of language brokering among Arab, Asian, and Latin immigrants. *Journal of Multilingual and Multicultural Development, 37*(2), 150–166.

Guinier, L. (2004). From racial liberalism to racial literacy: *Brown v. Board of Education* and the interest-divergence dilemma. *Journal of American History, 91* (1), 92–118. https://doi.org/10.2307/3659616

Gundaker, G. 1998. *Signs of diaspora / diaspora of signs: Literacies, Creolization, and vernacular practice in African America.* Oxford University Press.

Gutiérrez, K. D. (2008). Developing a sociocritical literacy in the third space. *Reading Research Quarterly, 43*(2), 148–164. https://doi.org/10.1598/rrq.43.2.3

Gutiérrez, K. D., Cortes, K., Cortez, A., DiGiacomo, D., Higgs, J., Johnson, P., Lizárraga, J. R., Mendoza, E., Tien, J., & Vakil, S. (2017). Replacing representation with imagination: Finding ingenuity in everyday practices. *Review of Research in Education, 41*(1), 30–60.

Halliday, M. A. K. (2013, October 23). *Language in a changing world* [Research seminar]. University of Hong Kong.

Hamel, E. C. (2006). *Exploring possibilities of home and community literacies within a space for conversation, engagement, and reflection: Epiphanies, celebrations, and challenges* [Unpublished doctoral dissertation]. University of South Carolina.

Hancock, I. F. (2015). Texan Gullah: The Creole English of the Brackettville Afro-Seminoles. In J. L. Dillard (Ed.), *Perspectives on American English* [Originally published 1980], Vol. *29* (pp. 305–334). De Gruyter.

Harris, L. (1993). *Just another girl on the IRT* [Videocassette recording]. Live Home Video.

Harrison, L. (1992). *Who Prospers?* Basic Books.

Hartlep, N. D. (2012). Reconsidering the model minority and Black Mormon discourses. *NERA Conference Proceedings 2012*, 8. https://digitalcommons.lib.uconn.edu/nera_2012/8/

Hebblethwaite, B. (2012). French and underdevelopment, Haitian Creole and development: Educational language policy problems and solutions in Haiti. *Journal of Pidgin and Creole Languages, 27*(2), 255–302. https://doi.org/10.1075/jpcl.27.2.03heb

Heller, M., & McElhinny, B. S. (2017). *Language, capitalism, colonialism: Toward a critical history*. University of Toronto Press.

Henry, A. (1998). "Speaking up" and "speaking out": Examining "voice" in a reading/writing program with adolescent African Caribbean girls. *Journal of Literacy Research, 30*(2), 233–252. https://doi.org/10.1080/10862969809547997

Herdina, P., & Jessner, U. (2002). *A dynamic model of multilingualism: Perspectives of change in psycholinguistics*. Multilingual Matters.

Hickling-Hudson, A. (2015). *Caribbean schooling and the social divide – What will it take to change neo-colonial education systems?* [Conference presentation]. CIES, Washington, DC, United States.

Holdstein, D. (Ed.). (2008). *College Composition and Communication, 59*(3).

Holm, J. (2015). The Creole "Copula" that highlighted the world. In J. L. Dillard (Ed.), *Perspectives on American English* [Originally published 1980], Vol. *29* (pp. 367–376). De Gruyter.

hooks, b. (1992). *Black looks: Race and representations*. South End Press.
  ——— (1994). *Teaching to transgress: Education as the practice of freedom*. Routledge.
Hornberger, N. H. (2002). Multilingual language policies and the continua of biliteracy: An ecological approach. *Language Policy, 1*(1), 27–51.
Horowitz, R. (2012). Border crossing: Geographic space and cognitive shifts in adolescent language and literacy practices. In H. Romo, C. A. G. de la Calleja, & O. Lopez (Eds.), *A bilateral perspective on Mexico-U.S. migration* (pp. 147–164). Instituto de Investigaciones Histórico.
Hunter, L. (1992). *Diary of Latoya Hunter: My first year in junior high*. Vintage.
Hymes, D. (1972). On communicative competence. In J. Pride & J. Holmes (Eds.), *Sociolinguistics* (pp. 269–293). Penguin Books.
Ibrahim, A. (1999). Becoming Black: Rap and hip-hop, race, gender, identity, and the politics of ESL learning. *TESOL Quarterly, 33*(3), 349–369. https://doi.org/10.2307/3587669
  ——— (2019). *Black immigrants in North America: Essays on race, immigration, identity, language, hip-hop, pedagogy, and the politics of becoming Black*. Myers Education Press.
  ——— (2020). Immigration, language, and racial becoming. In H. S. Alim, A. Reyes, & P. V. Kroskrity (Eds.), *The Oxford handbook of languge and race* (pp. 167–185). Oxford University Press.
Ibrahima, A. B., & Mattaini, M. A. (2019). Social work in Africa: Decolonizing methodologies and approaches. *International Social Work, 62*(2), 799–813. https://doi.org/10.1177/0020872817742702
Irizarry, Y., & Cohen, E. D. (2019). Of promise and penalties: How student racial-cultural markers shape teacher perceptions. *Race and Social Problems, 11*(2), 93–111. https://doi.org/10.1007/s12552-018-9231-7
Ivanic, R., Edwards, R., Barton, D., Martin-Jones, M., Fowler, Z., Hughes, B., Mannion, G., Miller, K., Satchwell, C., & Smith, J. (2009). *Improving learning in college: Rethinking literacies across the curriculum*. Routledge.
James, C. L. R. (1992). From Toussaint L'Ouverture to Fidel Castro. In A. Grimshaw (Ed.), *The C.L.R. James Reader* (pp. 296–314). Wiley-Blackwell.
Janesick, V. (2010). *Oral history for the qualitative researcher: Choreographing the story*. Guilford Press.
Jennings, Z. (2001). Teacher education in selected countries in the Commonwealth Caribbean: The ideal of policy versus the reality of practice. *Comparative Education, 37*(1), 107–134.
Jiménez, R. T., Eley, C., Leander, K., & Smith, P. H. (2015). Transnational immigrant youth literacies: A selective review of the literature. In P. Smith & A. Kumi-Yeboah (Eds.), *Handbook of research on cross-cultural approaches to language and literacy development* (pp. 322–344). IGI Global.
Jiménez, R. T., Smith, P. H., & Teague, B. L. (2009). Transnational and community literacies for teachers. *Journal of Adolescent & Adult Literacy, 53*(1), 16–26. https://doi.org/10.1598/jaal.53.1.2
Johnson, E. (2005). WAR in the media: Metaphors, ideology, and the formation of language policy. *Bilingual Research Journal, 29*(3), 621–640.
Johnson, L. L., Bryan, N., & Boutte, G. (2019). Show us the love: Revolutionary teaching in (un)critical times. *The Urban Review, 51*(1), 46–64.

Joseph, V. (2012). How Thomas Nelson and Sons' *Royal Readers* textbooks helped instill the standards of whiteness into colonized Black Caribbean subjects and their descendents. *Transforming Anthropology, 20*(2), 146–158. https://doi.org/10.1111/j.1548-7466.2012.01156.x

Jules, D. (2008). Rethinking education for the Caribbean: A radical approach. *Comparative Education, 44*(2), 203–214.

(2010, December 13). Rethinking education in the Caribbean. *Caribbean Examinations Council.* www.cxc.org/?q=media-centre/cxcs_blog

Kaba, A. (2008). Race, gender and progress: Are Black American women the new model minority? *Journal of African American Studies, 12*(4), 309–335. https://doi.org/10.1007/s12111-008-9043-8

Kachru, B. B. (1992). *The other tongue: English across cultures* (2nd ed.). University of Illinois Press.

Kachru, B. B., & Nelson, C. (2001). World Englishes. In A. Burns & C. Coffin (Eds.), *Analysing English in a global context: A reader* (pp. 9–25). Routledge.

Kalantzis, M., & Cope, B. (2012). *Literacies.* Cambridge University Press.

(2020). *Adding sense: Context and interest in a grammar of multimodal meaning.* Cambridge University Press.

Kalmijn, M. (1996). The socioeconomic assimilation of Caribbean American Blacks. *Social Forces, 74*(3), 911–930. https://doi.org/10.1093/sf/74.3.911

Kan Kan Riddim. (2015). *Benjai – Phenomenal* [Video]. YouTube. www.youtube.com/watch?v=fdzqSzk5QsA

Katende, C. (1995). *Population dynamics in Africa* [Discussion]. University of Pennsylvania.

Kates, I. C. (2010). Creativity as soul work. In I. C. Kates & C. L. Harvey (Eds.), *The wheels of soul in education: An inspiring international dynamic* (pp. 113–129). Brill.

Kendi, I. X. (2019). *How to be an antiracist.* One World.

Kent, M. M. (2007). Immigration and America's Black population. *Population Bulletin, 62*(4), 1–16.

Kes the Band. (n.d.). About. https://kestheband.com/about-1

Keyes, C. L. M. (2002). The mental health continuum: From languishing to flourishing in life. *Journal of Health and Social Behavior, 43*(2), 207–222. https://doi.org/10.2307/3090197

Khan, T., Abimbola, S., Kyobutungi, C., & Pai, M. (2022). How we classify countries and people – and why it matters. *BMJ Global Health, 7*(6), e009704.

Kigamwa, J. C., & Ndemanu, M. T. (2017). Translingual practice among African immigrants in the US: Embracing the mosaicness of the English language. *Journal of Multilingual and Multicultural Development, 38*(5), 468–479. https://doi.org/10.1080/01434632.2016.1186678

King, J. E. (1992). Diaspora literacy and consciousness in the struggle against miseducation in the Black community. *The Journal of Negro Education, 61*(3), 317–340. https://doi.org/10.2307/2295251

(1995a). Culture-centered knowledge: Black studies, curriculum transformation and social action. In J. A. Banks & C. M. Banks (Eds.), *The handbook of research on multicultural education* (pp. 265–290). Palgrave Macmillan.

(1995b). Race and education: In what ways does race affect the educational process? In J. L. Kinchloe & S. R. Steinberg (Eds.), *Thirteen questions: Reframing education's conversation* (pp. 159–179). Peter Lang.

(1997). Thank you for opening our minds: On praxis, transmutation and Black studies in teacher development. In J. E. King, E. R. Hollins, & W. C. Hayman (Eds.), *Preparing teachers for cultural diversity* (pp. 156–169). Teachers College Press.

(2006). "If justice is our objective": Diaspora literacy, heritage knowledge, and the praxis of critical studyin' for human freedom. *The Yearbook of the National Society for the Study of Education, 105*(2), 337–360. https://doi.org/10.1111/j.1744-7984.2006.00089

(2021). Diaspora literacy, heritage knowledge and revolutionary African centered pedagogy in Black studies curriculum theorizing and praxis. In W. H. Schubert & M. F. He (Eds.), *Oxford encyclopedia of curriculum studies*. Oxford University Press.

King, J. E., & Swartz, E. E. (2016). *The Afrocentric praxis of teaching for freedom: Connecting culture to learning*. Routledge.

King, J. R. (2015). Sociolinguistic and educational perspectives on code switching in classrooms: What is it, why do it, and then, why feel bad about it? In P. Smith & A. Kumi-Yeboah (Eds.), *Handbook of research on cross-cultural approaches to language and literacy development* (pp. 345–366). IGI Global.

King, J. R., & Chetty, R. (2014). Codeswitching: Linguistic and literacy understanding of teaching dilemmas in multilingual classrooms. *Linguistics and Education, 25*, 40–50.

King, L. J. (2017). The status of Black history in U.S. schools and society. *Social Education, 81*(1), 14–18.

(2019). Interpreting Black history: Toward a Black history framework for teacher education. *Urban Education, 54*(3), 368–396.

(2020). Black history is not American history: Toward a framework of Black historical consciousness. *Social Education, 84*(6), 335–341.

Kinloch, V., Larson, J., Orellana, M. F., & Lewis, C. (2016). Literacy, equity, and imagination: Researching with/in communities. *Literacy Research: Theory, Method, and Practice, 65*(1), 94–112.

Kiramba, L. K. (2017). Multilingual literacies: Invisible representation of literacy in a rural classroom. *Journal of Adolescent & Adult Literacy, 61*(3), 267–277. https://doi.org/10.1002/jaal.690

Kiramba, L. K., Kumi-Yeboah, A., & Sallar, A. M. (2020). "It's like they don't recognize what I bring to the classroom": African immigrant youths' multilingual and multicultural navigation in United States schools. *Journal of Language, Identity, and Education, 22*(1), 83–98. https://doi.org/10.1080/15348458.2020.1832499

Kiramba, L. K., Kumi-Yeboah, A., Smith, P., & Sallar, A. M. (2021). Cultural and linguistic experiences of immigrant youth: Voices of African immigrant youth in United States urban schools. *Multicultural Education Review, 13*(1), 43–63. https://doi.org/10.1080/2005615x.2021.1890312

Kiramba, L. K., & Oloo, J. (2020). Identity negotiation in multilingual contexts: A narrative inquiry into experiences of an African immigrant high school student. *Teachers College Record, 122*(13), 1–24.

Kirkpatrick, A., & Deterding, D. (2011). World Englishes. In J. Simpson (Ed.), *The Routledge handbook of applied linguistics* (pp. 373–387). Routledge.

Kleyn, T., & García, O. (2019). Translanguaging as an act of transformation: Restructuring teaching. In L. C. de Oliveira (Ed.) *The handbook of TESOL in K-12* (1st ed., pp. 1–24). John Wiley & Sons.

Kperogi, F. A. (2009, March 22). African immigrants now America's new "model minority"? *Notes from Atlanta*. www.farooqkperogi.com/2009/03/african-immigrants-now-americas-new.html

Krueger, R. A., & Casey, M. A. (2009). *Focus groups: A practical guide for applied research* (4th ed.). Sage.

Kumi-Yeboah, A. (2018). The multiple worlds of Ghanaian-born immigrant students and academic success. *Teachers College Record*, *120*(9), 1–48.

Kumi-Yeboah, A., Onyewuenyi, A. C., & Smith, P. (2020). Teaching Black immigrant students in urban schools: Teacher and peer relationships and academic performances. *The Urban Review*, *53*(2), 218–242. https://doi.org/10.1007/s11256-020-00570-2

Kumi-Yeboah, A., & Smith, P. (2016). Critical multicultural citizenship education among Black immigrant youth: Factors and challenges. *International Journal of Multicultural Education*, *18*(1), 158–182. https://doi.org/10.18251/ijme.v18i1.10

Labov, W. (1969). Contraction, deletion, and inherent variability of the English copula. *Language*, *45*, 715–762.

(1972). *Language in the inner city: Studies in the Black English vernacular*. University of Pennsylvania Press.

Lacoste, V. (2007). Modelling the sounds of Standard Jamaican English in a grade 2 classroom. *Caribbean Journal of Education*, *29*, 290–326.

Lam, W. S. E. (2000). L2 literacy and the design of the self: A case study of a teenager writing on the internet. *TESOL Quarterly*, *34*(3), 457–482.

(2013). Multilingual practices in transnational digital contexts. *TESOL Quarterly*, *47*, 820–825. https://doi.org/10.1002/tesq.132

Lam, W. S. E., & Warriner, D. S. (2012). Transnationalism and literacy: Investigating the mobility of people, languages, texts, and practices in contexts of migration. *Reading Research Quarterly*, *47*(2), 191–215.

Lea, M. R., & Street, B. V. (1998). Student writing in higher education: An academic literacies approach. *Studies in Higher Education*, *23*(2), 157–172. https://doi.org/10.1080/03075079812331380364

Lee, E., & Alvarez, S. P. (2020). World Englishes, translingualism, and racialization in the US college composition classroom. *World Englishes*, *39*(2), 263–274.

Lee, H. (2021). "No more Korean at home." Family language policies, language practices, and challenges in Korean immigrant families: Intragroup diversities and intergenerational impacts. *Linguistics and Education*, *63*. https://doi.org/10.1016/j.linged.2021.100929

Lee, S., Xiong, C., Pheng, L. M., & Vang, M. N. (2017). The model minority maze: Hmong Americans working within and around racial discourses. *Journal of Southeast Asian American Education and Advancement*, *12*(2), 1–21. https://doi.org/10.7771/2153-8999.1153

Leu, D. J., Kinzer, C. K., Coiro, J., Castek, J., & Henry, L. A. (2017). New literacies: A dual-level theory of the changing nature of literacy, instruction, and assessment. *Journal of Education*, *197*(2), 1–18.

Lewis, G. K. (2004). *The growth of the modern West Indies*. Ian Randle Publishers.

Lin, A. M. (2019). Theories of trans/languaging and trans-semiotizing: Implications for content-based education classrooms. *International Journal of Bilingual Education and Bilingualism, 22*(1), 5–16.

Lincoln, C. E., & Mamiya, L. (1990). *The Black church in the African American experience*. Duke University Press.

Lincoln, Y., & Guba, E. G. (1985). *Naturalistic inquiry*. Sage.

Lippi-Green, R. (1997). *English with an accent*. Routledge.

Lituchy, T. R., & Michaud, J. (2016). A cultural perspective of Africa. In T. R. Lituchy, B. L. Galperin, & B. J. Punnett, *LEAD: Leadership effectiveness in Africa and the African diaspora* (pp. 19–31). Palgrave Macmillan.

Lizárraga, J. R., & Gutiérrez, K. D. (2018). Centering Nepantla literacies from the borderlands: Leveraging "in-betweenness" toward learning in the everyday. *Theory Into Practice, 57*(1), 38–47. https://doi.org/10.1080/00405841.2017.1392164

Lorde, A. (2003). The master's tools will never dismantle the master's house. In R. Lewis & S. Mills (Eds.), *Feminist postcolonial theory: A reader* (pp. 25–27). Routledge.

Louis, D., Thompson, K. V., Smith, P., Williams, H. M. A., & Watson, J. (2017). Afro-Caribbean immigrant faculty experiences in the American academy: Voices of an invisible Black population. *The Urban Review, 49*(4), 1–24. https://doi.org/10.1007/s11256-017-0414-0

LRA. (2016, November 29). *The role of literacy research in racism and racial violence. Statement endorsed by the Literacy Research Association*. https://literacyresearchassociation.org/wp-content/uploads/2022/05/LRA-role-of-literacy-research-in-racism-and-racial-violencejanuary2017final.pdf

Luczak, E. B., Dayal, S., & Pochmara, A. (2019). *New cosmopolitanisms, race, and ethnicity: Cultural perspectives*. De Gruyter.

Luke, A. (2018). *Critical literacy, schooling, and social justice: The selected works of Allan Luke*. Routledge.

MacSwan, J. (2017). A multilingual perspective on translanguaging. *American Educational Research Journal, 54*(1), 167–201.

Madowo, L., & Attiah, K. (2018, February 16). Opinion | 'Black Panther': Why the relationship between Africans and Black Americans is so messed up. *The Washington Post*. www.washingtonpost.com/news/global-opinions/wp/2018/02/16/black-panther-why-the-relationship-between-africans-and-african-americans-is-so-messed-up/

Mahboob, A., & Szenes, E. (2010). Construing meaning in world Englishes. In A. Kirkpatrick (Ed.), *The Routledge handbook of world Englishes* (pp. 580–598). Routledge.

Mahmud, T. (1999). Postcolonial imaginaries: Alternative development or alternatives to development. *Transnational & Contemporary Problems, 9*, 25–34.

Malcolm, Z. T., & Mendoza, P. (2014). Afro-Caribbean international students' ethnic identity development: Fluidity, intersectionality, agency, and performativity. *Journal of College Student Development, 55*(6), 595–614. https://doi.org/10.1353/csd.2014.0053

Maldonado-Torres, N. (2005). Frantz Fanon and C.L.R. James on intellectualism and enlightened rationality. *Caribbean Studies, 33*(2), 149–194.

Marshall, P. (1983). *Praisesong for the widow*. Plume.
Martin, D. (2012, August 8). Roy S. Bryce-Laporte, who led Black studies at Yale, dies at 78. *The New York Times*. www.nytimes.com/2012/08/09/nyregion/roy-bryce-laporte-who-led-black-studies-program-at-yale-dies-at-78.html
Martin, T. G., Martin, A. J., & Evans, P. (2017). Student engagement in the Caribbean region: Exploring its role in the motivation and achievement of Jamaican middle school students. *School Psychology International*, *38*(2), 184–200. https://doi.org/10.1177/0143034316683765
Martínez, R. A. (2010). "Spanglish" as literacy tool: Toward an understanding of the potential role of Spanish–English code-switching in the development of academic literacy. *Research in the Teaching of English*, *45*(2), 124–149.
Martin-Kerr, K. G. (2019). Fostering critical colonial consciousness through queer pedagogy. In S. Blackman, D. Conrad, & L. Brown (Eds.), *Achieving inclusive education in the Caribbean and beyond* (pp. 193–203). Springer.
Martinot, S. (2003). *The rule of racialization: Class, identity, governance*. Temple University Press.
Matsinhe, D. M. (2007). Quest for methodological alternatives. *Current Sociology*, *55*(6), 836–856. https://doi.org/10.1177/0011392107081988
Mattix, B. (2018, August 23). Is the proper term 'illegal aliens' or 'undocumented immigrants'? ABC 30 News. https://abcstlouis.com/news/nation-world/is-the-proper-term-illegal-aliens-or-undocumented-immigrants#
Maxwell, J. A. (2013). *Qualitative research design: An interactive approach*. Sage.
McAuliffe, M., & Khandria, B. (2020). *World Migration Report 2020*. IOM UN Migration. https://publications.iom.int/system/files/pdf/wmr_2020.pdf
McClintock, P. (2018, April 7). Box office: 'Black Panther' sails past 'Titanic' to become no. 3 title of all time in U.S. Billboard. www.billboard.com/music/music-news/box-office-black-panther-sails-past-titanic-to-become-no-3-title-of-all-time-8297508/
McGill, L. D. (2005). *Constructing Black selves: Caribbean American narratives and the second generation*. New York University Press.
McInnis, J. C. (2019). A corporate plantation reading public: Labor, literacy, and diaspora in the global Black south. *American Literature*, *91*(3), 523–555.
McLean, C. A. (2010). A space called home: An immigrant adolescent's digital literacy practices. *Journal of Adolescent & Adult Literacy*, *54*(1), 13–22. https://doi.org/10.1598/jaal.54.1.2
 (2020). Racialized tensions in the multimodal literacies of Black immigrant youth. *Teachers College Record*, *122*(13), 1–22.
McNerney, M. (1978). The Trinidadian Creole speaker: Performance, awareness, and attitude. *TESL Talk*, *1*(2), 132–140.
Merriam, S. B. (2009). *Qualitative research: A guide to design and implementation*. John Wiley and Sons.
Merriam Webster. (2021, October 30). What is the 'metaverse'? www.merriam-webster.com/wordplay/meaning-of-metaverse
Mesthrie, R. (2019). African-Indian-American South and Caribbean worlds: Connecting with John R. Rickford's language contact research. In R. Blake & I. Buchstaller (Eds.), *The Routledge companion to the work of John R. Rickford* (pp. 26–34). Routledge.

Mfum-Mensah, O. (2005). The impact of colonial and postcolonial Ghanaian language policies on vernacular use in schools in two northern Ghanaian communities. *Comparative Education, 41*(1), 71–85.

Michel, A. (2017). The contribution of PISA to the convergence of education policies in Europe. *European Journal of Education, 52*(2), 206–216.

Migration Policy Institute. (2013). *Major US immigration laws, 1790–present: Timeline*. Migration Policy Institute.

Millar, P., & Warrican, J. (2015). Constructing a third space: Positioning students' out-of-school literacies in the classroom. In P. Smith & A. Kumi-Yeboah (Eds.), *Handbook of research on cross-cultural approaches to language and literacy development* (pp. 87–117). IGI Global.

Miller, E. (1989). Caribbean primary education: An assessment. *Caribbean Journal of Education, 16*(3), 136–171.

Mills, C. W. (1997). *The racial contract*. Cornell University Press.

Milner, R. H. (2012). Beyond a test score: Explaining opportunity gaps in educational practice. *Journal of Black Studies, 43*(6), 693–718. https://doi.org/10.1177/0021934712442539

Milson-Whyte, V. (2014). Working English through code-meshing: Implications for denigrated language varieties and their users. In B. Horner & K. Kopelson (Eds.), *Reworking English in rhetoric and composition: Global interrogations, local interventions* (pp. 103–115). Southern Illinois University Press.

(2018). Caribbean Creole-speaking cultures, language, and identity. In J. Liontas & M. DelliCarpini (Eds.), *The TESOL encyclopedia of English language teaching* (pp. 1–7). John Wiley & Sons.

Milu, E. (2021). Diversity of raciolinguistic experiences in the writing classroom: An argument for a transnational Black language pedagogy. *College English, 83*(6), 415–441.

Mislevy, R., & Durán, R. P. (2014). A sociocognitive perspective on assessing EL students in the age of Common Core and Next Generation Science Standards. *TESOL Quarterly, 48*(3), 560–585. https://doi.org/10.1002/tesq.177

Mitchell, S. A. (2007). Acquiring basic reading skills: An exploration of phonetic awareness in Jamaican primary schools. *Caribbean Journal of Education, 29*(2), 327–358.

Model, S. (1991). Caribbean immigrants: A Black success story? *International Migration Review, 25*, 248–276.

(1995). West Indian prosperity: Fact or fiction? *Social Problems, 42*, 535–553.

Mogaka, E. N. (2013). *Characteristics of high-achieving Kenyan immigrant students* [Unpublished doctoral dissertation]. Capella University.

Moje, E., McIntosh Ciechanowski, K., Kramer, K., Ellis, L., Carrillo, R., & Collazo, T. (2004). Working toward Third Space in content area literacy: An examination of everyday funds of knowledge and discourse. *Reading Research Quarterly, 39*(1): 38–70.

Moll, L. C., Amanti, C., Neff, D., & Gonzalez, N. E. (2005). Funds of knowledge for teaching: Using a qualitative approach to connect homes and classrooms. In N. Gonzalez, L.C. Moll, & C. Amanti (Eds.), *Funds of knowledge: Theorizing practices in households, communities, and classrooms* (pp. 71–88). Routledge.

Morgan-Trostle, J., & Zheng, K. (2016). The state of Black immigrants Part I: A statistical portrait of Black immigrants in the United States. *Black Alliance for Just*

Immigration. https://baji.org/wp-content/uploads/2020/03/sobi-fullreport-jan22.pdf

Morrell, E. (2002). Toward a critical pedagogy of popular culture: Literacy development among urban youth. *Journal of Adolescent & Adult Literacy, 46*(1), 72–77.

Morrison, S., & Bryan, J. (2014). Addressing the challenges and needs of English-speaking Caribbean immigrant students: Guidelines for school counselors. *International Journal for the Advancement of Counselling, 36*(4), 440–449. https://doi.org/10.1007/s10447-014-9218-z

Morrison, T. (2020). *Toni Morrison: The pieces I am* [Audio podcast]. PBS. www.pbs.org/wnet/americanmasters/toni-morrison-the-pieces-i-am-documentary/16971/

Moss, B., & Lapp, D. (2010). *Teaching new literacies in grades 4–6: Resources for 21st-century classrooms*. Guilford Press.

Mufwene, S. S. (2001). *The ecology of language evolution*. Cambridge University Press.

(2004). Language birth and death. *Annual Review of Anthropology, 33*, 201–222.

Muhammad, G. (2020). *Cultivating genius: An equity framework for culturally and historically responsive literacy*. Scholastic Incorporated.

Murdoch, H. A. (2009). A legacy of trauma: Caribbean slavery, race, class, and contemporary identity in "Abeng." *Research in African Literatures, 40*(4), 65–88.

Mustonen, S. (2021). 'I'll always have black hair': Challenging raciolinguistic ideologies in Finnish schools. *Nordic Journal of Studies in Educational Policy, 7*(3), 159–168. https://doi.org/10.1080/20020317.2021.2000093

Mwangi, C. A. G., & English, S. (2017). Being Black (and) immigrant students: When race, ethnicity, and nativity collide. *International Journal of Multicultural Education, 19*(2), 100–130.

Myhill, J., & Ash, S. (1986). Linguistic correlates of inter-ethnic contact. In D. Sankoff (Ed.), *Diversity and diachrony* (pp. 33–44). John Benjamins.

Nalubega-Booker, K. (In press). *How raciolinguistic ideologies shape literacy assessment among African immigrants: A reflection on WIDA access* [Doctoral dissertation, University of Illinois, Urbana–Champaign].

Nalubega-Booker, K., & Willis, A. (2020). Applying critical race theory as a tool for examining the literacies of Black immigrant youth. *Teachers College Record, 122*(13), 1–24. https://doi.org/10.1177/016146812012201309

NAMI. (2022, June). Mental health by the numbers. www.nami.org/mhstats

Nderu, E. N. (2005). *Parental involvement in education: A qualitative study of Somali immigrants in the Twin Cities area* (Publication No. 3160164) [Doctoral dissertation, University of Minnesota–Twin Cities]. ProQuest Dissertations & Theses Global.

Nero, S. (2000). The changing faces of English: A Caribbean perspective. *TESOL Quarterly, 34*(3), 483–510. https://doi.org/10.2307/3587740

(2001). *Englishes in contact: Anglophone Caribbean students in an urban college*. Hampton Press.

(2006). Language, identity, and education of Caribbean English speakers. *World Englishes, 25*(3/4), 501–511. https://doi.org/10.1111/j.1467-971X.2006.00470.x

(2014). Classroom encounters with Caribbean Creole English: Language, identities, pedagogy. In A. Mahboob & L. Barratt (Eds.), *Englishes in multilingual contexts* (pp. 33–46). Springer.

New London Group. (1996). A pedagogy of multiliteracies: Designing social futures. *Harvard Educational Review*, *66*(1), 60–92.

Ngo, B. (2008). Beyond "culture clash" understandings of immigrant experiences. *Theory Into Practice*, *47*(1), 4–11.

Nicolescu, B. (1999, April). *The transdisciplinary evolution of learning* [Conference presentation]. American Educational Research Association, Montreal, Quebec.

(2010). Methodology of transdisciplinarity: Levels of reality, logic of the included middle and complexity. *Transdisciplinary Journal of Engineering & Science*, *1*(1), 19–38.

Nwanosike, O. F., & Onyije, L. E. (2011). Colonialism and education. *Mediterranean Journal of Social Sciences*, *2*(4), 41–47.

Obeng, C., & Obeng, S. (2006). African immigrant families' views on English as a Second Language (ESL) classes held for newly arrived immigrant children in the United States elementary and middle schools: A study in ethnography. In M. Firmin & P. Brewer (Eds.), *Ethnographic and qualitative research in education* (Vol. 2, pp. 105–116). Cambridge Scholars Publishing.

Obinna, D. N. (2016). A study of academic performance by immigrant generation with an emphasis on the Black immigrant experience. *International Journal of Sociology and Social Policy*, *36*(1/2), 18–35. https://doi.org/10.1108/IJSSP-02-2015-0026

Ogbu, J. U. (1987). Variability in minority school performance: A problem in search of an explanation. *Anthropology and Education Quarterly*, *18*(4), 312–334.

(2014). Variability in minority responses to schooling: Nonimmigrants vs. immigrants. In G. Spindler & L. Spindler (Eds.), *Interpretive ethnography of education at home and abroad* (pp. 269–294). Psychology Press.

Ogbu, J. U., & Simons, H. D. (1998). Voluntary and involuntary minorities. A cultural ecological theory of school performance with some implications for education. *Anthropology and Education Quarterly*, *29*(2), 155–188.

Okonofua, B. A. (2013). "I am blacker than you": Theorizing conflict between African immigrants and African Americans in the United States. *SAGE Open*, *3*(3). https://doi.org/10.1177/2158244013499162

Olatunji. (2015). *Ola* [Video]. YouTube. www.youtube.com/watch?v=PAIW2FHgF5g

Omogun, L., & Skerrett, A. (2021). From Haiti to Detroit through Black immigrant languages and literacies. *Journal of Literacy Research*, *53*(3), 406–429. https://doi.org/10.1177/1086296X211031279

Onwuegbuzie, A. J., & Frels, R. K. (2013). Introduction: Toward a new research philosophy for addressing social justice issues: Critical dialectical pluralism 1.0. *International Journal of Multiple Research Approaches*, *7*(1), 9–26. https://doi.org/10.5172/mra.2013.7.1.9

Onyewuenyi, A. (2018). *The unexplored voices of the "New African Diaspora": An examination of the impact of race, ethnicity, and teacher discrimination on academic performance for Nigerian and Black American adolescents* [Doctoral dissertation, University of Washington]. ProQuest Dissertations & Theses Global.

Orellana, M. F. (2015). *Immigrant children in transcultural spaces: Language, learning, and love*. Routledge.

Orellana, M. F., & García, O. (2014). Language brokering and translanguaging in school. *Language Arts*, *91*(5), 386–392.

Orelus, P. W. (2012). Facing with courage racial and linguistic discrimination: The narrative of an ELL Caribbean immigrant living in the U.S. diaspora. *Diaspora, Indigenous, and Minority Education, 6*(1), 19–33. https://doi.org/10.1080/15595692.2011.633130

Otheguy, R., García, O., & Reid, W. (2015). Clarifying translanguaging and deconstructing named languages: A perspective from linguistics. *Applied Linguistics Review, 6*(3), 281–307. https://doi.org/10.1515/applirev-2015-0014

Oxford Reference. (n.d.). West Indies. www.oxfordreference.com/display/10.1093/oi/authority.20110803121907924

Page, H. E., & Thomas, B. (1994). White public space and the construction of white privilege in US health care: Fresh concepts and a new model of analysis. *Medical Anthropological Quarterly, 8*(1), 109–116.

Pallotta, F. (2022, November 13). 'Black Panther: Wakanda Forever' notches record opening for November. CNN. www.cnn.com/2022/11/13/media/black-panther-wankanda-forever-box-office/index.html

Palmer, G. (1996). *Toward a theory of cultural linguistics*. State University of Austin Press.

Paraskeva, J. M. (2011). *Conflicts in curriculum theory: Challenging hegemonic epistemologies*. Palgrave Macmillan.

Paris, D., & Alim, H. S. (2014). What are we seeking to sustain through culturally sustaining pedagogy? A loving critique forward. *Harvard Educational Review, 84*(1), 85–100. https://doi.org/10.17763/haer.84.1.982l873k2ht16m77

Paris, S. G. (2005). Reinterpreting the development of reading skills. *Reading Research Quarterly, 40*(2), 184–202.

Park, J. S.-Y. (2022). Raciolinguistic construction of Southeast Asia in Korean cartographies of language. In J. W. Lee (Ed.), *The sociolinguistics of global Asians* (pp. 11–23). Routledge.

Park, J. Y. (2017). Responding to marginalization: Language practices of African-Born Muslim refugee youths in an American urban high school. *SAGE Open, 7*(1). https://doi.org/10.1177/2158244016684912

Patel, S. G., Barrera, A. Z., Strambler, M. J., Muñoz, R. F., & Macciomei, E. (2016). The achievement gap among newcomer immigrant adolescents: Life stressors hinder Latina/o academic success. *Journal of Latinos and Education, 15*(2), 121–133. https://doi.org/10.1080/15348431.2015.1099529

Pavlenko, A. (2022). Multilingualism and historical amnesia: An introduction. In A. Pavlenko (Ed.), *Multilingualism and history* (pp. 1–49). Cambridge University Press.

Peercy, M. M. (2011). Preparing English language learners for the mainstream: Academic language and literacy practices in two junior high school ESL classrooms. *Reading & Writing Quarterly, 27*(4), 324–362. https://doi.org/10.1080/10573569.2011.596105

Pence, A. R., & Marfo, K. (2008). Early childhood development in Africa: Interrogating constraints of prevailing knowledge bases. *International Journal of Psychology, 43*(2), 78–87.

Pennycook, A. (2001). *Critical applied linguistics: A critical introduction*. Lawrence Erlbaum.

(2021). Entanglements of English. In R. Rudby & R. Tupas (Eds.), *Bloomsbury World Englishes: Vol. 2. Ideologies* (pp. 9–26). Bloomsbury.

Phelps, J. T. (2000). Communion ecclesiology and Black liberation theology. *Theological Studies, 61,* 672–699.

Pierre, J. (2004). Black immigrants in the United States and the "cultural narratives" of ethnicity. *Identities: Global Studies in Culture and Power, 11*(2), 141–170.

Pihama, L., & Lee-Morgan, J. (2019). Colonization, education, and Indigenous peoples. In E. A. McKinley & L. T. Smith (Eds.), *Handbook of Indigenous education* (pp. 19–27). Springer.

Pinder, P., Prime, G., & Wilson, J. (2014). An exploratory quantitative study comparing and correlating parental factors with environmental science achievement for Black American and Black Caribbean students in a Mid-Atlantic state. *The Journal of Negro Education, 83*(1), 49–60. https://doi.org/10.7709/jnegroeducation.83.1.0049

Poddar, P., & Johnson, D. (2005). *A historical companion to postcolonial thought in English.* Columbia University Press.

Portes, A. (2019). Bifurcated immigration and the end of compassion. *Ethnic and Racial Studies, 43*(1), 2–17. https://doi.org/10.1080/01419870.2019.1667515

Poza, L. (2017). Translanguaging: Definitions, implications, and further needs in burgeoning inquiry. *Berkeley Review of Education, 6*(2), 101–128.

Pratt-Johnson, Y. (1993). Curriculum for Jamaican Creole-speaking students in New York City. *World Englishes, 12*(2), 257–264. https://doi.org/10.1111/j.1467-971x.1993.tb00026.x

Prou, M. (2009). Attempts at reforming Haiti's education system: The challenges of mending the tapestry, 1979–2004. *Journal of Haitian Studies, 15*(1/2), 29–69.

Raff, J. (2017, December 30). The 'double punishment' for Black undocumented immigrants. *The Atlantic.* www.theatlantic.com/politics/archive/2017/12/the-double-punishment-for-black-immigrants/549425/r

RAICES. (2020). Black immigrant lives are under attack. www.raicestexas.org/2020/07/22/black-immigrant-lives-are-under-attack/

Ramcharan-Crowley, P. (1961). Creole culture: Outcast in West Indian schools. *The School Review, 69*(4), 429–436. www.jstor.org/stable/1083804

Ramjattan, V. A. (2019). Raciolinguistics and the aesthetic labourer. *Journal of Industrial Relations, 61*(5), 726–738.

(2023). Engineered accents: International teaching assistants and their microaggression learning in engineering departments. *Teaching in Higher Education, 28*(6), 1119–1134.

Rampton, B. (1985). A critique of some educational attitudes to the English of British Asian schoolchildren, and their implications. In C. Brumfit, R. Ellis, & J. Levine (Eds.), *English as a second language in the United Kingdom: Linguistic and educational contexts* (pp. 187–198). Pergamon Press.

(1997). Second language research in late modernity: A response to Firth and Wagner. *The Modern Language Journal, 81*(3), 329–333.

Razfar, A. (2012). Narrating beliefs: A language ideologies approach to teacher beliefs. *Anthropology and Education Quarterly, 43,* 61–81.

Redding, J., & Brownsworth, V. (1997). *Film fatales: Independent women directors.* Seal Press.

Reece, R. (2012). *King of the Hill's Souphanousiphones, the new model minority, and the subversive model minority* [Master's thesis, University of Mississippi]. eGrove Electronic Theses and Dissertations. https://egrove.olemiss.edu/etd/241

Reid, I. (1939). *The Negro immigrant*. AMS Press.
Reyes, A. (2020). Coloniality of mixed race and mixed language. In H. S. Alim, A. Reyes, & P. V. Kroskrity (Eds.), *The Oxford handbook of language and race* (pp. 186–206). Oxford University Press.
Ricento, T. (2000). Historical and theoretical perspectives in language policy and planning. *Journal of Sociolinguistics, 4*(2), 196–213.
Richardson, J., & Stroud, C. (2021). Multilingualism as racialization. *Multilingual Margins: A Journal of Multilingualism from the Periphery, 8*(1), 2–11.
Rickford, J. R. (1985). Ethnicity as a sociolinguistic variable. *American Speech, 60*, 90–125.
(2006). Linguistics, education, and the Ebonics firestorm. In S. J. Nero (Ed.), *Dialects, Englishes, Creoles, and education* (pp. 71–92). Routledge.
Rickford, J. R., & McNair-Knox, F. (1994). Addressee-and topic-influenced style shift: A quantitative sociolinguistic study. In D. Biber & E. Finegan (Eds.), *Sociolinguistic perspectives on register* (pp. 235–276). Oxford University Press.
Rickford, J. R., & Rickford, A. E. (1995). Dialect readers revisited. *Linguistics and Education, 7*(2), 107–128. https://doi.org/10.1016/0898-5898(95)90003-9
(2015). Cut-eye and suck-teeth: African words and gestures in new world guise. In J. L. Dillard (Ed.), *Perspectives on American English* [Originally published 1980], Vol. *29* (pp. 347–366). De Gruyter.
Ritchie, W. C., & Bhatia, T. K. (2010). Psycholinguistics. In B. Spolsky & F. M. Hult (Eds.), *The handbook of educational linguistics* (2nd ed.) (pp. 38–52). Wiley-Blackwell.
Robertshaw, M. (2018). Occupying Creole: The crisis of language under the US occupation of Haiti. *Journal of Haitian Studies, 24*(1), 4–24. https://doi.org/10.1353/jhs.2018.0000
Robinson, C. (2000). *Black Marxism: The making of the Black radical tradition* (2nd ed.). University of North Carolina Press.
Rodriguez, S. H. (2015). *Watering seeds: The socialization of African American adolescent male masculinity* [Unpublished doctoral dissertation]. University of Illinois, Urbana–Champaign.
Rogoff, B. (2003). Developing understanding of the idea of communities of learners. *Mind, Culture and Activity, 1*, 209–229.
Rong, X. L., & Brown, F. (2007). Educational attainment of immigrant and non-immigrant young Blacks. In S. J. Paik & H. J. Walberg (Eds.), *Narrowing the achievement gap: Strategies for educating Latino, Black, and Asian students* (pp. 91–107). Springer.
Rong, X. L., & Fitchett, P. (2008). Socialization and identity transformation of Black immigrant youth in the United States. *Theory Into Practice, 47*, 35–42. https://doi.org/10.1080/00405840701764714
Rosa, J. D. (2016). Standardization, racialization, languagelessness: Raciolinguistic ideologies across communicative contexts. *Journal of Linguistic Anthropology, 26*, 162–183, https://doi.org/10.1111/jola.12116
Rosa, J. D., & Flores, N. (2017). Unsettling race and language: Toward a raciolinguistic perspective. *Language in Society, 46*(5), 621–647. https://doi.org/10.1017/s0047404517000562
Ross, T. (1990). The rhetorical tapestry of race: White innocence and Black abstraction. *William & Mary Law Review, 32*(1). https://scholarship.law.wm.edu/wmlr/vol32/iss1/2

Rubinstein-Ávila, E. (2007). From the Dominican Republic to Drew High: What counts as literacy for Yanira Lara? *Reading Research Quarterly*, *42*(4), 568–589. https://doi.org/10.1598/rrq.42.4.6

Sabourin, L., & Stowe, L. A. (2010). Neurobiology of language learning. In B. Spolsky & F. M. Hult (Eds.), *The handbook of educational linguistics* (2nd ed.) (pp. 27–37). Wiley-Blackwell.

Said, E. W. (1978). *Orientalism*. Pantheon Books.

Santos, B. S. de (2007). Beyond abyssal thinking: From global lines to ecologies of knowledges. *Review (Fernand Braudel Center)*, *30*(1), 45–89.

Saunders, J. (2022, September 7). *A USF professor, student and organization file a lawsuit against Florida race-related teaching*. WUSF. https://wusfnews.wusf.usf.edu/politics-issues/2022-09-07/usf-professor-student-organization-lawsuit-florida-race-based-teaching

Savignon, S. J. (2018). Communicative competence. In J. I. Liontas (Ed.), *The TESOL encyclopedia of English language teaching* (pp. 1–7). John Wiley & Sons.

Schutz, A. (1967). *The phenomenology of the social world*. Northwestern University Press.

Schwartz, S. J., Unger, J. B., Zamboanga, B. L., & Szapocznik, J. (2010). Rethinking the concept of acculturation: Implications for theory and research. *American Psychologist*, *65*(4), 237–251. https://doi.org/10.1037/a0019330

Sealey-Ruiz, Y. (2021). The critical literacy of race: Toward racial literacy in urban teacher education. In H. R. Milner IV & K. Lomotey (Eds.), *Handbook of urban education* (pp. 281–295). Routledge.

Sedlacek, Q. C., Hudley, A. H. C., & Mallinson, C. (2023). Surveying the landscape of college teaching about African American Language. *Linguistics and Education*, *77*. https://doi.org/10.1016/j.linged.2023.101189

Seidman, I. (2012). *Interviewing as qualitative research: A guide for researchers in education and the social sciences*. Teachers College Press.

Sewell, S. (1978). *British decolonization in the Caribbean: The West Indies Federation* [Unpublished master's thesis]. Oklahoma State University.

Sexton, J. (2018). Unbearable Blackness. In *Black men, Black feminism: Lucifer's nocturn* (pp. 75–105). Palgrave Macmillan.

Sharifian, F. (2013). Globalisation and developing metacultural competence in learning English as an international language. *Multilingual Education*, *3*(7), 1–11. https://doi.org/10.1186/2191-5059-3-7

Sheares, A. (2022). Who should be provided with pathways toward citizenship? White and Black attitudes toward undocumented immigrants. *Sociology of Race and Ethnicity*, *9*(1). https://doi.org/10.1177/23326492221125116

Shizha, E. (2013). Reclaiming our Indigenous voices: The problem with postcolonial sub-Saharan African school curriculum. *Journal of Indigenous Social Development*, *2*(1), 1–18.

Shizha, E., Abdi, A. A., Wilson-Forsberg, S., & Masakure, O. (2020). African immigrant students and postsecondary education in Canada: High school teachers and school career counsellors as gatekeepers. *Canadian Ethnic Studies*, *52*(3), 67–86.

Shockley, E. T. (2021). Expanding the narrative of the Black-White gap in education research: Black English learners as a counterexample. *The Journal of Negro Education*, *90*(1), 7–25.

Shohamy, E. (2006). *Language policy: Hidden agendas and new approaches.* Routledge.

Siegel, J. (1997). Formal vs. non-formal vernacular education: The education reform in Papua New Guinea. *Journal of Multilingual and Multicultural Development, 18*(3), 206–222. https://doi.org/10.1080/01434639708666315

(2012). Two types of functional transfer in language contact. *Journal of Language Contact, 5*, 187–215.

Simmons, A. B. (1999). Economic integration and designer immigrants: Canadian policy in the 1990s. In M. Castro (Ed.), *Free markets, open societies, closed borders? Trends in international migration and immigration policy in the Americas* (pp. 53–69). University of Miami North-South Center Press.

Simmons-McDonald, H. (2004). Trends in teaching Standard English varieties to Creole and vernacular speakers. *Annual Review of Applied Linguistics, 24*, 187–208.

(2006). Attitudes of teachers to St. Lucian language varieties. *Caribbean Journal of Education, 28*(1), 51–84.

Sireci, S. G., & Faulkner-Bond, M. (2015). Promoting validity in the assessment of English learners. *Review of Research in Education, 39*(1), 215–252. https://doi.org/10.3102/0091732X14557003

Skerrett, A. (2006). Looking inward: The impact of race, ethnicity, gender, and social class background on teaching sociocultural theory in education. *Studying Teacher Education, 2*(2), 183–200.

(2012). Languages and literacies in translocation. *Journal of Literacy Research, 44*(4), 364–395. https://doi.org/10.1177/1086296x12459511

(2015). *Teaching transnational youth: Literacy and education in a changing world.* Teachers College Press.

(2020). Investing in the learning of transnational youth: Considerations for English/literacy educators and researchers. *Research in the Teaching of English, 54*(3), 287–290.

Skerrett, A., & Omogun, L. (2020). When racial, transnational, and immigrant identities, literacies, and languages meet: Black youth of Caribbean origin speak. *Teachers College Record, 122*(13), 1–24.

Skutnabb-Kangas, T. (1988). Multilingualism and the education of minority children. In T. Skutnabb-Kangas & J. Cummins (Eds.), *Minority education: From shame to struggle* (pp. 9–44). Multilingual Matters.

(2013). Today's indigenous education is a crime against humanity: Mother-tongue-based multilingual education as an alternative? *TESOL in Context, 23*(1/2), 82–125.

Smalls, K. A. (2018). Fighting words: Antiblackness and discursive violence in an American high school. *Journal of Linguistic Anthropology, 28*(3), 356–383.

(2020). Race, signs, and the body: Towards a theory of racial semiotics. In H. S. Alim, A. Reyes, & P. V. Kroskrity (Eds.), *The Oxford handbook of langue and race* (pp. 232–260). Oxford University Press.

Smith, A. (2020, February 10). *Meghan Markle and British racism: What her saga says to Black Britons.* NBC News. www.nbcnews.com/news/world/meghan-markle-british-racism-what-her-saga-says-black-britons-n1132181

Smith, C. W. (2013). Ethnicity and the role of group consciousness: A comparison between African Americans and Black immigrants. *Politics, Groups, and Identities, 1*(2), 199–220.

Smith, M. G. (1965). *The plural society in the British West Indies*. University of California Press.

Smith, P. (1978). *Christopher Columbus: Four voyages to the New World: Letters and selected documents*. Corinth Books.

(2013a). Accomplishing the goals of multicultural education: A transdisciplinary perspective. *Curriculum and Teaching Dialogue, 15*(1/2), 27–40.

(2013b). *Crossing cultural boundaries: Explorations in multilingual teaching and learning* (Publication No. 1432179476) [Doctoral dissertation, University of South Florida]. ProQuest Dissertations & Theses Global.

(2016). A distinctly American opportunity: Exploring non-standardized English(es) in literacy policy and practice. *Policy Insights from the Behavioral and Brain Sciences, 3*(2), 194–202. https://doi.org/10.1177/2372732216644451

(2017). Nonstandardized Englishes in mainstream literacy practice. *Oxford Research Encyclopedia of Education*. https://doi.org/10.1093/acrefore/9780190264093.013.18

(2018). Learning to know, be, do, and live together with in the cross-cultural experiences of immigrant teacher educators. *Teaching and Teacher Education, 69*, 263–274. https://doi.org/10.1016/j.tate.2017.10.018

(2019a). (Re)positioning in the Englishes and (English) literacies of a Black immigrant youth: Towards a *transraciolinguistic* approach. *Theory Into Practice, 58*(3), 292–303. https://doi.org/10.1080/00405841.2019.1599227

(2019b). [Review of the book *Caribbean discourse in inclusive education: Historical and contemporary issues*, by S. Blackman & D. Conrad (Eds.)]. *Teachers College Record*. https://doi.org/10.13140/RG.2.2.36662.75849

(2020a). "How does a Black person speak English?" Beyond American language norms. *American Educational Research Journal, 57*(1), 106–147.

(2020b). Silencing invisibility: Toward a framework for Black immigrant literacies. *Teachers College Record, 122*(13), 1–42. https://doi.org/10.1177/016146812012201301

(2020c). The case for translanguaging in Black immigrant literacies. *Literacy Research: Theory, Method, and Practice, 69*(1), 192–210.

(2021). Beyond anti-Blackness in bilingual education: Looking through the lens of the Black immigrant subject. *American Educational Research Association Bilingual Education Research Special Interest Group Newsletter*, Spring Edition, 4–5.

(2022a). Black immigrants in the United States: Transraciolinguistic justice for imagined futures in a global metaverse. *Annual Review of Applied Linguistics, 42*, 109–118. https://doi.org/10.1017/S0267190522000046

(2022b). A transraciolinguistic approach for literacy classrooms. *The Reading Teacher, 75*(5), 545–554.

(2022c, December). *Racialized entanglements and the promise of liberatory Caribbean imaginaries: An interactive panel presented in response to the Oscar S. Causey Address by Dr. Arlette I. Willis* [Panel presentation]. Literacy Research Association Annual Conference, Phoenix, AZ, United States.

(2022d, December). *Why multiliteracies? Black immigrant literacies as a vehicle for raciosemiotic architecture* [Conference session]. Literacy Research Association Annual Conference, Phoenix, AZ, United States.

(2022e). *(Dis)entanglements of racialized Englishes and peoples across "Black" and "white" worlds* [Video]. YouTube. www.youtube.com/watch?v=WdcLqrWNMm4

(2023a). *Black immigrant literacies: Intersections of race, language, and culture in the classroom*. Teachers College Press.

(2023b, March). *Transraciolinguistics for (re)imagining entanglements of racialized languages and peoples* [Conference presentation]. American Association for Applied Linguistics, Portland, OR, United States.

(2023c, November 30). Beyond dichotomies in the quest for raciosemiotic architecture: Black immigrants in the United States. *Teachers College Press*. www.tcpress.com/blog/dichotomies-quest-raciosemiotic-architecture-black-immigrants-united-states/

(2024). *Leveraging a language of forgiveness for flourishing* [Conference presentation]. University of the Southern Caribbean, Trinidad. https://usc.edu.tt/2024/03/20/exploring-the-nexus-of-spirituality-forgiveness-and-health-highlights-from-the-usc-research-conference-2024/

(In press). Contested inheritances of racialized entanglements: Cultivating liberatory Caribbean imaginaries. In T. Esnard (Ed.), *Social justice and higher education in the Caribbean*. Routledge.

Smith, P., Berends, J., Ibrahim, A., McMillion, G., Watson, V., Willis, A., & Zaidi, R. (2021, April). *Critical literacy for racial justice: Equity through intersectionality* [Presentation]. American Educational Research Association Annual Meeting. Virtual.

Smith, P., Cheema, J., Kumi-Yeboah, A., Warrican, S. J., & Alleyne, M. L. (2018a). Language-based differences in the literacy performance of bidialectal youth. *Teachers College Record, 120*(1), 1–36. https://doi.org/10.1177/016146811812000105

Smith, P., Cremin, T., Kucirkova, N., & Collier, D. R. (2023). *Literacy for social justice: Charting equitable global and local practices* [Special Issue]. United Kingdom Literacy Association (UKLA).

Smith, P., & Kumi-Yeboah, A. (2015). Consolidating commonalities in language and literacy to inform policy: Bridging research cultures in the multilingual English-speaking Caribbean. In P. Smith & A. Kumi-Yeboah (Eds.), *Consolidating commonalities in language and literacy to inform policy: Bridging research cultures in the multilingual English-speaking Caribbean*. IGI Global.

Smith, P., Kumi-Yeboah, A., Chang, R., Lee, J., & Frazier, P. (2019). Rethinking "(under) performance" for Black English speakers: Beyond achievement to opportunity. *Journal of Black Studies, 50*(6), 528–554. https://doi.org/10.1177/0021934719851870

Smith, P., Lee, J., & Chang, R. (2022). Characterizing competing tensions in Black immigrant literacies: Beyond partial representations of success. *Reading Research Quarterly, 57*(1), 59–90.

Smith, P., & Murillo, L. A. (2012). Researching transfronterizo literacies in Texas border colonias. *International Journal of Bilingual Education and Bilingualism, 15*(6), 635–651.

Smith, P., & Warrican, S. J. (2021). Migrating while multilingual and Black: Beyond the '(bi)dialectal' burden. In E. Bauer, L. Sánchez, Y. Wang, & A. Vaughan (Eds.), *A transdisciplinary lens for bilingual education: Bridging*

translanguaging, sociocultural research, cognitive approaches, and student learning (pp. 102–128). Routledge.
Smith, P., Warrican, S. J., & Alleyne, M. L. (2020). "You hear my funny accent?!": Problematizing assumptions about Afro-Caribbean "teachers turned educators." *International Multilingual Research Journal, 14*(3), 248–269. https://doi.org/10.1080/19313152.2019.1710042
Smith, P., Warrican, S. J., Kumi-Yeboah, A., & Karkar-Esperat, T. (2023). Rethinking race in research on migration: Transnational literacies as a tool. In E. Shizha & E. Mazwaarimba (Eds.), *Immigrant lives: Intersectionality, transnationality, and global perspectives* (pp. 37–57). Oxford University Press.
Smith, P., Warrican, S. J., Kumi-Yeboah, A., & Richards, J. (2018b). Understanding Afro-Caribbean educators' experiences with Englishes across Caribbean and U.S. contexts and classrooms: Recursivity, (re)positionality, bidirectionality. *Teaching and Teacher Education, 69*, 210–222. https://doi.org/10.1016/j.tate.2017.10.009
Smith, P., Warrican, S. J., & Williams, G. (2017). Towards transculturalism in tackling diversity for literacy teacher education. In R. Zaidi & J. Rowsell (Eds.), *Literacy lives in transcultural times* (pp. 191–215). Routledge.
Smitherman, G. (1977). *Talkin and Testifyin: The language of Black America*. Houghton Mifflin.
Soja, E. (1996). *Thirdspace: Journeys to Los Angeles and other real-and-imagined places*. Blackwell.
Solano-Flores, G., Trumbull, E., & Nelson-Barber, S. (2002). Concurrent development of dual language assessments: An alternative to translating tests for linguistic minorities. *International Journal of Testing, 2*(2), 107–129. https://doi.org/10.1207/S15327574IJT0202_2
Solomona, R. P., Portelli, J. P., Daniel, B. J., & Campbell, A. (2005). The discourse of denial: How white teacher candidates construct race, racism and 'white privilege.' *Race Ethnicity and Education, 8*(2), 147–169.
Sowell, T. (1978). Three Black histories. In T. Sowell (Ed.), *Essays and data on American ethnic groups* (pp. 7–64). The Urban Institute.
Spears, A. (1988). Black American English. In J. Cole (ed.), *Anthropology for the nineties* (pp. 96–113). The Free Press.
Steele, C., Dovchin, S., & Oliver, R. (2022). 'Stop measuring Black kids with a white stick': Translanguaging for classroom assessment. *RELC Journal, 53*(2), 400–415. https://doi.org/10.1177/00336882221086307
Steinberg, S. (2005). Immigration, African Americans, and race discourse. *New Politics, 10*(3), 42–54.
Stewart, M. A., Hansen-Thomas, H., Flint, P., & Núñez, M. (2022). Translingual disciplinary literacies: Equitable language environments to support literacy engagement. *Reading Research Quarterly, 57*(1), 181–203. https://doi.org/10.1002/rrq.381
St. Hilaire, A. (2007). National development and the language planning challenge in St. Lucia, West Indies. *Journal of Multilingual and Multicultural Development, 28*(6), 519–536. https://doi.org/10.2167/jmmd531.0
St-Hilaire, A. (2011). *Kwéyòl in postcolonial Saint Lucia: Globalization, language planning, and national development*. John Benjamins.
Stornaiuolo, A., Smith, A., & Phillips, N. C. (2017). Developing a transliteracies framework for a connected world. *Journal of Literacy Research, 49*(1), 68–91.

Street, B. (1995). *Social literacies: Critical approaches to literacy in development, ethnography and education*. Routledge.

Stuesse, A., Staats, C., & Grant-Thomas, A. (2017). As others pluck fruit off the tree of opportunity: Immigration, racial hierarchies, and intergroup relations efforts in the United States. *Du Bois Review*, *14*(1), 245–271. https://doi.org/10.1017/S1742058X16000394

Suárez-Orozco, C. (2017). The diverse immigrant student experience: What does it mean for teaching? *Educational Studies*, *53*(5), 522–534. https://doi.org/10.1080/00131946.2017.1355796

Suárez-Orozco, C., & Suárez-Orozco, M. M. (2009). *Children of immigration* [Originally published 2001]. Harvard University Press.

Sutcliffe, D. (1992). *System in Black language*. Multilingual Matters.

Taira, B. W. (2019). (In)visible literacies of transnational newcomer youth in a secondary English classroom. *Global Education Review*, *6*(2), 74–93.

Tamir, C. (2021, March 25). The growing diversity of Black America. *Pew Research Center*. www.pewresearch.org/social-trends/2021/03/25/the-growing-diversity-of-black-america/

Temple, C. N. (2010). The emergence of Sankofa practice in the United States: A modern history. *Journal of Black Studies*, *41*(1), 127–150.

Thomas, E. E. (2019). *The dark fantastic: Race and the imagination from Harry Potter to the Hunger Games*. New York University Press.

Thomas, O. N., Caldwell, C. H., Faison, N., & Jackson, J. S. (2009). Promoting academic achievement: The role of racial identity in buffering perceptions of teacher discrimination on academic achievement among African American and Caribbean Black adolescents. *Journal of Educational Psychology*, *101*(2), 420–431.

Thompson, B. P., Warrican, S. J., & Leacock, C. J. (2011). Education for the future: Shaking off the shackles of colonial times. In D. Dunkley (Ed.), *Readings in Caribbean history and culture: Breaking ground* (pp. 61–86). Lexington Books.

Thornton, M. C., Taylor, R. J., Chatters, L. M., & Forsythe-Brown, I. (2017). African American and Black Caribbean feelings of closeness to Africans. *Identities*, *24*(4), 493–512. https://doi.org/10.1080/1070289X.2016.1208096

Tillery, A. B., & Chresfield, M. (2012). Model Blacks or "Ras the Exhorter." *Journal of Black Studies*, *43*(5), 545–570. https://doi.org/10.1177/0021934712439065

Tillman, L. C. (2009). *The SAGE handbook of African American education*. Sage.

Tollefson, J. (2011). Ideology, language varieties, and ELT. In J. Cummins & C. Davison (Eds.), *International handbook of English language teaching* (pp. 25–36). Springer.

Tomlinson, S. (2014). *The politics of race, class and special education: The selected works of Sally Tomlinson*. Routledge.

Toussaint, L., Worthington, E. L., Webb, J. R., Wilson, C., & Williams, D. R. (2023). Forgiveness in human flourishing. In M. L. Heras, M. Grau-Grau, & Y. Rofcanin (Eds.), *Human flourishing: A multidisciplinary perspective on neuroscience, health, organizations and arts* (pp. 117–131). Springer.

Trow, M. (1957). Comment on participant observation and interviewing: A comparison. *Human Organization*, *16*(3), 33–35.

Tuckett, A. G., & Stewart, D. E. (2004). Collecting qualitative data: Part I Journal as a method: Experience, rationale and limitations. *Contemporary Nurse*, *16*(1/2), 104–113. https://doi.org/10.5172/conu.16.1-2.104

References

Ukpokodu, O. N. (2018). African immigrants, the "New Model Minority": Examining the reality in U.S. K-12 schools. *The Urban Review, 50*(1), 69–96. https://doi.org/10.1007/s11256-017-0430-0

Ukpokodu, O. N., & Ojiambo, P. O. (2017). *Erasing invisibility, inequity and social justice of Africans in the diaspora and the continent*. Cambridge Scholars Publishing.

U.S. Census Bureau, American Community Survey. (2013). English learner (EL) students who are Black: Fast facts (No. 1066637963). Office of English Language Acquisition.

U.S. Department of Health and Human Services. (2022). *Language and literacy*. https://health.gov/healthypeople/objectives-and-data/social-determinants-health/literature-summaries/language-and-literacy

U.S. Department of Justice. (1970). Annual report. Immigration and Naturalization Service.

U.S. Department of State. (n.d.). *The Immigration and Nationality Act of 1952 (The McCarran-Walter Act)*. https://history.state.gov/milestones/1945-1952/immigration-act

van Manen, M. (1990). *Researching lived experience*. State University of New York Press.

Viesca, K. (2013). Linguicism and racism in Massachusetts education policy. *Education Policy Analysis Archives, 21*(52), 1–37.https://doi.org/10.14507/epaa.v21n52.2013

Vigouroux, C. B. (2017). The discursive pathway of two centuries of raciolinguistic stereotyping: 'Africans as incapable of speaking French.' *Language in Society, 46*(1), 5–21.

Voice. (2011, January 8). *Regional linguists meet at UWI international conference on language rights and policy*. www.thevoiceslu.com/local_news/2011/january/08_01_11/Regional.htm

Waitoller, F. R. & Thorius, K. A. K. (2016). Cross-pollinating culturally sustaining pedagogy and universal design for learning: Toward an inclusive pedagogy that accounts for dis/ability. *Harvard Educational Review, 86*(3), 366–389.

Waldron, C., Willis, A., Tatum, A., Salas, R. G., Cole, J. J., Croom, M., Deroo, M. R., Hikida, M., Machado, E., Smith, P., & Zaidi, R. (2023). Reimagining LRA in the spirit of a transcendent approach to literacy. *Literacy Research: Theory, Method, and Practice, 72*, 50–73.

Wallace, D. (2017a). Distinctiveness, deference and dominance in Black Caribbean fathers' engagement with public schools in London and New York City. *Gender and Education, 29*(5), 594–613.

(2017b). Reading 'race' in Bourdieu? Examining Black cultural capital among Black Caribbean youth in south London. *Sociology, 51*(5), 907–923.

(2023). *The culture trap: Ethnic expectations and unequal schooling for Black youth*. Oxford University Press.

Wallace, D., & Joseph-Salisbury, R. (2022). How, still, is the Black Caribbean child made educationally subnormal in the English school system? *Ethnic and Racial Studies, 45*(8), 1426–1452.

Warrican, S. J. (2005). *Hard words: The challenge of reading and writing for Caribbean students and their teachers*. Ian Randle.

(2006). Promoting reading amidst repeated failure: Meeting the challenges. *The High School Journal, 90*(1), 33–43. https://doi.org/10.1353/hsj.2006.0014

(2009). Literacy development and the role of the Eastern Caribbean joint board of teacher education. *Journal of Eastern Caribbean Studies, 34*(2), 71–85.

(2020). Toward caring language and literacy classrooms for Black immigrant youth: Combating raciolinguistic ideologies and moral licensing. *Teachers College Record, 122*(13), 1–22. https://doi.org/10.1177/016146812012201306

(2021, June 25). *Students of color in the Caribbean share the same plight as counterparts in white dominated countries*. USApp – American Politics and Policy Blog.

Warrican, S. J., Leacock, C., Thompson, B., Alleyne, M., Smith, P., Burnett, A., Thomas, K., & Collins, D. (2020). *Factors that influence academic performance of students in the Caribbean: An empirical study: Report on preliminary analysis of data* [Brief]. https://doi.org/10.13140/RG.2.2.10093.51683

Warrican, S. J., & Smith, P. (In press). Reconciling raciolinguistic ideological tensions across nation states: Insights from educators' Caribbean Englishes for anti-racist language education. In R. Figuera (Ed.), *World Englishes and the politics of internationalisation: Critical perspectives from the Anglophone Caribbean*. Routledge.

Wartofsky, M. W. (1979). Perception, representation, and the forms of action: Towards an historical epistemology. In R. S. Coher & M. W. Wartofsky (Eds.), *A portrait of twenty-five years* (pp. 215–237). Springer.

Waters, M. C. (1994). *Differing perceptions of racism: West Indians, African Americans, and whites in the workplace* [Conference presentation]. Annual meetings of the American Sociological Association, Los Angeles, CA, United States.

Waters, M. C., Kasinitz, P., & Asad, A. L. (2014). Immigrants and African Americans. *Annual Review of Sociology, 40*, 369–390. https://doi.org/10.1146/annurev-soc-071811-145449

Watson, V. W. M. (2018). Envisioning the already-present literacy and learning of youth. *English Journal, 107*(5), 10–13.

Watson, V. W. M., & Beymer, A. (2019). Praisesongs of place: Youth envisioning space and place in a literacy and songwriting initiative. *Research in the Teaching of English, 53*(4), 297–319.

Watson, V. W. M., & Knight-Manuel, M. G. (2017). Challenging popularized narratives of immigrant youth from West Africa: Examining social processes of navigating identities and engaging civically. *Review of Research in Education, 41*(1), 279–310.

(2020). Humanizing the Black immigrant body: Envisioning diaspora literacies of youth and young adults from West African countries. *Teachers College Record, 122*(13), 1–28.

Watson, V. W. M., Knight-Manuel, M. G., & Jaffee, A. T. (2014). Beyond #Talking and #Texting: African immigrant youth's social–civic literacies and negotiations of citizenship across participatory new media technologies. *Citizenship Teaching & Learning, 10*(1), 43–62. https://doi.org/10.1386/ctl.10.1.43_1

Watson, V. W. M., Knight-Manuel, M. G., & Smith, P. (In press). *Educating African immigrant youth: Schooling and civic engagement in K–12 schools*. Teachers College Press.

Watson, V. W. M., Reine Johnson, L. E., Peña-Pincheira, R. S., Berends, J. E., & Chen, S. (2022). Locating a pedagogy of love: (Re)framing pedagogies of loss in popular-media narratives of African immigrant communities. *International Journal of Qualitative Studies in Education, 35*(6), 588–608. https://doi.org/10.1080/09518398.2021.1982057

Watts, D. (1990). *The West Indies: Patterns of development, culture, and environmental change since 1492.* Cambridge University Press.

Wee, L. (2005). Intra-language discrimination and linguistic human rights: The case of Singlish. *Applied Linguistics, 26*(1), 48–69.

Wekker, G. (2016). *White innocence: Paradoxes of colonialism and race.* Duke University Press.

Wilentz, G. (1992). Toward a diaspora literature: Black Women writers from Africa, the Caribbean, and the United States. *College English, 54*(4), 385–405. https://doi.org/10.2307/377831

Wiley, T. G. (2014). Diversity, super-diversity, and monolingual language ideology in the 65 United States: Tolerance or intolerance? *Review of Research in Education, 38*(1), 1–32.

Williams, K. (2016). Caribbean literature in English. *Soka University English Literature Society, 28*(2), 107–149.

Willis, A. I. (1995). Reading the world of school literacy: Contextualizing the experience of a young African American male. *Harvard Educational Review, 65*(1), 30–50.

(2002). Literacy at Calhoun colored school 1892–1945. *Reading Research Quarterly, 37*(1), 8–44.

(2003). Parallax: Addressing race in preservice literacy education. In S. Greene & D. Abt-Perkins (Eds.), *Making race visible: Literacy research for cultural understanding* (pp. 51–70). Teachers College Press.

(2008). Critical race theory. *Encyclopedia of Language and Education, 2*, 15–28.

(2012). *Reading comprehension research and testing in the US: Undercurrents of race, class, and power in the struggle for meaning.* Routledge.

(2015). Literacy and race: Access, equity, and freedom. *Literacy Research: Theory, Method, and Practice, 64*(1), 23–55.

(2018). Re-positioning race in English language arts research. In D. Lapp & D. Fisher (Eds.), *Handbook of research on teaching the English language arts* (pp. 30–56). Routledge.

(2019). Race, response to intervention, and reading research. *Journal of Literacy Research, 51*(4), 394–419.

(2022, December). *Revolutionizing literacy: The life of Omar ibn Said, written by himself* [Conference speech]. Literacy Research Association Annual Conference, Phoenix, AZ, United States.

(2023). Revolutionizing literacy: The life of Omar ibn Said, written by himself. *Literacy Research: Theory, Method, and Practice, 72*(1). https://doi.org/10.1177/23813377231168586.

Willis, A. I., & Harris, V. J. (2000). Political acts: Literacy learning and teaching. *Reading Research Quarterly, 35*(1), 72–88. https://doi.org/10.1598/RRQ.35.1.6

Willis, A. I., McMillon, G. T., & Smith, P. (2022). *Affirming Black students' lives and literacies: Bearing witness.* Teachers College Press.

Willis, A. I., & Smith, P. (2021). Advancing antiracism in literacy research. *Literacy Research: Theory, Method, and Practice*, *70*(1), 152–169. https://doi.org/10.1177/23813377211027554

Willis, A. I., Smith, P., Kim, J., & Hsieh, B. (2021). *Racial justice in literacy research*. Literacy Research Report, Literacy Research Association.

Wilson-Akubude, N. L. (2016). Black male success in mathematics: The development of a positive mathematics identity in urban schools [Unpublished doctoral dissertation]. University of Massachusetts.

Wilson-Forsberg, S., Masakure, O., Shizha, E., Lafrenière, G., & Mfoafo-M'Carthy, M. (2018). Disrupting an imposed racial identity or performing the model minority? The pursuit of postsecondary education by young African immigrant men in southern Ontario, Canada. *Race Ethnicity and Education*, *23*(5), 693–711. https://doi.org/10.1080/13613324.2018.1497965

Windle, J. A., & Muniz, K. (2018). Constructions of race in Brazil: Resistance and resignification in teacher education. *International Studies in Sociology of Education*, *27*(2/3), 307–323.

Winer, L. (1988). *The story of English*. By Robert McCrum, William Cran, and Robert MacNeil. *Journal of Pidgin and Creole Languages*, *3*(1), 141–145.

(1993). Teaching speakers of Caribbean English Creoles in North American classrooms. In A. W. Glowka & D. M. Lance (Eds.), *Language variation in North American English* (pp. 191–198). MLA.

(2006). Teaching English to Caribbean English Creole-speaking students in the Caribbean and North America. In S. J. Nero (Ed.), *Dialects, Englishes, Creoles, and education* (pp. 105–118). Routledge.

Winer, L., & Jack, L. (1997). Caribbean English Creole in New York. In O. García & J. A. Fishman (Eds.), *The Multilingual Apple: Languages in New York City* (pp. 300–337). De Gruyter.

Winford, D. (2003). Ideologies of language and socially realistic linguistics. In A. Ball, S. Makoni, G. Smitherman, & A. K. Spears (Eds.), *Black linguistics: Language, society and politics in Africa and the Americas* (pp. 33–51). Routledge.

(2019). Another look at the Creolist hypothesis of AAVE origins. In R. Blake & I. Buchstaller (Eds.), *The Routledge companion to the work of John R. Rickford* (pp. 64–78). Routledge.

Wingate, U. (2015). *Academic literacy and student diversity: The case for inclusive practice*. De Gruyter.

(2018). Academic literacy across the curriculum: Towards a collaborative instructional approach. *Language Teaching*, *51*(3), 349–364. https://doi.org/10.1017/s0261444816000264

Wirtz, K. (2020). Racializing performances in colonial time-spaces. In H. S. Alim, A. Reyes, & P. V. Kroskrity (Eds.), *The Oxford handbook of language and race* (pp. 207–229). Oxford University Press.

Wolfram, W. (1971). Black-White speech relations revisited. In W. Wolfram & N. H. Clarke (Eds.), *Black-White speech relations* (pp. 139–161). Center for Applied Linguistics.

Woodson, C. G. (1933). *The mis-education of the Negro*. Associated Publishers.

Wright, S. C., & Bougie, É. (2007). Intergroup contact and minority-language education: Reducing language-based discrimination and its negative impact. *Journal of Language and Social Psychology*, *26*(2), 157–181.

Wynter-Hoyte, K., & Smith, M. (2020). "Hey, Black child: Do you know who you are?" Using African diaspora literacy to humanize Blackness in early childhood education. *Journal of Literacy Research, 52*(4), 406–431. https://doi.org/10.1177/1086296X20967393

Yoon, B. (2012). Junsuk and Junhyuck: Adolescent immigrants' educational journey to success and identity negotiation. *American Educational Research Journal, 49*(5), 971–1002.

Zaidi, R. (Host). (2021, March). *A (trans)raciolinguistic approach for literacy classrooms* [Audio podcast]. voicEd Radio. https://voiced.ca/podcast_episode_post/a-transraciolinguistic-approach-for-literacy-classrooms-ft-dr-patriann-smith/

Zéphir, F. (2010). The languages of Haitians and the history of Creole: Haiti and its diaspora. In A. Spears & C. Berotte Joseph (Eds.), *The Haitian Creole language: History, structure, use and education* (pp. 55–80). Lexington Books.

Zoboi, I. (2017). *American street.* Balzer & Bray.

Zong, J., & Batalova, J. (2019, February 13). Caribbean immigrants in the United States. *Migration Policy Institute.* www.migrationpolicy.org/article/caribbean-immigrants-united-states-2017

Index

"abyssal thinking" (Santos), 69–70, 109
"alien" (status), 7, 117, 125–126, 136–138
"collective imaginaries" (Mahmud), 8, 68
"double consciousness" (Du Bois), 122, 144, 225, 230–231
"fictive kinship" (Fordham and Ogbu), 27
"interstices" (Bhabha), 121, 206
"new beings" (Freire), 13, 20, 118, 206, 209, 213, 219, 238
"New Childhoods" framework, 234
"oppressor vs. oppressed dynamic" (Freire), 13, 15, 20, 118, 126, 143, 209
"The Hill We Climb" (Gorman), 23–24, 72, 108, 133, 155, 211
"transcendent literacy" (Willis), 75, 78–79, 104–105, 110, 118, 139, 207, 209, 212
academic attainment, *see also* model minority frame; success
    achievement and opportunities, 39–41, 52–53, 71
    African Americans, *see* African Americans: academic attainment
    and "underachievement," 39
    challenges faced by Black immigrant youth, 27
    disaggregation of Black student data, 54–55
    in general, 5, 18, 25–28
    and immigration law, 45–47
    of Indigenous minorities vs. immigrants, 26
    literacy, academic, 5, 111–114, 135, 212
    meritocracy, myth of, 40–41, 116
    and model minority frame, 54
    motivations, 39
    narratives of
        achievement, 51–56
        ethnicity and culture vs. race, 56–59
        in general, 47
        invisibility, 47–51
        peer relations, 59–62, 99
        possibility, 62–66, 70–71
    accent, 88, 95, 171–172, 174, 178, 180, 183, *see also* dialects

Achebe, Chinua, 63
Africa
    Africanness, 61
    Afrocentrism, 78, 230, 234
    Afrofuturism, 3
    Afronography, 78
    colonialism, effects of, 73
    diaspora, African, 72, 75–79, 240
    immigrants from, 27, 46, 49–51, 63
    slavery, African, 105
African Americans, *see also* Black immigrant youth; Black people
    "descendants of slaves" (DOS) demarcation, 228
    academic attainment
        achievement, narratives of, 51–54
        invented illiteracy, 106
        and model minority frame, 4, 18, 59–62
        peer relations, 59–62, 99
        reading literacy performance, 28
    accents, 180
    African American Language (AAL), 124
    and African immigrants, 50–51
    diversity of, 47, 183–184
    intraracial responses to, 190
    perceived superiority of Black immigrants, 4, 106, 170–171, 219
    racism experienced by, 36
African Diaspora Participatory Literacy Communities (ADPLCs), 77
agency, 36, 67, 76, 97, 120, 129, 132, 150, *see also* self-determination
Agyepong, M., 61–62
Alim, H. S., 5, 20, 94, 109, 117–118, 127, 135–137, 143, 215–217, 228, 232, 236
Allen, K. M., 50
American Anthropological Association (AAA), 14
American Association of Applied Linguistics (AAAL), 14
American Educational Research Association (AERA), 14

278

Index

American Psychological Association (APA), 14
Ancient Egyptian language, 72
animation, 234–236
anti-racism, 43
Anya, Uju, 42
applied linguistics, 103–104, 110–111, 236–237
Archie of Sussex, 24
Asian immigrants, 25, 44, 61, 70
assessments and tests, 87–88, 112, 162, 187, *see also* National Assessment of Educational Progress (NAEP); Programme for International Student Assessment (PISA)
athletic pursuits, 160, 191
attention deficit hyperactivity disorder (ADHD), 38
Attiah, Karen, 2
authenticated knowledge, 75–79, 105, 110
Awokoya, J., 58

Bachoo, Ryan, 32–34
Bahamian Creolized English
  as 'broken English,' 157–160
  accentuating, 171, 189
  comprehension of, 176–177, 195
  delegitimization of, 163–165, 173–176, 178
  legitimization of, 163
  paradoxical expectations about, 160
  wish for US engagement with, 183
Bahamian Standard English, 158, 160, 178, 188, 195
Bailey, E.K., 38
Barbadian Creolized English (Bajan), 196
Barro, Maimouna Abdoulaye, 104
Barth, E. A. T., 14
Barthes, R., 39
Bartlett, L., 43
Bennett, Lerone, 49
Bernal, M., 72
Beymer, A., 131
Bhabha, Homi K., 34, 121, *see also*
bidialectalism, 87–88, 94, 166
Bilingual Education Project (BEP), 86
bilingualism, 83, 94, 122, 166, *see also* multilingualism; translanguaging; translingualism
binaries, 13, 37, 66, 121, 159, 165
Black Caribbean peoples, 15, 55
Black Englishes, 85–86, 187–188, 215–217, 227
Black gaze, 209–210, 223
Black immigrant literacies framework, *see also* holistic literacies; model minority frame; transraciolinguistics
  elements of
    in general, 202–204, 219

justice, claim to the struggle for, 103–104, 184, 189–190, 202, 227, 236–237
  local-global connection, 30, 201–203, 225
  in general, 98
  model for conceptualizing, *203*
  and racialization of language, 236–237
Black immigrant youth, *see also* flourishing; holistic literacies; language architecture; self-determination; semiolingual innocence; translanguaging
  academic challenges faced by, 27
  academic research on, 89–92
  agency, 67, 97, 120, 129, 150
  assets, 5, 50, 52–54, 62, 67, 70
  author's experience with, 133–134
  ecological framework, 67
  emotions, 161, 184–191, 199
  ESL classrooms, put in, 27, 95, 158, 160
  in general, 3–6, 18–21, 30, 191–192
  identities, 4
  qualitative research on
    credibility, 153–154
    data sources, 147–153
    in general, 141
    participants, 145–147, 153
    questions, 144, 148
  reading literacy performance, 28, 52, 102
  resilience, 67–68, 100, 102
  social adjustment, 102–103
Black immigrants
  "becoming Black," 5, 66, 125–126, 136, 144, 170, 219
  "ethnic distinctiveness," discourses of, 56–58
  accents, 180–181
  and *Black Panther*, 2
  heterogeneity, 49
  historical overview of, 24–47
  in general, 22
  ICE detention rates, 67
  invisibility, 47–51
  linguistic richness, 64
  myths about, 116
  statistics, 22, 24–47
Black innocence (*inonsans jan nwè*), *see also* semiolingual innocence
  definition, 7, 9
  in general, 1–3, 5–6, 18
  and Olatunji, 238
  performance of, 166
Black Lives Matter, 223
Black Panther (film), 1–3, 139, 212
Black Panther: Wakanda Forever (film), 2–3, 139, 233

Black people, *see also* African Americans; Black immigrant youth; Blackness
   divisiveness among, 4, 171
   invented illiteracy of, 72, 81, 104–106
   literacies, 106–107
   murders of, 13, 41, 66, 223, 228
   peer relations, 59–62, 99, 184
   and rational acceptability, 236
   solidarity, 2, 171
Black studies, 76–78
Blackledge, A., 127
Blackman, S.
   Caribbean Discourse in Inclusive Education, 37–38
Blackness
   "becoming Black," 5, 66, 125–126, 136, 144, 170, 219
   and Africanness, 61
   and body as transraciosemiotic marker, 170–172
   global language of, 75
   heterogeneity, 99–101, 183–184, 191
   intraracial responses, 189
   opposition to, 23, 106
body, as tranraciosemiotic marker, 167–168, 189, 191
Boseman, Chadwick, 1
Braden, E., 58
Brazil, 42
Breakfast Program (1969), 2
Bristol, L., 39
Britain, 25, 54
British and Foreign School Society (BFSS), 35
Brown v. Board of Education, 76
Brown, D. S., 73
Brownsworth, V., 91
Bryce-Laporte, Roy Simon, 3, 48–49
bullying, 186
Burkhard, T., 64
Bustos Flores, Belinda, 220

Calzada, E., 54–55
Campbell, Carl, 33
Canada, 66
Canagarajah, Suresh, 130
Caribbean, *see also* Black immigrant youth; specific Caribbean islands, *e.g. St. Lucia*
   'racelessness' of peoples from, 43
   about, 31–32
   educational landscape, 32–36, 39
   liberatory Caribbean imaginaries, 230–234
   linguistic identity, 86–89
   literary scholarship, 80
   migration to US, 46
   occupations and earnings, 55
   postcolonial project, 15, 36
Caribbean Community (CARICOM), 89
Caribbean Discourse in Inclusive Education (Blackman and Conrad), 37–38
Caribbean Englishes (CEs), 82–86, 88–89, 92–93, 96
Caribbean Secondary Education Certification (CSEC), 84
Carpenter, Karen, 85
casting decisions, 19
Catherine, Princess of Wales, 26
Chawawa, Munya, 24
Chetty, R., 73
Christian student organizations, 192–193
civil rights movement, 44–45
Clachar, A., 95–96
Clark, Vèvè A., 76, 79
class, 4, 226–227
Clayton, K. E., 53
Coard, Bernard, 14
codeswitching, 73
Cohen, L., 61
colonialism, coloniality, and colonialization, *see also* decolonizing perspective; Eurocentrism; postcolonialism and postcoloniality
   and education, 73, 88
   historical overview, 32–36
   and linguistic hegemony, 72–74, 230
   and race, 36, 72, 74
   and raciolinguistics, 117
   and transcendent literacy, 79, 118
   trauma inherited from, 228
communication, *see also* language; speech
   literacies, communicative, 200–201
   nonverbal, 14, 85, 97
   and translanguaging, 181
   and transnational literary curriculum, 30
community, 16, 78, 142, 173, 220
Concordat (documentary), 33–34
conformity, 182
Conrad, D.
   Caribbean Discourse in Inclusive Education, 37–38
constructivism, 38
cosmopolitanism, 29
COVID-19 pandemic, 69
Cowley, S. J., 123
Creese, A., 127
Creole, *see also* Bahamian Creolized English; Barbadian Creolized English (Bajan); dialects; Jamaican Creolized English
   and bilingualism, 83
   in general, 83–86

Index

Haitian, 34–35, 41–42
Jamaican Creole (JC), 86–87
St. Lucian French, 6, 35
as official language, 93
vs. Standard English, 4, 91
critical applied linguistics, 110–111, *see also* applied linguistics
critical dialectical pluralism, 5, 141, 143, 157
critical language awareness (CLA), 9
critical literacy, 110–111
Critical Race Theory, 78, 115, 223
Critical Studyin', 76–78
Cuba, 117
Cultural-Ecological Theory of School Performance, 51
culture, 53, 56–59, 193–194, *see also* ethnicity; metacultural understanding

Daoud, N., 55
Davies, Carole Boyce, 36, 80
Dávila, L. T., 54, 65
De Lisle, J., 36
decolonizing perspective, 5, 17, 38–40, 69, 140–145, *see also* colonialism, coloniality, and colonialization; Eurocentrism; postcolonialism and postcoloniality
Dei, G. J. S., 142–143
Delva, R. J., 41
deportation, 67, 118
Devonish, Hubert, 85
dialects, *see also* accent; Englishes
bidialectalism, 87–88, 94, 166
and Englishes, 4, 7, 81, 92–93
in general, 80–81
and named languages, 93–94
and personhood, 94, 163
and privilege, 140
diaspora, 72, 75–79, 240
Diaspora Literacy, 62–63, 76–79
dichotomies, 13, 20, 37, 70, 96, 115, 121, 212
Dillard, C. B., 78
discrimination, 27, 44, *see also* racism
diversity, 25, 183, 190, 194
Dodoo, F., 49, 55
Donaldson, John, 34
Dornan, I., 35
Dovchin, S., 82
Du Bois, W.E.B. (William Edward Burghardt), 226, *see also* "double consciousness" (Du Bois)
dual-language classrooms, 214, 227

Early Childhood Longitudinal Study, 61
earnings attainment, 55

education and educational systems, *see also* schools; teachers; tests and assessments
and colonialism, 73, 88
Eurocentrism in, 68–70
focus on intellect, 233
inclusive education, 37–38
interrelationship of language and race in, 16
and liberatory Caribbean imaginaries, 232–234
national landscapes
Caribbean, 32–36, 39
St. Lucia, 35–36
US, 24–47
racialization, 14
transnational literacy curriculum, 30, 58
educators, *see* teachers
Egyptian language, Ancient, 72
E-languages, *see also* Englishes; individual linguistic repertoires (I-languages); specific E-languages
accentuating, 171–172, 180–181, 189
in general, 12, 122–125, 127
perceived inferiority of, 159, 164, 173, 175, 192–193, 214
positive emotions attached to use of, 161
and raciolinguistic ideology, 158
self-determination, 158, 162, 166, 172, 176, 180
and semilingual innocence, 199, 204–205
switching on and off of, 173–174, 181–182, 189, 194–195, 197–198
emotions and feelings, 161, 184–191, 199–200
English as a Second Language (ESL), 27, 64, 95–96, 158, 160
English language, *see also* Black Englishes; Caribbean Englishes (CEs); Englishes; Global English Language Teaching (GELT); Standard American English (SAE); Standard English; standardized Englishes; World Englishes
'broken English,' 157–160, 196–197
as "master discourse," 91
linguistic hegemony, 74–75
native vs. non-native speakers, 102
Englishes, *see also* dialects; non-standardized Englishes; standardized Englishes; specific Englishes, *e.g. Bahamian Creolized Englishes*
Black Englishes, 85–86, 187–188, 215–217, 227
Caribbean Englishes (CEs), 82–86, 88–89, 92–93, 96
comportment rules, 4
cross-circle, 82–83, 89
definition, 7, 80

Englishes (cont.)
  and dialects, 4, 7, 81, 92–93
  disentangling from, 225, 231
  in general, 1–5
  naming practices, 92–93, 129
  New Englishes, 80
  paradoxical expectations about, 160–162
  and racialization, 116, 127–129
  translanguaging with Englishes (TWE), 165, 209, 218
  translingual, 82
  white Englishes, 226–227
  World Englishes, 57, 81–82, 87, 129–130
Enrivo, Cynthia, 19
E-semiotics, 13, 125, 127, 168, 173, 204–205, *see also* individual semiotic repertoire (I-semiotics)
Esperanto, 73
ethnicity, 56–59, *see also* culture; race
Eurocentrism, *see also* colonialism, coloniality, and colonialization; decolonizing perspective; postcolonialism and postcoloniality
  and academic achievement, 41, 68–70, 105, 107, 209
  and Black innocence, 7
  and coloniality, 32
  and invented illiteracy, 105, 107
  and knowledge, 142
  and multilingualism, 109
  and racialized language, 15
  and transraciolinguistics, 121
exclusivity, 183–184, 191–192

Fanon, Frantz, 42, 238
feelings and emotions, 161, 184–191, 199
Fergus, Claudius, 33
Fisher, M. T., 77
Flores, N., 11, 65, 67, 70, 94, 111, 113, 115–116, 128, 161, 165, 167, 188, 201, 213
Florida, 106, 223
flourishing
  and academic literary success, 5, 31
  and Black innocence, 3, 7, 9
  definition, 11
  and semiolingual innocence, 206–207, 222
  and transracialization, 228
Floyd, George, 13, 41, 66, 223, 228
food, 172–173
Fordham, S., 27
forgiveness, 226
François, R., 34
Freire, Paulo, 13, 15, 20, 118, 126, 143, 206, 209, 213, 219
Frels, R. K., 141, 143

French Creole, 6, 35
French language, 41–42
friendliness, 169–171
Fulani (Pulaar), 104

García, Ofelia, 12, 68–71, 109, 111, 122–124, 126, 129–130, 218, 232
gender, 51, 170
generational status, 51–52
gestures, 14, 85
Ghong, M., 49
Gilbert, S. C., 51–52
Global English Language Teaching (GELT), 129–130, 218
Global Englishes, 57, 81–82, 87, 129–130
Global Majority, 109
global metaverse, 103–104, 221, 236–238
globalization, 75
Goodwin, A. Lin, 66
Goopta, Primnath, 34
Gordon, April, 62
Gorman, Amanda
  "The Hill We Climb," 23–24, 72, 108, 133, 155, 211
grade point averages (GPAs), 52, 62
grammar, 94, 122
Greek language, 72
greetings, 168–171
group memory (Heritage Knowledge), 76
Gullah, 86
Gundaker, G., 15
Gutiérrez, K. D., 30
Guyana, 34

Haitian Creole, 34–35, 41–42
Haitian immigrants, 67
Halliday, M. A. K., 12
Hamel, E. C., 112
Harlem Renaissance, 78–79, 89
Harris, Leslie, 91
Hart–Cellar Immigration Reform Act, 44–46, 55–57
Hartlep, N. D., 25
Harvey, C. L., 236
Hebblethwaite, B., 41
Heller, M., 72
Henry, Annette, 90–92
Heritage Knowledge, 76
heteroglossic norms, 84, 102, 111–112, 114, 129, 131
Hickling-Hudson, A., 36
Hmong Americans, 25
Holdstein, Deborah, 15
holistic literacies
  communicative, 200–201

in general, 17, 156, 201–203
  of human sensitivity, 199–200
  and interdependence, 229
  of intraracial and interracial
    interdependence, 201
  of paradox, 200
  of perceived success, 198–199
  of possibility, 201
  and semiolingual innocence, 213–214,
    222
home languages, 89, 111–113, 160, 196,
  232
homogeneity, 192–194
hooks, bell, 223
humanity, shared, 12, 208, 222–224, 229, 234
Hunter, Latoya, 90

Ibrahim, Awad, 66, 118, 170
ICE detention, 67
identity, *see also* class; ethnicity; gender;
    personhood; race
  and bilingualism, 83
  of Black immigrant youth, 4
  national, 81–82, 89
I-languages, *see* individual linguistic repertoire
    (I-languages)
illiteracy, invented, 72, 81, 104–106
imaginaries
  collective imaginaries, 8, 68
  definition, 8
  of innocence (*imajinè inosan*), 3, 8, 18, 23,
    127, 141
  liberatory Caribbean imaginaries,
    230–234
  and translanguaging, 221–226
imagination, 12, 68, 208, 235–236
immigration, *see also* Black immigrant youth;
    Black immigrants
  "alien" (status), 7, 118, 125–126, 136–138
  "illegality" of immigrants, 117
  "languagelessness" of immigrants, 103
  and academic attainment, 45–47
  and Blackness, 5, 66, 125–126, 136, 144,
    170, 219
  in Caribbean culture, 89
  contemporary US policy, 23
  deportation, 67, 118
  Hart-Cellar Immigration Reform Act, 44–46,
    55–57
  historical overview, 44–45, 55
  invisibility of, 47–51
  laws curtailing, 44
  non-Black immigrants, 4
  and raciolinguistic ideology, 137
  and translanguaging, 125–126

Indigeneity
  colonialism's effect on, 32, 72–74
  and food culture, 172
  and greeting others, 170
  knowledge, Indigenous, 50, 73, 77, 79,
    141–143, 145
  minorities, Indigenous, 27
Individual Freedom Act, 223
individual linguistic repertoire (I-languages),
    see also E-languages
  and being comfortable with others, 174
  perceived inferiority of, 159
  positive emotions attached to use of, 161
  and translanguaging, 12, 18, 122–124,
    126–127, 204
individual semiotic repertoire (I-semiotics), 13,
    124, 127, 204, *see also* E-semiotics
individuality, 169–170, 173, 220
Indo-European languages, 72
Indofuturism, 3
industrialization, 105, 107
innocence, *see also* Black innocence (*inonsans
    jan nwè*); semiolingual innocence
  definition, 8
  imaginaries of (*imajinè inosan*), 3, 8, 18, 23,
    127, 141
  linguistic, 18, 79, 204
  white, 9, 221–223
institutions, *see* schools
interdependence, 12, 170, 201, 208, 220–224,
    229–230, 233
intersectionality, 5, 38, 63–65
invented illiteracy, 72, 81, 104–106
Irizarry, Y., 61
isolation, 192–194

Jack, L., 90
Jagan, Cheddy, 34
Jamaica, 36, 85, 87, 92
Jamaican Creole (JC), 86–87
Jamaican Creolized English, 158, 186–187,
    194
Johnson, Lyndon B., 44
Joseph, V., 43
Just Another Girl on the IRT (film), 91
justice, 103–104, 184, 189–190, 202, 227,
    236–237

Kaba, A., 25
Kachru, Braj B., 82
Kates, I. C., 236
Kent, M. M., 45
Kigamwa, J. C., 64
King, J. E., 43, 76–77
King, J. R., 73

King, L. J., 123
King, Martin Luther, Jr., 226–229
Kiramba, L., 50, 65
Kleyn, T., 122–124, 126
Knight-Manuel, M. G., 62–64
knowledge
  authenticated, 75–79, 105, 110
  evidence of, 142
  Heritage Knowledge, 76
  Indigenous, 50, 73, 77, 79, 141–143, 145

Labov, W., 216
Lacoste, V., 87
language, *see also* communication; E-languages; named languages; pronunciation; raciolinguistics; semiolingual innocence; semiotics; transraciolinguistics; writing; individual linguistic repertoire (I-languages); specific languages, *e.g. English language*
  "brokering," 70, 220
  Blackness, global language of, 75
  home languages, 89, 111–113, 160, 197, 232
  ideology, 9, 29
  policy, 29
  racialization of, 15, 27, 30, 102–104, 107, 212, 236
  social constructedness of, 122
  standardized, 9, 20, 213–214
  twining of race and, 13, 16, 117, 167, 171, 182, 184, 225
  unnamed languages, 214–215, 217–218, 227
language architecture
  definition, 9
  foregrounding assets, 70
  in general, 3, 113
  and holistic literacies, 203
  and liberatory Caribbean imaginaries, 232
  and power relations, 128
  and raciosemiotic architecture, 11
  and semiolingual innocence, 212
languaging, *see also* translanguaging
  academic research on, 15
  in *Black Panther*, 1–2
  definition, 9
  and E-languages, 123
  and semiolingual innocence, 11
  and solidarity, 2
LeBlanc, Rodney, 155–156, 206–207, 212
LGBTQI+ students, 38
Li, Wei, 12, 232
liberatory Caribbean imaginaries, 230–234
liminality, 10, 37
linguicism, 27

linguistic hegemony, 42, 72–74, 116, 135, 230
linguistic innocence, 18, 79, 204
linguistic repertoires, *see* E-languages; individual linguistic repertoire (I-languages)
linguistic supremacy, 20, 217
literacies, *see also* Black immigrant literacies framework; holistic literacies; multiliteracies; translanguaging
  definition, 10
  disciplinary, 131
  frameworks, 28–29
  in general, 5–6
  invisible, 112–114, 212
  of Black people, 106–107
  transliteracies, 114
literacy
  "functional," 106–107
  academic, 5, 111–114, 135, 212
  autonomous perspective of, 111–112
  critical, 110–111
  Diaspora Literacy, 62–63, 76–79
  ideological perspective of, 111–113
  reading literacy, 27, 51–52, 87, 91, 102, 162
  transcendent, 75, 78–79, 104–105, 110, 118, 139, 207, 209, 212
Literacy Research Association (LRA), 14, 74
literate potentiality, 231–232, 234, 236
love, 62, 78

MacSwan, J., 123–124, 127
Mahboob, A., 81
Mahmud, T., 8
Majority World, 16, 106, 108–110
Malcolm, Z. T., 50
Mandela, Nelson, 228
Marshall, Paule
  Praisesong for the Widow, 80
Martin-Kerr, K. G., 39
masculinities, 170
McElhinny, B. S., 72
McKay, Claude, 89
McLean, C., 29, 62, 99, 114
McQueen, Steve, 14
meaning-making modes, 113, 128, 162
Meghan, Duchess of Sussex, 24–25
Mendoza, P., 50
mental health, 38, 69
meritocracy, myth of, 40–41, 116
metacultural understanding, 119–121, 162, 169, 173–175, 179, 182–183, 185, 193
metalinguistic understanding, 119–121, 157, 159, 161, 164–165, 171, 174–176, 179–180, 182
metaracial understanding, 119–121, 188

Index

metaverse, 103–104, 221, 236–238
Mfum-Mensah, O., 73
Michael, Princess, of Kent, 24
Mico school missionaries, 35
migration, *see* immigration
Millar, P., 39, 87
Mills, Charles, 72, 74, 98, 105
Milner, Richard, 40, 52
Milu, Esther, 64, 74
Minority World, 16
missionaries, 35
mixedness, 117
model minority frame, *see also* academic attainment; flourishing; success
   and academic achievement, 54
   author's experience with, 137
   children's behavior, 168
   in general, 4–5, 18, 202
   perceived inferiority of African Americans, 4, 18, 59–62
Mollien, Gaspard Theodore, 34
monoglossic ideology, 10, 31, 94, 103, 111–112, 114, 129, 131, *see also* raciolinguistic ideology
monolingualism, 96, *see also* translanguaging
moral licensing, 100–101, 138
Mufwene, Salikoko S., 92
Muhammad, Gholnescar (Gholdy), 232
multilingualism, *see also* bilingualism; translanguaging; translingualism
   heteroglossic perspective on, 114
   historical overview of, 108–110
   and meaning-making modes, 176
   and metalinguistic awareness, 114
   multilingual uses of Englishes (MUE), 94
   and semiolingual innocence, 204
   and translanguaging, 122–124, *151*, 165–166, 204–205, 217
   and translingualism, 96
multiliteracies
   definition, 10, 113
   in general, 16, 131–132
   historical overview of, 109
   and semiolingual innocence, 156
   and transgressive transracialization, 201
multimodality, 109–110, 172
Muniz, K., 42
murders, 13, 41, 66, 223, 228
Murdoch, H.A., 35
myths, 40–41, 116, *see also* model minority frame

Nalubega-Booker, K., 65
named languages, 37, 70, 94, 122, 127, 130, 160, 208, 214, 217–218
National Assessment of Educational Progress (NAEP), 106
National Center for Education Statistics (NCES), 52, 106
National Council of Teachers of English (NCTE), 14–15
national identity, 81–82, 89
National Survey of American Life (NSAL), 60
native English speakers, 102
Ndemanu, M. T., 64
Négritude (movement), 79
Nero, Shondel, 82–83, 88–90, 92–97, 187–188
New Englishes, 80
New London Group, 235
new model minority, *see* model minority frame
New Negro Movement, 79, *see also* Harlem Renaissance
Ngo, B., 53, 58
Nichols, Tyre, 228
Nicolescu, B., 233
Nigerian immigrants, 55
non-native English speakers, 102
non-standardized Englishes, *see also* standardized Englishes
   and "attitudinal schizophrenia," 88–89
   and Blackness, 85
   Caribbean variants of, 84, 87–89
   definition, 7, 80, 82
   perceived inferiority of, 83, 160
   as symbol of national identity, 89
nonverbal communication, 14, 85, 97
Nwanosike, O. F., 73

Obama, Barack, 118
Obinna, D. N., 52
occupational status, 55
Ogbu, J. U., 26–27, 51
Ojiambo, Peter Otiato, 47
Okonofua, B. A., 60
Olatunji (songwriter), 211–212
Oloo, J., 65
Omar ibn Said, 74–75, 104–105
Omogun, L., 62, 99
online spaces, 82, *see also* global metaverse
Onwuegbuzie, A. J., 141, 143
Onyewuenyi, A., 53–55
Onyije, L. E., 73
opportunity gap explanatory framework, 40, 52–53
oral language, 95, 159, 177–178, *see also* accent; dialects
Orellana, M. F., 114, 130, 219–220, 234–235
Orelus, Pierre, 57
Organization for Economic Development (OECD), 14, 53

Orientalism, 15
Oscar S. Causey Award, 74

Palmer, G., 95
Park, J. Y., 64
Patel, S. G., 54
Pavlenko, A., 108–109
personhood
 and dialects, 94, 163
 erasure of, 190, 231
 inferiority, linked to, 158–159, 171, 192
 and model minority frame, 47
 preservation of, 165–166, 204
 and racialized languaging, 30
 and third space, 121
 and transracialization, 118
 and twining/entanglements, 167, 175, 225, 231
Phenomenal (song by LeBlanc), 155–156, 206–207, 212
phenomenality, 156, 212, 225
philosophy, Ubuntu, 36, 142, 222, 234
phonics, 87, 158, 198
Pierre, J., 56
poetry, 77
Portes, A., 23
postcolonialism and postcoloniality, *see also* colonialism, coloniality, and colonialization; decolonizing perspective; Eurocentrism
 and education, 16, 36, 73
 and linguistic hegemony, 42
 and race, 36–39, 42–44
 and raciolinguistics, 117
Praisesong for the Widow (Marshall), 80
prayer, 33
private schools, 160–161
privilege, 87–89, 105, 140, 214–215, 221–222
Programme for International Student Assessment (PISA), 28, 52, 87
Progress in International Reading Literacy Study (PIRLS), 51
pronunciation, 95
protests, 223
Prou, M., 34
psycholinguistic processes, 164
public schools, 161
Pulaar (Fulani), 104
pursuits, 232–234

race, *see also* Blackness; skin color; whiteness; people of specific races, *e.g.* Black people
 centralizing of, 16, 97–100, 117, 132, 202
 and coloniality, 36, 72, 74
 and dialects, 94
 and Englishes, 85–86, 89–90, 92–93
 injustice, racial, 14, 228
 metaracial understanding, 119–121, 188
 and postcoloniality, 36–39, 42–44
 and raciolinguistics, 117
 reckoning, racial, 13, 236
 and semiolingual innocence, 217
 and translanguaging, 126
 and transracialization, 132
 and transraciolinguistics, 121–122
 and transsemiotics, 126, 219
 vs. ethnicity and culture, 56–59
racialization, *see also* transracialization
 author's experience with, 136
 denial of, 43
 of language, 15, 27, 30, 102–104, 107, 212, 236
 and postcolonialism, 41
 and translanguaging, 110, 125–126
 and white audit, 115–116
raciolinguistic ideology, *see also* monoglossic ideology
 and accent, 175
 and Black immigrant literacies framework, 31
 conformity, 182
 definition, 10
 deligitimization of home language, 178–183
 depicted, *152*
 and Englishes, 81
 erasure of holistic voices, 157
 and feeling of emotions, 185
 in general, 115–116
 and immigration, 126, 137
 and language discrimination, racialized, 27
 perceived inferiority of non-standardized Englishes, 83, 160
 and phonics, 158
 rewards for approximating Standard English, 187–188
 transgeographic aspect of, 219
 and white gaze, 132, 138, 162
raciolinguistic perspective
 and colonialism, 161–162
 and decolonizing perspective, 5
 definition, 11
 in general, 117, 131
 and holistic literacies, 202
 and multiliteracies, 132
 and standardized language, 213
raciolinguistics, *see also* transraciolinguistics
 academic research on, 13–17
 epistemologies, raciolinguistic, 110
 in general, 5, 19–20

Index

markers, raciolinguistic, 83–84
twining, 13, 16, 117, 167, 171, 182, 184, 225
raciosemiotics, *see also* transraciosemiotics
  architecture, raciosemiotic, 11, 20, 128, 170, 201, 212, 232
  definition, 13
  ideology, raciosemiotic, 156, 185, 205, 219
  injustice, raciosemiotic, 194
  and peer relations, 184
racism, *see also* raciolinguistic ideology; white supremacy
  and anti-racism, 43
  in contemporary US, 106, 217
  denial of, 36, 188, 190
  effect on language use, 103
  experienced by African Americans, 36
  experienced by all Black people, 41
  statistics, 70
Rampton, B., 113
reading literacy, 27, 51–52, 87, 91, 102, 162
Redding, J., 91
Refugee and Immigrant Center for Education and Legal Services in the US (RAICES), 67
Reid, L., 55
religion, 32–36, 192–193, 226
Rickford, A., 14
Rickford, J., 14
Robertshaw, M., 42
Rogoff, B., 235
Roman Catholic church, 32–35
Rosa, J. D., 65, 67, 94, 115–116, 161, 165, 167, 188, 201, 213
Royal Readers textbooks, 43
Rubenstein-Ávila, E., 29
Ryan, Finbar, 33

safety, 190–191
SAGE Handbook of African American Education, 75
Said, Edward, 15, 73
Said, Omar ibn, 74–75, 104–105
Sankofa, 8, 78
Santos, Boaventura de Sousa, 69
Schneider, Jenifer Jasinski, 137
schools, *see also* education and educational systems; teachers; tests and assessments
  areas for improvement, 175, 177, 182–183, 190, 193–194, 221
  basic services, provision of, 101
  private, 160–161
  public, 161
second-language learners (SLLs), 70, *see also* English as a Second Language (ESL)

Seidman, I., 149
self-determination, *see also* agency
  E-languages, use of, 158, 162, 166, 172, 176, 180
  E-semiotics, influence of, 168
  in general, 19, 31
  and semiolingual innocence, 191
semiolingual innocence, *see also* Black innocence (*inonsans jan nwè*); flourishing
  all skin colors' claim to, 222–224, 226–230
  and authenticated knowledge, 79
  author's experience with, 137–141
  definition, 7, 11–12
  in general, 17, 156, 191, 212
  heuristic of, 213, 225, 235
  and interdependence, 220, 222–224, 226–230
  and liberatory Caribbean imaginaries, 230–231
  promise of, 208–210
  reinscribing of, 216, 222–226, 229
  trauma's effect on, 228
  and translanguaging, 214–218, 226
semiolingual transgressiveness, 137, 139, 179
semiotics, *see also* individual semiotic repertoire (I-semiotics); transraciosemiotics; transsemiotics and transsemiotizing
  E-semiotics, 13, 125, 127, 168, 173, 204–205
  and semiolingual innocence, 11
  supremacy, semiotic, 20
Shepherd School Programme (Ghana), 73
Shizha, E., 73
shootings, 190
Simons, H. D., 51
Skerrett, A., 29, 62, 99
skin color, 26, 140
slavery, 105, 228
Small Axe (television series), 14
Smith, M. G., 32
Smitherman, Geneva, 74, 117
social adjustment, 102–103
socioeconomics, 40, 55–56
solidarity, 2, 171
sororities, 184, 193
South Africa, 73
Sowell, T., 55
Spanglishes, 214, 227
Spears, A., 90
speech, 95, 159, 177–178, *see also* accent; dialects
spoken word poetry, 77
St. Lucia, 6, 35–36

Index

Standard American English (SAE)
  approximating, 158, 164, 179, 182, 187–188, 192
  and model minority frame, 1–5
  monoglossic ideology, 111
  translating E-languages to, 177
  vs. (non-)standardized Englishes, 7
Standard English
  linguistic hegemony of, 74, 116, 135
  and model minority frame, 4
  privileging of, 87–89
  and raciolinguistic ideologies, 10
  teaching, 194–198
  vs. (non-)standardized Englishes, 7, 92
Standard Jamaican English (SJE), 86–87, 195
standardized Englishes, *see also* non-standardized Englishes; Standard American English (SAE); Standard English
  and academic literacy, 111
  author's experience with, 140
  definition, 7, 81–82
  superiority of, assumed, 83, 158, 160, 163
  vs. Caribbean Englishes (CEs), 89–90
Stewart, M. A., 131
Stop WOKE Act, 223
student organizations, 133, 183–184, 190, 192–193
Stuesse, A., 59
Suárez-Orozco, Carola, 66–68, 70
success, *see also* academic attainment; flourishing
  academic literacy, focus on, 3–5, 39, 102–103, 105, 111, 114
  and Englishes, 82, 85, 197
  and flourishing, 5, 31
  literacies of perceived success, 198–199
  metacultural understanding of, 184–185
  and model minority frame, 25–27
  vs. opportunity, 71
Sutton, Constance, 48
Sylvain, Georges, 42
synaesthesia, 173, 199
Szenes, E., 81

Tamir, C., 46
teachers, 50, 83–84, 88, 146–147, 194–198
tests and assessments, 87–88, 112, 163, 187, *see also* National Assessment of Educational Progress (NAEP); Programme for International Student Assessment (PISA)
Texas Success Initiative (TSI), 187–188
textbooks, 43, 77
third space, 13, 30, 37, 87, 121–122, 206

Thorne, B., 235
Thornton, M. C., 60
transcendence, 104
transculturation, 219
translanguaging, *see also* E-languages; individual semiotic repertoire (I-semiotics); languaging; literacies
  "both-and" approach to, 12, 16, 20, 126, 128, 138, 200, 230
  academic research on, 122–124
  and comprehension, 176, 181, 195, 197, 200
  definition, 12
  and E-languaging, 125
  in general, 3, 5, 18, 124, 131, 156
  and Global English Language Teaching (GELT), 129–130, 218
  and global metaverse, 237
  history, 108–110
  and immigration, 125–126
  and interdependence, 220–226
  and multilingualism, 122–124, *151*, 165–166, 204–205, 217
  and race, 126
  and racialization, 110, 125–126
  rejection of, 179
  and semiolingual innocence, 214–218, 226
  strategic use of, 171, 189
  transgeographic aspect of, 218–219
  as transgeographic practice, 189, 205, 219
  translanguaging with Englishes (TWE), 165, 209, 218
translating E-languages, 176–177
translingualism, 64, 96, *see also* bilingualism; multilingualism
transliteracies, 114
transnational literacy curriculum, 30, 58
transracialization, *see also* racialization
  "both-and" approach to, 127
  definition, 118
  in general, 17, 143, 228, 236
  and semiolingual innocence, 156
  transgressive, 201
  and white gaze, 156, 168, 228
transraciolinguistics, *see also* raciolinguistics
  "both-and" approach to, 206, 222
  definition, 118
  in general, 17, 30, 101, *119*, 120–122, 203
  injustice, transraciolinguistic, 191
  justice, transraciolinguistic, 103–104, 236–237
  and semiolingual innocence, 221
  transgeographic aspect of, 219
transraciosemiotics, *see also* raciosemiotics
  body as marker of, 167–168, 189, 191
  injustice, transraciosemiotic, 191

Index

transsemiotics and transsemiotizing
　"both-and" approach to, 13, 16
　definition, 12
　and food culture, 173
　in general, 18, 131
　and global metaverse, 237
　and greeting people, 168–171
　and race, 126, 219
transgressiveness, transsemiotic, 171
transworld pedagogy, 191, 220
trauma, 228
Trinidad and Tobago, 32–34, 87, 211
Tubman, Harriet, 19
twining, 13, 16, 117, 167, 171, 182, 184, 225

Ubuntu philosophy, 36, 142, 222, 234
Ukpokodu, Omiunota, 47, 54
United Kingdom (UK), 25, 54
United States (US)
　Black immigrants, 22, 24–47, 66
　educational landscape, 24–47
　food culture, 172–173
　individuality, culture of, 169–170, 173
　racism, contemporary, 106, 217
University of South Florida (USF), 223
unnamed languages, 214–215, 217–218, 227,
　see also Creole; dialects; non-
　standardized Englishes
upward social mobility, 4

virtual spaces, 82, *see also* global metaverse
Vodou, 34

Wakanda, 1–2, *see also Black Panther* (film)
Warrican, S. Joel, 39–40, 83, 86, 93–94, 100–101
Watson, V., 62–64, 131
West African immigrants, 27, 50, 63
West Indian immigrants, 55
West Semitic language, 72
white audit, 115–116, 132, 158, 187–188
white Englishes, 226–227
white gaze, *see also* Black gaze; white audit
　and Black innocence, 7

　and linguistic supremacy, 165, 172
　and raciolinguistic ideology, 10
　and semiolingual innocence, 11, 79, 139,
　　207, 209, 222–223
　and transracialization, 156, 168, 228
white innocence, 9, 221–223
white people, 222, 226–228
white supremacy
　and "the master's language," 225, 230–234
　and Black liberation, 2
　and colonialism, 74, 79, 228
　denial of, 74
　and food culture, 173
　and invented illiteracy, 79, 81
　and linguistic supremacy, 21, 116, 165
　and model minority frame, 19
　and slavery, 228
　and struggle for justice, 202
　and transraciolinguistics, 121
whiteness
　'unmarked narrative' of, 223
　and anti-racism, 43
　and colonialism, 74
　approximating, 168, 175
　hegemonic, 116
　passing for white, 26
　privilege, white, 105, 222
whitewashing, 184
Williams, Eric, 33, 105, 143
Willis, Arlette, 2, 9, 65, 74–75, 79, 104–105,
　108, 110, 118, 132, 228, *see also*
　"transcendent literacy" (Willis)
Windle, J., 42
Winer, L., 89–90
Women's March (2017), 223
World Englishes, 57, 81–82, 87, 129–130
World Migration Report, 14
writing, 95–96, 159, 164, 177–178, 196, 215

Yearwood, Olatunji, 211–212

Zéphir, F., 41
Zusho, A., 53

Milton Keynes UK
Ingram Content Group UK Ltd.
UKHW021943041124
450744UK00008B/195